HISTORY

OF THE

WACO BAPTIST ASSOCIATION

OF TEXAS.

BY

J. L. WALKER AND C. P. LUMPKIN.

"We all have the glorious privilege of praying for the advancement of the Redeemer's kingdom, and each one of us can do something personally to advance His cause."—*Adopted by the Association in 1865.*

"Lo, I am with you alway, even unto the end of the world."—*Matt. 28:20.*

WACO, TEXAS:
BYRNE-HILL PRINTING HOUSE,
1897.

PREFACE.

No apology is offered for giving this book to the public. The struggles, privations, labors and triumphs of our honored pioneer fathers ought to be recorded. It is God's glory that the queen of American bodies is the fruit of the toils of His early servants in this section. "Herein is my Father glorified that ye bear much fruit." The compilers are deeply conscious of the many imperfections contained in the work, and they very much regret that after many and repeated efforts only vague and unsatisfactory data could be obtained of some beloved workers. Yet the hope is cherished that the production will be kindly received by a generous public. It has seemed wise to present historical facts in brief statement with little or no comment, carefully retaining all the shining gems. That nothing should be written even of real history, unless it will tend to the betterment of posterity, is a principle that has been scrupulously observed. To the blessing of Him who from the beginning has been our God and Guide this volume is most humbly and sincerely commended.

INTRODUCTION.

The Baptists have been negligent concerning their history. This is true not only with reference to important associational history, but of historical events in the wider fields of denominational activity. In view of this widespread delinquency concerning this most important matter, it is supremely gratifying to note the compilation of so valuable a work as brethren Walker and Lumpkin have given to the Baptists of Waco Association and the state at large. There are several points about the history of Waco Association worthy of special note. Great labor has been expended in gathering materials, and most diligent research has been made to secure correct data of every church, preacher, or leading worker within our bounds. The life sketches have been carefully prepared and are true records of the lives of the brethren whom we know and love so well. The work is a veritable picture album, and the cuts presented would do credit to a book of much larger pretensions than the one before us. The organization of Waco Association was foundation work. The men who laid this foundation were among the greatest and wisest men our state has ever known. The constitution of the Association was at that day unique and struck boldly into new thoughts and plans for the great world-wide work of apostolic evangelization. It was just such a constitution as was needed for the foundation of a great Association, and that those who laid this Association builded well, is evidenced in the fact that Waco Association is to-day the leading Association of Texas in its contributions to missions, in the compactness of its organization, and in its supreme loyalty to the general organized work of the denomination. The Articles of Faith are the most widely accepted compendium of Baptist principles known to me. They were adopted by Waco Association before Pendleton's "Manual" was published and only one year after the publication of the first edition of Hiscox's "Directory."

In some respects it is a more carefully worded document than is found in either Hiscox or Pendleton. If I were asked to suggest a model declaration of Baptist principles, I would not go further than the Articles of Faith of Waco Association. Of course these Articles are popularly known as the New Hampshire confession.

It will be noted that this history carefully records every development in the work of the churches which compose it. There are only fifteen Associations in Texas older than Waco Association, viz: Austin, Bethlehem, Central, Cherokee, Colorado, Dallas County (formerly Elm Fork), Leon River, Little River, Mount Zion, Navarro County (formerly Richland), Rehoboth, San Marcos, Soda Lake, Trinity River and (old) Union. The largest of these is the Cherokee Association, which has sixty churches, and a total membership of 4,207. Waco Association has 37 churches and 4,212 members. The Lord has been gracious to us here, and it is a matter of no small moment that the beloved brethren who prepared this history have given us such an excellent contribution to the historical literature of the Baptists of the state. May God bless this book to every one who reads it, and as the struggles, successes, discouragements and achievements of those whose names are recorded here are studied in aftertimes may the Holy Spirit lead the student of this history to redouble his efforts for the advancement of the kingdom of our Lord and his Christ.

Not only do I most heartily commend the work to all the churches of the Waco Association, but bespeak for it state wide circulation. It seems to me that it is rendering good service to our people to place such a history within their reach. It will not only be useful to Waco Association, but may be made very helpful to others, and I indulge the hope that it may lead to the compilation of similar associational histories of the various bodies of the state. B. H. CARROLL.

HISTORY
OF THE
WACO BAPTIST ASSOCIATION.

CHAPTER I.
INTRODUCTORY.

"We believe that a visible church of Christ is a congregation of baptized believers associated by covenant in the faith and fellowship of the gospel," etc.—*Articles of Faith of Waco Association.*

A tree may stand alone in the midst of a vast plain; it is then beautiful, helpful, an object of admiration. So a Baptist church may stand aloof from other churches, and be a blessing. But it is not to the lone oak, but to the great forests that workmen go for wood to build the mighty ocean vessels. So it is not to dissociated churches, but the well organized associations of churches that the wise master-builders look for means to aid the grand old ship of Zion while she bears cargoes of the Bread of Life to all the nations of earth.

BAPTIST ASSOCIATIONS.

It was the custom of the apostolic churches to co-operate together in carrying on the Master's work. See 2 Cor. 8:16-23. Here "a brother was *appointed by the churches* to travel," etc. God's people have always been a blessing to the world when they have associated themselves together for benevolent ends. One of the earliest associations of modern times was the London, formed in 1689. It was composed of messengers of more than 100 churches, scattered over England and Wales. The Confession of Faith adopted by this body, which formed the basis of what is now known as the Philadelphia Confession, was like the rising of a new sun, chasing away the clouds of doubt and misrepresentation respecting the Baptist people and their belief. By the London Association it was resolved, "That whatever is determined by us in any case shall not be binding upon any church till the consent of that church be first had." Baptists universally hold that "a church of Christ is the highest ecclesiastical authority on the earth."

The first Association in America was the Philadelphia, organized in 1707, which lives till this day, and is the mother of all American associations. Some fine utterances of this grand body in her youthful days could be republished with profit. Example: "Each particular church hath a complete power and authority from Jesus Christ to administer all gospel ordinances, * * * as baptism and the Lord's supper, and to receive and cast out, and also to try and ordain her own officers, and to exercise every part of gospel discipline and church government independent of any other church or assembly whatever." These words were written by Benjamin Griffith and signed by the whole Association in 1749, three years before the birth of any other American Association.

The earliest associations were: (1) the Philadelphia, 1701; (2) the Charleston, S. C., 1751; (3) the Sandy Creek, N. C., 1758; (4) the Kehukee, N. C., 1765; (5) the Ketocton, Va., 1766; (6) the Warren, R. I., 1767; (7) the Stonington, Conn., 1772; (8) the Red Stone, Penn., 1776; (9) the New Hampshire, N. H., 1776; (10) the Shaftesbury, Vt., 1781; (11) the Woodstock, Vt., 1783; (12) the Georgia, Ga., 1784. The number of Associations in the United States now reaches 1,500.

TEXAS.

The fairest land, the sweetest clime, the brightest skies, the balmiest air, the richest soil, the gayest fields, Texas stands unmatched, the paradise of ages. Demons have seen but one Alamo; angels have rejoiced over one San Jacinto. Richer in examples of exalted heroism than ancient Sparta, and in instances of devoted patriotism than imperial Rome; surpassing in beauty the fabled home of the undying gods—this is Texas. Happy the child of highest culture and purest christianity, yet to be born, who shall write the Texas epic.

BAPTISTS IN TEXAS.

The first evangelical sermon ever heard in Texas was preached by Elder Freeman Smalley, 1822. In the then far-away Northwest Territory (now Clinton county, O.) on March 3, 1791, was born this first Texas preacher. His education was such as the country afforded at that time—"reading, writing and ciphering as far as the Rule of Three." He visited New Orleans in 1822, and traveled 500 miles along on foot through the wilderness from New Orleans to North Texas. On the Texas side of Red River, opposite the mouth of Boggy creek, now Lamar county, Brother Smalley preached the first sermon in Texas. The services were held at the house of William Newman. The echo of that preacher's voice in 1822 has bounded from hill to hill throughout the length and breadth of Texas, and has multiplied into 2,500 voices. At the ripe old age of 83 this good man passed to his reward. His body sleeps in Kansas. He was an enthusiastic Missionary Baptist.

Elder Joseph Bays was the second Texas preacher. He preached his first sermon in Texas at the home of Moses Shipman, in South Texas, in 1825. He afterwards went to San Augustine, where he was for a time greatly hindered on account of opposition on the part of the authorities.

The third preacher, Elder Thos. Hanks, came from Tennessee in 1829. He also preached at the house of Moses Shipman. Under his ministry Mrs. Lydia Allcorn, the wife of James Allcorn, afterward deacon, made a profession of religion. This is probably the first profession in Texas.

During the same year, 1829, T. J. Pilgrim, a Baptist deacon, organized the first Sunday school in Texas. Brother Pilgrim came from New York. The story of his voyage down the Alleghany, the Ohio, the Mississippi and across the gulf to Texas is full of thrilling incidents. He gathered his pioneer Sunday School in the old town of San Felipe. It numbered thirty-two.

The fourth preacher was Elder Z. N. Morrell. He preached his first sermon in Texas to a camp of forty land hunters on Little River, December 30, 1835. Brother Morrell organized his first church in the town of Washington, in 1837. This was the first church on strictly gospel principles in the state. The church afterward went to pieces.

The first Association in Texas was organized at Travis, in Austin county, on October 8, 1840. Messengers from three churches went into the organization—Independence church, Washington county; La Grange, Fayette county, and Travis, Austin county. This was the origin of Union Association, the mother of all Texas associations. All Texas was her territory, and all the Baptist churches her constituents. The daughters of Union Association are Colorado, Trinity River, Tryon and Little River Associations. The granddaughters are Austin, Leon, Richland and Waco. The mother of Waco Association is Trinity River.

HISTORY

OF

THE WACO BAPTIST ASSOCIATION

From its Organization in 1860 to the Year 1897.

CHAPTER II.

FIRST HALF OF FIRST DECADE—HISTORY FROM DATE OF
ORGANIZATION TO CLOSE OF THE CIVIL WAR.

1860-1864.

The territory of Waco Association was originally part of the field of Trinity River Association, and later of both Trinity River and Richland. Prior to the formation of the Waco Association the rich country of Falls and McLennan counties, was but sparsely settled. It was the Texas frontier. Except in the Brazos bottom the lands were thought to be worthless, save for grazing purposes. Wild beasts, long horn cattle and skulking Indians disputed every acre of the territory with the advancing tide of population. Here and there little settlements formed, villages came into existence and the wild desert rapidly changed into fruitful fields of corn and broad, snowy "patches" of cotton. With the first people came Baptists, who organized themselves into churches at Waco, Marlin, Bosqueville, Bold Springs, Union Springs, White Rock, Blue Ridge, Cow Bayou (now Mooreville), Caddo and Perry (now Moody).

Waco, Marlin, Bosque (now Bosqueville), Perry, Blue Ridge and Caddo previously held membership in Trinity River Association. Perry church withdrew from Trinity River in 1859 and united with Leon River; afterwards went into the organization of McGregor Association; did not unite with Waco Association till 1890.

White Rock, Bold Springs and Union Springs were connected with Richland Association. At the meeting of Richland (third session), with Bold Springs church, October 15, 1860, the following was adopted:

"*Whereas*, It is contemplated by some of the churches of this Association to enter into a new Association to be formed at Waco, on Friday before the second Sabbath in November next, therefore

"Resolved, That at therequest of delegates of said churches, they, or any of them, may, in event of the formation of such new Association, by act of joining the same, be dismissed from this body in fellowship and order."

This act dismissed Bold Springs, Union Springs and White Rock.

Some complications were the cause of friction in Trinity River Association as soon as it was known that the new Association was contemplated. The complications were these:

Trinity River had a Male Classical School at Waco, with two-story brick building. Trinity River also had a Book Depository at Waco, under the management of Elder S. G. O'Bryan, and a similar Depository at Springfield, under the management of R. W. Swain. The interests at Waco, to which the brethren had made contributions, they were loath to surrender. And there were fears that Springfield might be induced to join the new organization. However, the influence of such diplomats as S. G. O'Bryan, J. W. Speight and N. W. Crain (Waco members) brought the matter to a successful issue, and at the thirteenth session of Trinity River, held with Leona church, Leon county, September, 1860, the churches at Waco, Bosqueville, Marlin and Blue Ridge were dismissed in fellowship and order.

Cow Bayou was newly organized and was hitherto unassociated.

On Friday, November 9, 1860, delegates from nine churches met in convention in Waco. They came together at the hour of 11 o'clock A. M.

The introductory sermon was preached by Elder Z. N. Morrell from Acts 11: 21, 22, "And the hand of the Lord was upon them; and a great multitude believed and turned unto the Lord. Then the tidings of these things came unto the ears of the church which was in Jerusalem; and they sent forth Barnabas that he should go as far as Antioch." After the sermon, adjourned till 2 o'clock P. M.

At 2 P. M., re-assembled. On motion of J. W. Speight, Elder Z. N. Morrell was called to the chair for temporary organization. Bro. Morrell called the assembly to bow with him in earnest prayer.

On motion of Elder N. W. Crain, Deacon L. Magee was chosen temporary Secretary.

Brethren J. W. Speight and N. W. Crain were appointed to read the letters from the churches. Letters were read from seven churches, and delegates' names enrolled as follows:

Bosque, A. H. Rhodes and H. Rodgers.
Blue Ridge, Z. N. Morrell and A. S. Trigg.
Waco, J. W. Speight, N. W. Crain and D. B. Arnold.
Union Springs, G. T. Holman and R. K. Williams.
Marlin, W. B. Eaves, L. Magee and W. A. Mason.
Bold Springs, Clay Cobb, H. Vaughn and Thomas Horseley.
White Rock, W. R. Bird, M. A. Bates and J. Y. Riddle.
These delegates were all present.

Permanent officers of the convention were now elected: Moderator, Z. N. Morrell, and Secretary, J. W. Speight.

Visiting brethren, J. J. Riddle of Richland Association and pastor of Bold Springs church, W. R. Kellum and I. H. Earle, were invited to, and accepted seats in the convention.

The following committees were appointed:

On Constitution—J. W. Speight, J. Y. Riddle, N. W. Crain, Thomas Horseley and Z. N. Morrell. The three last named were ordained ministers.

On Articles of Faith—W. A. Mason, H. Vaughn, J. J. Riddle, W B. Eaves, A. S. Trigg and B. D. Arnold. The four first named were ordained ministers.

On Rules of Order and Decorum—W. B. Eaves, H. Vaughn, W. R. Bird, Clay Cobb, R. K. Williams, and G. T. Holman. The two first named were ordained ministers.

The convention adjourned till night.

At night sermon by J. J. Riddle, followed with exhortation by W. B. Eaves.

SATURDAY MORNING, NOVEMBER 10.

W. A. Thompson was seated as delegate from Waco church.

Robert More, delegate from Cow Bayou, presented his letter and was seated.

The committee on constitution made their report, which, after discussion by Brethren Magee, Speight, Eaves and Crain, was unanimously adopted. The Constitution does not follow in form or substance the Constitution of Richland or of Trinity River, nor yet that of the State Convention. It was written by J. W. Speight, and is a grand document; and has never been altered or amended, though in some instances it has been construed on certain points by the Association. Following is the full text:

CONSTITUTION OF WACO BAPTIST ASSOCIATION.

ARTICLE I.

STYLE, TIME OF MEETING, REPRESENTATION, OBJECTS, ETC.

Section 1. This Association shall be styled the "Waco Baptist Association."

Sec. 2. It shall assemble annually at such time and place as shall best suit the conveniences of the churches.

Sec. 3. This Association shall be composed of five delegates from each church in union with us, who shall produce letters from their respective churches, certifying their appointment as such delegates.

Sec. 4. The objects of this Association shall be to establish and perpetuate a union, correspondence and fellowship between her respective churches, to spread the Gospel and disseminate Bible truth by all proper means.

ARTICLE III.

DUTIES OF CHURCHES, STATISTICS, FUNDS, ETC.

Section 1. It shall be the duty of the several churches of this Association to send up in their letters annually by their delegates a statement of the number received by letter or voucher, the number received by experience and baptism, the number dismissed, excommunicated, and died, since the last report, and the total number in fellowship, with such other information as may be deemed important, or that the Association may from time to time require.

Sec. 2. It shall also be the duty of said churches to send up to the Association annually by their delegates, according as they feel willing and able, funds to defray all necessary expenses, and to further and promote the objects of our union.

ARTICLE III.

OFFICERS, THEIR DUTY, ETC.

Section. 1. This Association shall elect annually by ballot (a majority of the delegates present being necessary to a choice) a Moderator, Clerk and Treasurer, and such other officers as the Association shall from time to time think necessary; and such officers, so elected, shall serve till their successors be duly elected.

Sec. 2. It shall be the duty of the Moderator to preside over the deliberations of the Association, preserve order, maintain decorum, state and put all questions, and declare the vote thereon, decide all points of order, (from which decisions, however, an appeal may be taken to the Association) and to vote only in the case of a tie.

Sec. 3. It shall be the duty of the Clerk to keep a minute of the proceedings of the Association, to keep a file of all important papers and documents, and to superintend the printing and distribution of the minutes, under the direction of the Association.

Sec. 4. It shall be the duty of the Treasurer to safely keep all monies and other funds of the Association, to disburse the same only by order of the Association, and to make in writing at each annual session a report of his official proceedings.

ARTICLE IV.

INDEPENDENCE OF CHURCHES—RESTRICTIONS ON AND PRIVILEGES OF THE ASSOCIATION.

Section. 1. A church of Jesus Christ being the highest ecclesiastical authority known on earth, it is therefore declared that the churches of this Association are absolutely independent of each other, and of any other organization or earthly power—that they acknowledge no soverign head but Christ, the Supreme Lawgiver, and consequently this Association shall never of right, interfere with the internal rights of, or dictate to, the said churches, exercise appellate jurisdiction or in any manner whatever lord it over God's heritage.

Sec. 2. This Association admits the right of any of her churches at any time to withdraw from her, and she claims the right to withdraw from, and disfellowship any church which shall depart from the principles of this compact, or become heterodox in faith or disorderly in practice, and to this end she may institute inquiry concerning fellowship and order.

Sec. 3. This Association, with respect to her authority over her churches, is merely an advisory council, and it shall be her duty to exercise her office as such, in all cases of disagreement or difficulty in or between any of her constituent churches.

ARTICLE V.

ADMISSION OF OTHER CHURCHES AND GENERAL DUTIES OF ASSOCIATION.

Section 1. Other churches may be admitted into this Association by letter and delegates, provided they be found to be orderly and orthodox; and upon such admission, the Moderator shall extend to the delegates the right hand of fellowship.

Sec. 2. It shall be the duty of the Association to make provision for the appropriation and employment of all funds in and for the specific purposes for which they have been sent up and received.

Sec. 3. This Association shall adopt and publish her "Articles of Faith," shall enact, publish and maintain her "Rules of Order and Decorum," and to this end she may admonish, reprove and rebuke through her Moderator, and in extreme cases may, by a unanimous vote, exclude an individual from a participation in her councils and deliberations.

Sec. 4. It shall be the duty of this Association to cultivate the most fraternal feelings for and among all brethren of our faith and order, and for all her sister Associations and kindred organizations; and to this end she may invite visiting brethren to sit with us and participate in our deliberations, may correspond with other bodies, and take any other legitimate and proper step to extend the sphere of her influence and usefulness.

Sec. 5. No query shall be received by this Association until it shall have been taken up and acted on in the church where it originated; then, if the church shall fail to get satisfaction, by inserting query in her letter, and certifying the facts, it may be received.

ARTICLE VI.
VOTING, AMENDMENTS, ETC.

Section 1. All questions coming before the Association, except in cases herein otherwise provided, shall be decided by a majority vote of the members present.

Sec. 2. Upon the admission or dismission of a church to or from this Association the vote shall be unanimous.

Sec. 3. Upon demand of the united delegation from any church the vote upon any question (except one merely of order or decorum) shall be taken by churches, and each church shall have one vote.

Sec. 4. The Articles of Faith of this Association shall not be altered or amended except by the unanimous concurrence of all churches expressed in their annual letters.

Sec. 5. This Constitution may be amended upon application of any church, which application shall be made by stating the proposed amendment, specifically in her annual letter; and if said proposed amendment shall be received by a two-thirds vote, it shall be entered on the minutes, and lie over till next annual meeting, when, if voted for by two-thirds of the churches of this Association in the manner prescribed in Section 3d, of this Article, it shall be a part and parcel of this Constitution.

During the Thirty-second annual session with Moody church, 1891, the Association construed Article IV, Section 2, of her Constitution to mean this: "This Association admits the right of any of her churches to withdraw from her at any time when the Association is in session, the Association consenting to the same," etc.

During the Thirty-fourth annual session held with Geneva church, 1893, a paper was adopted, "On Church Order in Seeking to Form or Withdraw from Associational Relations," which, *see*.

The *letter* of the Constitution (Art. I, Sec. 3), has not always been strictly observed. We refer to the words, "Who shall produce letters," etc. For instance at the Nineteenth Session with White Rock church, 1878, J. R. Shelton, from Mastersville church, was seated without a letter. Again, at the Thirty-first Session with Lorena church, 1890, against the ruling of Moderator W. D. Gaines, the Association by vote seated M. L. Garrett, delegate from Rock Creek church without a letter.

After the adoption of the Constitution more delegates of Waco church appeared and were seated in the Convention, viz: J. E. Harrison and J. C. West.

The committee on Articles of Faith made their report.

An amended version of the New Hampshire Declaration was presented, and adopted. In 1859 "The Baptist Church Directory" was published by Dr. E. T. Hiscox, and the document adopted by the Convention was almost an exact copy of the Articles of Faith found in "Hiscox's Directory," and later in Dr. J. M. Pendleton's "Church Manual." The Aritcles adopted differ from those in Hiscox and Pendleton, in substituting "Holy Spirit" for "Holy Ghost" in Article I, and in Article XIV.

The Articles of Faith have never been altered, amended or construed. There is no more complete uninspired compendium of Baptist faith to be found in all literature.

ARTICLES OF FAITH OF WACO ASSOCIATION.

I.

OF THE SCRIPTURES.

We believe that the Holy Bible was written by men Divinely inspired, and is a perfect treasure of heavenly instruction; 1 that it has God for its author, salvation for its end; 2 and truth, without any mixture of error, for its matter; 3 that it reveals the principles by which God will judge us; 4 and therefore is, and shall remain to the end of the world, the true center of Christian union; 5 and the supreme standard by which all human conduct, creeds and opinions shall be tried.

II.

OF THE TRUE GOD.

We believe there is one, and only one, living and true God, an infinite, intelligent Spirit, whose name Jehovah, the Maker and supreme Ruler of heaven and earth; 1 inexpressibly glorious in holiness, 2 and worthy of all possible honor, confidence and love, 3 that in the unity of the Godhead there are three persons, the Father, the Son, and the Holy Spirit, 4 equal in every divine perfection, 5 and executing distinct but harmonious offices in the great work of redemption.

III.

OF THE FALL OF MAN.

We believe that man was created in holiness, under the law of his maker; 1 but by voluntary transgression, fell from that holy and happy state; 2 in consequence of which all mankind are now sinners; 3 not by constraint, but choice; 4 being by nature utterly void of that holiness required by the law of God, positively inclined to evil; and therefore under just condemnation to eternal ruin; 5 without defense or excuse.

IV

OF THE WAY OF SALVATION.

We believe that the salvation of sinners is wholly of grace; 1 through the mediatorial offices of the Son of God; 2 who by the appointment of the Father, freely took upon Him our nature, yet without sin; 3 honored the Divine law by his personal obedience; 4 and by His death made a full atonement for our sins; 5 that having risen from the dead, He is now enthroned in heaven; 6 and uniting in His wonderful person the tenderest sympathies with the Divine perfections, He is every way qualified to be a suitable, a compassionate and an all-sufficient Savior.

V

OF JUSTIFICATION.

We believe that the great Gospel blessing which Christ 1 secures to such as believe in him is Justification; 2 that Justification includes the pardon of sin; 3 and the promise of eternal life on principles of righteousness; 4 that is bestowed, not in consideration of any work of righteousness, which we have done, but solely through faith in the Redeemer's blood; 5 by virtue of which faith his perfect righteousness is freely imputed to us of God; 6 that it brings us into a state of most blessed peace and favor with

God, and secures every other blessing needful for time and eternity.

VI.
OF THE FREENESS OF SALVATION.

We believe that the blessings of Salvation are made free to all by the gospel; 1 that it is the immediate duty of all to accept them by a cordial, penitent and obedient faith; 2 and that nothing prevents the salvation of the greatest sinner on earth, but his own determined depravity and voluntary rejection of the Gospel; 3 which rejection involves him in eternal condemnation.

VII.
OF GRACE IN REGENERATION.

We believe that in order to be saved, sinners must be regenerated, or born again; 1 that regeneration consists in giving a holy disposition to the mind; 2 that it is effected in a manner above our comprehension by the power of the Holy Spirit, in connection with the Divine truth, 3 so as to secure our voluntary obedience to the Gospel; 4 and that its proper evidence appears in the holy fruits of repentance and faith, and newness of life.

VIII.
OF REPENTANCE AND FAITH.

We believe that repentance and faith are sacred duties and also inseparable graces, wrought in our souls by the regenerating influences of the Spirit of God, 1 whereby being deeply convinced of our guilt, danger and helplessness, and of the way of salvation by Christ, 2 we turn to God with unfeigned contrition, confession and supplication for mercy; 3 at the same time heartily receiving the Lord Jesus Christ as our Prophet, Priest and King, and relying on Him alone as the only and all-sufficient Savior.

IX.
OF GOD'S PURPOSE OF GRACE.

We believe that election is the eternal purpose of God, according to which he graciously regenerates, sanctifies and saves sinners; 1 that being perfectly consistent with the moral agency of man, it comprehends all the means in connection with the end;

2 that it is a most glorious display of God's sovereign goodness, being infinitely free, wise, holy and unchangeable; 3 that it utterly excludes boasting, and promotes humility, love, prayer, praise, trust in God, and active imitation of his free mercy; 4 that it encourages the use of means in the highest degree; 5 that it may be ascertained by its effects in all who truly believe the Gospel; 6 that it is the foundation of Christian assurance, 7 and that to ascertain it with regard to ourselves, demands and deserves the utmost diligence.

X.

OF SANCTIFICATION.

We believe that Sanctification is the process by which, according to the will of God, we are made partakers of His holiness; 1 that it is a progressive work; 2 that it is begun in regeneration; 3 and that it is carried on in the hearts of believers by the presence and power of the Holy Spirit, the Sealer and Comforter, in the continual use of the appointed means—especially the word of God—self-examination, self-denial, watchfulness and prayer.

XI.

OF THE PERSEVERANCE OF THE SAINTS.

We believe that such only are believers as endure to the end, 1 that their persevering attachment to Christ is the grand mark which distinguishes them from superficial professors; 2 that a special providence watches over their welfare; 3 and they are kept by the power of God through faith unto salvation.

XII.

OF THE HARMONY OF THE LAW AND GOSPEL.

We believe that the law of God is the eternal and unchangeable rule of his moral government; 1 that it is holy, just and good; 2 and that the inability which the Scriptures ascribe to fallen men to fulfill its precepts, arises entirely from their love of sin; 3 to deliver them from which, and restore them a mediator to unfeigned obedience to the holy law, is one great end of the Gospel, and of the means of grace connected with the establishment of the visible church.

XIII.
OF A GOSPEL CHURCH.

We believe that a visible church of Christ is a congregation of baptized believers, 1 associated by covenant in the faith and fellowship of the Gospel; 2 observing the ordinances of Christ; 3 governed by His laws; 4 and exercising the gifts, right, and privileges invested in them by His word; 5 that its only scriptural officers are Bishops or Pastors and Deacons, 6 whose qualifications, claims and duties are defined in the Epistles to Timothy and Titus.

XIV.
OF BAPTISM AND THE LORD'S SUPPER.

We believe that Christian Baptism is the immersion in water of a believer, 1 in the name of the Father, and Son and Holy Spirit; 2 to show forth in a solemn and beautiful emblem, our faith in the crucified, buried, and risen Savior, with its effect, in our death to sin and resurrection to a new life; 3 that it is pre-requisite to the privileges of a church relation, and to the Lord's Supper, 4 in which the members of the church, by the sacred use of bread and wine, are to commemorate together the dying love of Christ; 5 preceded always by solemn self-examination.

XV.
OF THE CHRISTIAN SABBATH.

We believe that the first day of the week is the Lord's Day, or Christian Sabbath; 1 and is to be kept sacred to religious purposes, 2 by abstaining from all secular labor and sinful recreations; 3 by the devout observance of all the means of grace, both private 4 and public; 5 and by preparation for that rest that remaineth for the people of God.

XVI.
OF CIVIL GOVERNMENT.

We believe that Civil Government is of Divine appointment, for the interests and good order of human society; 1 and that magistrates are to be prayed for, conscientiously honored, and obeyed; 2 except only in things opposed to the will of our Lord

Jesus Christ, 3 who is the only Lord of the conscience, and the Prince of the kings of the earth.

XVII.

OF THE RIGHTEOUS AND THE WICKED.

We believe that there is a radical and essential difference between the righteous and the wicked; 1 that such only as through faith are justified in the name of the Lord Jesus, and sanctified by the Spirit of our God, are truly righteous in His esteem; 2 while all such as continue in impenitence and unbelief, are in His sight wicked, and under the curse; 3 and this distinction holds among men both in and after death.

XVIII.

OF THE WORLD TO COME.

We believe that the end of this world is approaching; 1 that at the last day Christ will descend from heaven, 2 and raise the dead from the grave to find retribution; 3 that a solemn separation will then take place; 4 that the wicked will be adjudged to endless punishment, and the righteous to endless joy; 5 and that this judgment will fix forever the final state of men in heaven or hell, on principles of righteousness

During the afternoon session (Nov. 10.) and after the adoption of Articles of Faith, delegates from Caddo church arrived with their letter and were seated in the Convention. They were John Knight, Joseph Harris and J. C. Newcum.

The Committee on Rules of Order and Decorum presented a document, which was adopted, but which has been amended at different times to suit the convenience of the Association. Originally it appeared as follows:

RULES OF ORDER AND DECORUM.

I. The sessions of the Association shall be opened and closed by prayer.

II. The following shall be the order of business:

1. Read the letters from the churches and enroll the names of the delegates.

2. Call the roll and make corrections if any are needed.

3. Elect officers according to the order in which they are named.

4. Call for petitionary letters.

5. Invite visiting brethren to sit with us.

6. Call for and invite corresponding messengers.

7. Enquire concerning the fellowship and order of the churches of this Association.

8. Appoint the following committees, viz: On Foreign Missions, on Home Missions, on Schools and Education, on Sabbath Schools, on Literature and Periodicals, on Colored Missions, on Temperance, on Finance, on Divine Service, on Ordained and Licentiate Ministers, and any other subject which at this time the Association may choose.

9. Read the Rules of Order and Decorum.

10. Return correspondence.

11. Call for reports of committees in the order of their appointment.

12. Appoint ministers to preach the introductory, missionary and closing sermons at next session of this body.

13. Select the time and place for holding the next session of this body.

14. Call for Treasurer's report.

15. Miscellaneous business.

III. The order of business may be temporarily suspended for a specified purpose by a vote of the Association.

IV. The Moderator shall appoint all committees, except otherwise ordered.

V. No appellation shall be used but that of brother.

VI. When a person is about to speak, he shall arise and respectfully address the Moderator. He shall confine himself to the subject under discussion; shall not deal in remarks personally offensive, or calculated to wound feelings, and shall not occupy the floor more than twice on the same subject, or speak longer than 30 minutes at any one time without permission from the Association.

VII. But one person shall occupy the floor at a time, and should two rise, the Moderator shall designate the one to speak.

VIII. While a person is speaking he shall not be interrupted, except, by a call to order, or by his own permission for some one to explain.

IX. When the discussion on any subject is ended, and before the question is put, the Moderator may speak by way of advice; but in that event he shall call some brother to the chair.

X. No motion shall be entertained till the same is seconded; nor shall any new subject be introduced till the matter under consideration has in some manner been disposed of.

XI. A motion to adjourn, to postpone, or to lay on the table is always in order.

XII. No appeal from the decision of the chair shall be taken, except on the same day on which the decision is made.

XIII. No member shall absent himself from the sessions of the Association without leave of the body.

XIV. The Minutes of the Association shall be read, amended if need be, approved, and signed by the Moderator and Clerk, before the Association rises.

The latest (1896) form of this document presents the order of Business and Rules of Decorum separated as follows:

ORDER OF BUSINESS.

1. Read letters from churches and enroll names of messengers.
2. Call roll and make corrections.
3. Elect Moderator, Clerk and Treasurer.
4. Call for petitionary letters.
5. Appoint committees on Divine Service, Nominations, Finance and other special committees.
6. Invite correspondence from other bodies.
7. Invite visiting brethren to seats in the Association.
8. Return correspondence.
9. Elect delegate to Southern Baptist Convention.
10. Refer all documents to appropriate committees.
11. Appoint the following committees to report at next session: Foreign Missions, Home Board, Schools and Education, Ministerial Education, Buckner Orphans' Home, State Missions, Obituaries and Sabbath Desecration.
12. Report of Associational Mission Board.
13. Organize new Board.

14. Reports of Standing committees.
15. Reports of special committees.
16. Treasurer's report.
17. New business.

RULES OF DECORUM.

1. The Sessions of this body shall be opened and closed with prayer.

2. The order of business may be temporarily suspended by a vote of the Association.

3. The Moderator shall appoint all committees unless otherwise ordered.

4. No appellation other than that of "Brother" shall be used.

5. When a person is about to speak, he shall rise and respectfully address the Moderator. He shall confine himself to the subject under discussion; shall not deal in remarks personally offensive or otherwise calculated to wound feelings, and shall not occupy the floor more than twice on the same subject, or speak longer than thirty minutes at any one time without permission from the Association.

6. But one person shall occupy the floor at one time, and should two rise, the Moderator shall designate the one to speak first.

7. While a person is speaking he shall not be interrupted, except by a call to order, or by permission of the speaker for some one else to explain.

8. When discussion on any subject is ended and before the question is put, the Moderator may speak by way of advice, but in that event he shall call some brother to the chair.

9. No motion shall be entertained till seconded, nor shall any new subject be introduced until the matter under consideration has in some way been disposed of.

10. A motion to adjourn, to postpone, or to lay on the table, is always in order.

11. No appeal from the decision of the chair shall be taken except on the same day the decision was made.

12. No member shall be absent from the Sessions of the Association without leave of the body.

13. The Minutes of the Association shall be read, amended (if need be) and signed by the Moderator and Clerk before the Association adjourns.

After adopting the Rules of Order and Decorum, this resolution was adopted:

"*Resolved*, That this Convention do now close, and that we proceed to organize as an Association under our Constitution, that the present officers act temporarily, and that the members of this Convention act as delegates accredited by their respective letters from their several churches."

The Convention closed with prayer by W. A. Mason.

The brethren then proceeded to organize the Waco Baptist Association in the afternoon of November 10, 1860.

There were present delegates from nine churches representing membership as follows: Blue Ridge, 12 members; Bosque, 41; White Rock, 19; Waco, 181; Union Springs, 44; Marlin, 133; Bold Springs, 52; Cow Bayou, 19; Caddo, 60. Total, 531.

Z. N. Morrell was pastor of Blue Ridge, N. W. Crain of Bosque and White Rock, W. H. Bayliss of Waco, H. Vaughn of Union Springs, W. B. Eaves of Marlin, J. J. Riddle of Bold Springs, Wm. Wright of Caddo. Cow Bayou had no pastor.

Z. N. Morrell was elected moderator of the Association, J. W. Speight clerk, and L. Magee treasurer.

B. D. Arnold, John Knight and J. Y. Riddle were appointed a finance committee. They reported $26.00 for publishing minutes.

The Association decided to open correspondence with Trinity River Association, Richland, Leon River and the Baptist State Convention.

It was ordered that any delegate "attending either of those bodies, and presenting a copy of our minutes, may act as our corresponding messenger to the same."

The next session was appointed to be held at Marlin, commencing Friday before the fourth Sunday in September, 1861. N. W. Crain was elected to preach the introductory sermon, W. H. Bayliss the missionary sermon, and Z. N. Morrell the closing sermon.

The following resolution passed with one dissenting voice:

Resolved, That we undertake to conduct our own missionary operations in our own bounds, and that the churches of this Association be requested to send up money and pledges for home missions at our next meeting to be expended during the succeeding year.

The clerk added: "Any funds, therefore, intended for this purpose will not be paid over to any agent of the Baptist State Convention, but retained and sent up to our next session at Marlin, or forwarded to Brother L. Magee, treasurer, at Marlin."

The Association, by vote, accepted the "Waco Classical School," "on the terms and conditions of its charter."

Brethren J. W. Speight, N. W. Crain and W. B. Eaves were appointed a committee "to correspond with Trinity River Association on the subject of the two Book Depositories of said Association now within our bounds, and request of said body a division of books, funds, etc."

The Association adjourned. Prayer by Z. N. Morrell, "after which, during the singing of an appropriate hymn, the brethren extended to each other the right hand of fellowship, and amidst the best of feelings the meeting dispersed."

SESSION OF 1861 AT MARLIN.

This was the year in which began the great civil war, and, of course, not much was done in the way of advancing the interests of the Association during the next four years. But the cause of Christ was not forgotten. Though all the able-bodied men were off east, in the war, yet the Association did not fail to meet regularly.

In 1861 the Marlin church had a membership of 108. It had a feeble beginning nine years previously with seven members.

At this session of the Association all the churches were represented except Union Springs. Additions by baptism reported: Waco 3, Bold Springs 2, Cow Bayou 4. By letter: Waco 22, Bosque 2, Bold Springs 2. Total membership, 505. (This does not include Union Springs).

Churches and pastors: Blue Ridge, Z. N. Morrell; Bosque, Bold Springs and Cow Bayou, N. W. Crain; Waco, W. H. Bayliss; Marlin, W. B. Eaves.   There were present 18 delegates.

The brethren came together on Friday at 11 o'clock a. m., September 20, 1861, in the upper story of the only brick building in the town. The building was the property of Mr. Z. Bartlett.

Elder N. W. Crain preached the introductory sermon. Text: "Ye are my witnesses, saith the Lord." Isa. 43:10. Adjourned till 2:30.

Re-assembled. The old officers were re-elected.

Jasper McKinney was received as a corresponding messenger from Little River Association, and Prof. D. R. Wallace of Waco University was seated as a visitor.

The following committees were appointed:

Foreign Missions—W. B. Eaves, W. H. Bayliss, D. Barclay.

Home Missions—N. W. Crain, J. Y. Riddle, R. Rogers.

Schools and Education—M. D. Herring, L. Magee, M. R. Shields.

Sabbath Schools—J. A. Fortune, S. F. Sparks, W. Z. Dixon.

Colored Missions—A. G. Perry, R. Rogers, T. P. Aycock.

Temperance—E. C. Hardin, A. G. Perry, J. W. Speight.

Literature and Periodicals—W. H. Bayliss, J. W. Speight.

Finance—M. D. Herring, T. P. Aycock.

Divine Service—The pastor and deacons of Marlin church.

On Ordained and Licentiate Ministers—W. B. Eaves, J. W. Speight.

All these committees presented written reports which were published.

Following are extracts:

Foreign Missions: "It is a cause dear to every Baptist heart."

Home Missions: "In view of the condition of the country, engaged as we are in a bloody and expensive war for our liberties, and the stringent condition of money matters, * * *we cannot see how we could sustain missions in our midst. We would recommend to the Association not to make any provision for a missionary in the field for the present, but to mature their plan for carrying on missions, so that when times shall alter and we can sustain them, we will be ready to commence operations. We recommend to the Association to appoint a committee of experienced, discreet brethren to report a plan to the next meeting of this body."

The committee provided for in this report was appointed: N. W. Crain, W. B. Eaves and J. W. Speight.

Schools and Education:

"By its charter the Waco University and Classical School is under the patronage and fostering care of our Association. It is the most prominent and bids fair to be the most successful school, not only within our bounds, but in the entire state."

It should be stated in this connection that the former principal, John C. West, resigned on Jan. 1, 1861, and that Dr. R. C. Burleson, president of Baylor University at Independence, with the entire faculty of the male department of that institution, had been engaged by the trustees of Waco Classical School. The school under Dr. Burleson had been in operation just three weeks at the time of this meeting of the Association. The library consisted of nearly 700 volumes. They had assumed the name of "Waco University," though the charter for that name was not yet granted. There were over sixty pupils.

Extract from report on Sabbath Schools: "Organize a school of a half dozen scholars, teach them diligently, and they will be better children, you a better Christian, and the church a better church."

Extract from report on Literature and Periodicals: "There is a small depository of books located at Waco, in the hands of our brother, J. W. Speight, subject to your directions. Said books were transferred to the Waco Association by the Trinity River Association at its last session, and amount to between $50 and $60 at sale prices. Your committee recommend that the depository be continued at Waco as the most suitable location; and that Bro. E. H. Hardin be appointed your agent. * * * The 'Texas Baptist,' formerly the organ of the denomination in this state, has fallen under the pressure, and in the opinion of your committee is not likely ever to revive again."

The Texas Historical and Biographical Magazine (August, 1892), says the old Texas Baptist suspended in 1862. We prefer to accept the statement of Waco Association. The paper was dead in

September, 1861. It never revived. The above report was written by Elder W. H. Bayliss.

Extract from report on Colored Missions: "We recommend that the several churches do what they can towards evangelizing our colored population, * * * at least till we shall be able to employ a special missionary for the purpose."

Be it said to their praise that our dear old Southern Baptist fathers were always solicitous about the spiritual welfare of their slaves. And when the colored people were converted they were baptized into the fellowship of the churches with the whites.

Extract from report on Temperance: "It is a noticeable and lamentable fact that many of the exclusions from our churches may be traced directly or indirectly to the use of ardent spirits."

The minute fund was $27. The fund for associational missions $15.80. Nothing was sent by the churches for missions. The $15.80 was the result of public collection during the Association at Marlin.

N. W. Crain was elected corresponding secretary of the Association.

At 9 o'clock on Sunday morning the Association met in earnest and solemn prayer to God for "the protection of the Southern armies and for the success of our country's cause."

At 11 o'clock a. m. Elder W. H. Bayliss preached; at 3 p. m. W. B. Eaves, and at night N. W. Crain.

Ordained Ministers: Z. N. Morrell, Alto Springs; W. B. Eaves and W. A. Mason, Marlin; Thomas Horseley, Bold Springs; W. H. Bayliss, N. W. Crain, R. C. Burleson and R. B. Burleson, Waco.

Licentiates: M. M. Vanderhurst, Waco; Jno. A. Fortune, Jr., Marlin; J. K. Horseley, Bold Springs.

SESSION OF 1862 AT BOSQUEVILLE.

Bosqueville was before the war quite a thriving village. It was the seat of Bosqueville College, a chartered institution. The church was called at that time "Bosque Church." Bosqueville is four miles northwest of Waco. It was with this church the third annual session of the Association was held.

Two new churches were received at this session, Antioch and Searsville.

Antioch, in the northeastern part of Bosque county, was newly organized. Elder F. A. Mound was pastor. The church reported a fine revival in which twelve were received by baptism and twenty-four by letter. She reported a total membership of forty-five. The Association met with Antioch in 1863. After that the church never was represented again.

Searsville is near Valley Mills, in Bosque county. It was a new church in 1862, and came into the Association with 11 members. The delegates bearing the petitionary letter were F. F. Bloodworth and S. Preston. In 1864 the Association met with Searsville. This church continued a member of the Association till 1874, when she withdrew with 43 members. The church still exists, is a member of Meridian Association, and has about 100 members.

At the third session of the Waco Association only five churches were represented, viz: Waco, Bosqueville, Searsville, Bold Springs and Antioch. Blue Ridge, Cow Bayou, Caddo, Marlin and Union Springs failed to represent. Blue Ridge, Caddo and Union Springs did not again represent till after the close of the war.

Two churches reported additions by baptism: Waco 6, and Antioch 12. There were only 15 delegates present.

The introductory sermon was preached by R. C. Burleson, from Dan. 2:44: "And in the days of these kings shall the God of heaven set up a kingdom which shall never be destroyed; and the kingdom shall not be left to other people, but it shall break in pieces and consume all these kingdoms, and it shall stand forever."

Officers were elected as follows: Moderator, N. W. Crain; clerk, W. E. Oakes; treasurer, R. B. Wilson.

Elder L. D. Stringer was welcomed as a corresponding messenger from Leon River Association and Elder J. J. Riddle, from Richland.

Corresponding messengers were appointed to other bodies as follows: Trinity River Association, R. C. Burleson and F. F.

Bloodworth; Little River, W. B. Eaves and Van Diver; Richland, N. W. Crain and J. Y. Riddle; Leon River, R. C. Burleson, N. W. Crain and S. Preston; Bosque River, Van Diver, W. A. Mason and S. Preston; Baptist State Convention, W. R. Kellum, S. F. Sparks, S. Preston, J. Y. Riddle and F. F. Bloodworth.

Committees appointed: Foreign Missions—R. C. Burleson, S. Preston, M. R. Carroll.

Schools and Education—F. F. Bloodworth, S. F. Sparks, W. E. Oakes; N. W. Crain was added.

Colored Missions—H. Rogers, R. B. Wilson.

Sabbath Schools—J. Y. Riddle.

Temperance—A. H. Rhodes, L. D. Stringer.

Literature—R. C. Burleson, F. F. Bloodworth.

Finance—S. F. Sparks, W. S. Gill.

A committee was appointed on Home Missions, but was at their own request excused because there was a standing committee on this subject appointed at last session. Brethren S. F. Sparks and R. B. Wilson were added to this committee, and they were given another year to report.

An executive committee of nine were appointed to supply Home (associational) Missions for the ensuing year, to-wit: R. C. Burleson, N. W. Crain, W. B. Evans, F. F. Bloodworth, S. F. Sparks, W. R. Kellum, R. B. Wilson, J. Y. Riddle, W. E. Oakes.

Only four of the reports were published, viz: On Sabbath Schools, Temperance, Colored Missions and Finance.

From the report on Sabbath Schools we learn that there were three schools in the bounds of the Association.

From the report on Temperance, written by that consecrated deacon of Bosqueville, A. H. Rhodes, we make this extract: "Our own observation has taught us that the pathway of the dram drinker and rumseller is a slippery path, in which many have fallen to rise no more."

No funds were reported for missions; funds for printing minutes $23.50.

On motion of S. F. Sparks:

"*Resolved*, That this Association appoint the second Sabbath in November next as a day of thanksgiving and prayer to Almighty God for his great mercies vouchsafed to us in the recent victories he has given our armies over our wicked foes, and for a continuance of his providence to us as a nation."

On Sunday, at 11 A. M., Elder J. J. Riddle preached.

SESSION OF 1863 AT ANTIOCH.

Only two churches were represented, Antioch and Searsville. They convened Friday, Oct. 9, 1863.

Antioch reported 20 received by baptism and 7 by letter. Searsville reported 5 by baptism. The plucky brethren from Searsville were S. Preston, F. F. Bloodworth, J. H. Mabry, J. L. Sears and J. K. Helton. Antioch delegates: B. E. Lucas, J. Carroll, J. Parker, J. Lane, G. Powell, B. M. Willingham.

The introductory sermon was preached by L. D. Stringer. Text, John 8: 36, "If the Son, therefore, make you free, ye shall be free indeed."

Elder B. E. Lucas was elected moderator, Elder J. Carroll, clerk, and J. Lane, treasurer.

Elder J. J. Sledge and Brethren S. Dyer and W. Harrison were welcomed as corresponding messengers from Richland Association. Elders J. Hill and L. D. Stringer were seated as visitors.

Not having a copy of the Order of Business of the Association, those resourceful brethren made an Order of Business.

On Saturday, Oct. 10, at 4 P. M., Elder J. Hill preached.

On Sunday, at 11, Elder J. J. Sledge preached a powerful discourse from Isa. 11: 9. At the close of this sermon a collection for domestic missions was taken, amounting to $100.50.

In the midst of those perilous times and at a session when only two infant churches were represented, it is refreshing to read the following report on Home Missions:

"After taking into consideration the destitute condition of our Association, we recommend that an efficient missionary be employed to ride within said bounds, to visit families, and preach in destitute neighborhoods; and we recommend that Bro. (B. E.) Lucas be appointed to that work. We are of opinion that it will take $200 to pay him for this laborious service. We also recommend that a suitable agent be appointed to visit the churches in said bounds, and collect money to assist in paying said missionary; that the missionary appointed be requested to make collections whenever he may think it practicable.

"(Signed) JAMES LANE,
F. F. BLOODWORTH."

It is presumed that Bro. Lucas did not accept, as no report was made at the next Association, and as funds ($257) in the hands of Missionary Board were turned over to the finance committee at that meeting.

Our readers will be pleased with this report on Temperance, signed by J. K. Helton and J. Parker:

"Your committee on Temperance beg leave to make the following report:

"'Who hath woe? Who hath sorrow? Who hath contentions? Who hath babblings? Who hath wounds without cause? Who hath redness of eyes?' 'They that tarry long at the wine,' 'they that go to seek mixed wine.' 'Look not thou upon the wine when it is red, when it giveth its color in the cup,' 'when it moveth itself aright.' 'At last it biteth like a serpent and stingeth like an adder.'"

The report on Sabbath Schools states that there were three schools in the Association, Waco, Marlin and Searsville.

An Executive Board was appointed with J. K. Helton, chairman; J. L. Sears, secretary, and F. F. Bloodworth, treasurer.

The Treasurer's report showed funds on hand as follows:

Cash in current money ....$ 74 50
Cash in money not current 26 00
Subscription 100 00

Total $200 50

Dr. R. M. Barnes and F. F. Bloodworth were appointed to visit churches and collect funds.

A collection was taken for the benefit of the Clerk, amounting to $14.50.

The next meeting of the Association was appointed at Searsville on Friday before the second Sunday in October, 1864.

"Prayer by J. J. Sledge. An hymn was then sung, and the brethren bade each other farewell."

SESSION OF 1864 AT SEARSVILLE.

The fifth annual Session was held at Searsville, near Valley Mills, commencing Friday before the second Sabbath in October and ending Monday, 1864.

The introductory sermon was preached by R. C. Burleson, from Matt. 28: 18, 19, 20. Subject, the "Commission."

Three new churches were received, Beulah and Sunset, near Marlin, and Pleasant Grove, near Speegleville. Beulah exists till this day. Pleasant Grove dissolved, and Speegleville was afterward organized in the same community. Sunset ceased to exist long ago. Sunset had 41 members, Beulah 36, and Pleasant Grove 38.

Delegates with letters were present from Searsville, Waco, Marlin, Caw Bayou, Bosque, Sunset, Beulah, Pleasant Grove and Bold Springs. There were present 23 delegates. Blue Ridge, Caddo, Union Springs and Antioch failed to represent.

Received by baptism: Waco, 5; Searsville, 1; Marlin, 30; Cow Bayou, 15; Bosque, 2; Beulah, 12; Pleasant Grove, 9; Bold Springs, 3. Total, 77. Total received by letter, 74. Total membership (not counting absent churches) 620.

Officers elected: R. C. Burleson, moderator; J. W. Speight, clerk; L. Magee, treasurer.

Churches and Pastors: Searsville, William Manning; Waco, W. H. Anderson; Marlin, W. B. Eaves; Cow Bayou, John McLain; Bosque, N. W. Crain; Sunset and Pleasant Grove, R. B. Burleson; Beulah, C. Magee; Bold Springs, E. J. Billings.

Elders John McLain, S. G. O'Bryan and L. D. Stringer were welcomed to seats as visitors.

Committees were appointed on various subjects as required in the Order of Business.

Corresponding messengers were appointed as follows: To Little River Association, W. Manning, R. C. Burleson, L. Magee; to Leon River, F. F. Bloodworth, S. Preston, N. C. Crain, J. W. Speegle; to Richland, W. S. Grimes, R. C. Burleson, N. W. Crain; to Trinity River, A. G. Perry, J. W. Speight.

Extracts from report on Schools and Education: "We are to report that Waco University, under the direction of this Association, is in a flourishing condition, and is accomplishing much good. Three young preachers have been educated in this institution, two of whom are efficient chaplains in the army, and the other gives promise of great usefulness."—Written by A. G. Perry, of Sunset church.

After stating that Waco University had been put "upon a footing equal to that of the most favored institutions of learning in the Confederate States," the Trustees of the University report: "The institution matriculated last year 192 students, fully twice as many as any other college in the State."

The report on Foreign Missions, written by A. G. Perry, showed the association to be fully alive and loyal to the Richmond Board. The report on Home Missions, by the same author provided for a mission committee to be composed of a member from each church with the Moderator and Clerk of the Association. Following are the names of this committee: Waco, R. B. Burleson; Searsville, W. Manning; Marlin, Jno. Barton; Cow Bayou, Robert Moore; Bosque, W. S. Gill; Sunset, J. T. Waller; Beulah, L. Magee; Pleasant Grove, I. W. Speegle; Bold Springs, W. S. Grimes; R. C. Burleson, J. W. Speight.

The report on Sabbath Schools, written by Elder J. F. Pierson, declared that no church was excusable for neglect in this particular. That on Colored Missions declared, as former reports had done, that it was the intention of the Association, at some future time, to employ a special missionary to the colored people. However, this was never done, except in co-operation with other bodies.

The report on Temperance was written by J. K. Helton, of Searsville. He was in the front rank of temperance advocates. The report was a lengthy document. We give this extract: "Who among us now can defend moderate drinking on the same footing that they would moderate eating and moderate sleeping? * * * Do not the Scriptures make a difference? 'Look not upon the wine.' 'Go not among wine bibbers.' 'He shall drink neither wine nor strong drink.' How it would astonish any one of us to find a

Scripture like this: 'Look not upon the bread.' 'Go not among bread eaters!' "

Resolutions were adopted declaring their "fixed and unalterable attachment to the cause of Southern Independence."

The Treasurer's report showed funds for Associational missions:

Confederate notes $1212
County warrants 84
    Total $1296

All this currency died in the hands of the Treasurer.

Baptisms reported 5 years, 124; received by letter and vouchers in five years, 698. Decrease, 134.

Total raised for Missions, $1296; this being worthless currency, was all lost.

RESUME.

Nine churches were in the organization in 1860. Caddo and Union Springs did not again represent till after the Civil War, in 1866. White Rock united with Bold Springs. In '62 and '63 Cow Bayou and Blue Ridge failed to represent; Blue Ridge in '64.

In '62 Antioch and Searsville joined the Association. In '63 the Association met with Antioch, and besides Antioch, only Searsville was represented in that meeting. After '63, Antioch never represented again.

In '64 Beulah, Pleasant Grove and Sunset were received.

Membership reported in '60, 541. Membership reported in '64, 620.

CHAPTER III.

SECOND HALF OF FIRST DECADE.

1865-1870.

Never since the first colony settled at Jamestown in 1607, have Southern hopes and prospects been darker. The country prostrated, and with the new and untried social relations, was a picture to make the stoutest heart quake. But never was the cloud so dark as to cause the Baptists of the Waco Association to lose sight of the great object for which the body was formed "to spread the Gospel and to disseminate Bible truth by all proper means."

SESSION OF 1865 AT WACO.

The sixth annual session was held with the church at Waco, commencing Friday before the fourth Sunday in August, 1865. The churches represented were: Waco, R. C. Burleson, pastor; Searsville, Wm. Manning, pastor; Marlin, W. B. Eaves, pastor; Cow Bayou, J. McLain, pastor; Bosque, S. G. O'Bryan, pastor; Beulah, C. Magee, pastor; Pleasant Grove, R. C. Burleson, pastor; Blue Ridge, C. W. Wright, pastor; Bold Springs, E. J. Billings, pastor; Sunset, R. C. Burleson, pastor. Caddo, Union Springs and Antioch were not represented.

The name of Bosque church was changed during next year to "Bosqueville," though it does not so appear on the minutes of Association till 1870.

Union Springs church did not represent this or the following year—represented in 1867. This church was in the organization of Richland Association in 1858.

The introductory sermon was preached by Elder Wm. Manning, pastor of Searsville church, from Isa. 50: 10.

The association organized by electing Elder R. C. Burleson, moderator, J. W. Speight, clerk and L. Magee, treasurer.

Although the churches were just passing out of that awful period of the Civil War, which exhausted both the spirits and resources of our people, yet reports were adopted at this session on Foreign Missions, Home Missions, Schools and Education, Sabbath Schools, Literature and Periodicals, Colored Missions, Temperance and Finance. All these reports had the right ring, as the following extracts show:

"That being still in the providence of God cut off from communication with the Foreign Missions Board at Richmond, we are unable to inform you what is being done. * * * Resolved, That our interest in Foreign Missions as the work of God is unabated."—Report on Foreign Missions, by Wm. Manning.

"To urge upon the churches the importance of sustaining Home Missions is a needless task, as it is a cardinal principle with us to send the Gospel to the destitute. * * * We all have the glorious privilege of praying for the advancement of the Redeemer's

Kingdom, and each one of us can do something personally to advance His cause."—Report on Domestic Missions, by N. W. Crain.

"The committee would urge the claims of education with the same emphasis that has heretofore been given to this subject by the Association. The state of society, and changes that have taken place by no means suggest a diminution of zeal. * * * Brethren, educate your children, encourage good teachers and do not look upon the expenses as a matter of tax, but the most remunerative investment of money."—Report on Schools and Education, by Thos. P. Aycock.

The report on Waco University shows that no effort was made to keep up a collegiate department during the last three years of the war, in consequence of the enlistment of nearly all the young men into the military service. The primary and preparatory departments were kept up with good results. During this year a female department was added. The sexes were under the same faculty, though in separate buildings and occupying different grounds. They were only together during recitation. Faculty: R. C. Burleson, A. M., Pres., Professor Belle-Letters and Spanish; R. B. Burleson, A. M., V. P., Natural Science; D. R. Wallace, A. M., M. D., Latin, Greek and French; O. H. Leland, A. M., Mathematics, Mechanical Philosophy and Astronomy; W. H. Long, A. B., Adjunct Professor Greek, Latin and German; Mrs. H. M. Carter, Drawing, Painting and Embroidery; Miss S. C. Lambdin, Literary Department; E. W. Krause, Music.

The report on Sabbath Schools showed that there were only three in the Association.

Report on Colored Missions: "The change in the relations of the negro certainly does not lessen our duty to God in giving them moral and religious instructions. Heretofore the slave was dependent, and his master felt that there was a peculiar and special responsibility resting on him individually to cause him (slave) to be supplied with the Word of Life. Now, however, as the slave has been raised from the condition of a dependent to that of the responsibilities of a freeman, the interest of his late master ceases to be special and particular. * * * Heretofore the negro has never thought for himself—the white man has done his thinking. * * * God rules, * * * and we should be careful in our blind unbelief and impiety, not to err or scan his work in vain. He will interpret his own purposes and eventually turn all to his own glory." We wish we had space to reproduce this entire paper. It is a magnificent document—was written by the lamented Hon. J. W. Speight. No recommendations were made. It was "submitted to the churches whether it would not be better to organize the colored churches separate and distinct from white churches."

The Executive Committee on Missions appointed in 1864 (R. C. Burleson, chairman) reported that Elder N. C. Crain had been employed "to ride as missionary in the destitute portions of the upper part of the Association at $1.50 per day for time actually employed." He had labored 50 days and baptized 14 persons, and the Treasurer was ordered to pay him $75. He was paid $26.50 in specie; he donated $48.50, which was accepted. It was the intention to employ a man to supply Caddo church in Milam County, and the destitution in the Southern part of the Association; but after "vigorous effort" the committee failed to find a preacher.

The Association lost heavily in consequence of depreciation of Confederate currency—$1,296 died in the hands of the Treasurer.

The Association, as well as all Texas, was interested to have a Texas Baptist paper, and a report was adopted on that subject.

Visitors present: Elders F. Kiefer, W. H. Anderson, R. B. Burleson, R. H. Taliaferro, Brethren M. D. Herring, S. F. Sparks, D. R. Wallace, (Gen.) J. E. Harrison.

The total membership reported in 1864 was 542; in 1865 it was 623. Only four churches reported baptisms—Waco 9, Marlin 1, Searsville 19, Pleasant Grove 2.

SABBATH EXERCISES.

As every one knows, an important part of the exercises at associational meetings in the days of our fathers was Gospel preaching. And at this meeting we find the Lord's day pretty well filled up. Lecture on Sabbath Schools, by Elder T. P. Aycock 9 A. M. Baptist house 11 A. M., preaching by Elder S. G. O'Bryan, Methodist house, 11 A. M., preaching by R. H. Taliaferro. To the colored people at 3 P. M., preaching by Elders O'Bryan and J. F. Pinson. "The communion of the Lord's Supper was administered under the authority of church at Waco at 4 o'clock P. M." Night preaching at the Baptist house by T. P. Aycock, at Methodist house by J. A. Fortune.

All things considered, this session of '65 was one of the most important ever held by the Association. The great fact that Baptists can adapt themselves to any change of situation or environment is here beautifully illustrated. One is struck with the spirituality, harmony and business air of this meeting.

SESSION OF 1566.

The seventh annual Session was held with the church at Blue Ridge, Friday before the fourth Sunday in August, 1866.

At this meeting eight churches were represented: Waco, Searsville, Marlin, Cow Bayou, Bosqueville (formerly Bosque), Beulah, Pleasant Grove, Blue Ridge. Same Pastors as last year except Blue Ridge, which has C. B. Kincaid. Bold Springs, Sunset, Caddo, Union Springs, Antioch not represented. Baptisms—Waco 4, Cow Bayou 4, Bosqueville 4. Total 12. Received by letter—Waco 11, Marlin 4, Cow Bayou 12, Beulah 8, Pleasant Grove 1, Blue Ridge 7. Total 43.

Total dismissed 146, died 8, excluded 3. Membership this year 514. Decrease 109.

Officers elected: R. C. Burleson, moderator; J. W. Speight, clerk; W. R. Kellum, treasurer.

The following visiting brethren were invited to and accepted seats: Wm. Howard, agent of Southern Baptist Biennial Convention; J. W. D. Creath, agent of Texas Baptist State Convention; Elders Jonas Wood, T. M. Anderson, Little River Association; W. B. Eaves, Z. N. Morrell, Bro. W. A. Dunklin, Galveston church.

It was ordered that the "committees on Foreign, Home and Colored Missions be dispensed with, and that hereafter a committee on Missions be raised to consider the whole subject of Missions."

Reports were adopted on Missions, Sabbath Schools, Schools

and Education, Literature and Periodicals, Temperance, Waco University and Finance.

No missionary was kept on the associational field during the past year.

The report on Missions, after citing destitution on all fields, recommended:

1. "That we now appoint two missionaries for their whole time to preach the gospel to every creature, white and black, within the bounds of our Association during the ensuing associational year.

2. "That we now pledge our churches for a specific amount, to be paid quarterly, and that we take up in our churches weekly or monthly collections for the support of our missionaries.

3. "That we establish monthly concerts of prayer for missions, that the spirit of missions may be revived in our churches."

The report was written by R. C. Burleson.

The report on Schools and Education cited: "Our denomination is not behind any other in the extension of educational facilities." It recommends Waco University.

In the report on Waco University appear the following remarkable statements: "There were matriculated (in 1865-6) 130. * * * In the male department it (curriculum) is equal to any college in the South, and in the female department the standard of education is higher and more thorough than any female college in the South, the Mary Sharp College only excepted. The theological department is in successful operation, and two young men are preparing for the ministry." This, on the frontier of Texas and the first year after the civil war!

It will be remembered that the Waco University was now one of the enterprises of Waco Association. At this session the Association approved the selection of Col. Jno. T. Flint to fill a vacancy on the Board of Trustees. Col. J. W. Speight was president of the Board of Trustees.

The report on Sunday Schools shows only three schools within our bounds. The report hopefully chronicles a great awakening in other parts of the state on the subject.

Ringing reports adopted at this and the preceding session on

Temperance, show that our brethren of that day were not a step behind the most enthusiastic temperance advocates of later years.

The report on Literature and Periodicals recommended Bunyan, Winslow, Keach, Beddame, Fuller, Hall, Spurgeon, Gill, Ripley, Hackett, Conant, Carson, Booth, Pengilly, Howell, Dayton, Mrs. Ford, Jones, Robinson, Backus, Orchard and Benedict. Also the Texas Baptist Herald, published by J. B. Link, and the Companion, published by J. R. Clark.

The ministers of 1866 were R. C. Burleson, R. B. Burleson, S. G. O'Bryan, J. McLain, C. Magee, J. J. Riddle, N. C. Crain, Wm. L. Foster, T. P. Aycock, John A. Fortune, C. B. Kincaid.

The Executive Committee for the coming year: J. W. Speight, R. B. Burleson, B. D. Arnold, Sr.; F. F. Bloodworth, S. G. O'Bryan, R. C. Burleson. This committee was charged to carry out the recommendation of mission report.

The following amounts were pledged for missions: Waco Church $200, Marlin $25, Bosqueville $30, Beulah $25, Cow Bayou $25, Leonville $25. Leonville was not a member of the Association.

SABBATH EXERCISES.

At 11 o'clock Elder Wm. Howard preached "with great power," and a collection taken for the purpose of his mission of $100. At 3 p. m. Elder J. W. D. Creath preached to the white congregation, and T. M. Anderson to the colored. At night R. C. Burleson preached.

The Association decided to co-operate with the Texas Baptist Sunday School and Colportage Union, and delegates appointed to that body as follows: R. C. Burleson, A. G. G. Perkins, R. Moore, R. B. Burleson.

The thanks of the body were voted to Blue Ridge church.

Total for mission collected and pledged during the sittings, $425.

SESSION OF 1867.

This, the eighth session was held in Marlin at the usual time in August, 1867.

The introductory sermon was preached from James, 5:16: "Confess your faults one to another, and pray for one another that ye may be healed. The effectual, fervent prayer of a righteous man availeth much."

Five new churches were received: Bethel and Tehuacana, in McLennan county, Peoria, Hill county, and Ebenezer and Salem, from Trinity River Association. The right hand of fellowship was extended to the delegates of these new churches by the whole Association. Bethel, Peoria and Tehaucana were newly organized churches. In 1872 the name of Tehuacana was changed to Concord, and that of Bethel was changed to Robinson in 1877. Ebenezer was dismissed by letter in 1871.

There were now 18 churches on the rolls; 16 of these represented, viz: Waco, Bosqueville, Marlin, Beulah, Caddo, Pleasant Grove, Blue Ridge, Bold Springs (by letter only), Union Springs, Bethel, Tehuacana, Peoria, Ebenezer, Salem, Cow Bayou, Searsville; Sunset and Antioch not represented.

Officers elected: R. C. Burleson, moderator; N. W. Crain, clerk; Jno. A. Fortune, treasurer.

Marlin, Bold Springs, Union Springs and Bethel reported fine revivals. Marlin, under the pastoral care of Elder Calvin Magee-reported the greatest revival in her history before or since—77 were received by baptism, giving her a total membership of 216. And strangely enough she did not represent in the Association the two following years, and the next time we hear of her (1870) she has a new pastor and only 61 members.

Total increase reported: By baptism 164, letter 97. Decrease —by letter 73, excluded 10, died 9. Total membership 879.

The new churches brought into the Association two new ministers, Elder Benj. Walker, Tehuacana church, and T. J. Sparkman, Peoria church.

Visiting brethren: Elders J. W. D. Creath, agent of Baptist State Convention; J. M. McCraw, missionary of Association; Prof. W. H. Long of Waco University; Elder C. W. Kincaid, of this Association; W. A. Dunklin, Galveston, and J. W. Tabor, Millican.

The report of the Executive Committee showed an immense amount of labor done by missionary, Elder J. M. McCraw, in nine months. Miles traveled 2405, sermons preached 139, families visited 458, churches organized 2, churches visited, times 27, visited destitute places, times 14; baptized 2, etc. The report on missions, written by John A. Fortune, thus refers to Bro. McCraw's work: We have employed a missionary. He has worked faithfully, and God has blessed him."

The report on schools and education, written by N. W. Crain, notes "the fact that our people are very much alive to the importance of giving their children the advantages of a liberal education. The report on Waco University celebrates the fact that there were during the year past 253 matriculations. Prof. W. H. Long, A. M., is now in the chair of mathematics in the place of Prof. Foster, resigned.

The Association at this session passed resolutions endorsing the movement to organize the General Association, and appointed Brethren Sparkman, Crain, Aycock, Buck and Speight to aid in forming the same. The following resolution concerning the State Convention was passed:

"*Resolved*, That we entertain, in forming a new organization, the kindest Christian feeling for the Baptist State Convention, and that our only desire is to promote the efficiency and harmony of our churches."

It should be noted that in 1852 the Baptist State Convention met at Marshall. It was then proposed by the Baptist church at Tyler to establish a female high school at that place. The convention did not receive the proposition favorably; it was declared that their educational efforts only extended "to the aid of ministers," and that Baylor University was the convention school. The brethren of East Texas felt that they were pushed aside. They accordingly met at Larissa, Cherokee county, November, 1853, and organized the Texas Baptist General Association. Of course there was friction. The State Convention did not seem willing to admit the claims of the new body, while Elder G. S. Baggerly of the new organization charged Elder J. W. D. Creath, of the convention, with misappropriation of funds collected. Bro. Creath's accounts were adjusted, however, and harmony in a measure restored. The General Association met in Tyler, 1855, and dissolved, with the expressed purpose of forming the Eastern

Texas Convention, which was immediately done. At an adjourned meeting (eighth session) at Tyler, August 13, 1867, the Eastern Texas Convention reorganized as the "General Association." There were delegates present from Waco, Richland, Elm Fork, Saline, Cherokee and Soda Lake Associations, and from Ebenezer and Tyler churches.

Let us return to the Waco Association. Pledged for support of missionary the coming year as follows: Waco church $100, Bold Springs $35, W. A. Dunklin $10, John Flower $2.50, Benjamin Walker $2.50.

Executive Board: J. W. Speight, R. B. Burleson, D. B. Arnold, Sr., F. F. Bloodworth and J. E. Long. A brother from each church was appointed to collect funds to sustain missionary.

Resolution of thanks to Marlin church and community was offered and the Association adjourned to meet at Bold Springs.

SESSION OF 1868.

It was expected that the ninth session would be held at Bold Springs, twenty miles north from Waco. Brethren from quite a large number of churches met here at the time appointed. The introductory sermon was preached by that venerable and powerful preacher, W. C. Buck. His subject was "The Church." After reading several passages, particularly Matt. 16:13-19, he delighted the audience with one of the grandest discourses ever heard in Texas.

"Ecclesia" was carefully defined and its meaning sufficiently illustrated. Then came out with clearness and great power the following points:

1. The members of an "Ecclesia" must have certain well defined qualifications.

2. They must be called out and separated from the masses.

3. They must have a well-defined form of organization.

4. There must be certain outward, fixed rules of initiation and discipline.

5. The form of organization and fixed rules of initiation and discipline, like the laws of the Medes and Persians, change not forever.

6. There is one great purpose or end of this organization, to-

wit: The evangelization of the world, and to this end all means and talent must be consecrated. During this discourse the speaker observed some idleness in the room, and cried with a lion-like voice: "Brethren in the ministry, preach the word, whatever the surroundings. On one occasion I preached a sermon of two hours length to a congregation of six; two were attentive, two idle, and two slept the whole time!" Although this sermon was more than sixty minutes long, there was no more idleness in the congregation.

When Bro. Buck concluded his sermon, it was past 12 o'clock. The old moderator, R. C. Burleson, took the chair. Bro. J. W. Speight, of Waco, arose and said: "Bro. Moderator, I move you, sir, that we adjourn to Waco." The motion was immediately seconded. Elder Thomas F. Lockett, pastor of Bold Springs church, was instantly on his feet. He said: "Brethren, don't do that, for Christ's sake. You will break our hearts. It will be the joy of this church and community to entertain the Association. We have looked forward to the time when your coming in our midst would be our blessing."

Bro. Speight: "The dear brethren of Bold Springs by being conspicuously absent have manifested great pleasure in having the Association meet with their church."

Pastor Lockett: "I love my dear Bro. Speight, but must insist that he has spoken hastily. Brethren, the church at Bold Springs are not all absent. Some of them are away unavoidably. many of the good sisters are at home to-day cooking and preparing for you. You are here to attend to the Lord's business. I beg that you stay and do it."

Bro. Lockett's defense of his church was eloquent and pathetic, but of no avail. Bro. Speight's motion carried, and the entire Association that very August afternoon, without dinner or feed for horses, moved in a body through the burning sun to Waco. They arrived in Waco about sunset, and were received with open hearts and homes. Two delegates of Bold Springs, viz: P. Vaughn, with their pastor, came on with the brethren to Waco.

Letters were read from Bosqueville, Blue Ridge, Salem, Waco, Searsville, Caddo, Tehuacana, Cow Bayou, Bethel, Bold

Springs and Peoria. Great revivals were reported from Waco, Salem, Blue Ridge, Caddo, Bethel (McLennan), and Peoria. Indeed this was a year of ingathering. Whole number received by baptism 204, by letter 154. Total membership 773.

Seven churches failed to represent; namely, Ebenezer, Pleasant Grove, Union Springs, Antioch, Beulah, Sunset and Marlin.

Officers: M. B. Harden, moderator; J. W. Speight, clerk; J. H. Bagby, treasurer. Moderator Harden, being pastor at Waco, modestly asked Elder Benjamin Walker to take the chair, which he did and presided over the sittings of the body.

East Waco church, Elder B. Walker, pastor, was received at this meeting.

East Waco reported a fine revival and 44 members.

Two other new churches joined the Association this year: Bethel, Bosque county, P. O. Valley Mills; and Hopewell, Hill county, P. O. Patten's Mills. Bethel, with J. A. Land as pastor, had 13 members, and Hopewell, with J. Sandifer as pastor, reported 11 members. All three were but recently organized. Hopewell never represented again, and was soon afterward dissolved. Bethel failed to represent in 1869. In 1870 she reported 26 members, with Elder Sam Lacy as pastor. In 1871 her membership was 17, with J. Sandifer as pastor. After this she represented no more in the Waco Association. But in 1874 we find her on the rolls of Towash Association, with 51 members.

The usual reports on Misssions, Sabbath Schools, Literature and Periodicals, Temperance, Finance, Colored Population and Waco University, were adopted.

The report of the preceding year on Sabbath Schools recommended the work of the Texas Baptist Sunday School and Colportage Convention, and that convention had met in Waco a short time previous to this session.

The report on Waco University showed that there were matriculated during last session 163 students. The operations of the female department were commended.

The question of time and place being raised the Cow Bayou church put in application for the next meeting. Deacon A. D. Blackwell of Cow Bayou church asked for the meeting. Bro.

J. W. Speight asked: "Is your church able to take care of the Association?"

Deacon Blackwell: "I am able to take care of the whole body myself."

Elder Benj. Walker in the chair: "Some one move that we go with Bro. Blackwell to Cow Bayou."

The motion was made and carried.

Elder T. F. Lockett was appointed to preach the next introductory sermon.

The minutes of 1868 were signed: "Benj. Walker, moderator pro tem.; J. W. Speight, clerk."

The ordained ministers at this time were: W. C. Buck, R. C. Burleson, R. B. Burleson, M. B. Hardin, Benjamin Walker, J. J. Riddle, T. F. Lockett, J. W. McHorse, J. A. Fortune, J. K. Horseley, H. N. Reese, J. Sandifer, J. N. Kellis, C. W. Kinnard, A. W. Allege.

SESSION OF 1869.

This meeting was at Cow Bayou, according to previous appointment. Introductory sermon by Elder T. F. Lockett, from Nehemiah, 13:10-11: "And I perceived that the portions of the Levites had not been given them; for the Levites and the singers that did the work, were fled every one to his field. Then contended I with the rulers and said, Why is the house of God forsaken? And I gathered them together and set them in their place."

Letters were read from Bethel (McLennan), Bosqueville, Blue Ridge, Beulah, Caddo, Cow Bayou, East Waco, Ebenezer, Peoria, Tehuacana, Waco. Eight churches failed to represent, viz: Pleasant Grove, Union Springs, Antioch, Sunset, Marlin, Searsville, Bold Springs, Bethel (Bosque county), and Salem.

Two new churches were received: New Hope, R. C. Burleson, pastor, membership 49; and Union, Z. N. Morrell, pastor, membership 17. New Hope continued to represent till 1882—never represented after that date; was dropped from rolls in 1891.

Union church continued to represent, not missing once, till 1878. After that her name appears no more on our rolls. Her co-operation was full and hearty.

Officers: R. C. Burleson, moderator; J. W. Speight, clerk; J. H. Bagby, treasurer.

Peoria church was granted a letter of dismission to unite with Alvarado Association. This church was afterwards in the organization of Towash Association in 1873, and is now a member of Hillsboro Association.

Five churches reported fine revivals: Bethel, Cow Bayou, New Hope and Beulah. Total baptized 89, received by letter 69. Total membership 768.

Visiting brethren: Elder Z. N. Morrell and brethren J. C. Rogers, J. A. Head, W. D. Gaines. Bro. I. Elliott and Elder Josiah Leak were received as corresponding messengers from Richland Association. They were also recognized as corresponding messengers from Baptist General Association, and Elder Leak as general agent of the Bible Board of that body.

A special committee appointed to inquire concerning fellowship and order of Ebenezer church, reported the "fellowship broken and in discord," and recommended "that all parties who offer themselves for membership be declared ineligible to seats in this body." The committee suggested the "propriety of appointing a committee of wise, judicious and prudent brethren to visit Ebenezer church with the view of healing the breaches." In accordance with this suggestion, the following committee was appointed: Irvin Brown, J. P. Brown, R. M. Turner, Harrison Bryan, and J. V. Wright.

The usual reports were read and adopted.

That on Schools and Education recommended Waco University, and urged endowment and better buildings.

The report on Sabbath Schools complains (as did that of the preceding year) that churches failed to send up statistics.

The report on Colored Missions deserves to be inserted in full if we had space. Following are extracts:

"The subject referred to under consideration is one of no minor importance. * * * The eternal God was concerned on behalf of the Etheopian eunuch (Acts 7). * * * Something should be done and no time lost. * * * Important events are developing. An association of colored Baptists promising great usefulness has been organized during the present season. * *

* Dear brethren, this field is white for the harvest, waiting for Baptist preachers. Shall we not occupy? They are exceedingly solicitous for instruction. * * * Ignorance and superstition is the field for Catholicism. The Romanists boast of their prospects in these United States. Every effort is being made on their part to occupy this field. The Baptists are the only people in our conception that can successfully come in contact with this great error." This report was written by Elder Benjamin Walker.

It appears that some little missionary work was done during the year 1868-9, though no report of the Executive Board or of the work is found in the minutes. The treasurer reported that he had "paid missionary" $76.85 coin, and $2.40 currency.

Resolutions were adopted instructing Executive Committee to raise $500, employ a missionary, and pay him quarterly in advance.

A committee, consisting of J. W. Speight, C. W. Kinnard and Z. N. Morrell were appointed to visit Trinity River Association and propose a union with that body on "basis of the adoption of our Constitution, Articles of Faith and Rules of Decorum." As there was some opposition to this union in Trinity River Association, the proposition was withdrawn by committee.

The next meeting was appointed with Salem church at Eutaw.

Elder Banjamin Walker was appointed to preach the Introductory Sermon, with R. C. Burleson, alternate. With sorrow do we chronicle the fact that Elder Walker passed from his labor on earth to his reward in glory before the next meeting of the Association. On April 2, 1870, he went to sleep in the arms of Jesus.

The thanks of the body were voted to Cow Bayou church for their entertainment, and the body adjourned.

SESSION OF 1870.

The eleventh Session was held with Salem church at Eutaw, commencing Friday before fourth Sabbath in August, 1870. The following churches were represented: Bethel (McLennan), Bethel (Bosque) Bosqueville, Bold Springs, Blue Ridge, Cow Bayou, Caddo, East Waco, Marlin, New Hope, Salem, Searsville, Tehaucana, Union, Waco. Caddo was represented by letter only. Ebenezer was excluded from representation. Beulah and Pleasant Grove failed to represent. Antioch, Sunset and Union Springs having dissolved, were dropped from the rolls.

Three new churches were received at this meeting, Calvert, Bremond and White Rock. Calvert continued with the Association till 1874.

Bremond continued in Waco Association till 1880, failing to represent only once, in 1878.

Five churches reported revivals, viz.: Bosqueville, both Bethels, Union and Waco. Total baptized 71, received by letter 128, restored 3. Decrease 141. Whole membership, 1053.

Officers: M. B. Hardin, moderator; W. M. Gough, clerk; F. F. Bloodworth, treasurer.

A committee appointed to consider the application of certain colored churches, recommend that these "churches be received under the watchful care of the Association, and that a committee be appointed to aid the colored brethren, by counsel and correspondence, to organize them into an Association as soon as possible, and that the most cordial feeling and correspondence be maintained between our white and colored brethren." This report was written by the venerable pioneer, Z. N. Morrell. The committee appointed to carry out this recommendation were Z. N. Morrell, J. V. Wright and R. W. Kinnard.

Visiting brethren: J. A. Head, W. D. Anderson and J. B. Link. Bro. Link was invited to present the claims of the Texas Baptist Herald, which invitation he gladly accepted.

In addition to the usual reports, one was adopted this year on "Ministerial Support and Consecration." There was no report on Waco University. The report of the special committee appointed at last Session, on Ebenezer church, was read and re-committed. Again the committee reported the following resolution, which was adopted:

"*Resolved*, That after a full investigation of all the facts within our reach, we are forced to regard each party still in disorder, and we most affectionately advise the brethren to call in a council of judicious brethren from sister churches to aid them in the settlement of their difficulties, and in the event their differences cannot be reconciled, to advise them what course to pursue."

The resolution was signed by Z. N. Morrell, J. P. Brown, W. R. Kellum, J. V. Wright, R. W. Turner, R. C. Burleson, T. F. Lockett.

The report on Schools and Education, written by Elder Sam Lacy, recommended that Elder T. F. Lockett "present immediately the claims" of Waco University. Bro. Lockett embraced the opportunity thus offered, and raised in subscription $403.50.

The report on Ministerial Support and consecration set forth: "We believe it to be as much their (the churches') duty to support their pastors as it is to pray or to support their own families; for we are one family in Christ. * * * We recommend to the churches to send up at our next annual Association the number of Sabbaths occupied by their pastors, and the amounts paid them. * * * We believe it is the duty of the pastor to be wholly consecrated to his work, that his time is not his own." This report was signed by that grand old deacon and San Jacinto veteran, whose influence was so long felt in this Association—Deacon S. F. Sparks.

Report on Temperance, written by Z. N. Morrell, after stating that the use of ardent spirits "stands first in the catalogue of dark crimes," closes with these words: "That we, the Association, advise the churches, if their members visit drinking saloons, indulge in the use of ardent spirits with drinking assemblies, or make a practice of drinking, that they withdraw from all such members as daring violators of the Divine law." Happy day will it be for the churches when this advice is heeded!

The Executive Committee had been instructed to employ a missionary, but to incur no debt. Their report shows that Elder Samuel Lacy began work on Jan. 1, 1870, and labored 79 days, traveled 656 miles, preached 74 sermons, visited 80 families, sung and prayed with 50 families, baptized 4. Total amount paid him, $94.15. We copy from the report of Executive Committee these tender words:

"It is our sad duty to record the death of one of our members, Elder B. Walker, who, after a short but painful illness, was called up to a higher and happier sphere of service. He finished his course with joy." Bro. Walker was their Treasurer.

WACO BAPTIST ASSOCIATION.

The Mission Board was at this meeting made to consist of one member from every church with instructions to hold meetings each fifth Sunday. This plan of one member from every church was changed at the next Association.

Full Board for '70-71: W. G. Evans, R. C. Burleson, John Flowers, J. B. Puckett, A. H. Rhodes, S. M. Saxon, Robert Moore, J. E. Harrison, Jasper Garrett, J. H. McHorse, A. H. Stallworth, J. W. Speegle, W. M. Mathews, F. F. Bloodworth, Zach Davis, C. F. Clabaugh, R. W. Turner, J. F. Jackson, C. H. Fisher.

To this Board was committed the work of collecting funds and employing a missionary.

The report on Colored Missions, written by Thomas F. Lockett, recommended "that a missionary be appointed to visit their ((colored) churches and aid them in setting all things in order."

After the usual vote of thanks the body adjourned. Prayer by R. B. Burleson.

The pastors at this time were: Bethel (McLennan), R. C. Burleson; Bethel (Bosque), S. Lacy; Bosqueville, R. C. Burleson; Bold Springs, Thomas Hooker; Blue Ridge, J. V. Wright; Bremond, W. C. Boone, Cow Bayou, John McClain; Calvert, A. E. Vandiver; East Waco, M. B. Hardin; Marlin, R. F. Mattison; New Hope, B. H. Carroll; Salem, J. V. Wright; Searsville, B. T. Stephens; Tehuacana, A. W. Ellege; Union, J. V. Wright; Waco, R. C. Burleson.

Besides pastors there were within the bounds of the Association the following ordained ministers: N. W. Crain, T. F. Lockett, W. W. Smith, John Fortune, T. P. Aycock, Z. N. Morrell, R. B. Burleson, W. M. Gough.

The territory covered was 100 miles extending N. W. and S. E. on both sides of the Brazos, and 50 miles from east to west.

The total baptized during last half of decade so far as reported to the Association was 573. It was, no doubt, more than these figures as there were 31 failures to report. If the baptisms in the unreported churches averaged one-half as well as those reported, the whole number of baptisms, during the five years immediately after the war reached 670.

From meager reports of missionary work done in the bounds of the Association from August, 1864, to August, 1870, we compile the following: Missionaries: N. C. Crain ('65), J. M. McGraw ('66-'67), Sam. Lacy ('70). Miles traveled, 3,061; families visited, 538; days labored, 399; baptized, 17; organized churches, 2. Total cost of missionary labor, $477.61. Lost in Confederate currency, $1,296.

We have no means of ascertaining how much was paid by the churches of the Association to State, Domestic and Foreign Missions. Agents traveled among our people and collected funds each year. It is fair to presume that our people did as the average churches throughout the State. The vast destitution of the Associational field seems, however, to have claimed attention principally. Much of the missionary work in our hands consisted in nursing weak churches; and much gratuitous work of this kind was done by the consecrated pastors.

There were at the close of the war 350 churches in the State. One-twenty-seventh of these were in the bounds of Waco Association. Let it not be forgotten that during the last half of this first decade much manly strength was well spent in building up Waco University. The University was the property and pride of the Association. Though on the very frontier and without prestige (save what came to Waco with the great President, Rev. R. C. Burleson, A. M., and his faculty) this school matriculated in 1856, 130. Baylor University at Independence reported to the State Convention October, 1866, a total in all departments of 176. The Female Department at Independence had 70 pupils, at Waco 35 pupils. There was at that time a "Female College" at Fairfield (Freestone Co.), just on the borders of Waco Association, under President Henry L. Graves, A. M., and eight professors and instructors, which "enjoyed a liberal patronage."

CHAPTER IV.

FIRST HALF OF SECOND DECADE.

1871–1875.

Like cautious sailors on an untried sea, sounding the deep and taking observations, of currents, rocks and bars, so the Association, during the next five years, moved slowly but surely forward. One plan of work was tested and passed by; another method was suggested, tried and abandoned. The subject of efficient organization became a matter of intense interest and earnest prayer. Guided by the spirit of God and taught by that best of masters, experience, the brethren grew wiser every year. At length they fell upon the present form of organization, which, under the blessing of God, has put the Waco Association in the front of the great advancing Baptist brotherhood of Texas.

SESSION OF 1871—HELD WITH THE EAST WACO CHURCH, COMMENCING FRIDAY BEFORE THE FOURTH SUNDAY IN AUGUST.

This was the twelfth annual session.

The East Waco church at that time worshiped in the old first house near the east end of the town.

Twenty churches, including three new ones, were represented, viz.: Bosqueville and East Waco, V. G. Cunningham, pastor; Bethel (McLennan), R. C. Burleson, pastor; Beulah, C. Magee; Bremond, W. C. Boone; Bethel (Bosque), J. Sandifer; Blue Ridge, Salem and Union, J. V. Wright; Cow Bayou and Salem (new church, McLennan), John McLain; Ebenezer, W. T. Wright; Greenwood (new church, McLennan), and Pleasant Grove, R. B. Burleson; New Hope, W. M. Gough; Tehuacana, pastorless; Searsville, B. T. Stephens; Waco, B. H. Carroll; White Rock, Thos. Hooker; Bold Springs, Calvert and Marlin not represented.

Salem and Greenwood were newly organized churches. The name of Salem was changed to Mastersville in 1884. Greenwood continued till 1881, representing every year except 1876 and 1879. In 1882 the church ceased to exist. Greenwood reported 23 members, Salem 39 and White Rock 45.

Officers: J. E. Harrison, moderator; W. M. Gough, clerk; F. F. Bloodworth, treasurer.

Ebenezer church, reported in disorder the past two years, was allowed to represent, peace being restored. Ebenezer and Caddo were dismissed by letter. Caddo re-united with the Association in 1888.

The past year was one of blessing and revivals. Sixteen

churches reported additions by baptism, viz.: Bosqueville, 9; Bethel (McLennan), 19; Bethel (Bosque), 2; Beulah, 33; Blue Ridge, 18; Cow Bayou, 7; Caddo, 27; East Waco, 7; Ebenezer, 35; Greenwood, 8; New Hope, 7; Pleasant Grove, 2; Salem (Limestone), 18; Salem (McLennan) 11; Searsville, 8; Union, 13; Waco, 31; White Rock, 18. Total, 272.

Elder E. C. Eager, district secretary of the Domestic Mission Board, S. B. C., and Elder Thomas Hooker, of Alvarado Association, were seated as visitors.

The usual reports of committees—on Missions, Schools and Education, Sabbath Schools, Literature and Periodicals, Colored Missions, Temperance and Finance—were read and adopted.

The report on Missions, written by N. W. Crain, referred to the historical facts that missionary labors within the bounds of the Association had in the past been "greatly blessed, and that the people had shown a disposition to sustain the missionary beyond what we have been accustomed to witness."

The report on Literature and Periodicals, written by J. B. Puckett, recommended "a thorough Baptist literature for our Sabbath Schools." Only twice before in the history of the Association do we find definite, clear cut declarations in favor of Baptist literature in Sabbath Schools. The instances are in the reports on Sabbath Schools in 1864 and 1865. In the former, written by Elder. J. F. Pierson, we read: "We feel it our duty to warn our brethren of the evil, as we believe, of Union Sabbath Schools (so-called), and of union books."

In the latter, written by John A. Fortune, we read: "We would exclusively recommend Baptist Sabbath School books."

The reader will note that in those early days very many of our best pastors and brethren advocated "union" Sunday Schools. Because of the prevalence of this union sentiment, it was hard in many of our churches to have other than "union schools."

But experience is often the best teacher; and now, after giving the "union" schools a fair trial, the brethren were ready to take high ground in favor of Baptist schools. Accordingly, at this same session (1871) the report on Sabbath Schools, written by R. B. Burleson, recommends, "That the Association co-operate fully with he Sunday School Board of the Southern Baptist Convention."

The report on Schools and Education states: "The late school law, if our judgment of its working be just, effectually closes out the idea of Baptist interests in all schools below the grade of College." This was written by B. H. Carroll, and the thought was correct. Had there been no change in the public school law, Baptists would have been compelled to stand aloof.

Dr. Burleson had been employed just previous to this meeting to canvass the entire state for Waco University. He raised in cash and pledges $20,000. However, many of the pledges were never paid.

It was this year that Elder W. W. Harris ("Spurgeon" Harris) made his brilliant career as an evangelist of the Association. He was employed by the Executive Board in April, 1871, at a salary of $1,000 per annum. The great work of Brother Harris partly accounts for the revivals heretofore mentioned. He held meetings with Robinson, Bosqueville, Bethel, Marlin and Greenwood. Visited Waco, East Waco, White Rock, Searsville, Salem (McLennan) and Cow Bayou. Traveled 260 miles, preached 57 sermons, delivered 140 exhortations, baptized (in absence of regular pastors) 19, received for baptism 27. He was paid $368.95 in full for time employed.

Missionary Board for 1871-2: J. W. Speight, J. B. Puckett, J. A. Rentz, J. B. Sanderson, J. E. Harrison.

A resolution was adopted requesting each church to appoint a special agent to collect for missions.

R. C. Burleson, S. B. Humphreys, W. H. Trolinger, T. B. McComb, W. G. Caperton and R. C. Buckner were elected to fill vacancies in Board of Trustees of Waco University.

A special committee, consisting of B. H. Carroll, N. C. Crain and J. W. Speight, was appointed to report at next session on Ministerial Education.

W. C. Boone was chosen to preach the introductory sermon. J. V. Wright, alternate. Thus closed the session of 1871.

SESSION OF 1872.

This, the *thirteenth* session, was held with Union church, Falls county. Including three new churches received at this meeting (Antioch, Hope and Rock Creek), twenty churches were represented: Antioch, R. F. Matison, pastor; Bosqueville, Rock Creek, V. G. Cunningham, pastor; Bethel, Greenwood, New Hope, R. B. Burleson, pastor; Beulah, Calvin Magee, pastor; Bremond, W. C. Boone, pastor; Blue Ridge, Salem (Limestone), Union, J. V. Wright, pastor; Cow Bayou, Salem (McLennan), John McLain, pastor; East Waco, Tehuacana, N. W. Crain, pastor; Marlin, W. M. Gough, pastor; Waco, B. H. Carroll, pastor; White Rock, Thomas Hooker, pastor; Calvert and Hope, pastorless.

Antioch church does not now exist. Antioch was a new church in Limestone county, and came in with 51 members; remained with the Association five years and went out in 1877 with 106 members. Brother E. Spencer represented the church every year but the last, when she sent no messenger.

Hope, in the western part of Falls county, continued with the Association five years, representing regularly. She came in with 11 members, and had 44 when she went out by letter in 1877. In 1891 the church went into the organization of Falls County Association.

Rock Creek was a newly organized church in the northern part of McLennan county, on the west bank of the Brazos. This church came in with 34 members and continues a noble, co-operating body till this day.

Revivals were reported by Antioch, Bosqueville, Cow Bayou, Calvert, East Waco, Hope, Rock Creek, Salem (Limestone), Salem (McLennan), Tehuacana, White Rock. Total baptized, 121; received by letter, 190. Decrease, 239. Total membership, 1164. Bethel (Bosque), Pleasant Grove and Searsville not represented. Bethel (Bosque) and Pleasant Grove never represented again.

Officers elected: J. E. Harrison, moderator; W. M. Gough, clerk; C. E. Stephen, treasurer. Elder Z. N. Morrell preached the introductory sermon from Acts 2: 42,43.

The reports adopted at this meeting are remarkable for cogency and point. Witness the following extracts:

"To exclude a man for getting drunk on a gill of whisky and

pass by others who drink it by the pint without staggering is to the mind of your committee like paying a premium on intemperance."—Report on Temperance, by V. G. Cunningham.

"It seems to be taken for granted that any story, however silly or improbable, is well enough for this purpose, provided it is only pervaded by a vein of sickly sentimentalism, not unfrequently misnomered, piety."—Report on Literature and Periodicals, by D. R. Wallace.

The report of the Mission Board shows that Elder A. W. Ellege was employed as missionary of the Association from Sept. 6, 1871, to May 14, 1872, 7 1-2 months. He was a hero of Baptist faith and did a grand work . Traveled 1360 miles, visited 380 families, preached 100 sermons, received for baptism, 23; by letter, 30; ordained deacons, 2; organized churches, 3; Sabbath Schools, 2. Salary, $375.

There was raised also for Domestic Missions, S. B. C., $26, and for ministerial education, Waco University, $106.

Some changes in the Order of Business were adopted: (1) "That at each session of this Association, after the appointment of a minister and an alternate to preach the Introductory, another minister shall be appointed to preach a sermon at 11 o'clock, at the next session, on any one, more, or all of the peculiar doctrines of our denomination."

(2) "The the following standing committee be appointed at each session of the Association, to report at the next meeting of the body, viz.: On Foreign Missions of the Southern Baptist Convention; on Domestic Missions of the Southern Baptist Convention; on Schools and Education; Sabbath Schools; on Literature and Periodicals; on Colored Missions; on Temperance; on Ministerial Education."

After the 11 o'clock sermon Sunday a hymn was sung, parting hand taken and the body declared adjourned by Moderator J. E. Harrison.

SESSION OF 1873.

This was the fourteenth session and was held at Marlin August 22-25, 1893. At 11 o'clock Friday, Elder C. E. Stephen preached the introductory sermon from Rev. 20: 12, and Rev. 22: 12.

Two new churches, White Hall and Mt. Pisgah, came in at this meeting, and, including them, 22 were represented.

During the past year Tehuacana changed her name to Concord. The churches and pastors of 1873 are as follows: Antioch, A. E. Matison; Beulah and Cow Bayou, C. Magee; Blue Ridge, Salem (Limestone), and Union, J. V. Wright; Bosqueville, J. J. Riddle; Bremond, W. C. Boone; Calvert, W. H. Dodson; Concord, Rock Creek and White Hall, V. G. Cunningham; East Waco, R. C. Burleson; Bethel, Greenwood and Marlin, R. B. Burleson; Hope, J. J. Davis; Salem (McLennan) John McLain; Searsville, B. T. Stevens; Waco, B. H. Carroll; Mt. Pisgah, C. E. Stephen; New Hope, J. B. Parrock. Mt. Pisgah was in the S. E. corner of Falls county, and came into the Association with 15 members, remained three years, left us in 1875 with 34 members. During her short life she enrolled among her members some of Texas' most distinguished noblemen; as, Elders Jesse Tubb and Z. N. Morrell. Reagan is now in the same community.

White Hall was a new church; joined us with 20 members; has represented every year (in 1885 by letter only) from 1873 till this day, and continues one of the honored constituents of the Association.

White Rock and Pleasant Grove not represented.

Nineteen churches reported baptisms. The revival spirit was general. Baptisms as follows: Antioch, 7; Bethel, 16; Beulah, 4; Blue Ridge, 17; Bosqueville, 1; Bremond, 32; Concord, 5; Cow Bayou, 13; Greenwood, 2; Hope 35; Mt. Pisgah, 1; New Hope, 8; Rock Creek, 3; Salem (McLennan), 13; Salem (Limestone), 2; Searsville, 2; Union, 27; Waco, 19; White Hall, 9. Total, 215.

Officers: R. B. Burleson, moderator; C. E. Stephen, clerk; J. W. Speight, treasurer.

Visitors' names enrolled: J. W. Scarborough, J. B. Link, Z. N. Morrell, J. P. McCullough, W. T. Russell, agent Domestic Mission Board, S. B. C., J. B. Daniel, agent General Association.

We are pleased to chronicle the general advance of mission ideas and mission effort.

The report on Foreign iMssions, written by V. G. Cunningham, made special mention of Dr. W. N. Cote, missionary at Rome:

"We specially urge the importance of the Italian Mission, with which our noble Brother, W. N. Cote, of Rome, is connected."

The reader of mission history will recall the brilliant career of Dr. Cote at Rome, 1870-1873. Like a meteor shot across the dark sky of that priest-ridden land was the brief work of this zealous preacher. Italy was then for the first time in many centuries, open to the gospel. On September 23, 1870, the army of Victor Emanuel entered and took possession of Rome. Ever since that time the country has been open to missionary effort. Dr. Cote was the first evangelical missionary to enter Rome after the country was free. He did a magnificent work. Troubles arose, and though not a shadow rested on Bro. Cote's dectrines, morals, or his missionary ability, yet early in 1874 the Board of the Southern Baptist Convention found it necessary to request him "to withdraw from the mission and service of the Board." He died four years later of heart disease, supposed to have been caused by his troubles. He was a noble man, and the gospel light he planted on the hills of the eternal city grows brighter as the years go on.

No missionary was kept in the field from August, 1872, to August, 1873.

A new plan was now adopted. Instead of a Missionary Board, a Missionary Convention of Waco Association was organized with J. W. Speight president, J. H. Harrison, secretary; J. A. Rentz, treasurer, and fifteen vice-presidents. There was immediately pledged to the Missionary Convention $750. At the first meeting of this convention J. J. Riddle was elected president. It will be proper to state here that the plan of a "Missionary Convention" only continued one year.

Fine work in the way of ministerial education was being done at this time. The Ministerial Education Board of the General Association was located at Waco, and most of the funds received by that board was paid by brethren of Waco Association.

At this session of the Association pledges were taken to aid young ministers at Waco University, amounting to $240, 200 pounds of pork and 50 bushels of corn.

Following is the correct list of the Board of Trustees of Waco

University, August, 1873: J. W. Speight, Waco, president; D. R. Wallace, Waco, secretary; John T. Flint, Waco, treasurer; C. A. Westbrook, Waco; J. E. Harrison, Waco; R. B. Wilson, Waco; R. Coke, Waco; J. M. Anderson, Waco; S. A. Owens, Waco; S. B. Humphreys, Waco; J. E. Sears, Waco; R. C. Burleson, Waco; O. L. Battle, Waco; B. H. Carroll, Waco; M. D. Herring, Waco; H. J. Chamberlin, Davilla; W. A. Dunklin, Galveston; T. P. Aycock, Calvert; H. M. Watkins, Huntsville; W. G. Caperton, Tyler; R. C. Buckner, Paris; James Hogue, Cold Springs; W. B. Denson, Cold Springs; W. H. Trollinger, Whitesboro; T. B. McCombe, Farmington—25.

The University building and grounds were then estimated to be worth $40,000. The new boarding house of the female department was so far completed as to be in use. There was nearly $7,000 outstanding indebtedness.

SABBATH EXERCISES.

At 9 o'clock a. m. Sabbath school addressed by J. B. Link, W. H. Dodson and J. E. Harrison.

At 11 a. m. W. T. Russell preached at the school house from Micah 7:18; subject, "Jehovah, a pardoning God."

At 3:30 p. m. Sabbath school mass meeting. Addresses by J. J. Riddle, S. P. Hollingsworth, Z. N. Morrell, J. P. McCullough, J. B. Link and R. C. Burleson.

Night, J. B. Daniel preached from Isaiah 35:8; subject, "Highway to Heaven."

Collections on Sabbath $49.75, divided equally between associational missions and ministerial education.

The next session was appointed to be held at Bremond.

B. H. Carroll (J. J. Riddle, alternate), was appointed to preach the introductory sermon, and V. G. Cunningham (R. C. Burleson, alternate), the doctrinal sermon.

Rule 7, of section 2, of "Rules of Order and Decorum," which reads: "Inquire concerning the fellowship and order of the churches of the Association," was stricken out.

The change from Mission Board to Missionary Convention has already been mentioned. It is the request of the General Association that "missionary conventions auxiliary to the General Association, "be formed in the several associations co-operating with that body." This explains why change was made.

The Missionary Convention plan did not work well and it was abandoned the next session.

SESSION OF 1874.

The fifteenth session was held with Bremond church.

Elder B. H. Carroll preached the introductory sermon from Mark 12:41. It was a grand sermon.

All the churches except Bold Springs were represented. Pleasant Grove, having dissolved, was stricken from the rolls. One new church, Olive Branch, was received.

Pastorless—Antioch and Beulah; under the care of J. J. Riddle, Bethel, Bosqueville, Greenwood, White Rock; of J. J. Davis, Blue Ridge, Hope, Union; of C. E. Stephen, Bremond, Mount Pisgah; of V. G. Cunningham, Rock Creek, Concord; of C. Magee, Cow Bayou; of G. L. Jennings, East Waco; of S. King, Marlin, New Hope; of J. B. Parrock, Olive Branch; of W. T. Wright, Salem (Limestone); of John McLain, Salem (McLennan); of B. T. Stevens, Searsville; of B. H. Carroll, Waco; of J. S. Allen, White Hall.

During the year past there were fine revivals in six of the churches—Bremond, Olive Branch, Salem (McLennan), Waco, White Hall and White Rock. Nine others reported baptisms. The largest number baptized into one church was at White Hall, 36. The whole number baptized was 129. The preceding year it was 215. The year following 110.

Searsville represented the last time. Olive Branch came into the Association with 16 members; continued till 1895 and withdrew by letter, going out with 30 members. She represented every year except '82, '85, '86, '89; in '82 and '86 she represented by letter only; in '85 and '89 by neither letter nor delegate. This church is in the northeast part of McLennan county, near Axtell. At this session Elder J. J. Riddle was elected moderator; C. E. Stephen, clerk, and J. W. Speight, treasurer, were re-elected.

Elder G. L. Jennings was received as a corresponding messenger from Trinity River Association. Elders T. M. Anderson and W. J. Glazener were received as corresponding messengers from Little River Association.

The report of the missionary convention showed that Elder V. G. Cunningham had been employed at a salary of $50 per month, and that he had labored seven and one-half months, doing very satisfactory work.

Following is a synopsis of Brother Cunningham's work: Two churches organized; miles traveled, 2,423; families visited, 758; held family worships, 155; sermons, 204; baptized, 23; received by letter, 45.

The "Missionary Convention's" plan was now abandoned because "there were difficulties of a practical character effectually preventing its use by all the churches."

The present plan of a "Missionary Board," or "Mission Board,' composed of one member from each church, was organized at this Bremond meeting. For nearly a quarter of a century this plan has worked well. By it Waco Association has been developed and made the banner Association of the South, saving, perhaps, Dover of Virginia; St. Louis and Blue River of Missouri; Long Run and Elk Horn, of Kentucky. The plan of work is to hold four board meetings in connection with fifth Sundays each year. Each board member is chosen by his church and recommended to the Association for appointment. The Association is divided into four districts. There is a president of the board and four vice presidents chosen annually, a vice president in each district and each district has one board meeting every year. A new board is organized at each annual meeting and in open session of the Association, and all the board meetings for the ensuing year appointed. The proceedings of the organization of the board, together with a list of every board member and his postoffice, and a list of board meetings for coming year, are published in the minutes of the Association. Minutes of each appointed meeting are kept and recorded in the president's cash book. The president, in addition to the regular duties of his office, performs the duties of corresponding secretary and treasurer. He keeps the books and receives and disburses the funds of the churches.

At this first organization of the Mission Board, B. H. Carroll was elected president; C. E. Stephen, S. King, J. V. Wright and A. D. Blackwell were chosen vice presidents, and J. J. Riddle was chosen secretary.

It was made the duty of the president and secretary "to visit during the year every church in Waco Association, and hold mass meetings in the mission interest, and instruct the churches and impress missionary duty. That this visit be appointed after consultation with pastor of each church, and the meeting held under the sanction of the church."

B. H. Carroll held the position of president of the board continuously till 1888, when J. R. M. Touchstone, pastor at Marlin, was chosen. Brother Touchstone served thirteen months till October, 1889. B. H. Carroll was again chosen and served till the meeting of the Association in 1892. J. L. Walker was elected and served two years till October, 1894. B. J. Kendrick served one year till October, 1895, when J. L. Walker was again chosen. This plan was not fully developed and in complete working order till 1877, when Elder J. B. Parrock proposed the district system, which was adopted.

A proposition came from the First Church, Waco, to employ and sustain Elder V. G. Cunningham as city missionary in Waco, on condition that the other churches of the Association would employ Elder J. B. Parrock as associational missionary to work outside the city. This proposition was accepted by the Association. Elder Cunningham's salary was fixed at $500, that of Bro. Parrock at $600. Every church was asked to raise an average of 50 cents per member for Brother Parrock.

The report on domestic missions recommended the hearty cooperation of the Association with the general missionaries of the General Association.

It is proper to state that the Missionary Board of the General Association, located at Dallas, had recently appointed Elders E. B. Hardie and J. E. Sligh as general missionaries, Elder Hardie to occupy the southern part of the field.

In this report on domestic missions every pastor in the Association was requested "to preach upon the great missionary interests of the state, at least quarterly, and take up a collection for Brother Hardie's support. Prayers, sympathy and contributions are asked to aid in building the meeting house at Marlin." The report goes on: "We express our determination to heartily co-operate with the Home Mission Board, located at Marion, Alabama." This report was written by John H. Harrison.

The report on schools and education, by B. H. Carroll, states with regard to Waco University: "Its last session was the most successful in its history and the next promises still better results."

Extract from report on Sabbath schools, by C. E. Stephen: "Let no Sabbath pass without each church 'gathering the people together, men, women and children, and the stranger that is within thy gates that they may hear, and that they may learn, and fear the Lord your God.'"

Fine reports were also adopted on foreign missions and ministerial education. A collection to aid in building a hall for ministerial students of Waco University was taken—cash, $36.30; pledges, $68.00.

Touching resolutions were passed relative to Elder W. C. Boone, A. M., late pastor of Bremond.

The Association directed minutes to be printed at the office of the Religious Messenger, Paris, Texas.

The next session was appointed at Waco. Elder S. King (V. G. Cunningham, alternate), was apopinted to preach the introductory sermon, and C. E. Stephen (J. J. Riddle, alternate), the doctrinal sermon.

PREACHING SERVICES.

Saturday night S. King preached from John 3: 3, subject: "The New Birth." Sunday, 9 o'clock, a. m., R. C. Burleson, Z. N. Morrell, and G. L. Jennings delivered addresses to the Sabbath School. At 11 a. m. B. H. Carroll preached from Job 14: 10-14, subject, "Life in the Spirit World and the Resurrection." At 4 p. m., J. J. Riddle preached from Rom. 3: 28, subject, "Justification by Faith." At night R. C. Burleson, from John 19: 22, subject, "Individual Influence on Others."

Ordained ministers: R. C. Burleson, R. B. Burleson, B. H.

Carroll, V. G. Cunningham, Thos. Hooker, W. W. Smith, Waco; W. P. Hatchett, B. T. Stevens, Valley Mills; C. W. Kinnard, Z. N. Morrell, C. E. Stephen, J. V. Wright, Jesse Tubb, Bremond; S. King, C. Magee, Marlin; J. J. Riddle, Bosqueville; J. A. Simmons, Kosse.

Unordained ministers: T. P. Aycock, Calvert; T. H. Mills, J. H. Harrison, J. B. Puckett, J. B. Parrock, J. C. Rutledge, G. W. Scarborough, Waco; W. A. Smalley, Mastersville.

SESSION OF 1875.

According to previous appointment, the sixteenth session was held at Waco.

The introductory sermon was preached by G. W. Rogers, agent of Foreign Mission Board of S. B. C., from 1 Cor. 15: 58, theme, "Christian Labor."

All the churches represented with letters and delegates. Three new churches were received. The churches and pastors were as follows: Antioch and Salem (Kosse), A. W. Middleton; Bethel, Greenwood, Rock Creek, J. J. Riddle; Beulah, Carolina (new church), C. Magee; Blue Ridge, J. V. Wright; Bremond, L. R. Scruggs; Bosqueville, V. G. Cunningham; Concord, Olive Branch, J. B. Parrock (missionary pastor); Cow Bayou, J. M. Gambrell; East Waco, G. L. Jennings; Hope, J. L. Lattimore; Marlin, Union, S. King; Mount Pisgah, C. W. Kinnard; New Hope, J. H. Harrison; Sage Chapel (new church), T. A. Mangum; Salem (Mastersville), J. McLain; Waco, B. H. Carroll; White Hall, S. I. Caldwell; White Rock, J. J. Sledge; Deer Creek (new church), B. J. Bossel—25 churches.

The old moderator, J. J. Riddle, was re-elected. B. H. Carroll was chosen clerk, and C. E. Stephen, treasurer.

Carolina, near Durango, in Falls county, was organized by Elder Calvin Magee in 1875. This church came into the Association with 16 members, represented regularly till 1883, when she ceased to exist. In 1883 the church numbered 65. Many of the Carolina brethren afterward became members at Durango.

Sage Chapel was a newly organized church and joined the Association with 11 members. In 1883 the name was changed to Eddy. In '81, '86, '87, '88, '89, the church did not represent. It still exists, a noble church of this Association.

Deer Creek, in the N. W. part of Falls, a new church, joined with 20 members, and withdrew in 1885 to unite with Falls County Association. She represented every year except 1880; in '81 and '82 by letter only. She went out of the Association with 129 members.

Bold Springs this year joined the Towash Association with 60 members,—returned to the Waco Association in 1884 with 195 members.

The total baptisms in 1874-5 were only 110, less than any previous year since 1870, and less than any year afterward, except 1883, when the number was 89.

The following visitors accepted seats: J. B. Link, F. M. Law, E. F. Thuring, R. C. Buckner, E. B. Hardie, J. J. Sledge. Representing the Foreign Mission Board, S. B. C., G. W. Rogers; Bosque River Association, W. P. Hatchett, F. F. Bloodworth; Leon River, G. W. Scarborough, P. J. Nolin; Salado, H. J. Chamberlin, W. H. Robert.

Corresponding messengers were appointed to Associations and general bodies, as at last session.

At last session it was made the duty of the president and secretary of the Mission Board to visit every church in the Association. They visited all but one, and failed in that instance because of some mistake in mail matters. Mass meetings were held all over the Association, and Board meeting at Bremond, Cow Bayou, Marlin, Mastersville, Blue Ridge.

Never before in the history of the Association had a missionary been kept in the field the whole year. This year two were kept in the field, V. G. Cunningham in Waco and J. B. Parrock in the country. Elder Parrock traveled 2,498 miles, visited 752 families and held worship with 162 families; preached 189 sermons, baptized thirty-seven and organized two churches. Besides Bro. Parrock's work Bro. John H. Harrison, an unordained minister, and J. J. Riddle, moderator of the Association, did much gratuitous missionary work.

Bro. V. G. Cunningham's work in Waco is thus referred to

in the report of the board: "Waco city missionary, Elder V. G. Cunningham, employed by the Waco church, has labored a whole year in Waco with great success. If to visit, comfort and relieve the poor, to gather into Sunday schools the orphans and the uncared for, to save the erring from lives of shame, and deaths of eternal horror; if to go to jails and preach to the captives; if to divide the scanty store with the children of penury; if prayers, admonitions and watchings with the sick and dying; if all these and many other things not mentioned, constitute a faithful missionary, then no living intelligence can dispute Brother Cunningham's title to that name."

At least three times as much was given for missions this year as during any former year. Waco church paid Brother Cunningham $500. Brother Parrock lost two weeks' time and was paid $575. There were paid by the churches (outside of Waco) $593.80, and raised independently $19.35. On hand with which to begin the new year, $38.15.

The board of the General Association, located at Dallas, had kept a general missionary, Elder E. B. Hardie, in the field. The report on domestic missions states: "Some of our churches contributed largely to this board last year, under the agency of E. B. Hardie." We have no means of ascertaining what amounts were paid Elder Hardie. The churches were not yet in the habit of reporting sums paid through other agencies than the associational board. But they were encouraged by the Association to contribute to state, home and foreign missions. The amount reported for foreign missions was $46.95.

The reports on schools and education, Sabbath schools, temperance and literature and periodicals were all well written and show that the Association was wide awake on these matters.

On Saturday night a large congregation was addressed on the subject of foreign missions by S. I. Caldwell, G. W. Rogers, C. E. Stephen, W. H. Robert and B. H. Carroll.

Two months before this meeting of the Association (June 23, 1875), there was held in the town of Bremond an educational convention, which resolved to raise $250,000 for the purpose of establishing "a grand central university" for the entire state.

Resolutions by the Association were passed approving this action of the Bremond convention.

It should be stated that friction between the two schools, Baylor University at Independence, and Waco University, prevented the laudable purpose of the Bremond educational convention from being carried into effect.

Mission societies had been organized in nearly all the churches by B. H. Carroll and J. J. Riddle. A committee to whom the "rolls" of the societies were referred, reported: "Having examined all submitted to our inspection we declare the Mastersville roll, William McMullen, secretary, is, in our judgment, the best kept."

The following resolutions were adopted:

"*Resolved* 1, That we ought to have a Sabbath school in every church.

"2. That we can have a Sabbath school in every church.

"3. That we will have a Sabbath school in every church."

Touching memorial resolutions were adopted concerning Elder C. W. Kinnard, deceased.

The next session was appointed to be held with Blue Ridge church, Friday before the fourth Sunday in August, 1876. B. H. Carroll was chosen to preach the introductory, L. R. Scruggs, alternate. No one was selected to preach the doctrinal sermon.

Total churches in 1871, 23; total churches in 1875, 25; total membership in 1871, 1213; total membership in 1875, 1618, Bold Springs and Pleasant Grove did not represent during these five years. Calvert and Marlin did not represent in 1871. Pleasant Grove ceased to exist in 1873. Bethel (Bosque county) did not represent after 1871. Ebenezer and Caddo were dismissed by letter in 1871. Searsville, Bold Springs, Mount Pigah and Union ceased to belong to the Association in 1875. Salem, White Rock and Greenwood churches were received in 1871. Hope, Antioch and Rock Creek in 1872. White Hall and Mount Pisgah in 1873. Olive Branch in 1874. Carolina, Sage Chapel (afterwards Eddy) and Deer Creek in 1875.

Total baptized in five years, 841; received by letter, 921; restored, 61; increase, 1823.

Dismissed by letter, 836; excluded, 208; died, 109; decrease, 1153.

Contributed for missions: Associational, $1,764.41; domestic, S. B. C., $152.55; foreign, S. B. C., $46.95; ministerial education (Waco University), $382.10. Total (five years), $2,348.91. This is correct only so far as reported.

Missionary work within bounds of Association, 1871-5: Missionaries, W. W. Harris, A. W. Ellege, V. G. Cunningham, J. B. Parrock: miles, 3,978; visits, 2,090; sermons, 581; baptisms, 102. Besides this summary much gratuitous work was done.

CHAPTER V.

LAST HALF OF SECOND DECADE.

1876–1880.

"And besides this, giving all diligence, add to your faith virtue; and to virtue knowledge; and to knowledge temperance; and to temperance patience; to patience godliness; and to godliness brotherly kindness; and to brotherly kindness charity." (2 Pet. 1: 5, 6.)

The above paragraph is beautifully descriptive of the progress of the Association during the next five years.

Blessed with tireless, faithful, resourceful leaders, men of God, who taught and prayed and sacrificed for the glory of Christ, the Association moved grandly forward on her beneficent mission. The fallow ground was broken; error, ignorance and iniquity rooted up; and the precious seeds of evangelical truth were sown down everywhere. The harvest is here. These closing years of the nineteenth century are reaping priceless sheaves of spiritual joys and privileges of spiritual religion and spiritual life.

SESSION OF 1876 AT BLUE RIDGE.

At the seventeenth session, held with Blue Ridge church, Falls county, August 26 and 27, 1876, 26 churches were represented and 68 delegates were present. Included in the 26 are four new churches, Golinda, Groesbeck, Live Oak and Carolina. Greenwood and White Rock were not represented. Bosqueville was represented by letter only. Mt. Pisgah was changed to Reagan.

As they stood on the rolls at that time the churches and pastors were as follows:

Antioch and Salem (Limestone), W. C. Manning; Bethel, Greenwood and Rock Creek, J. J. Riddle; Beulah and Carolina, Calvin Magee; Blue Ridge, Hope, Marlin and Union, J. L. Lattimore; Bremond, L. R. Scruggs; Bosqueville and East Waco, V. G. Cunningham, Cow Bayou, Deer Creek and Sage Chapel, T. A. Mangum; Groesbeck, G. L. Jennings; Golinda, R. C. Burleson; New Hope, J. H. Harrison; Reagan, Jesse Tubb; Salem (Mastersville), John McLain; Waco, B. H. Carroll; White Rock, J. J. Sledge; Concord, Live Oak and Olive Branch, supplied by Missionary J. B. Parrock.

During the year past there were some glorious revivals—notably at Bethel, New Hope, Salem (Mastersville), Union, Waco and White Hall. At Bethel 85 were baptized, which more than doubled the membership. At Waco 157 were baptized and 116 received by letter. Had it not been that 82 withdrew by letter, the membership at Waco would have more than doubled. At this meeting Waco had a total of 439; at last meeting 249. New Hope received 23 by baptism, Salem 17 and White Hall 39. In all 22 churches reported additions by baptism. The whole number batptized in all the churches was 396, a larger number than during any preceding year in the history of the Association; and not for 15 years afterwards was so large a number reported. In 1891 the number was 594; in 1893, 538; 1894, 592. In no year has the number reached 600. The total in fellowship in 1876 was 2112, a net gain over 1875 of 432.

There were now 11 Sunday schools, with the following churches: Antioch, Bethel, Bremond, Bosqueville, Concord, Marlin, New Hope, Rock Creek, Salem (Kosse), Waco and White Hall. Whole number of teachers 85; scholars, 546.

Officers elected: J. W. Speight, moderator; C. E. Stephen, clerk; C. Stubblefield, treasurer.

The new churches were Groesbeck, Golinda, Live Oak and Carolina. These were all newly organized. Groesbeck came into the Association with 16 members, continued ten years until 1886, and departed with 35 members. During this time she represented at every meeting and entertained the Association in 1882. Groesbeck is now the county site of Limestone county, and the church is one of the most prominent in Limestone association. Golinda is five miles from the Brazos on the west side, on the line of Falls and McLennan. This church came into the Association with 20 members, represented every year till 1881. The church ceased to exist shortly afterwards. The last time represented, her membership number 65. Live Oak was the fruits of J. B. Parrock's missionary labors. This church is south of Lott five miles, joined the Association with 19 members, and continued 17 years. In 1893 she withdrew by letter to join Falls County Association. She failed to represent in 1883, 1888 and 1889. Membership at time of withdrawal, 53. Carolina lived 13 years; came into the Association with 26 members, represented every year till 1882. Had at that time 65 members. The Association met with this church in 1879.

The regular appointees to preach the introductory sermon, B. H. Carroll and L. R. Scruggs, were absent. The sermon was preached by G. L. Jennings, from Luke 15. Theme, "Salvation of a Sinner." G. L. Jennings and J. T. S. Park were received as corresponding messengers from Richland Association. Messengers of correspondence were appointed to the following associations and general bodies: Union Association, Leon River, Trinity River, Little River, Sister Grove, Bosque River, Richland, Towash, Waxahachie, Little Brazos, Comanche, Navasota River, General Association, State convention and Sunday school convention.

During the past year meetings of the Mission Board were held at New Hope and Reagan. Elder J. B. Parrock was kept in the field as missionary. His report shows: Miles traveled, 2119; sermons preached, 149; families visited, 590; family worship, 147; baptized, 29; churches organized, 2. Because of financial embarrassment of the Board, Bro. Parrock was not continued as missionary.

Extracts from reports adopted at this meeting:

Schools and education, by S. Durham and W. H. Jenkins—"The report of your worthy President of the Board of Trustees of

Waco University, Col. J. W. Speight, made to your body in August, 1861, shows the University opening with 50 students, and expresses the belief that but for the war and other depressing circumstances, the number would have been 150. In view of this report, it is a pleasing reflection that this institution, whose highest ambition in 1861 was to matriculate 150 students in the year ending June 19, 1876, during a financial crisis only less depressing to the community than the presence of an armed enemy on our coasts, matriculated over 400 students."

Foreign Missions by J. B. Parrock.—"A failure or refusal to contribute is to neglect our Savior."

Sabbath schools by B. L. Aycock and J. L. Long—"Let the first buddings of the mind catch the great central figure of the gospel, the death and resurrection of the Savior."

Literature and Periodicals by J. L. Lattimore—"We suggest that every church place a small sum of money in the hands of the pastor to be spent in the distribution of denominational tracts in their midst."

The amount raised during the year for associational missions was $355.30. This was paid J. B. Parrock.

The doctrinal sermon was preached by C. E. Stephen. Scriptures read: Mark 3:14, Matt. 28:20, John 14:20. Theme, "Restricted Communion."

Friday night W. C. Manning preached from the text, "It is finished;" Saturday night, J. B. Parrock from Rom. 1: 4; Sunday, 11 a. m., J. G. Nash, from Gal. 6:14; same hour at old house, C. E. Stephen, from Eph. 2: 1; night, B. L. Wright.

A Sunday school mass meeting was conducted by J. T. S. Park.

The next session was ordered to be held at Marlin on Friday before the fourth Sunday in August, 1877. J. S. Allen, J. L. Lattimore, alternate, was appointed to preach the introductory sermon, and B. H. Carroll, J. J. Riddle, alternate, the doctrinal sermon.

Ordained ministers: J. S. Allen, R. C. Burleson, R. B. Burleson, B. H. Carroll, V. G. Cunningham, T. D. Suttle, J. F. Duncan, J. H. Harrison, J. B. Parrack, J. B. Puckett, J. J. Riddle, W. W. Smith, Waco; J. L. Lattimore, A. W. Middleton, Kosse;

Calvin Magee, Marlin; Z. N. Morrell, Jesse Tubb, Reagan; J. V. Wright, L. R. Scruggs, C. E. Stephen, Bremond; J. W. Scarborough, Crawford.

Unordained: J. D. Brown, J. L. Brown, J. Jones, W. G. Smith, Kosse; P. S. Bruner, Thos. Burrows, Mastersville; L. L. Foster, Groesbeck; W. T. Compere, J. C. Robinson, Z. C. Taylor, Waco.

SESSION OF 1877 AT MARLIN.

Introductory sermon by J. L. Lattimore, 2 Tim. 4:2. Subject, "Responsibilities of the Ministry."

Pursuant to adjournment the Association in her eighteenth session met with the church at Marlin, Friday and Saturday, August 24 and 25, 1877. No new churches were received. Bethel's name is changed to Robinson. Concord not represented. Robinson had delegates present, but not statistical letter. The past was a year of revivals. Every church in the Association except Concord (not represented), Bosqueville, Reagan and Robinson, reported baptisms. Antioch reported 22; Blue Ridge, 41; Bremond, 31; Carolina, 14; Cow Bayou, 20; Deer Creek, 14; Greenwood, 15; New Hope, 10; Rock Creek, 22; Sage Chapel, 16; Salem (Kosse), 29; White Rock, 39; others smaller numbers. Whole number baptized, 309. Total in fellowship 2337, net gain over last year of 225.

Churches and pastors: Antioch and Salem (Kosse), W. C. Manning; Beulah and Live Oak, Calvin Magee; Blue Ridge and Union, J. L. Lattimore; Bremond, W. W. Harris; Bosqueville, V. G. Cunningham; Carolina and New Hope, T. D. Suttle; Cow Bayou, Deer Creek and Sage Chapel, T. A. Mangum; East Waco, J. G. Nash; Greenwood, J. H. Harrison; Groesbeck, G. L. Jennings; Golinda and Olive Branch, J. F. Duncan; Marlin (supply) and Reagan, J. V. Wright; Robinson, J. B. Parrock; Rock Creek and White Rock, J. J. Riddle; Salem (Mastersville), John McLain; White Hall, J. S. Allen; Waco, B. H. Carroll; Hope, pastorless.

Ten Sunday schools, 82 teachers, 619 scholars.

The old officers were re-elected.

Letters of dismission were granted Salem (Kosse), Hope and Antioch.

J. H. Thetfort and G. L. Jennings were received as corresponding messengers from Richland Association; F. F. Bloodworth, from Bosque River; R. H. Blanton and J. B. Osterhout, from Salado.

"It was ordered that hereafter any member of this Association attending any session of any of our Baptist Associations in this state is hereby authorized to represent this association as corresponding messengers to such body, and that a permanent statement hereof be made in the Order of Business. Further ordered, that this rule shall not apply to the appointment of corresponding messengers to Baptist State conventions, the Sunday School convention or to the General Association."

Corresponding messengers were appointed to the general bodies as heretofore.

During the past year the Mission Board held four meetings, one at Carolina, one at Rock Creek and two at Robinson. J. H. Harrison was employed as missionary two months. He was paid by the Waco church $100 for time employed. Following is Bro. Harrison's report: "Time, 79 days; miles, 615; sermons, 79; families visited, 119; family prayer, 34 times; visits to churches, 14; exhortations, 13; baptized, 10; professions at meetings held by missionary, 25." J. B. Parrock did some good work also visiting and preaching to New Hope, Carolina, Golinda and Marlin.

The Board states: "The church at Golinda is the banner church, it alone having contributed an average of 50 cents per member."

It was at this meeting that the plan of mission operations under the direction of the Mission Board was perfected. The following, recommended by the Board (B. H. Carroll, president, and Cortez Stubblefield, secretary), was adopted:

"*Resolved* 1. That our territory be equally divided into four districts, as near as situation and population will admit, to be numbered 1, 2, 3 and 4.

"2. That No. 1 consist of Waco, Bosqueville, Rock Creek, Greenwood, White Hall and Robinson. No. 2—Golinda, Cow Bayou, Mastersville, Sage Chapel, Deer Creek, Carolina, Beulah and Live Oak. No. 3—East Waco, White Rock, Olive Branch,

Concord and New Hope. No. 4.—Marlin, Blue Ridge, Union Bremond, Reagan and Groesbeck.

"3. That the Board members of each district elect for themselves a vice-president, whose duty it shall be to hold a mission meeting per month in the bounds of his district, reporting quarterly to the president.

"4. That there be held each fifth Sunday an entire Board meeting, once only in each district, the district selecting the place and the Board the time. At these meetings the president shall preside and in his absence the vice-president in whose district the meeting is held. Likewise, in the absence of the secretary, the secretary of the district in which the meeting is held, shall act as such."

Elder J. B. Parrock is the originator of this district system. It was he who planned it and made the suggestion to the Board.

The following was adopted:

Resolved, That the Mission Board of this Association take full charge of the Sunday school work, and that the Board be called the Mission and Sunday school Board of Waco Association.

The members of the M. S. S. B. were elected for the new year, and $415 pledged by the churches for associational mission work.

On Friday night, T. D. Suttle preached from Matt. 22:22. Subject, "Christ." Saturday night, V. G. Cunningham, from Psalm 85:6. Subject, "A Genuine Revival." Sunday morning, C. E. Stephen, from John 3:7. Subject, "Why Regeneration is Necessary." Sunday night, J. J. Riddle, from 1 John 3:1, "God's Love."

The minute closes with these words: "Thus ended a pleasant, profitable and harmonious meeting."

The ordained preachers were the same as the preceding year, except that R. L. Scruggs of Bremond moved out of the associational bounds and that B. F. Tatum moved in, locating at Waco.

SESSION OF 1878 AT WHITE ROCK.

On Friday, August 24, 1878, the Waco Association convenes in her nineteenth annual session with the White Rock church.

W. S. Huff preached the introductory sermon. Theme: "The Exaltation of Christ."

Four new churches came into the Association: Mount Calm, New Zion, Pleasant Grove, Willow Springs. Four of the old ones, Bremond, Beulah, Salem and Reagan, were not represented. Twenty-five churches were present with letters, represented by 68 delegates. All these but four, Golinda, Mt. Calm, Pleasant Grove and Waco, reported additions by baptism.

Carolina, New Hope, New Zion, Deer Creek, Robinson and Rock Creek reported fine revivals. The whole number baptized 168. Total membership 1793. If to these figures be added membership of last year of the churches failing to represent the footing is 2059, nearly 300 fewer than the total a year ago.

Churches and pastors: Blue Ridge and Union, J. L. Lattimore; Bosqueville, V. G. Cunningham; Carolina, New Hope, New Zion and Willow Springs, T. D. Suttle; Concord, A. P. Scofield; Cow Bayou and Deer Creek, T. A. Mangum; East Waco, B. F. Tatum, Golinda, J. B. Parrock; Groesbeck, G. L. Jennings; Greenwood, R. S. Taylor; Live Oak and Pleasant Grove, S. S. Johnson; Marlin and Rock Creek, J. J. Riddle; Olive Branch, J. F. Duncan; Robinson and White Hall, J. S. Allen; Sage Chapel, Thos Burrows; Waco, B. H. Carroll.

Mount Calm joined the Association with 33 members, continued ten years, represented every year except 1883, departed in 1888 with 65 members. New Zion was organized in 1877 by Elder Calvin Magee, and dissolved February 24, 1883. Represented regularly, dissolved with 57 members. Pleasant Grove came into the Association with 26 members, has represented regularly except in '80, '82, '83, '84, and still continues membership in the Association. Willow Springs had but 22 members, but she continues a fine co-operating church. In 1891 the name was changed to Mart. This church has never failed to represent in the Association; in 1880, however, by letter only. Mt. Calm is on the Cotton Belt Railroad, twenty miles east from Waco in Hill county. New Zion was near Chilton in Falls; Pleasant Grove is in the southern part of Falls, two miles west of the Brazos river and four miles north of the Falls and Milam line. Mart is in the southeastern corner of McLennan, twenty miles from Waco.

Messengers were appointed to the general bodies.

WACO BAPTIST ASSOCIATION.

T. H. Compere was received as corresponding messenger from Richland Association, and J. B. Pulis from Leon River.

The Mission and Sunday School Board held meetings (called "Board meetings") during the year at Blue Ridge, White Hall, Golinda and New Hope.

J. B. Parrock labored as missionary one month, and J. F. Duncan four months. Bro. Parrock preached 17 sermons, visited 3 churches and 31 families. No report of Bro. Duncan's work has been published.

The amount raised for Associational missions was $354.70. No statement is made of sums raised for Home and Foreign missions.

No report is made of the number of Sabbath schools.

The committees on Sabbath schools and Domestic missions were stricken from the list of standing committees, these subjects having been referred to the M. S. S. Board. Later (1891) it was made a part of the order to appoint a standing committee on "Home Board," or Home missions of S. B. convention.

Amended, the list of subjects assigned to standing committees, is as follows: Foreign missions, Schools and Education, Literature and Periodicals, Ministerial Education, Temperance, "and any other subject the Association may choose."

Occasionally a committee was appointed on Orphans' Home.

The report on Literature and Periodicals, adopted this year (written by J. F. Duncan), recommended, "That this Association co-operate with the Bible and Colportage Board of the General Association, located at Waco, by making contributions to that Board, by authorizing the missionary of the Association to act as colporteurs for that Board, and by recommending the books, tracts and periodicals circulated by that Board."

Appointed, the next session with Carolina church, beginning Saturday, August 23, 1879. To preach the introducory sermon, J. J. Riddle, J. S. Allen, alternate. To preach the doctrinal sermon B. H. Carroll, J. L. Lattimore, alternate.

Arranged and published in the Minutes of 1868 the following Order of Business of Board meetings:

1. Program of Ministers' meeting from 9 a. m. to 11:30 a. m. Saturday.
2. Sermon at 11:30 a .m.
3. Board meeting from 2 to 3 p. m.
4. Deacons' meeting from 4 to 6 p. m.
5. Sermon at 8 p. m.
6. Sunday school mass meeting at 9 a. m. Sunday .
7. Sermon at 11 a. m.
8. Sunday school institute 2 to 5 p. m.
9. Sermon at 8 p. m.

At 11 o'clock Saturday J. F. Duncan preached. Subject, "The Holy Spirit; who is He, and what is His Office Work." No other preaching noted in minutes.

Ordained ministers at this time: J. S. Allen, R. C. Burleson, B. H. Carroll, J. F. Duncan, W. S. Huff, J. B. Parrock, J. J. Riddle, V. G. Cunningham, J. H. Harrison, J. B. Puckett, W. W. Smith, T. D. Suttle, B. F. Tatum, Waco; C. E. Stephen, Bremond; J. L. Lattimore, Kosse; Z. N. Morrell, Jesse Tubb, Reagan; Calvin Magee, Marlin.

SESSION OF 1879 AT CAROLINA.

Pursuant to adjournment the Association met in her twentieth annual session with Carolina church, Falls county, Saturday, August 23, 1879. Session ended Monday, August 25.

J. J. Riddle preached the introductory sermon from Matt. 18:17. Subject, "Gospel Discipline."

Two new churches, Liberty and Union Grove, united with the Association at this meeting. Union, Beulah, Greenwood and Groesbeck failed to represent. Union never represented again.

Churches and pastors: Beulah, C. Magee; Bremond, C. C. Lee; Blue Ridge and Liberty, J. L. Lattimore; Bosqueville, R. B. Burleson; Carolina, New Zion and Willow Springs, T. D. Suttle; Cow Bayou and Deer Creek, T. A. Mangum; Concord and East Waco, B. F. Tatum; Golinda, T. P. Speakman; Groesbeck and Mount Calm, G. L. Jennings; Live Oak and Pleasant Grove, S. S. Johnson; Marlin and Rock Creek, J. J. Riddle; New Hope and Salem, A. P. Scofield; Union Grove, Thomas Hooker; Reagan, W. S. Huff; Robinson and White Hall, J. S. Allen; Sage

Chapel, John McLain; White Rock, J. H. Harrison; Waco, B. H. Carroll; Greenwood and Olive Branch, without pastor. Bremond withdrew from the Association.

The new churches were Liberty and Union Grove. Liberty, in the Eastern part of Falls, was a newly organized church, came into the Association with 105 members, did not represent the next year, afterwards represented every year till 1890, when she was dismissed by letter to go into the organization of Falls County Association. She departed with 81 members. Union Grove was but recently organized. In 1887 the name was changed to Geneva. This church come to us with 28 members and has never failed to represent with letter and delegates, except 1882, when she had present letter only. The church is at Elm Mott.

During the past year Waco, White Hall, Sage Chapel, Rock Creek, Robinson, Live Oak, Liberty, Golinda, Cow Bayou and Blue Ridge enjoyed precious revivals. Every church in the Association, save Salem, White Rock and Beulah, reported additions by baptism. The largest number by one church was 44 at Robinson. Total baptized 241, total in fellowship 2225. This is 432 more than was reported in 1878, but lacks 112 of the number reported in 1877.

At this meeting J. J. Riddle was elected moderator; C. E. Stephen, clerk, and M. H. Curry, treasurer. Officers of the M. S. S. Board: B. H. Carroll, president; W. G. Daniel, W. D. Gaines, T. M. L. Duncan and C. E. Stephen, vice-presidents.

Board meetings were held the past year at Mount Calm, Groesbeck, New Zion and Bosqueville.

W. S. Huff was appointed missionary. He began his work in September and closed in June. Salary $50 per month.

At last session of the Association the missionary was requested to work for the Bible and Colportage Board of the General Association. This character of work caused some dissatisfaction. Further dissatisfaction arose because the missionary had been instructed to take collections for ministerial students, retaining to himself a small per cent. of the collections. Funds for his support came in slowly. During the year Reagan petitioned for one-fourth of his time, promising to relieve the Board of one-fourth of the expense. This was accepted. Summary of missionary's labors: Sermons, 139; exhortations, 61; inquirers instructed, 140; visits, 600; organized Sunday schools, 3; prayer-meetings, 4; sold books, 340; gave away tracts (pages), 12,700. Amount paid W. S. Huff, $437.50.

Adopting the recommendations of the Board the Association, instead of employing a missionary for the coming year, asked pastors to supply the destitution.

The appointment of Cortez Stubblefield as financial agent by the General Association to labor in the bounds of Waco, Richland and Towash Associations, was heartily endorsed.

The following important recommendations of the M. S. S. Board were adopted:

"(1.) That of the funds collected in our bounds we appropriate one month's salary to the general superintendent of missions appointed by the General Association, and one month's salary to A. J. Holt, frontier missionary.

"(2.) That all the rest of the funds be appropriated to another missionary to the frontier to be appointed by the Mission Board of the General Association.

"(3.) That for this work we recommend to that Board as missionary, Elder J. B. Parrock, former missionary of this Association, whose praise is in all the churches. We would suggest as important points to be occupied, Breckenridge, in Stephens county, and Graham City, in Young county, provided these places are not supplied and will accept our aid."

We would be glad to reproduce the reports of standing committees this year. They are fine, but in the main, a reproduction of excellent thoughts in former reports.

The next session was appointed at White Hall. The time was now changed from August 10 to September, and this session was appointed for September 25, 1880. To preach the introductory sermon, C. Magee, alternate, B. H. Carroll; to preach the doctrinal sermon, C. E. Stephen, alternate, T. D. Suttle. To preach the missionary sermon Sunday at 11 o'clock, B. H. Carroll.

It was made a permanent order that the introductory sermon be preached on Saturday at 10 a. m. each year; the denominational (or doctrinal) sermon Saturday night and the missionary sermon on Sunday at 11 a. m.

Ordained ministers: J. S. Allen, R. B. Burleson, W. T. Compere, J. B. Parrock, A. P. Scofield, B. F. Tatum, R. C. Burleson, B. H. Carroll, J. F. Duncan, W. S. Huff, J. B. Puckett, W. W. Smith, T. P. Speakman, and R. S. Taylor, Waco; T. Burrows, Mastersville; T. M. L. Duncan, Chase; W. M. Garrett, Elm Mott; C. C. Hardwick and T. D. Suttle, Peyton; C. C. Lee and C. E. Stephen, Bremond; R. Moore, Mooreville; J. J. Riddle, Bosqueville; John Witt, Perry; J. Daffin and S. S. Johnson, West Falls; J. L. Lattimore, Kosse; Calvin Magee, Marlin; Jesse Tubb, Reagan.—29.

Unordained: P. S. Bruner, L. L. Foster, J. M. McFarland, J. Venable, J. T. Crawford, J. A. Lea, J. W. Scarborough, W. B. White.

SESSION OF 1880 AT WHITE HALL.

As appointed, the Association convened in her twenty-first annual session at White Hall, five miles west from Waco.

Elder Calvin Magee preached the introductory sermon from 1 Cor. 3:22.

Twenty-two churches were represented by letter and delegates. The total number of delegates 49. Two churches, Willow Springs and New Hope, were represented by letter only. Concord, Liberty, Reagan and Pleasant Grove, failed to represent.

(No statistics of this year have ever been published).

Churches and pastors: Blue Ridge, S. L. Morris; Bosqueville and Reagan, W. S. Huff; Beulah, Calvin Magee; Carolina, New Zion and Willow Springs, T. D. Suttle; Cow Bayou and Deer Creek, T. A. Mangum; East Waco, Rock Creek and Concord, B. F. Tatum; Golinda, Greenwood and White Rock, T. P. Speakman; Groesbeck, G. A. Coulson; Liberty, J. L. Lattimore; Live Oak, J. T. Crawford; Marlin, T. J. Drane; Mount Calm, G. L. Jennings; New Hope, without pastor; Olive Branch and Union Grove, Thomas Hooker; Robinson and White Hall, J. S. Allen; Salem, A. J. Shelton; Waco, B. H. Carroll.

Officers elected: J. J. Riddle, moderator; S. L. Morris, clerk; M. H. Curry, treasurer.

Corresponding messengers present: From Leon River Association, Elder J. M. Wright, W. Hickerson; from Hamilton County Association, Elder R. S. Hurt; from Bosque River, Elder W. B. Hatchett; from Comanche, Elder J. T. Harris; from Richland, Elder G. A. Coulson and S. N. Wilson; from Union Association, W. B. Bagby.

The M. S. S. Board reported: Paid to superintendent of missions of General Association $100; to A. J. Holt, frontier missionary, $75; to W. Lee, frontier missionary, $3.75; to C. Stubblefield, financial secretary of General Association, $28.35; to W. T. Compere, S. S. evangelist, $22.25; to W. B. Long, frontier missionary, 7 months, $225; Bible Board of General Association, for ministerial education, $19.35; J. B. Parrock, frontier missionary, $140.15; to building meeting house in Hamilton county, $60; to foreign missions, $34. Total $805.45.

VOLUNTEER AND UNPAID MISSIONARY LABOR.

J. S. Allen kept up two regular appointments, one at Miller Moore's school house, south of Waco eight miles, and the other at a school house ten miles southwest of Waco. Besides, he spent three weeks in protracted meetings not connected with pastoral labors.

J. J. Riddle supplied four destitute points on nights during the week.

W. S. Huff did some good work and reports 2 baptized.

J. H. Harrison also did some volunteer work.

FRONTIER WORK.

J. B. Parrock labored three months, secured lot for house in town of Graham.

W. B. Long labored seven months. Summary of his report: Stations regularly supplied, 16; sermons, 207; exhortations, 74; baptisms, 54; received by letter, 58; restored, 11; miles, 1311; Sunday schools organized, 9; deacons ordained, 4; pages of tracts distributed, 2460; collected on field, $154.30.

As the work during the past year was fruitful of much good, the Board recommended to the Association that the same plan be continued; that W. B. Long be continued on the same terms ($35.00 per month); that the General Association be requested to appoint Elder R. S. Hurt as frontier missionary, our new board to pay his salary. These recommendations were adopted.

The churches were requested to organize Mission societies and endeavor to collect an average of 50 cents per member for missions.

Officers of M. S. S. Board for coming year: President, B. H. Carroll; vice-presidents, C. Stubblefield, W. D. Gaines, S. F. Sparks, M. H. Curry.

Extracts from reports of standing committees:

Foreign missions by B. F. Tatum—"Today the largest Baptist church in the world is at the mission station of Ongale, India, among the Teloguse, where there are 14,000 members in one congregation."

Temperance, by L. L. Foster—"If there were no moderate dram drinkers there would be no drunkards."

The report on Schools and Education, written by J. S. Allen, briefly rehearses the history of Waco University from its incipiency. From this we learn that from 1870 to 1880 there were matriculated 1167 females and 1492 males. This is considered a good showing for the second decade of the University.

The next session was appointed at Groesbeck. To preach the introductory sermon, B. F. Tatum, alternate, T. P. Speakman; to preach the denominational sermon, W. S. Huff or S. L. Morris; to preach the missionary sermon, John S. Allen or B. H. Carroll.

Four new ministers moved into the Association; S. L. Morris, T. J. Drane, J. T. Crawford, S. H. Ragan. Two moved away, C. C. Lee, A. P. Scofield.

RESUME.

During the second half of the second decade the following churches held membership in the Association: Antioch, Bethel, Blue Ridge, Beulah, Bremond, Bosqueville, Carolina, Concord, Cow Bayou, Deer Creek, East Waco, Golinda, Greenwood, Groesbeck, Hope, Live Oak, Liberty, Marlin, Mount Calm, New Hope, New Zion, Olive Branch, Pleasant Grove, Reagan, Robinson, Rock Creek, Sage Chapel, Salem (Kosse), Salem (Mastersville),

Union, Union Grove, Willow Springs, Waco, White Hall, White Rock.—35.

Total churches in 1876, 26; total churches in 1880, 31.

Membership in 1876, 2112; in 1879, 2225; no statistics of 1880 were published.

Golinda, Carolina, Groesbeck and Live Oak joined the Association in 1876; Mount Calm, New Zion, Pleasant Grove and Willow Springs (afterwards Mart) in 1878; Liberty and Union Grove, in 1879.

Salem, Hope and Antioch were dismissed by letter in 1877. Bremond did not represent after 1879.

Total baptized in 1867-9, 915; received by letter, 1007; gain, 1922; loss by letter, exclusion and death, 1220.

Moderator, 1876-8, J. W. Speight; 1879-80, J. J. Riddle.

President of Mission and S. S. Board, B. H. Carroll.

Sunday schools 11.

Missionaries, 1876-7, J. B. Parrock; 1877, J. H. Harrison, 4 months; 1877-8, J. B. Parrock, 40 days, J. F. Duncan, 5 months; 1878-9, W. S. Huff, 9 months; 1879-80, J. B. and W. B. Long, and others on frontier.

Funds reported for Associational mission, five years, $1747.05; ministerial education, $17.20; all other purposes, $6200.20. Total $7964.45.

CHAPTER VI.

FIRST HALF OF THIRD DECADE.

1881–1885.

Years of Glory! Earnest, solid, systematic work. "Go forward" is the motto. How beautiful, the advancing columns of the Lord's hosts! If harmonious labor, if earnest, active co-operation, if prayer and sacrifice are acceptable to the Lord Jesus, surely this half decade is well pleasing in His sight. That our Savior smelled a sweet savor is proved in the fact that He came down and blessed His people. Everywhere the seeds sown by our missionaries sprang up and brought fruit. New churches came into existence at strategic points. Old ones, weak, grew strong. Cultured, consecrated pastors fed the flocks. The wilderness and solitary place was glad; the desert rejoiced and blossomed as the rose.

WACO BAPTIST ASSOCIATION.

SESSION OF 1881 AT GROESBECK.

Since the meeting of the last Association, the moderator, Dr. J. J. Riddle, passed to his blessed reward. His work was done. It pleased the Master to take him. Touching mention of his life and work is made in the minutes of this year.

This was the twenty-second annual session. T. P. Speakman preached the introductory from Eph. 5:22-29.

East Waco, New Hope, Robinson, Rock Creek, Sage Chapel and Concord failed to represent. White Hall represented by letter only.

Two new churches were received, Mount Zion, near Harrison, and Mount Antioch, near Mt. Calm.

On rolls, 31 churches.

Churches and pastors: Blue Ridge, Cow Bayou, Beulah, Golinda and New Zion, S. L. Morris; Bosqueville and Reagan, W. S. Huff; Marlin and Carolina, T. J. Drane; Deer Creek and Sage Chapel, T. A. Mangum; East Waco, Robinson and White Hall, J. S. Allen; Greenwood and White Rock, T. P. Speakman; Groesbeck, G. A. Coulson; Liberty, J. L. Lattimore; Live Oak, J. T. Crawford; Mount Antioch, J. R. Malone; Mount Zion and Willow Springs, T. D. Suttle; Mount Calm, T. M. L. Duncan; Olive Branch and Union Grove, Thos. Hooker; Pleasant Grove, W. J. Glazener; Rock Creek, B. F. Tatum; Salem, A. J. Shelton; Waco, B. H. Carroll; Concord, without pastor.

Mount Zion joined with 13 members, represented next year with name changed to Trading House, 39 members and never represented again.

Mount Antioch came to us from Richland with 99 members, continued till 1888, failed to represent in 1885, represented by letter only in 1886, and departed with 123 members.

Total baptized, 117; in fellowship, 2049.

Officers: J. W. Speight, moderator; S. L. Morris, clerk; M. H. Curry, treasurer.

Visitors: From Little Brazos Association, James Newman; from Richland, E. Bowman, G. A. Coulson, G. L. Jennings, Mrs. Jane Armour and Miss Florence Coulson.

The Order of Business authorizing any member to represent

the Association who might be present at the meetings of other district bodies was not observed at this or the last session and was indifferently observed during all the succeeding history.

Report of the Mission and S. S. Board condensed: Co-operating with the General Association, missionaries—W. B. Long and R. S. Hurt, frontier; W. B. Bagby, Brazil. Board meetings at White Rock, Reagan, Rock Creek, Live Oak. Volunteer work in Association—Much destitution supplied by T. D. Suttle, T. M. L. Duncan, J. Daffin and J. T. Crawford.

Appropriations: To R. S. Hurt, $110; W. B. Long, $420, treasurer of General Association, $10.00; foreign missions for W. B. Bagby, $276.95; orphans home, $376.35; other purposes, $76.70. Total, $1,270.25.

Officers of the new Board: President, B. H. Carroll; vice-presidents, W. S. Huff, W. D. Gaines, R. H. Fowler, G. W. Holland.

For twenty years Waco University was the property of Waco Association and under the supervision of a Board of Trustees appointed by the Association.

At this session in 1881 the following was adopted: "The General Association is a much larger body than this and comprehends in its scope of operation a much more extensive territory than ours. That body desires the supervision and control of Waco University so far as the provisions of the charter will allow, and it has authorized negotiations through committee to accomplish this object.

"The Board of Trustees has assented to the proposition, and while it is believed that this assent of the Board might complete the transfer without being a derogation of charter, nevertheless it has been deemed a due respect and courtesy to Waco Association to solicit its formal consent.

"With this view your committee is authorized by the Board, whose president is president and moderator of this body to recommend the adoption of the following:

"*Resolved*, That the supervision of Waco University, as heretofore exercised by the Waco Association under the provision of the charter of that institution, be, and the same is hereby transferred to the Baptist General Association of Texas, at the request of that body and by the assent of the Board of Trustees of said university."

In the writer's judgment this was the greatest mistake ever made by the Waco Association. Reasons briefly: (1) Nearly all the funds for building up the University, before and since have been raised within the bounds of the Association. (2) Patronage of the school did not increase materially. (3) Disintegration of Waco Association began after losing the school.

The Order of Business was amended by adding: "Organization of new Mission and Sunday School Board."

Willow Springs church was requested to nominate a missionary, "who shall devote a part of his time to missionary work, to supply destitution in that section." Elder T. D. Suttle was named and appointed.

The reports of standing committees were splendid documents, and served well for educational purposes.

Ordained ministers—J. S. Allen, S. L. Morris, J. B. Puckett, Jesse Tubb, R. S. Taylor, R. C. Burleson, B. H. Carroll, J. H. Harrison, W. S. Huff, J. B. Parrock, Waco; T. Burrows, A. J. Shelton, Mastersville; T. M. L. Duncan, Chase; W. M. Garrett, Elm Mott; C. C. Hardwick, Peyton; S. S. Johnson, West Falls; R. Moore, Mooreville; T. D. Suttle, Mart; J. T. Crawford, C. Magee, Landrum; T. J. Drane, Marlin; J. L. Lattimore, Stranger; J. Witt, Perry.

Unordained—P. S. Brunner, L. L. Foster, J. M. McFarland, J. W. Scarborough, W. B. White, J. Venable, J. S. Dinton, J. A. Lea, W. O. Hudson, W. J. Reid, Thos Tutts.

SESSION OF 1882 AT MART.

This, the twenty-third annual session, was held September 23-25, 1882.

The introductory sermon was preached by Robert Moore, Phil. 1: 27.

Received one new church, Mexia.

Name of Sage Chapel is changed to Eddy, that of Mount Zion to Trading House. This church appears no more on our records. Concord does not again appear 'till 1890.

Total churches, 30; not represented, Eddy, New Hope and Salem.

Churches and Pastors: Beulah, New Zion and White Hall, A. J. Shelton; Blue Ridge, B. H. Beal; Carolina, T. J. Drane; Cow Bayou and Marlin, S. L. Morris; Deer Creek, John Witt; East Waco, J. S. Allen; Eddy, T. A. Mangum; Groesbeck and Mexia, H. W. Watson; Liberty, James Newman; Live Oak, Trading House and Willow Springs, T. D. Suttle; Mt. Calm and Olive Branch, J. Scarborough; Union Grove, W. B. Brantly; Reagan, W. S. Huff; Robinson, C. P. Lumpkin; Rock Creek, J. L. Walker; White Rock, T. P. Speakman; Waco, B. H. Carroll, Bosqueville, Greenwood, New Hope, Pleasant Grove and Salem without pastors.

East Waco, Mexia, Reagan, Rock Creek, Trading House, Willow Springs and Waco reported revivals. The largest number baptized was at Willow Springs, 46.

Total baptized, 205; otherwise received, 132; loss by letter and otherwise, 258; present number, 2245.

Officers: G. W. Holland, moderator; S. L. Morris, clerk; M. H. Curry, treasurer.

Correspondence received: Hamilton County Association, R. S. Hurt; Little Brazos, J. Newman; Prairie Grove, E. B. Smyth.

Reports of Mission and Sunday School Board; meetings at Waco, Marlin, Olive Branch and Beulah:

(1) To promote Sunday School work, Sunday School Institutes were held in connection with Board meetings.

(2) Missionaries—in Association, T. D. Suttle, J. T. Crawford; on frontier, W. B. Long, R. S. Hurt; traveling agent in Association, S. F. Sparks.

J. T. Crawford's field, mainly in the forks of Pond creek, West Falls county; T. D. Suttle's field, country near Mart; R. S. Hurt's field, Hamilton County Association; W. B. Long's field, Cisco, Breckenridge, Graham, Eastland City, Providence, Albany and other points.

Great and permanent good was done by these missionaries. Willow Springs, under care of Missionary Pastor T. D. Suttle, became a good working church, and is to-day the strongest country church in the Association.

Bro. Hurt organized one church and ordained one minister.

W. B. Long organized six churches; received into church by baptism 70, by letter and restoration, 144; organized six Sunday Schools. Lot secured and meeting house erected in Eastland City worth $700, house built in Cisco worth $1000, Breckenridge house improved $70, ordained ministers 4.

Appropriations: J. T. Crawford, $50; T. D. Suttle, $8.50; R. S. Hurt, $100; W. B. Long, $560; ministerial education, $10; L. S. Knight, frontier missionary of Alvarado Association, $80.40; Cisco church building, $10; foreign missions, $262.20; Buckner Orphans' Home, $261.50; other purposes (state mission work), $78.25. Total, $1,410.85.

The Board recommended the appointment of Elder J. R. Kelley, of Alvarado, as frontier missionary in place of W. B. Long, resigned, and that R. S. Hurt be continued.

The preaching on Sunday was by S. L. Morris (Matt. 16: 18), B. H. Carroll (Tit. 2: 13, 14) and H. W. Watson.

Mission and Sunday School Board for new year: B. H. Carroll, president; J. E. Brown, W. D. Gaines; J. T. S. Park and G. W. Holland, vice presidents.

Ordained ministers: J. S. Allen, S. L. Morris, J. B. Puckett, Jesse Tubb, R. C. Burleson, B. H. Carroll, J. H. Harrison, W. S. Huff, J. B. Parrock, R. S. Taylor, Waco; T. Burrows, A. J. Shelton, Mastersville; T. M. L. Duncan, Chase; W. M. Garrett, Elm Mott; C. C. Hardwick, Peyton; S. S. Johnson, West Falls; R. Moore, Mooreville; J. T. S. Park, H. W. Watson, Mexia; T. D. Suttle, Mart; J. T. Crawford, C. Magee, Landrum; T. J. Drane, Marlin; J. L. Lattimore, Stranger; T. P. Speakman, Ross; John Witt, Perry.

SESSION OF 1883 AT ROCK CREEK.

The twenty-fourth session was with Rock Creek church, beginning Saturday September 22, and closing Monday, September 24, 1883.

Introductory sermon by J. S. Allen, John 9: 15.

On rolls, 32 churches.

Four new churches received, Chilton, Elm Grove, Lorena, Speegleville.

Golinda appears no more on our rolls. Pretty Valley, organized in the same community, appointed delegates to this meeting, but they failed to attend.

Churches and pastors: Blue Ridge and Reagan, L. W. Duke; Bosqueville and Rock Creek, J. L. Walker; Chilton, Cow Bayou and Salem, L. H. Ewing; Deer Creek, G. G. Gibson; East Waco, J. S. Allen; Eddy, Robert Moore; Elm Grove and Groesbeck, G. L. Jennings; Liberty, W. S. Huff; Live Oak, M. F. Whatley; Mexia, — Lacy; Mt. Antioch, H. R. Puryear; New Hope, J. B. Parrock; Olive Branch and White Hall, A. A. Hensler; Pretty Valley, John Harris; Robinson, C. P. Lumpkin; Waco, B. H. Carroll; White Rock, T. P. Speakman; Beulah, Carolina, Greenwood, Lorena, Marlin, Mt. Calm, Pleasant Grove, Speegleville, Union Grove and Willow Springs without pastors.

Revivals were reported in Blue Ridge, Bosqueville, Elm Grove, Mt. Antioch and Robinson.

Total baptized, 99; received by letter and restoration, 168; loss, 242. Membership, 2091.

Officers: G. W. Holland, moderator; S. L. Morris, clerk; W. D. Gaines, treasurer.

Correspondence received from Towash Association, Elder J. L. Walker; Hamilton County, Elder R. S. Hurt.

Correspondence returned: Elected messenger to General Association,

"*Resolved*, That any messenger of this Association present at any session of a body with whom we correspond be recognized as our correspondent."

The report of the Sunday School and Mission Board is very elaborate, and recites a vast deal of work done.

Frontier missionaries: R. S. Hurt, field, Hamilton County Association; J. R. Kelly, field, "Putnam, Baird, Clyde and Abilene, situated on the line of the Texas and Pacific railway, with a territory of fifteen or twenty miles in width, lying south of those points, and along the line of the railroad."

Appropriated to R. S. Hurt for year's labor, $100; to J. R.

Kelly for year's labor, $744.75; to foreign missions (for W. B. Bagby and wife and Z. C. Taylor and wife, Brazil, and W. D. Powell and wife, Mexico), $573.29; to Buckner Orphans' Home, $314.31; to Maggie Houston Hall (Waco University), $32; to Home Board, S. B. C., $50; to General Association, $3.50; E. B. Hardie, Sunday School evangelist, $10; to Hillsboro church building, $100; to Wesley Smith for Indian missions, $46.03. Total, $2,148.31.

Recommendations by Board: "That we raise, next year, for frontier missions, $1,000; foreign missions, $500; Orphans' Home, $250; for work in our bounds, $250; Sunday School work, $250.

"(2) That we engage Bro. (Deacon) S. F. Sparks to visit all the churches in our Association and organize a plan of systematic co-operation work, and raise funds for the purposes indicated above.

"(3) That we heartily co-operate with L. W. Coleman in the Sunday School work, calling upon our Sunday Schools to contribute to his support, in amount $250. That he be invited to attend our Board meetings and work up the churches of our Association in regard to Sunday Schools.

"(4) That we heartily co-operate with the Southern Baptist Convention in foreign mission work in Brazil and Mexico.

"(5) That Elder J. R. Kelley be continued as frontier missionary at a salary of $75 per month.

"(6) That in parting from Bro. R. S. Hurt, we express our undiminished love for, and confidence in him. That we commend him to all Baptists, as a venerable man of God, who has served the Lord as a missionary from the mountains of Virginia to the frontier of Texas."

The report on Schools and Education: "We hail with pleasure the double effort, by the city of Waco to raise $20,000 building fund, and by the General Association to raise $60,000 endowment. We therefore welcome among us Elder S. L. Morris, the agent appointed to raise this endowment fund." It needs only to be stated that the endowment was raised on paper, but it never materialized.

The report on Literature and Periodicals recommended, The

Texas Baptist, Dallas; The Home and Sunday School, Belton; Kind Words, lesson sheets; the Foreign Mission Journal, Richmond; and the Heathen Helper, Louisville.

Sunday devotional services by H. R. Puryear, Sunday School Institute by A. Goddard, mission sermon by B. H. Carroll; collection for frontier missions, $100; denominational sermon by C. P. Lumpkin; foreign sermon by W. S. Huff; collection $36.53.

After adjournment on Monday "a hymn was sung and the brethren joined in an affectionate farewell."

SESSION OF 1884 AT ROBINSON.

This was the twenty-fifth annual session. Robinson, the place of meeting, was six miles south of Waco, about the center of the Association's territory. The representation was large, thirty-one churches and ninety delegates were present.

Elder W. S. Huff preached the introductory sermon, from Luke 17: 5: "Lord Increase Our Faith."

The old officers were re-elected.

Three new churches were received, Center, Pretty Valley and Social Circle. Bold Springs, an old church of the Association who left us in 1875, joined the Towash Association in 1876, now returned with 195 members. This church continues; present name, West.

Pretty Valley, a new church, appointed messengers a year ago, but they failed to be present. This chuch is in the southern part of McLennan county, west of the Brazos, in the neighborhood of old Golinda, deceased. Many of the Golinda brethren became members of Pretty Valley. This church joined the Association with fifty-six members. The name was changed to Hill Side in 1891; has never failed to represent; by letter only, however, in 1888. Social Circle was a newly organized church, came in with thirty-five members, has never failed to represent; name changed to Battle in 1892. The church worships at town of Battle. Center was organized September 6, 1883, with nine members, joined Little Brazos Association and remained with that body one year; joined Waco Association in 1884, with thirty-six members; represented every year except 1895-6. Salem's name was changed to Mastersville.

Churches and pastors: Blue Ridge, Liberty and Reagan, L. W. Duke; Bold Springs, Pretty Valley and Olive Branch, T. P. Speakman; Bosqueville and Rock Creek, J. L. Walker; Center and Marlin, A. E. Baten; Chilton, J. R. M. Touchstone; Cow Bayou, A. J. Shelton; Deer Creek, G. G. Gibson; East Waco, J. S. Allen; Elm Grove, G. L. Jennings; Groesbeck, J. J. Harris; Live Oak and Pleasant Grove, M. F. Whatley; Lorena and Mastersville, W. S. Huff; Mexia, J. H. Roland; Mount Antioch and Social Circle, T. D. Suttle; Robinson, C. P. Lumpkin; Speegleville, J. B. Parrock; Waco, B. H. Carroll; White Rock and Willow Springs, H. R. Puryear; Beulah, Eddy, Union Grove and White Hall without pastors. Beulah and New Hope were not represented; Mexia by letter only.

During the past year, Bold Springs, Center, Chilton, Liberty, Reagan, Robinson, Rock Creek, Union Grove, Waco and Willow Springs enjoyed revivals. At Bold Springs the largest number, forty-two, was baptized. Whole number baptized, 242. Beulah, Blue Ridge, Eddy, East Waco, Groesbeck, Live Oak, Mexia, New Hope, Pleasant Grove and Social Circle reported no baptisms. Membership this year, 2687; last year, 2090.

During the year past Board meetings were held Waco, East Waco, Mount Antioch and Blue Ridge. The Board reports: "These meetings are the glory and power of our Association. They reach the masses, help the churches where held, inspire the mission spirit where there is none, and revive it when cold."

The Board was expected to co-operate with the Sunday school Convention Board (located at Waco), which it did. The Sunday School Board was assisted by our Board in paying a balance due Elder E. B. Hardie, in sustaining his successor, Elder L. W. Coleman, missionary, during the six months he was in the field, and Elder Kit Williams, last appointed.

Bro. J. R. Kelley was kept in the field during the entire year, at a salary of $75 per month. Miles traveled, 3,152; sermons, 152; baptisms, 26.

The total amounts raised during the year are as follows: Home (state) missions, $1,540.91; foreign missions, $780.57 1-2; Orphans' Home, $363.39 1-2. Total, $2,684.48.

During the year Deacon S. F. Sparks traveled among the churches and organized a uniform plan of systematic giving, which did much towards advancing the work. Also, in company with Deacon W. P. Martin, he visited Buckner Orphans' Home, and made report of same. The Home had at that time twenty-eight girls and twelve boys. The Home school was taught by Miss Carrie Smith.

Work outlined for next year: To frontier missions, to be sent to A. J. Holt, superintendent of missions, General Association, $600; to sustain Kit Williams, Sunday School missionary in bounds of General Association, $500; to sustain V. G. Cunningham, Sunday School missionary in bounds Waco, Towash and Richland Associations, $250; to Orphan's Home, $500; to foreign missions, $500. Total $2,350.

New Board: President, B. H. Carroll; vice presidents, A. M. Harris, W. D. Gaines, John Flowers and G. W. Holland.

Corresponding messengers received: Hamilton County Association, R. S. Hurt; Leon River Association, T. J. Everett; Towash Association, J. L. Walker and N. C. Sparks.

Visitors enrolled: Elders A. T. Hawthorn, Austin, and John Harris, Eddy.

Correspondence returned to General Association and adjacent district bodies.

Extract from report on foreign missions, written by Elder C. P. Lumpkin: "Through constant and earnest prayer, liberal and systematic contributions, by every individual member of the several churches, composing this Association, multitudes who are to-day bowing down to stocks and stones, might hear the gospel and be led to Christ."

Extract from report on Ministerial Education, written by Deacon B. J. Kendrick and Elder John Harris: "The apostles of our Savior who, it is alleged, were unlearned fishermen, were kept in the school of Christ for three years."

Sunday exercises:

10 a. m., Sunday School speeches by L. L. Foster, J. R. M. Touchstone, M. P. Martin.

11 a. m., preaching at Baptist house by B. H. Carroll, Matt.

28: 18, 19; collection for State missions, $58.85. At Presbyterian house, by S. B. McJunkin, Ps. 84: 11; collection for State missions, $10.10.

3 p. m., Sunday School mass meeting, conducted by Elder Kit Williams. Speeches by S. B. McJunkin, W. R. Kellum, M. P. Matheny and J. R. M. Touchstone.

7:30 p. m., preaching at Baptist house, by S. L. Morris, John 8: 36. At Presbyterian house, by M. P. Matheny; collection for foreign missions, $10.55.

SESSION OF 1885 AT CHILTON.

Chilton is ten miles west from Marlin, on the San Antonio and Aransas Pass railroad. At the time the Association was held there the railroad was not yet built. This is the home church of Deacon W. D. Gaines, who had been vice president of the Mission and Sunday School Board since 1877, who continued vice president 'till 1893, and was moderator of the Association four years, 1889-1892.

This was the twenty-sixth annual session. Elder G. W. Greene of Temple, visiting brother, preached the introductory sermon, Rom. 1: 16.

L. L. Foster was elected moderator, S. L. Morris clerk and W. D. Gaines, treasurer.

One new church, Little Deer Creek, was received. Five of the old ones, Beulah, Bold Springs, New Hope, Concord and Speegleville, failed to represent. Total present, thirty-one churches, represented by seventy-seven delegates.

Churches and pastors: Blue Ridge and Center, J. F. McLeod; Bold Springs and Pretty Valley, T. P. Speakman; Bosqueville and Rock Creek, J. L. Walker; Chilton and Live Oak, J. R. M. Touchstone; Cow Bayou and Mastersville, A. J. Shelton; Deer Creek, Thos. Burrows; East Waco, J. S. Allen; Elm Grove and Willow Springs, G. L. Jennings; Groesbeck, J. J. Harris; Liberty and Reagan, L. W. Duke; Little Deer Creek and Pleasant Grove, Robert Moore; Lorena, C. D. Daniel; Mexia, J. H. Roland; Mt. Calm, R. S. Taylor; Robinson and White Hall, S. B. McJunkin; Union Grove and White Rock, T. E. Muse; Waco, B. H. Carroll; Beulah, Marlin, Eddy, Mt. Antioch, New Hope Olive Branch, Social Circle and Speegleville, pastorless.

Little Deer Creek, the new church, joined the Association with twenty-nine members. It meets at a point on Little Deer creek in Falls county, about three miles north from the town of Lott. This church never failed to represent at the meetings of the Association 'till dismissed, by letter, in 1893. She departed with seventy-one members.

Correspondence received: From Salado Association, J. Jenkins; Leon River, John Witt.

Vistors: Elder G. W. Greene, J. T. Duggan, Emma Duggan, Temple; Elders S. J. Anderson and John A. Campbell, Dallas; Elder E. A. Puthuff, representing the Foreign Mission Board Southern Baptist Convention.

The Mission and Sunday School Board during the year held four "successful meetings," at Groesbeck, West Speegleville and East Waco.

Good work was done in the Association by V. G. Cunningham, Sunday School missionary.

The amounts raised were: For home (State) missions, $1,600; foreign missions, $642.68; orphans' home, $923.15. Total, $3, 165.83.

Work outlined for new year, as recommended by the Board and adopted by the Association: Appropriated $250 to W. R. Maxwell, general superintendent of Sunday School Convention; to V. G. Cunningham, Sunday School missionary and colporter, $400; to Saltillo church (Mexico), $100; to frontier missions, to be disbursed by A. J. Holt, $600.

The new Board organized: President, B. H. Carroll; vice presidents, district No. 1, A. Goddard; district No. 2, W. D. Gaines; district No. 3, John Flower; district No. 4, M. H. Curry.

Sunday, 11 a. m., mission sermon, by B. H. Carroll, Acts 10: 4. Denominational sermon at 3 p. m., by S. J. Anderson, Acts 8: 12. Foreign mission sermon at night, by L. W. Duke, Phil. 3: 8.

Extract from Foreign Mission report, written by Elder B. H. Carroll: "In general terms, it will suffice to say, that in both Brazil and Mexico the work prospers beyond our most sanguine expectations; and as the mission force in both is made up of Texans, and mainly supported by Texas contributions, there is the greater reason why we should continue the most hearty co-operation. An additional incentive in this direction is furnished in the fact, that the Foreign Mission Board at Richmond has recently appointed Rev. E. A. Puthuff and Rev. C. D. Daniel to the Brazilian field." These brethren went to Brazil, but soon returned.

All the committees on Literature and Periodicals, since 1877, recommended the Texas Baptist as the organ of the General Association, the next year (year of consolidation) The Texas Baptist and Texas Baptist Herald, were both recommended.

Ordained ministers: J. S. Allen, W. S. Huff, R. S. Taylor, R. C. Burleson, B. H. Carroll, C. D. Daniel, S. B. McJunkin, T. E. Muse, S. L. Morris, E. A. Puthuff, Waco; W. B. Brantley, W. M. Garrett, T. M. L. Duncan, Elm Mott; L. H. Ewing, T. Burrows, Mastersville; W. L. Farmer, J. T. S. Park, Mexia; R. Moore, A. J. Shelton, Mooreville; G. G. Gibson, Durango; C. C. Hardwick, T. D. Suttle, Mart; J. F. McLeod, Reagan; T. P. Speakman, West; J. R. M. Touchstone, M. F. Whatley, J. Daffin, Rupee; E. Taylor, Robinson; E. J. Billington, H. R. Puryear, Mt. Calm; Peter S. Bruner, Eddy; John H. Harrison, Peyton; John Holland Carthage.

RESUME.

During these five years the following churches held membership in the Association: Beulah, Blue Ridge, Bold Springs, Bosqueville, Concord, Center, Chilton, Carolina, Cow Bayou, Deer Creek, Eddy, East Waco, Elm Grove, Golinda, Greenwood, Groesbeck, Liberty, Live Oak, Little Deer Creek, Lorena, Mastersville (formerly Salem), Marlin, Mexia, Mount Antioch, Mount Calm, New Hope, Olive Branch, Pleasant Grove, Pretty Valley, Reagan, Robinson, Rock Creek, Speegleville, Social Circle, Trading House, Union Grove, Waco, White Hall, White Rock, Willow Springs, 40. Concord and New Hope, nominally members, did not represent these five years, and New Hope, though continued on the rolls 'till 1890, never represented again.

Total churches in 1881, 31.

Total churches in 1885, 36.

Membership in 1881, 2,049; in 1885, 2,749.

Mt. Zion and Mt. Antioch united with the Association in 1881, Mexia in 1882, Chilton, Elm Grove, Lorena and Speegleville in 1883, Center, Pretty Valley and Social Circle in 1884, Bold Springs, formerly a member, came back in 1884, Little Deer Creek in 1885.

Golinda and Greenwood never represented after 1881. Carolina and Trading House never represented after 1882.

In 1882 Sage Chapel was changed to Eddy, and Mt. Zion was changed to Trading House.

Salem was changed to Mastersville in 1884.

Total baptized 1881-85, 970; received by letter, 1057; gain, 2027; loss by letter, exclusion and death, 1136.

Missionaries: Associational field, T. D. Suttle, T. M. L. Duncan, J. Daffin, J. T. Crawford, V. G. Cunningham, S. F. Sparks; frontier, R. S. Hurt, W. B. Long, J. R. Kelly; general, L. W. Coleman, Kit Williams, A. J. Holt; foreign, W. B. Bagby, Z. T. Taylor, (Brazil), and W. D. Powell, Mexico.

Total contributions, missions and Orphans' Home, five years, $10,679.42.

CHAPTER VII.

SECOND HALF OF THIRD DECADE.

1886–1890.

Sunshine and shadows! Obstacles, formidable and threatening, lay across the Association's pathway. The faith of God's people was tested and proved. As this decade drew to a close the Lord's hosts advanced on their knees, but advanced. The thorns of Martinite heresy were plucked up. Never once did the armies of God think of turning back, even when the battle was hottest.

SESSION OF 1886 AT LIBERTY.

Liberty church is ten miles west of Marlin, in Falls county. The church had at the time of this meeting seventy-three members, with that grand preacher, Elder L. W. Duke, as pastor.

This session at Liberty was the twenty-seventh annual session.

The introductory sermon was preached by Elder J. B. Link, from 1 Cor. 15: 56-58.

On rolls thirty-five churches; not represented, Beulah and New Hope. New Hope never represented again. Bold Springs, Lorena, Olive Branch and Speegleville were represented by letter only.

Eddy left us and went into the McGregor Association.

Two new churches united with the Association at this meeting, Durango and Prairie Hill.

Durango church is in the town of Durango, in the western part of Falls county, in the neighborhood of old Carolina, dissolved two years before.

Prairie Hill is in the northwestern part of Limestone county. She came into the Association with thirty-three members, remaining with us two years, and went out in 1888 with forty members.

Total baptized, 296; total membership, 3,176.

Churches and pastors: Blue Ridge and Center, J. F. McLeod; Bold Springs and Pretty Valley, T. P. Speakman; Bosqueville, Rock Creek and Speegleville, J. L. Walker; Chilton and Marlin, J. R. M. Touchstone; Cow Bayou, A. J. Shelton; Deer Creek, Durango, Live Oak and Little Deer Creek, A. A. Hensler; Elm Grove H. J. E. Williams; East Waco, J. S. Allen; Groesbeck, J. J. Harris; Liberty and Reagan, L. W. Duke; Lorena and White Hall, S. B. McJunkin; Mastersville, D. M. Ayers; Mount Antioch and Social Circle, T. D. Suttle; Mount Calm, R. S. Taylor; Olive Branch, W. S. Huff; Pleasant Grove, R. Moore; Prairie Hill, G. L. Jennings; Robinson and Union Grove, T. E. Muse; Waco, B. H. Carroll; White Rock, J. T. Stanton; Willow Springs, C. P. Lumpkin.

Officers elected: J. S. Allen, moderator; S. L. Morris, clerk; W. D. Gaines, treasurer.

No correspondence from other bodies.

Visitors: A. J. Holt, superintendent of missions; Jeff D. Ray, superintendent of Sunday School missions; E. R. Carswell, field editor Texas Baptist and Herald.

The General Convention of Texas meets in October of each year. So that the meeting of that body in 1887 came after the next meeting of the Waco Association. Hence there were no messengers appointed to the General Association at this meeting.

Board meetings during the past year: With Live Oak in November, with Marlin in January, with Willow Springs in May and with White Hall in August. The collections at the Marlin Board meeting were larger than at any previous meeting in the history of the Association, either of the Board or of the Association itself. They amounted to $150.35.

The amount raised for State and Sunday School missions was $1,619.50; for foreign missions $1,182.75; for Buckner Orphans' Home, $1,463.40. Total, $4,265.65. This amount exceeds the recommendations of last year ($2.350) by $1,815.65. The amount for Orphans' Home was the largest given during any one year in the previous history of the Association, and is accounted for in the fact that $1,000 was donated by one man, Thomas Parker, of Waco.

Extract from the report of the Board: "The marvelous fruit of our appropriation to destitute frontier missions appears in the report of Rev. A. J. Holt for the Baptist General Association, as submitted to the consolidated General Convention, held in Waco last July. It was the grandest report of modern times, and without a parallel since apostolic times."

Recommendations, adopted:

"(1) That we hail with joy the consolidation of the General Association, State Convention and other bodies, and that we appropriate to this Baptist General Convention the usual sum of $600 for frontier missions, to be sent to its superintendent of mission work, Rev. A. J. Holt.

"(2) That we congratulate the State Sunday School Convention on securing the services of Rev. Jeff D. Ray, as general superintendent, and we hereby appropriate on his salary $250.

"(3) That we appropriate to Rev. J. L. Walker, Sunday School missionary and colporter for this and Salado Association, $400, or $33 1-3 per month.

"(4) That we heartily approve the action of Waco church, in appropriating $500 to V. G. Cunningham as city missionary.

"(5) That all our churches remember and help the Orphans' Home."

New Board organized: President, B. H. Carroll; vice president district No. 1, A. Goddard; vice president district No. 2, W. D. Gaines; vice president district No. 3, John Flower; vice president district No. 4, M. H. Curry.

Extract from report on Schools and Education: "By the terms of consolidation agreed upon at Temple, December 10, 1885, Baylor University was moved to Waco and consolidated with Waco University, under the name of "Baylor University, at Waco." Baylor Female College was located at Belton. The buildings and property at Independence were turned over to Union Association, and the school there, to be carried on under the fostering care of that association. Baylor Female College opened September 13, at Belton, under president J. H. Luther, with an able faculty. They have one of the best buildings in the State; it is a stone building, three stories high, all furnished and will accommodate about 200 students. The endowment of old Baylor is to come to Waco, except such as the donors desire to remain at Independence.

"The city of Waco was to furnish a building site, of not less than twenty acres, and raise $45,000, and the trustees of Waco University to appropriate the present University buildings and grounds, to be used in the erection of new buildings on the new grounds in South Waco. The buildings planned and in process of erection will combine many modern conveniences. The buildings and site will cost $110,000, and will accommodate about 500 students.

"The Baptists of Texas have agreed to raise the endowment to $500,000 for Baylor University of Waco, and an additional building fund of $50,000. The plan adopted at the General Convention at Waco, in July last, was to raise the salaries of agents, independent of the endowment and building funds, and on the floor of the Convention over $1,600 was subscribed, and a good deal more has been added since. The new Board of Trustees have procured a Charter for Baylor University at Waco, and are fully organized. The main building is being put up as rapidly as possible; it is a grand building, that will cost about $45,000. The female boarding house will be let out to contractors soon. * * * Baylor University at Waco opened on September 20, 1886, with a greater number of students than at any previous year. Dr. R. C. Burleson is at the head of the new school as president, and Dr. Reddin Andrews as vice president. They have a full and able faculty associated with them." This report was written by the late Rev. John S. Allen. Two magnificent buildings stand imposingly on the sight, but the $500,000 endowment has never been raised. J. T. Boynton was adopted as the ministerial student of the Association.

We are unable to say how many Sunday schools were in the Association at this time. Suffice to state that nearly all the churches kept up schools for a part or all the year.

The Association had advanced from giving 50 cents per capita to $1.30 per capita.

PREACHING SERVICES.

Saturday night, foreign mission sermon, by B. H. Carroll, text Acts 13: 4.

Sunday, 9:30 a. m., Sunday School mass meeting, conducted by Jeff D. Ray; speeches by J. B. Link, J. R. M. Touchstone, J. S. Allen. 11 a. m., preaching at the Baptist house, by A. J. Holt, Matt 28: 19, 20; at the Union house, by Jeff D. Ray, from Eph. 2: 8 (latter clause).

Sunday night, by J. R. M. Touchstone, Matt. 8:11. Sermon in interest of Orphans' Home.

Districts at this time:

No. 1—Bosqueville, Lorena, Pretty Valley, Robinson, Rock Creek, Speegleville, White Hall, Waco.

No. 2.—Beulah, Chilton, Cow Bayou, Deer Creek, Durango, Little Deer Creek, Live Oak, Mastersville, Pleasant Grove.

No. 3—Bold Springs, East Waco, Elm Grove, Mount Antioch, Union Grove, White Rock, Willow Springs.

No. 4—Blue Ridge, Center, Liberty, Marlin and Reagan.

Duties of vice presidents: "Each vice president must visit every church in his district once a year, to stimulate mission interests, and report in writing to the president."

Duties of Board members: "Each Board member receives all money from his church and forwards the same to the president of the Board. It is also his duty to report in writing, (1) the Sunday

School statistics of his church; (2) all funds contributed by his church, not forwarded through the Board; (3) attend particularly the Board meeting in his own district, and secure as large attendance as possible; (4) organize in his own church the plan of systematic co-operation adopted by the Association."

Ordained ministers: J. S. Allen, W. S. Huff, R. S. Taylor, J. T. Stanton, R. C. Burleson, B. H. Carroll, S. B. McJunkin, T. E. Muse, S. L. Morris, Waco; T. M. L. Duncan, W. B. Brantley, W. M. Garrett, Elm Mott; L. H. Ewing, T. Burrows, Mastersville; G. G. Gibson, A. A. Hensler, Durango; J J. Harris, Groesbeck; C. C. Hardwick, T. D. Suttle, Mart; A. J. Shelton, R. Moore, Mooresville; T. P. Speakman, West; Elihu Taylor, T. J. Everett (M. D.), Robinson; J. R. M. Touchstone, F. M. Whatley, Jackson Daffin, Rupee; J. L. Walker, Patrick; E. J. Billington, H. R. Puryear, Mount Calm; Peter S. Brunner, Eddy; J. F. McLeod, L. W. Duke, Reagan; John Holland, Carthage; John H. Harrison, Peyton.

Unordained: R. O. Dewberry, J. W. George, J. W. Harlan, A. M. Hope, J. W. Roberts, J. L. Stuckey, G. W. Walker, W. H. Baten, L. E. Howard, Holmes Nichols, J. A. Stephen, S. W. Smedley, I. H. Venable.

SESSION OF 1887 AT EAST WACO.

At this twenty-eighth session thirty-four churches were represented by ninety-five delegates.

The introductory sermon was preached by Elder J. R. M. Touchstone, from Luke 19: 13.

Not represented: New Hope, Reagan and Speegleville.

Three new churches were received, Eldorado, China Springs and Lone Oak.

China Springs was organized March 13, 1887, by J. L. Walker, with eight members. It meets in the town of China Springs, twelve miles northwest from Waco. This church has never failed to represent in the Association. Membership in 1896, 45.

Eldorado, a new church organized by Elder G. S. Harris, with twelve members, is in the southern part of Falls county, five miles east from Rosebud. She came into the Association with fourteen members, failed to represent in 1890, withdrew in 1891, with seventy members, to go into the organization of Falls County Association.

Lone Oak is near the line of Hill and McLennan counties, about six miles west of the town of West. This church was located in a fine section of country and prospered for a few years. But during the years from 1893 to 1897 it only had occasional meetings. When Lone Oak represented last (1892) she had seventy-eight members.

Groesbeck was dismissed this year.

Churches and pastors: Beulah and Marlin, J. R. M. Touchstone; Blue Ridge and Center, J. F. McLeod; Bold Springs, S. B. McJunkin; Bosqueville and White Hall, J. L. Walker; Chilton, Durango, Live Oak and Little Deer Creek, A. A. Hensler; Cow Bayou, J. W. Roberts; Deer Creek, G. G. Gibson; Eldorado, G. S. Harris; East Waco and Lorena, J. S. Allen; Elm Grove, H. J. E. Williams; Geneva and Robinson, T. E. Muse; Lone Oak and Pretty Valley, T. P. Speakman; Mastersville, J. A. Lea; Mount Antioch and Social Circle, T. D. Suttle; Mount Calm and Willow Springs, C. P. Lumpkin; Prairie Hill, G. L. Jennings, Pleasant Grove, R. Moore; Waco, B. H. Carroll.

China Springs, Liberty, New Hope, Olive Branch, Reagan, Speegleville and White Rock without pastors.

Baptized, 201. Membership, 2693.

The old officers were re-elected.

Visitors received: Representing foreign missions, Elder and Mrs. Z. C. Taylor and W. R. Selvidge; Salado church, Miss Crawford; Sunday School missions, Jeff D. Ray; Ministers' Relief Board, S. E. Brooks; Texas Baptist and Herald, T. E. Muse; Perdinales Association, J. M. Marshall; Rehoboth Association, W. E. Riddle; Enon Association, W. T. Garrett; State Mission Board, J. S. Daugherty.

The following were appointed messengers to the Baptist General Convention: R. C. Burleson, B. J. Kendrick, J. E. Parker, S. L. Morris, B. H. Carroll, A. H. Rhodes, Jeff D. Ray, W. R. Selvidge, Kit Williams, T. E. Muse, J. L. Walker, J. B. Cranfill, M. T. Martin, J. R. M. Touchstone.

Board meetings were held during the past year with Mount Antioch church in October, with Mastersville church in January, with Center church in April, and with Pretty Valley church in June.

Missionaries: In Waco Association and Salado Association, J. L. Walker; in Waco, V. G. Cunningham.

J. L. Walker was directed to give two-thirds of his time to Waco Association and one-third to Salado. It was while missionary that he sustained the heavy stroke of providence that took away his companion, Mrs. P. Evie Walker. Mrs. Walker departed this life March 2, 1887, in the full triumphs of a living faith in Christ. Her husband remained at home with his three little children ten days, then arranged with his sister, Mrs. Elizabeth Jane W. Franklin, to care for the motherless little ones, and continued his work as missionary. His first work after the decease of his wife was to organize China Springs church, March 13.

Summary of J. L. Walker's work:

"His labors commenced October 11, 1886, and ended September 19, 1887, being eleven months and eight days, for which we engaged to pay him at the rate of $400 per annum. During this time he traveled 3,500 miles; organized one church and thirteen Sunday schools; baptized 25 converts; made 614 religious visits; held 24 prayer meetings; preached 253 sermons and delivered 40 Sunday school addresses. He sold 421 Bibles and Testaments, donated 278; sold 354 other religious books and donated 65; and distributed 5,967 pages of tracts." Copied from the report of the Mission and Sunday School Board.

Summary of V. G. Cunningham's work: "He was employed as city missionary in Waco. His work has been very faithful and profitable. During the year he has collected and disbursed for mission chapels, lots, etc., $943.65. His time has been devoted unceasingly to preaching, colportage and Sunday school work. His labors have been signally blessed."

Collected during the year for home (state) and Sunday school missions, $2,917.72; for foreign missions, $457.30; for Buckner Orphans' Home, $282.55; total, $3,657.57.

The year 1887 was one of the driest in the history of Central Texas. Crops were almost a failure. The large amount for missions was raised at a heavy sacrifice on the part of some brethren. F. L. Carroll, Waco; W. R. Kellum, Waco; Parker Kellum, S. F. Sparks and wife, B. H. Carroll and wife, and others contributed largely. And here it should be recorded that these brethren and others have done handsome things in the way of making large personal contributions to missions, many, many times.

From the report of the board: "The most noticeable feature of the exhibit is the extraordinary cash collection on Sunday at 11 a. m. during the session of the Association. It amounts to $326.85. It is believed that no such amount has been before collected by a district Association in Texas under similar conditions. It discloses the reserve power of the Waco Association. This collection saved the honor of the Association and enabled us to pay in full all outstanding obligations. The scene was very impressive. The Mission Board had announced the necessity of the hour. The Association had not failed for ten years. But the terrible and excessive drouths had dried up the resources of the people. The board meeting collections had been unusually small. The obligations assumed were larger than ever before. It seemed that the Waco Association would lose its prestige. The president of the board put down Waco church for $100. Many churches and generous individuals responded. But the most impressive part of the scene was the contribution from the East Waco church. The pastor, J. S. Allen, who is moderator of the Association, made a solemn appeal to his church, leading off with his own contribution. They promptly responded, one and all, male and female, until the amount reached $85; that ever faithful brother, W. R. Kellum, advancing the money for such of his church as had not the cash with them. When the general result was announced, there was a deep feeling of joy and relief."

Recommendations adopted for the new year:

"1. That we continue our co-operation in state mission work with the Baptist General Convention. And that we appropriate $500 to frontier missions and $250 for our own bounds on the co-operative plan.

"2. That we continue our co-operation with the State Sunday School Convention and appropriate therefor $150 outside of collections on children's day.

"3. That we again indorse and commend the city mission work inaugurated by Waco church, to which it agrees to pay $500.

"4. That we make special effort to secure some contributions to Foreign Missions and Orphans' Home from every church in the Association, and pledge ourselves anew to these great and deserving enterprises."

Extract from report on schools and education: "Baylor Female College matriculated last year 221 students. With the ample and suitable grounds which she has been blessed in securing, the three-story building which will afford accommodations for 200 students, and the consecrated Christian men and women who stand at the helm, we cannot but expect that success will be the portion of this home of learning for Texas girls.

"Baylor University at Waco has just begun a session which bids fair to be *the* session since the organization. Many things combine to make us proud, as an Association, that we have this grand school in our bounds. Her grounds and buildings are valued at $100,000."

The report was written by J. R. M. Touchstone. Very little of the endowment materialized. Baylor University ought to have $1,000,000 endowment.

Extract from report on literature and periodicals, written by V. G. Cunningham: "We suggest that our churches arrange to keep libraries of religious and denominational books, as our Sunday schools do, and that the pastors call public attention to the importance of reading them." Only one church acted on this suggestion. That was Olive Branch. That church distributed through her appointed agency 150 Testaments, 20 Bibles and 9,815 pages of tracts.

SESSION OF 1888 AT MARLIN.

Marlin was now a strong church of 138 members, and was keeping her pastor for full time at a salary of $800 per year. The session of 1888, the twenty-ninth annual session, was held with this church.

The introductory sermon was preached by Elder J. L. Walker, from Acts 17:11: "These were more noble than those of Thessalonica, in that they received the word with all readiness of mind, and searched the Scriptures daily, whether these things were so."

On rolls 39 churches; represented, 31; delegates present, 74; not represented, Beulah, Bosqueville, China Springs, Lone Oak, New Hope, Speegleville and White Rock.

Two new churches received, Caddo and Second Waco.

Churches and pastors: Blue Ridge and Pleasant Grove, J. F. McLeod; Bold Springs and Lone Oak, T. P. Speakman; China Springs, J. T. Boynton; Cow Bayou and Deer Creek, G. G. Gibson; Caddo, L. W. Duke; Durango, R. O. Dewberry; Eldorado, J. W. Roberts; Second Waco, S. B. McJunkin; Elm Grove, W. C. Manning; Geneva and Rock Creek, T. E. Muse; Little Deer Creek, J. Daffin; Lorena, Mastersville and White Hall, J. L. Walker; Marlin, J. R. M. Touchstone; Mount Antioch, Prairie Hill and Social Circle, T. D. Suttle; Olive Branch, W. S. Huff; Mount Calm and Willow Springs, C. P. Lumpkin; East Waco and Pretty Valley, W. W. Finley; Robinson, Kit Williams; Reagan, J. H. Roland; Waco, B. H. Carroll; Beulah, Bosqueville, Center, Chilton, Liberty, Live Oak, New Hope, Speegleville and White Rock, without pastors.

Caddo was an old church of the Association, withdrew by letter in 1871, A. E. Vandivere, pastor, with 129 members; went into Little River Association; continued sixteen years, and now came back with 157 members. This is our extreme southern church, and is in the northwest corner of Milam county, two miles west of the Brazos. Vice President of the Board, Deacon W. E. Bozeman, is a member of Caddo church.

Second Waco was organized by Elder V. G. Cunningham and the church is the fruit of his work as Waco city missionary. She came into the Association with 83 members, has never failed to represent; had September, 1886, 195 members.

Total baptized, 223; membership, 3,018.

Fine revivals were reported at Bold Springs, Cow Bayou, Deer Creek, Mount Calm, Mastersville, Marlin, First Waco and Second Waco. The greatest number baptized was 45 at Marlin, the second greatest number was 35 at Second Waco.

Officers elected: L. W. Duke, moderator; S. L. Morris, clerk; W. D. Gaines, treasurer.

Visitors: W. A. Mason, representing the Aged Ministers' Relief Board of Texas; B. F. Clayton, representing the State Sunday School and Colportage Convention; A. J. Holt, representing the mission work for Texas of the General Convention; T. E. Muse, representing the Texas Baptist and Herald.

The following was adopted:

"*Resolved*, That any member of this Association, upon presentation of minutes of this session, be recognized as our correspondent."

The following was adopted:

"That the regular Order of Business be suspended and amended so as to provide for an election of a messenger from this Association to the Southern Baptist Convention, and to come in as Article II. in Order of Business."

Elder B. H. Carroll was elected messenger to the Southern Baptist Convention and J. R. M. Touchstone, alternate. This was done in response to change in the constitution of that body, admitting Associational delegates.

It was ordered that the list of standing committees be so amended as to read as follows: "Foreign Missions, Schools and Education, Literature and Periodicals, Ministerial Education, Temperance, Buckner Orphans' Home, Sunday Schools and Colportage, Aged Ministers' Relief Board, Ordained and Licensed Ministers."

Report of the Board, condensed: "We commenced the year discouraged by four successive years of drouth, each passing over to its successor the accumulated burden of preceding years.

"We expected small things, attempted small things, and achieved small things. A summary of the practical results of this year as embodied in unexplained facts and figures, would indicate, upon comparison with the work of some preceding years, the most unsatisfactory year's work in the last decade. Last year three churches pledged nothing; this year seven. Last year only one church paid nothing; this year six. Last year ten churches were up to their estimate and thirteen above it; this year twelve are up to it and four above it. Last year ten churches paid to Orphans' Home and fifteen to foreign missions; this year seven paid to Orphans' Home and six to foreign missions.

"The condition of our Sunday Schools is far from being satisfactory. Upon this point and with reference to colportage there is much need of missionary work in our own bounds. To provide properly and adequately for this destitution is one of the greatest problems requiring solution by this Association. Bro. J. L. Walker, who last year labored in this department, was appointed to gather and tabulate statistics for this occasion. The following is his report to the Board:

"I have received reports from ten schools: Blue Ridge, Chilton, Lorena, Marlin, Reagan, Waco, West, White Hall and Willow Springs. From these reports it appears that, during the year, the attendance, contributions and literature taken are:

"Average attendance of ten schools: Teachers, 74; advanced pupils, 138; intermediate, 184; primary, 169. Total average attendance, teachers and pupils, 678. Total collections for all purposes, $468.32; copies of Baptist lesson helps taken, 771. Some of these schools have made no report of collections, others none of helps taken. Other churches have carried on schools for all or a part of the year, but we have no data from which to furnish statistics.

J. L. WALKER,
Secretary of S. S. Institute of Waco Association.

"Summary of V. G. Cunningham's work: This brother has given his entire time to the work assigned him with a fidelity and consecration never surpassed in the history of missionary labors. Without at all weakening existing churches he has organized one church which now numbers 83 members, is self-sustaining, has a house of worship, a good Sunday school and a pastor for his full time. Besides much for charity, he has collected and disbursed $450 for mission chapel and new lots. In several parts of the city he has in operation various mission Sunday schools and prayer meetings. He has preached 110 sermons, made 650 family visits, distributed 6,000 pages of tracts and kept up regular services at the county jail and poor-house."

Board meetings were held at Lorena, Reagan, Mart and Chilton. The receipts from these meetings and at the Association amounted to $175.42.

Summary of contributions: Home (state) and Sunday School Missions, $1,907.64; Foreign Missions, $236.58; Buckner Orphans' Home, $157.90. Total, $2,302.12.

Recommendations of the Board for the coming year (adopted by the Association):

"1. That we enlarge our work by increasing the amount to State Missions and Foreign Missions, and by making arrangements to supply Sunday School and colportage destitution in our bounds.

"2. That we continue our co-operation in State Missions with the Baptist General Convention, and appropriate $600, to be paid quarterly to Rev. A. J. Holt, superintendent of State Missions, or to his successor in office.

"3. That we continue our co-operation with the Southern Baptist Convention in both Home and Foreign Missions. That we endorse the plan submitted by Rev. A. T. Hawthorn, calling upon each Association to select one foreign missionary and make provisions for his support. That to this end, we select our beloved brother, W. B. Bagby, of Rio Janeiro, Brazil, as our missionary, and that we appropriate $600 for his support, to be paid quarterly to Rev. A. T. Hawthorn, State Superintendent of Foreign Missions.

"4. That we continue our co-operation with the State Sunday School Convention and appropriate for that work, exclusive of Children's Day contributions, $150, to be paid to B. F. Clayton, superintendent.

"5. That we re-affirm our endorsement of the employment of a city missionary in Waco, at a salary of $600, to be paid by the First Baptist Church of that place."

It should be stated that these "recommendations," outlining the work for each new year were written by the President of the Board and first submitted to the Board for their endorsement, then with the report of the Board to the Association. Indeed the entire report of the Board is each year treated in same way.

This year attached to the report of the Board is the following paper:

RESIGNATION OF THE PRESIDENT OF THE BOARD.

"Brethren, for fourteen years I have served as President and Treasurer of this Board. It has been the most joyful and perhaps the most successful service of my life.

"During this long period, your paper has never gone to protest. No man living can claim that we owe him anything but good will. Some who entered with me on the work have fallen asleep. Some have moved away. The love of some has waxed cold, and alas! some have deserted. A few of the original guard are yet at their post of duty.

"Your long continued appreciation, far beyond my deserving, touches my heart. Your co-operation for years awakens my lasting gratitude. Allow me, in surrendering back into your hands the responsible trust conferred upon me to bespeak for my successor, whoever he may be, the same generous sympathy, the same lovely charity, the same appreciation and united co-operation manifested for so many long years to

"Yours respectfully,

B. H. CARROLL."

No man among the Baptists has ever made his impress, on not only his own Association, but on the entire denomination in the State of Texas, as has B. H. Carroll. He held the responsible position of President of the Board of his Association continually for 14 years. And he has held the far more responsible position as pastor of one church, the First Baptist church of Waco, for more than a quarter of a century. The Waco church, under his leadership, has grown to be the leading church of the entire Southwest. His church contributes more than one-tenth of all the mission money raised among the Baptists of Texas.

The above paper made the entire Association sad. The brethren well knew that no other such leader and organizer would be found for our Association in the nineteenth century.

During Bro. Carroll's administration, many individuals stood by the work with their personal contributions. Some individuals contributed hundreds of dollars.

Among those who stood nobly by the work with personal contributions were J. M. Anderson, Mrs. S. A. Owens, Annie

Battle, Belle Battle, O. L. Battle, F. L. Carroll, B. H. Carroll, Mrs. B. H. Carroll, L. W. Duke, R. L. Lawson, Mrs. Georgia McDonald, S. B. Humphrey, I. T. Martin, W. P. Martin, W. S. Huff, B. F. Tatum, Miss Celia Axtel, C. A. Pruett, Dr. O. I. Halbert, E. Dickey, R. H. Harrison, A. W. Sears, Mrs. A. E. Harlan, R. H. Hill, H. T. Vaughn, Jasper Howard, J. W. Gooch, J. N. Gallagher, Frank Wells, Homer Wells, W. H. Jenkins, N. Stallworth, A. A. Hensler, A. H. Rhodes, D. N. Crenshaw, B. J. Kendrick, J. L. Walker, C. P. Lumpkin, M. H. Standifer, J. T. S. Park, L. L. Foster, Misses S. T. and A. E. Earle, Thomas Parker, L. M. Strickland, J. H. Bagby, R. C. Burleson, George Murphy, W. D. Eastland, Mrs. L. B. Chilton, T. E. Muse, W. D. Gaines, E. A. McKinney, W. R. Kellum, E. G. P. Kellum, A. J. Shelton, L. H. Ewing, Mrs. A. Davis, Mrs. Lem Chambers, Dr. C. Sams, S. P. Ross, A. G. Breland, T. D. Suttle, A. R. Seago, O. H. Leland, J. A. Lea, A. D. Blackwell, W. C. Gates, H. R. Puryear, E. P. Kirkland, G. W. Holland, J. P. Holcomb, A. Webb, R. H. Fowler, E. R. Edwards, Misses Mary and Lizzie Keel, W. M. Skipper and many others. The total personal contributions during these 14 years is $3,293.06.

During this period (1874-1888) the total amounts received from the churches for all purposes were as follows:

Antioch, $35.60; Blue Ridge, $300.99; Beulah, $74; Bold Springs (now West), $124.15; Bremond, $113; Bosqueville, $411; Caddo, $33.75; Carolina, $63.75; Center, $76.86; China Springs, $14.45; Chilton, $76.51; Concord, $92.45; Cow Bayou, $176.55; Deer Creek, $66.98; Durango, $10.55; East Waco, $993.14; Eddy, $81.50; Elm Grove, $30.55; Geneva (formerly Union Grove), $77.02; Liberty, $145.04; Little Deer Creek, $29.70; Live Oak, $205.55; Lone Oak, $7.50; Lorena, $47.55; Golinda, $56.10; Greenwood, $45.60; Groesbeck, $213; Mexia, $85.25; Mt. Zion, $5; Mt. Calm, $126.30; Marlin, $500.60; Mastersville (Bruceville), $156; Olive Branch, $181.17; Pleasant Grove, $50.60; Prairie Hill, $17.10; Hope, $73.80; New Hope, $119; New Zion, $45.35; Mt. Antioch, $179.90; Pretty Valley, $77.97; Reagan, $238.60; Robinson, $538.79; Rock Creek, $281.60; Social Circle, $27.10; Salem, $30.75; Speegleville,

$22.70; White Hall, $370.55; Union, $56.45; White Rock, $201.88; Willow Springs (now Mart), $235.16; Waco, $10,610.54. Total from the churches, $21,375.78.

It will be observed that First Church, Waco, lacked $154.70 of contributing as much as all the other churches together.

The various public collections during these years at board meetings amounted to $2,235.72; at associational meetings, $1,270.18. Total, $3,505.80.

During the period the amounts collected in the entire Association are $28,174.64. This does not include contributions for minutes or expenses of churches in their work at home.

There were collected from various places outside of the Assosiation's territory during the same period $782.25, making a grand total of $28,956.89.

Nearly all the Board meetings were held with churches out of Waco. However, one session of the Association was held with the Waco church in 1885 and one with East Waco church in 1887. Board meetings were held with the Waco Church in October, 1882; October, 1884, and December, 1887. With the East Waco Church in February, 1881; December, 1884; August, 1885, and January, 1888.

But the greatest service rendered during this period was not that of collecting, but it was organizing the Association for permanent and efficient work. And had it not been for the Martinite heresy that two years later caused dissension and alienation, and laid the foundation for immediate and hurtful disintegration, there can be no doubt that Waco Association would have grown to be the banner Association in the South by the year 1900.

The new board organized by electing J. R. M. Touchstone president; B. J. Kendrick, vice president, District No. 1; W. D. Gaines, vice-president, District No. 2; John Flower, vice-president, District No. 3; M. H. Curry, vice-president, District No. 4.

Extract from report on Temperance, written by B. H. Carroll: "In the language of the report adopted by the late Baptist General Convention of Texas, the attitude of Baptists towards this traffic should be one of eternal, truceless war."

Extract from report on Literature and Periodicals, written by J. L. Walker: "Two stupendous truths stare us in the face. (1) The people are starving to death for spiritual literature. (2) They are being poisoned to death by an iniquitous stuff in its stead."

Extract from report on Ministers' Relief Board, by J. B. Scarborough: "There was organized in 1885 and chartered by the state the Ministers' Relief Board. * * * We rejoice to know that this department of Christian beneficence is being pushed under the management of H. M. Burrows, corresponding secretary, and W. A. Mason, state agent."

Suitable and touching notice of the decease of the beloved Elder J. S. Allen was adopted in the form of a report on Obituaries, written by J. L. Walker.

On Sunday at 9:30 after a speech by A. J. Holt, a collection was taken for Orphans' Home, amounting to $17.

At 11 a. m. mission sermon, by B. H. Carroll. Text, John 12:35 (latter clause) with 2 Cor. 4: 3. Collection, $56.

2 p. m. Sermon by G. W. Clark of McGregor. Text, 1 John 4:16.

4 p. m. Sunday school service. Speeches by Brethren J. C. F. Kyger, B. F. Clayton, J. L. Walker, B. H. Carroll, A. J. Holt.

8 p. m. Sermon by A. J. Holt. Text, 1 John, 3:2. Collection $13.40.

Ordained ministers: Reddin Andrews, R. C. Burleson, T. E. Muse, M. T. Martin, J. T. Boynton, B. H. Carroll, V. G. Cunningham, P. W. Eldridge, G. S. Harris, S. L. Morris, S. B. McJunkin, Kit Williams, Waco; Peter S. Brunner, Eddy; R. O. Dewberry, Wilderville; J. T. Everett, E. Taylor, Robinson; C. C. Hardwick, T. D. Suttle, Mart; A. A. Hensler, Mooreville; J. F. McLeod, Reagan; J. W. Roberts, Chilton; J. L. Walker, Lorena; E. J. Billington, Mt. Calm; D. Jackson, Rupee; G. S. Harris, Lang; A. J. Shelton, Bruceville; Holmes Nichols, T. P. Speakman, West.

Licensed: J. A. Lee, Durango; J. L. Stuckey, Viesca; S. W. Smedley, Waco.

SESSION OF 1889 AT WEST.

The thirtieth annual session of the Association was held with the Bold Springs Church in the town of West, twenty miles north from Waco, on the Missouri, Kansas and Texas railroad. This town is in one of the best sections in Central Texas. It is a growing town of schools and churches and commercial enterprise; has about 2000 inhabitants. The town was named for Mr. Thomas West, an old and honored citizen, the first settler on the site. T. P. Speakman was the pastor of the Baptist church which numbered in 1888 178, in 1896 numbered 292.

On the rolls thirty-seven churches. One new church, Cottonwood, received.

Three of the old churches, Mount Calm, Mount Antioch and Prairie Hill, did not represent at this meeting, or at any succeeding meeting, and they appear no more on rolls.

These churches went into Hubbard City Association.

The new church, Cottonwood, was in the western part of Limestone county, five miles northwest of Mart. It had only a few members, and does not now exist. This church reported a membership of 27; next year, 37; in 1891, 35. The pastor, Elder J. J. Harris, died September 10, 1891, and the church soon afterward ceased to exist. The membership was absorbed by neighboring churches, principally by Mart.

Churches and pastors: Blue Ridge, Center, Chilton and Pleasant Grove, J. F. McLeod; Bold Springs and Geneva, T. P. Speakman; Bosqueville, S. L. Morris; China Springs, P. W. Eldridge; Cow Bayou and Deer Creek, G. G. Gibson; Concord, L. T. Richie; Cottonwood, J. J. Harris; Eldorado, J. W. Roberts; East Waco, John Bateman; Durango and Little Deer Creek, R. O. Dewberry; Liberty, J. A. Sowders; Lone Oak and White Rock, Holmes Nichols; Lorena, Mastersville and White Hall, J. L. Walker; Marlin, J. R. M. Touchstone; Olive Branch, W. S. Huff; Pretty Valley, W. W. Finley; Rock Creek, T. E. Muse; Reagan, J. H. Roland; Social Circle, T. D. Suttle; Speegleville, T. A. Mangum; First Waco, B. H. Carroll; Second Waco, S. B. McJunkin; Caddo, Elm Grove; Beulah, Live Oak, Robinson and Willow Springs, without pastors.

Beulah, Caddo, Live Oak, Eddy, Pleasant Grove and Olive Branch failed to represent. Thirty-two churches represented with eighty-seven delegates.

Bold Springs, Blue Ridge, Center, Chilton, Cow Bayou, Deer Creek, Durango, Geneva, Lone Oak, Marlin, Pretty Valley, Reagan, Speegleville, Willow Springs, First Waco and Second Waco reported revivals. The largest number baptized was thirty at Chilton, the result of a meeting held by J. L. Walker. The whole number baptized was 239.

Officers elected: W. D. Gaines, moderator; J. L. Walker, clerk; B. J. Kendrick, treasurer.

The introductory sermon (denominational) was preached by Elder S. B. McJunkin, from Isaiah 28:20: "For the bed is shorter than that a man can stretch himself on it; and the covering narrower than that he can wrap himself in it."

Correspondence received: From German Association, F. J. Gleiss and H. C. Gleiss; from Hubbard City Association, W. T. Compere.

Visitors: A. M. Johnson, Alvarado church; Joseph Gronde, Antioch church; Dallas county; A. C. Burroughs, Waco church; H. P. Tyra, Geneva church; Dr. W. J. Morris, Kyle church, Gonzales county; S. A. Hayden, Texas Baptist and Herald, Dallas, Texas; J. R. Shumate, Austin, Second church.

B. H. Carroll was elected messenger to the Southern Baptist Convention.

The Mission and Sunday School Board reported:

"Of the four Board meetings, three can be put down as failures. The main reason for this is found in the fact that many of those who have helped to make the Board meeting a success in the past, did not attend the meetings this year. Another reason is found in the fact that many of our churches have been in mission drouths. Still we are thankful that the spirit of missions is with us in part at least.

Board meetings were held at Pleasant Grove in October, at Waco (First church), in December; at Blue Ridge in March and at East Waco in June. The collections at these meetings amounted to $152.07.

The total receipts for Sunday School Missions and Bible fund were $215.60, for Orphans' Home, $168.62; for State Missions, $718.05; for Foreign Missions, $697.75; for Ministers' Relief Board, $44.00; for Ministerial Education, $41.35.

Of the amount for Ministerial Education, $32 were paid to R. O. Dewberry, ministerial student of the Association. The other amounts were disbursed through the regular channels.

The total sum collected and disbursed was $1885.37." The above is condensed from the report of the Board.

"Recommendations (adopted):

"1. That we continue to co-operate with the General Convention and the Sunday School and Colportage Boards.

"2. That we continue our pledge of $600 to W. B. Bagby (Brazil).

"3. That we try to raise $300 for Associational work.

"4. That we pledge $150 for Sunday School Missions.

"5. That we pledge $600 for State Missions."

A special committee, consisting of J. L. Walker, John Bateman and W. S. Huff were appointed on "One Hundred Years of Religious Liberty," to report next year.

Extract from report on German work, by J. B. Cranfill:

"It is estimated that we have within the bounds of Waco Association as many as 5,000 Germans. Many of these people do not speak our language, and are therefore entirely cut off from gospel privileges. The importance of this work cannot be too strongly emphasized. * * * We therefore recommend that Brother Joseph Gronde be appointed as missionary of this Association to work especially among the Germans; that we appropriate $300 toward his salary, and ask the State Board to supplement it with enough additional to sustain him in the field; and that we instruct our delegate to the Southern Baptist Convention to place this especial work before that body, and endeavor to procure their co-operation and help in Texas." This report was turned over to Mission and Sunday School Board. That Board reported it back to the Association with amendments as follows:

"That Joseph Gronde be requested to give a part of his time to work among the Americans under the direction of the Board."

Messengers to General Convention: W. N. Griffith, Homer Wells, M. H. Standifer, W. D. Gaines, Holmes Nichols, W. S. Huff, S. L. Morris, J. R. M. Touchstone, J. L. Walker, R. O. Dewberry, G. W. Stubblefield.

The following was adopted:

"*Whereas*, There is want of information relative to our Articles of Faith,

"*Resolved*, That the Articles of Faith and Constitution of this Association be published in this minute."

It was accordingly done.

Saturday night—Foreign mission sermon, by S. A. Hayden, from Isaiah, 53. Collection for foreign missions, $97.75, cash and pledges.

Sunday, 9 a. m. Addresses to children by S. E. Whipkey, R. O. Dewberry, W. T. Compere.

At 11 o'clock B. H. Carroll preached at Baptist house from Luke, 24:46, 47. J. B. Cranfill preached at the Presbyterian house from Matt. 13: 38. Total collections, $31.05.

At 4 p. m. the Association met and requested B. H. Carroll to prepare his sermon (preached at 11 o'clock) for publication in the Texas Baptist and Herald.

Sunday night. A. M. Johnson preached. Collection for Buckner Orphans' Home, $33.28. Total collections during the sittings of the Association for all purposes (exclusive of $6.15 collected to increase minute fund), $599.43.

SESSION OF 1890 AT LORENA.

Lorena is in McLennan county, fifteen miles south from Waco, on the Missouri, Kansas and Texas railroad. The church numbered at that time seventy-two members, J. L. Walker, pastor.

For more than a year serious trouble had been brewing which culminated at this meeting of the Association in charges being preferred by the Waco church against the Marlin church.

As early as March, 1889, the elders and deacons of Waco church held with Elder M. T. Martin, a member of that church, what was called a "fraternal conference," seeking to reclaim him, the said M. T. Martin, from the doctrinal heresies into which he had fallen, and further seeking to avoid, if possible, a church trial. This "conference" did not avail, and M. T. Martin soon afterward "forced the issue upon the church by demanding a letter of dismission." "Such letter would have committed the church irrevocably and forever to doctrines and practices at wide variance with our commonly accepted standards of faith."

As the matter now stood the church met the issue. Accordingly on July 14, 1889, the deacons were instructed by the church in conference "to prepare and prefer such charges against our brother, Rev. M. T. Martin, concerning his departure from the Baptist faith and polity, as the facts in the case may warrant."

Following are the charges:

"Rev. M. T. Martin, member and ordained minister of this church, has at various places and times since his connection with this church and responsibility to it, taught doctrines contrary to our acknowledged standards of faith and polity, thereby causing division and trouble in our denomination. We further charge that after the pastor had privately and kindly called his attention to those matters and admonished him more than once to be more careful and circumspect in his publications and pulpit utterances; and when trouble and confusion, excited by his ministerial course and practices, had assumed such proportions that the elders and deacons of the church invited him to a private and fraternal conference concerning these matters, and when assembled in such conference, he being voluntarily present and participating, they did by long and painstaking labor, seek earnestly to find some safe ground of adjustment, and did kindly admonish him and implore him to benefit by the lessons of the past, yet since that time the trouble and confusion following his ministerial labors, and excited by them, have increased rather than diminished. And we regret further to charge that some of his statements in the fraternal conference, a partial result of which was published for his benefit in the form of answers to direct questions, and referring to what he had taught in various places, have not been confirmed but refuted rather by the testimony of many pastors with whom he labored and which testimony he invoked.

"And we further charge that, even in so short a time, in some places where his doctrines have been received and his spirit imbibed, the effect has been detrimental to prayer meetings, Sunday schools, mission work and other denominational activities." Signed by F. L. Carroll, S. B. Humphreys, W. H. Long, A. H. Sneed, J. T. Battle, J. C. McCrary, deacons.

These charges were particularized in six specifications, which, condensed, are as follows:

1. *Violation of Art. vii. of his Church* (New Hampshire Declaration). This article he violates in that he teaches two new births instead of one; a birth or generation by the spirit and a later birth or generation by the Word, thus contrary to all Baptist interpretation, contradistinguishing regeneration not from a fleshy birth, but from a previous generation of the Spirit, thereby making regeneration to consist, not as this article affirms, "in giving a holy disposition to the mind," but *in the belief of the truth*, and in making it the effect, not of the Holy Spirit, but of the truth believed.

2. *Violation of Art. x. on Sanctification.* (Art. xiii. of the Philadelphia confession). He opposes these articles, in that he makes sanctification precede conversion and faith, confounds it with regeneration, logically denies its progressive character, and that it fits one for heaven.

3. *On Faith and Assurance.* He makes a full comprehension of all that is revealed concerning the object of faith or the promises to it, essential to its saving exercise. He makes assurance or absence of doubt so essential to faith as that the latter cannot exist without the former. By this he adds a condition to salvation itself and to the ordinances, and to the office of the ministry unknown to the Scriptures and to our standards. (See Art. ix. of New Hamp. Dec. and Art. viii. of the Phila. Con.)

4. *Making Assurance a Prerequisite to Baptism.* By making assurance, or absence of doubt, an essential to saving faith and prerequisite to baptism, he has so brought great confusion in our denomination and so caused a repetition of baptism and ordination as is without a parallel in our denominational history.

5. *On Repentance.* His definition: "Repentance is knowing God and turning from dead works." "As might be expected from such a definition he minifies and depreciates this doctrine. He justifies the failure to preach repentance by the inappropriate illustration, "When a physician wants a patient to vomit he doesn't tell him to vomit, but gives him an emetic and it vomits itself." We submit that aside from the lack of analogy in this illustration, which shows a physical effect not dependent upon the will, it would equally justify a failure to preach faith or any other duty. Art. viii. of our confession: "We believe that repentance is a sacred duty and grace wrought in our souls by the regenerating Spirit of God, whereby, being deeply convinced of our guilt, danger and helplessness, we turn to God with unfeigned contrition, confession and supplication for mercy."

6. *On Prayer.* Brother Martin usually not only reduces his prayer services in protracted meetings to a minimum startling to Baptist ministers, and not only lays exceptionally little stress on its importance in his preaching, but his teachings are against the duty and privileges of sinners praying for forgiveness, and the privilege and duty of Christians praying that sinners may be forgiven.

No specification was voted down by the church. Specification 2, on Sanctification, was withdrawn on M. T. Martin's stating that "he did not mean to write about the Baptist doctrine of Sanctification of the Spirit."

Specification 5, on repentance, was not pressed because, as was stated, "enough had been proven and the church was worn out with five long conferences."

"Three of the specifications were sustained by a vote of more than two to one. And one, perhaps the most important, by unanimous vote; we refer to the one on prayer."

On specification 3. Resolved, that so much of specification 3 as relates to assurance be declared sustained.

During this trial Elder S. B. McJunkin, pastor of Second Waco church, and Elder John Bateman, pastor of East Waco church, on invitation, sat with the First church and concurred in the decision, in these words: "The trial was fair, the spirit good, and in our judgment the decision of the church was wise."

It should be stated that before voting on the general charge the church bestowed in fervent prayer for divine direction. "Many rose in tears; a deep and holy awe pervaded the assembly."

"Whereupon a motion prevailed, by more than three to one, that the general charge, so far as based upon the four specifications considered, be declared sustained."

M. T. Martin's credentials as a minister of the gospel were recalled.

A motion was made to grant him a letter as a layman. This was followed by a substitute that the fellowship of the church be withdrawn. This last motion, at the earnest solicitation of the pastor, B. H. Carroll, and the venerable R. C. Burleson, was withdrawn and the letter granted.

In the light of subsequent events, it is clear that the fellowship of the church ought to have been withdrawn from M. T. Martin.

In the goodness of their hearts, the sympathies of Bro. Carroll and others turned towards the man on trial, and they earnestly plead for the latter to be granted.

The quotations and condensations above submitted are taken from the "Official Report," published by the Waco church Sept. 7, 1889.

Concerning this "official report," an article signed R. A. (Reddin Andrews) in the Standard Expositor (M. T. Martin's magazine, Atlanta, Georgia) Nov., 1889, begins with these words: "Dr. B. H. Carroll's pamphlet is before me. He may be proud of it now, but he will not be proud of it a few years hence. His was a wordy and labored effort to sustain the action of 45 members out of more than 500 in the deposition of M. T. Martin." It is now "a few years hence," and Martinism is repudiated by the Baptist denomination.

Mr. Martin went to Georgia, joined the Baptist church at Woodstock in that state, and was soon afterwards licensed to preach by the Woodstock church. In a very short time he returned to Texas and joined the Marlin church, on invitation of Marlin members.

On November 28, 1889, a council composed of Elders J. H. Roland, moderator; P. Harris, G. W. Cappes, S. W. Smith, A. J.

Wharton, J. F. McLeod and Peter S. Bruner, met at Marlin (on invitation of that church) examined M. T. Martin and declared he, the said M. T. Martin, "should be restored to his former ministerial functions." They advised the church: "That in order to do this in the scriptural, speedy and amicable way, you should appoint a committee of judicious brethren from your body to bear the finding of this council, with your petition to the First Baptist church at Waco, praying said church to restore Bro. Martin's credentials, or waive her right in said restoration in favor of the Marlin church, of which he is a member."

J. L. Walker was present in Marlin and sat with the council during the most of their proceedings, but he did not concur in the findings of the council, and asked that record be so made.

The Marlin church sent her pastor and deacons to Waco with a respectful petition:

The Baptist Church at Marlin, Texas, to the First Baptist Church at Waco, Texas, greeting:

Dear Brethren:—In compliance with the advice of a council of ministers, whose findings accompany this petition, we send you our brethren, pastor and deacons of our church, to bear you our petition and represent us before your body, asking you if in your judgment you can conscientiously do so, to restore the credentials of Brother M. T. Martin, who has been recently deposed from the ministry by your church, and who is now a member of our church.

If in your judgment you cannot conscientiously comply with this request, we ask that you by act of your body inform us that you will not on your part regard us as violating the fraternal relations between us if we should invest him with credentials.

The council, whose advice we send you, have declared their convictions that Brother Martin should preach. As a church we declare our belief that he should preach.

We do not argue the case, but fraternally ask you to answer this, our request, referring you to our committee for reasons, information, etc. Fraternally,

MARLIN BAPTIST CHURCH,
In conference assembled Dec. 1, 1889,

WACO BAPTIST ASSOCIATION.

Marlin, Nov. 29, 1889.

We, the undersigned members of a council called by the Baptist church at Marlin, having convened with said church at 10 o'clock a. m., November the 28th, 1889, for purpose of advising the said church in reference to restoring Brother M. T. Martin to the full work of a gospel minister, from which he has been deposed, beg leave to offer the following as the findings of the council:

Having entered into a prayerful and critical investigation of the allegations affecting his moral character, we find that the evidence did not justify or sustain said allegations.

Brother Martin was then examined on his doctrinal views, on prayer, repentance, faith and assurance, regeneration and the office work of the Holy Spirit; and we find him in accordance with the Bible.

We do, therefore, solemnly declare that it is the sense and advice of this council that he should be restored to his former ministerial functions, and that in order to do this in the most scriptural, speedy and amicable way, you should appoint a committee of judicious brethren from your body to bear the findings of this council, with your petition, to the First Baptist church at Waco, praying said church to restore Brother Martin's credentials, or waive her right in said restoration in favor of the Marlin church, of which he is a member.

May the great head of the church bless, guide and sustain you, and the Waco church, and enable you all to do his blessed will, is the prayer of your council. Respectfully,

   J. H. ROWLAND, Moderator, Bremond,
   PINCKNEY HARRIS, Flatonia,
   G. W. CAPPES, Henrietta,
   S. W. SMITH, Gonzales,
   A. J. WHARTON, Comanche,
   I. R. DEAN, Waxahachie,
   J. F. McLEOD, Blue Ridge Church,
   P. S. BRUNER, Deer Creek Church.

(A true copy from the records of the council.)

        M. H. CURRY, Clerk.

This communication from Marlin church was referred to a committee consisting of R. C. Burleson, S. B. Humphreys, A. H. Sneed, J. T. Battle, W. H. Jenkins and B. H. Carroll.

Bro. Carroll stated that he wished to propound to the Marlin committee certain interrogatories. This he wished to do for needed information:

The Marlin pastor explained that as the questions were written and doubtless carefully prepared it might not be well to give off-hand answers. It was replied that a copy of the questions would be furnished them, that they might take all necessary time for rejoinder and would not be bound except by their final and revised answers.

We here insert the interrogatories and their final answers:

INTERROGATORIES PROPOUNDED TO THE COMMITTEE BEARING PETITION FROM MARLIN CHURCH CONCERNING M. T. MARTIN.

Brethren—We have respectfully and fraternally heard your petition with accompanying statements, and it has been referred to a committee for the preparation of a suitable response, afterwards to be submitted to this church for final approval and then to be forwarded to you.

But before that committee begins to consider your communication we desire to ask certain questions concerning the council itself, its methods and findings, the action of your church, and the import of your petition.

The answer to these interrogatories are necessary to our proper understanding of what you want us to do, and to our giving due weight to the advice upon which you base your petition.

If you decline to answer these questions we will be left to deliberate without a proper knowledge of essential facts, and to conjecture concerning your meaning upon points which you can best explain.

1. There appeared yesterday in the Waco Day what purports to be a correct report of the proceedings at Marlin, all of it over the signature of M. H. Curry, as clerk of the council. Is the publication, which we here submit for your inspection, a correct re-

port and authoritatively published? The question is asked, because what you have read before us as the council proceedings contains only the latter part of that publication, and because there are several statements in the first part of that publication of interest to us.

2. Do you consider the council of eight, by whose advice you are acting and whose several names are signed to these findings, to be an impartial, disinterested, nonpartisan and representative council of Texas Baptist ministers?

3. Did the Rev. J. L. Walker, whose name you publish as a member of this council, act and vote with the council as a regular member, concurring with its findings up to the time he left?

4. If so, please state specifically what topics of the number cited were considered and decided in his presence?

5. Your publication states that "W. D. Gaines of Chilton church and J. W. Lawless of Waco church were seated with the council. In what capacity were they so seated? Did they participate in the deliberations, vote on the motions, concur in the findings? If not why are their names published in such connection?

6. Was J. W. Lawless a witness as to matters before the council? and if so, do you think it proper for a witness to aid in the deliberations of a court?

7. In the examination of M. T. Martin was the case and its evidence as before Waco church reviewed by the council, or did they conduct a new and independent investigation, by interrogating him as to his present views on the doctrines in question?

8. Did M. T. Martin, before the council recant any of his published views or make confession of any wrong done by him? If so, please state specifically what published views he recanted, and what wrongs he confessed, that he may have the benefit with us of such recantation or confession.

9. Had any member of your council in answer to your interrogatories or of others committed themselves in writing or by other statement, before the council met, to the effect that M. T. Martin ought not to have been deposed from the ministry? If so, state which ones.

10. Did the moderator of your council, Rev. J. H. Rowland, announce substantially, and in the presence of council or church, or both, that Waco church had acted wrong, and that her action ought to be ignored, and did he say substantially that he would not aid in reordaining Bro. M. T. Martin because, reordination, unlike restoration, would concede or seem to concede, that Waco church had rightfully deposed him? Were such statements, or either of them or any of similar purport made before the investigation?

11. Did Marlin church invite M. T. Martin to unite with them?

12. In the invitation, by whomsoever sent, and by whatever authority, was there a promise of restoration, directly or inferentially given?

13. Will you grant a respectful request from this church for a true copy of the invitation sent to him to unite with Marlin church, and if you have no copy will you secure one for us from him? We ask this because it must be part of the evidence upon which he was exonerated on one of the moral counts.

14. Was such a paper submitted in evidence before your council?

15. The exculpation of M. T. Martin of any immorality on the two counts presented is simply announced as a result. Now, as we are asked to restore him, and as outside of doctrinal matters, these two points are difficulties in our way, we ask you to answer the following general and particular questions:

Were the facts alleged, and supported by what some of us supposed sufficient testimony disproved, or being conceded as established, were they adjudged as not amounting to an immorality?

To particularize: It was alleged and evidence accompanied the allegation, (1) That public use was made both orally and by printing in the Gospel Standard, of a part of a strictly private letter marked "private" in the caption, in large letters and doubly underscored, and also more than once so marked in the body of the letter.

(2.) That the matter of the letter came legitimately under the head of private affairs in that it asked a brother minister a question about the personal heart history of the writer.

(3.) That the part so made public stops in the middle of a sentence, thus depriving it of the modification in the concluding part and in its context.

(4.) That such use of his private letter did sorely grieve and wound the author.

Now my question is: Were these facts disproved or were they, though established, merely adjudged as outside the domain of morals and therefore proper things for a Baptist minister to do?

If the facts were disproved, will you kindly furnish us the disproof, that our own minds may be relieved?

As to the second allegation we repeat the same question and make the same request.

There are certain numbered statements on page 4 of the letter sent you accompanied by written certificates of several members of this church. Certificates concerning matters of fact to which they were witnesses. Upon them the question recurs: Were they disproved? If so, will you send us the disproof?

If not disproved, were they adjudged as not constituting an immorality?

16. In asking us to restore M. T. Martin's credentials, tell us what you mean; for instance:

(1.) Do you mean for Waco church to confer credentials upon a man not a member of Waco church?

(2.) Or do you mean for us to rescind our action deposing him from the ministry and thereby asknowledge that we were wrong?

(3.) Or do you mean that he desires, the council advises, and you petition that he be placed again at the bar of Waco church for a new trial?

Please tell us plainly just which one of these three things you mean.

17. If you mean either restoration or a rescinding of our action do you ask either one on our judgment of the case or yours or on the mere opinion of the council?

We say opinion because neither your publication nor your petition furnishes us one jot of the ground for that opinion.

18. And as we have nothing before us but the opinion of your council, and as in the case of most of them, at least, their opinions

were expressed beforehand and as well known as the men themselves, why should we be influenced more by the expression of their opinion jointly than we were by its expression separately?

19. Your council, after giving it as their sense and advice that he be restored to ministerial functions, proceeds to designate the way it should be done, and declares as the most scriptural, speedy and amicable way that you petition the church which deposed to also restore. We are gratified that they by their advice, and you by your acceptance of it, thus distinctly recognize that the scriptural plan is for the deposing church to be the restoring church. But while the council concedes that the right to restore vests in this church, and you also concede it by your presence and petition, you both also concur in the proposition that Waco church may waive her right in favor of another church, and they do accordingly advise and you petition, that if we will not restore, we waive the right in favor of the Marlin church. Now, after all this preface, our question is: If Waco church, for reasons satisfactory to herself, decline most respectfully to waive this conceded right, does she thereby forfeit it?

20. There appeared in the Waco Day the morning after the trial of M. T. Martin closed, an article, which, among other things, declared that Marlin church would restore M. T. Martin's credentials and that Waco church might make the best of it. Upon inquiry it was ascertained (testimony of the reporter) that this article was written from notes furnished by a member of Marlin church, then stopping at Pacific hotel, and that he telephoned the reporter to come to him there for the interview in question. That this article was also substantially wired to other leading secular papers and reproduced in the Baptist News of Dallas. That the Marlin church, through its pastor and others, was duly apprised of these matters and the suggestion made that the church ought to disavow or endorse said article as it was fairly getting the credit over the state of an avowed purpose to restore M. T. Martin. Now our question is: Has the church of Marlin ever taken any action whatever about this? And if so, what action?

21. Will you please explain why, when notices of your meet-

ing on the 27 ult., were sent out to others early in November, the one inviting this church to be present was not written till the 23d and did not reach us until the 25th, with only one day intervening before your meeting, so that it was impossible to get the church together in time to answer?

ANSWERS.

Marlin, Texas, Dec. 23, 1889.

To the Committee of First Baptist church, Waco, Texas:

Dear Brethren—Hereby is acknowledged the receipt of a number of questions addressed to the pastor of the Marlin Baptist church.

The communication is without date or signature.

But on examination of the communication it is found to be substantially the same as that which the pastor of Waco Baptist church produced and proceeded to read immediately after the petition from Marlin church had been read and referred to a committee, even before that committee had been appointed, and which he persisted in reading over the repeated protests of the visiting brethren from Marlin.

Since said communication is without date and signature, we are left to presume that it is also without authority. But since we are enabled to recognize it as the one that was read as above stated in the conference of the First Baptist church of Waco, Texas, December 8, 1889, and since we were willing to do all we can as best we can to assist your committee and church to a just and speedy decision concerning the petition of the Marlin church, we offer you our answers to your questions.

With this one additional statement: Since it is a fact that these questions were asked by the pastor of your church against the repeated objections of the committee from Marlin church, in your open conference, we think it nothing but simple justice to us for our answers to be read in your conference.

We there leave it for you as brethren to say whether you will give to us this justice.

In answering your questions we will simply number them and write our answers:

Ques. 1. The publication in the Waco Day is not authoritative. The name of M. H. Curry appears simply to attest the resolution that is given just above it in said publication. We refer you to the report as published in Texas Baptist and Herald as the authorized publication.

Ques. 2. As we understand and regard the council that met with us, they are well known to you. They need no defense.

For answers to questions 3 and 4, we respectfully refer you to J. L. Walker.

Ques. 5. Brethren Gaines and Lawless were invited to seats with the council, but not as members of the council. They were at liberty to ask questions and express opinions, but not to vote.

Ques. 6. We answer this in our answer to question 5.

Question. 7. The council conducted its own investigation, by examining Bro. Martin on his past and present views on the doctrines in question.

Ques. 8. Bro. Martin made no confessions or recantations whatever.

Ques. 9. You say in your question 18 that most of the council had committed themselves to you. Then why ask us about it?

Ques. 10. We do not remember hearing Bro. Rowland or any other member of the council make such statements as you are asking about. The speeches made were not spread upon the minutes. We have had too much to think about to remember them. We give you Bro. Rowland's answer: "That if Waco church did right, Martin should not be restored. If Waco, did wrong he should be restored, not re-ordained."

In answer to question 11, 12 and 13 we send you an exact copy of letter.

Ques. 14. The letter was read before the council.

In answer to question 15, we send you all the testimony that was before the council, except your own, which you have.

In answer to questions 17 and 18, we respectfully refer you to our petition.

Ques. 19. This question involves a complicated point in

ecclesiastical laws which is vitally connected with the doctrine of church sovereignty. Time and space forbid our answering it now.

Ques. 20. Marlin church does not understand it to be her duty to employ her time in looking up and correcting statements that appear in secular papers, for which she is in no wise responsible.

Ques. 21. The invitation sent the pastor and deacons were intended for them as representatives of the church. Later on lest we might be misunderstood, we sent an invitation on the 23d of November, 1889, to the church. Fraternally,

PASTOR AND DEACONS,
Of Marlin Baptist church.

These were not satisfactory to the Waco church, for several reasons, perhaps the most prominent among others, this: "The history of the case at Waco, all the evidence and its applications were published, making a pamphlet of sixty pages. But there has been no scrap of evidence, whatever, sent to us or published to the world to justify the findings of the Marlin council in regard to M. T. Martin's doctrine. There is not an atom of evidence to show how they reached any of these doctrinal conclusions. We are asked to restore M. T. Martin's credentials upon a naked *ipse dixit*. The council seems to consider that the mere announcement of their names and opinions ought to be sufficient for the Waco church."

In February, 1890, the Marlin church, against the protest of the Waco church and several other churches of the Waco Association, adopted the following preamble and resolution, thus investing M. T. Martin with authority to preach the gospel and administer the sacred ordinances thereof:

PREAMBLE AND RESOLUTION.

Whereas, Bro. M. T. Martin, now a member of this church, was deposed from the Christian ministry (without the advice of the council) on the charge of heresy by the First Baptist church of Waco, Texas; and

Whereas, The First Baptist church at Waco, after deposing Bro. M. T. Martin from the ministry, gave him a letter in full fellowship to join any other church of the same faith and order; and

Whereas, Upon the letter above mentioned Bro. Martin was received into full fellowship by the Baptist church at Woodstock, Ga., and by the same church was granted a license to preach the gospel; and

Whereas, Afterward at the solicitations of many of our members, he united with this church upon a letter from Woodstock church; and

Whereas, At the request of Bro. M. T. Martin, a council of ministers was called by the church to examine Bro. Martin with reference to moral character (against which charges had been made to the pastor of this church by the pastor of the First Baptist church of Waco), and also his views and teaching of Christian doctrine; and

Whereas, Said council, after careful investigation of the whole case, decided that the charges of immoral conduct were not sustained by the facts, and that Bro. Martin's views of Christian doctrine were scriptural and in harmony with those held by Baptists generally; and

Whereas, This church having unanimously endorsed the finding of the council, and having by the advice of said council petitioned the First Baptist church of Waco to restore Bro. Martin's credentials, or to waive their rights in favor of this church; and

Whereas, The First Baptist church of Waco has refused to grant our request; and

Whereas, We believe that Bro. Martin's views are not heritical; and

Whereas, We believe that Bro. Martin has in a pre-eminent degree both the natural and spiritual qualification for the work of the ministry, and that he is called of God to preach; therefore be it

Resolved, That Bro. M. T. Martin is hereby authorized to preach the gospel and to administer the Christian ordinances, and to perform all other duties belonging to a regularly ordained Baptist minister wherever the providence of God may open up to him a field of usefulness.

Adopted by a unanimous vote of the church.

J. R. M. Touchstone, H. G. HOUGHTON,
    Moderator.   C. C.

It is proper to state that the "allegations affecting Mr. Martin's moral character," mentioned in the finding of the Marlin council and again mentioned in Marlin's preamble and resolution, refer to what the Waco church considered a violation of good faith on the part of Martin. Martin had promised not to "make trouble," not to "join at Marlin," not to put his letter "in any church soon." His words, "*I do not intend*," etc., were understood by the Waco brethren to be equal to a promise. They also construed his conduct in reading a part of a letter, from Dr. H. H. Tucker, of Georgia (during his trial), and not reading it all, and conveying a different idea from that intended by the author, as morally wrong.

It is but just here to state that Elder J. R. M. Touchstone has long since publicly withdrawn all indorsement of the peculiar doctrinal views of Martin. Elder J. H. Roland, now gone to his reward, did the same. J. F. McLeod perhaps never indorsed his extreme views.

The Waco church served notice on the other churches of the Association, and on the Marlin church, that charges would be preferred against that church at the Lorena meeting, for violating the associational compact.

We have given this brief history of the Martin trouble in order that the reader might the better understand some things in connection with this.

MEETING IN 1890 AT LORENA.

The First Baptist church at Waco had asked all the churches to send up to the Association their wisest and best messengers.

On rolls 49 churches, among them New Hope, which had not represented in ten years, which did not then exist and which was dropped from the rolls next year.

Several new churches came in at this meeting: From McGregor Association, which had recently dissolved, Shiloh, McGregor, Eddy, Moody, Crawford; from German Baptist State Convention, Cottonwood German; new churches, recently organized, Rosebud, Lott, First German church, Waco, Goshen; (old church of Towash Association recently revived), Oak Grove.

Shiloh church was a member of Leon River Association and came from that Association to McGregor at its second session in November, 1886, with 34 members, came to us with 43.

Eddy left our Association in 1885 with 48 members, came back with 96.

McGregor came to us with 235 members, Moody with 225, Crawford with 35, and Cottonwood German with 36.

Rosebud was a new church, organized in March, 1890, by J. L. Walker and A. J. Shelton, came into the Association with 14 members. Worships in town of Rosebud, 38 miles south from Waco, in the southern part of Falls county. It is on the San Antonio and Aransas Pass Railroad.

Lott is in the town of Lott, on the same railroad, and near the center of Falls county. She was but recently organized (by A. J. Shelton) and came into the Association with 15 members.

Waco German had been but recently organized (by Joseph Gronde) and came into the Association with 11 members.

Lott and Rosebud were the fruits of Elder A. J. Shelton's labor, and Waco German the fruit of Elder Joseph Gronde's labor. These brethren were missionaries of Waco Association.

Oak Grove came to us with 52 members and Goshen with 31.

Churches and pastors: Blue Ridge and Center, J. F. McLeod; Bold Springs, E. A. Puthuff; Bosqueville, S. L. Morris; Caddo, Chilton, Lorena and Mastersville, J. L. Walker; China Springs, P. W. Eldridge; Cow Bayou and Deer Creek, G. G. Gibson; Cottonwood, J. J. Harris; Crawford and Shiloh, J. M. Wright; Cottonwood German, F. J. Gleiss; East Waco and Robinson, John Bateman; Eddy, T. E. Muse; Eldorado, J. W. Roberts; Geneva, Lone Oak and White Rock, Holmes Nichols; Goshen, W. O. Millican; Liberty, J. A. Sowders; Little Deer Creek and Pleasant Grove, R. O. Dewberry; Pretty Valley, W. W. Finley; Live Oak, W. B. White; Lott, A. J. Shelton (missionary); Marlin, J. R. M. Touchstone; McGregor, J. S. Daugherty; Moody, C. P. Lumpkin; Oak Grove, L. T. Ritchie; Olive Branch, M. L. Davis; Rock Creek and Willow Springs, B. F. Tatum; Rosebud, A. J. Shelton (missionary); Waco, B. H. Carroll; Second

WACO BAPTIST ASSOCIATION.

Waco, V. G. Cunningham, Waco German, Joseph Gronde (missionary.)

A year of revivals. Thirty-eight churches reported additions by baptism. The greatest number baptized at one place was 38 at Lorena. The second largest number was 27 at Cow Bayou.

The whole number baptized, 342. Total memberships, 4141.

Officers elected: W. D. Gaines, moderator; J. L. Walker, clerk, and M. H. Curry, treasurer.

The introductory sermon was preached by R. O. Dewberry, from Acts 18:27, "And when he was disposed to pass into Achaia, the brethren wrote, exhorting the disciples to receive him; who when he was come, helped them much which had believed through grace."

Correspondence was received as follows: Salado Association, St. Clair Lawrence; Hubbard City Association, C. P. Lumpkin.

Invited to seats as visitors: W. W. Finley, G. L. Jennings, S. Lewis, A. C. Burrows (representing the old ministers' Relief Board); A. J. Holt, financial secretary of Baylor University; J. T. Harris, Northwest Texas mission agent; G. W. Clark, agent Baylor Female College, Belton, Texas.

R. C. Burleson was elected messenger to the Southren Baptist Convention.

The letter from the First Baptist church, Waco, was accompanied with charges against Marlin church.

These charges were read to the Association and referred to a committee of nine persons (known in the history of this affair as "The Committee of Nine,") consisting of L. Magee, J. B. Cotton, Henry Smilie, F. J. Gleiss, J. S. Daugherty, A. P. Smyth, James H. Gilliam, George Harlan and T. E. Muse. The documents were placed in the hands of the Committee of Nine on September 26, first day of the session, with instructions to "report to-morrow at 10 o'clock." Following is their report:

10 a. m. The report of the Committee of Nine, being the special order of this hour, the following was read:

Your committee to whom was referred the charges of the Waco church against the Marlin church, respectfully submit the following report:

That the brethren of the Marlin church having waived any

pleading to the charges of the Waco church, we recommend that the Waco church, through their selected representative, be allowed one hour to present their case before the Association, and the Marlin church be given one hour and a half to reply, and the Waco church then be given thirty minutes in final rejoinder; after which, the Association, proceed without discussion, to vote upon the question as to the merits of the charge.

Respectfully submitted,

    L. MAGEE,
    J. B. COTTON,
    HENRY SMILIE,
    F. J. GLEISS,
    J. S. DAUGHERTY,
    A. P. SMYTH,
    GEORGE HARLAN,
    T. E. MUSE.

(Note.—The committee to investigate the charges against Marlin proceeded in the absence of one of its members, James H. Gilliam, the parties interested consenting.—Clerk.)

An amendment was offered by J. R. M. Touchstone to strike out the recommendations and discharge the committee. The amendment was lost and the report adopted as read.

The representatives of Marlin church insisted that the charges against them should be preferred by the Association, and not by a church; and to save further dilatory proceedings the Association, by special resolution, made the charges her own for purposes of investigation.

CORRESPONDENCE AND CHARGES.

Waco, Texas, September 1, 1890.

To the Baptist Church at Marlin, Texas:

Dear Brethren—By order of the First Baptist church, Waco, Texas, the undersigned appointed and expressly instructed for that purpose, in our regular July Conference of this year, and in accordance with due and official notification, sent you and all other sister churches of the Association, November 25, 1889, do now transmit to you a true copy of charges and specifications to be preferred against you by our messengers, at the forthcoming session of the Waco Association, to be held at Lorena, Texas, in this month.

The facts, dates and circumstances upon which these charges are based, have been presented to you in previous documents.

For your better preparation in defense, we notify you that in material particulars the evidence will tend to substantiate the line of facts set forth in that part of our final reply to your church under the caption: "Marlin's Radical Mistakes." A copy of which is herewith enclosed. Fraternally,

PASTOR AND DECONS,
First Baptist Church, Waco.

Waco, Texas, September 1, 1890.

To the Waco Baptist Association Assembled at Lorena, McLennan Co., Texas:

Dear Brethren—While most painfully regretting the necessity, we feel constrained from an imperious sense of duty, to call your attention to what we regard as a manifest infraction of the principles of our associational compact.

Before taking this step we have, in the interest of peace, exhausted every other measure known to us.

Distrusting our own convictions, we have sought the counsel of sister churches in our Association, and quite a number of them have, by official action, labored with us to avert the necessity of this procedure.

We are not ignorant of the fact, so well known to all Baptists, and so clearly set forth in our Constitution, that Associations have neither jurisdiction nor power over the life or existence of its constituent churches. The charges hereinafter preferred, are not predicated upon the mistaken idea that associations can make or unmake churches, nor upon the erroneous hypothesis that it is essential for a church to belong to an association at all. On the contrary, we heartily endorse Section 1, Article IV of our Constitution, which unequivocally asserts the independence and sovereignty of Baptist churches.

Therefore the charges relate, and are designed to relate only to such matter as, by our Constitution, the Association may properly consider, and extend in possible consequence only to the limits of associational fellowship.

They are based upon that inalienable right inherent in all organizations and essential to organization, the right of the Association to prescribe and enforce the conditions of admission into the fellowship and continuance therein. A right asserted and exercised by Baptist Associations from time immemorial, and most expressly set forth in Article IV, Section 2, of our Constitution.

This Constitution was framed and adopted at the organization of our Association, thirty-one years ago. The church now charged with violation of its provisions, and the church which prefers the charge, were both in that organization and both were represented by messengers on the committee which drafted that wise instrument. Their committeeman is yet a living witness; ours has passed away. Associated with them on that committee was the venerable and now deceased Z. N. Morrell.

The church now charged with its violation, not only helped to draft it, but voluntarily subscribed to it herself, prescribed it to other churches seeking admission into our fellowship, helped to enforce it in the case of the Ebenezer church, uncomplainingly worked under its provisions for thirty years, and has never sought to amend it. It is presumed, therefore, they are not unwilling for their course in the matters charged to be now tested by it. If they have not violated its provisions, they will be abundantly able to show it.

In presenting the charges and specifications we have not been solicitous to follow the technicalities and forms prescribed in civil and criminal courts, but have put matters plainly and simply for the easy comprehension of a plain Baptist body, which knows the law and desires only to know the facts.

The facts which substantiate the charges, together with all the necessary dates and circumstances, have been presented in previous official documents sent to the church under charges, and we are now ready to submit them in order to you.

Charges and Specifications Against the Baptist Church at Marlin, Preferred by the First Baptist Church at Waco.

CHARGE.

In her several proceedings relative to M. T. Martin, a minister deposed by a sister church in the same association, the Baptist church at Marlin has repeatedly, willfully, and in spite of timely admonition and labors of sister churches, violated the principles of associational compact embodied in our Constitution, thereby disrupting the peace and harmony of the Association.

SPECIFICATIONS.

I. We charge a violation of the law involved in Art. I, Sec. 4, of the Constitution which declares that: "The objects of this Association shall be to establish and perpetuate a union, correspondence and fellowship between her respective churches," etc.

II. A violation of the law involved in Art. 5, Sec. 1, construed with Sec. 3, and construed with Art. IV, Sec. 2, which reads:

Art. V, Sec. 1. "Other churches may be admitted into this Association by letter and delegate, provided they be found to be orderly and orthodox; and upon such admission, the moderator shall extend to the delegates the righthand of fellowship."

Sec. 3. "This Association shall adopt and publish her articles of faith."

Art. IV, Sec. 2. "This Association claims the right to withdraw from, and disfellowship any church which shall depart from the principles of this compact, or become heterodox in faith, or disorderly in practice, and to this end may institute inquiry concerning fellowship and order."

III. A violation of the law involved in Art. IV, Sec. 3, which reads: "This Association, with respect to her authority over her churches, is merely an advisory council, and it shall be her duty to exercise her office as such, in all cases of disagreement or difficulty in or between any of her constituent churches."

IV. We charge, as unbecoming existing associational ties binding the churches, the disrespect shown by Marlin church in her treatment of the affectionate and respectful petition and admonition of several sister churches, urging a stay of her proceedings until counsel of the Association could be obtained.

V. We charge, that by the foregoing disregard of associational ties, and on the assumption that Waco church had done any wrong in the deposition of M. T. Martin, as is implied in the course of the accused church, then that church adopted a method of procedure calculated to defeat rather than promote the righting of such wrong by the proper party; on the other hand, it was proven to the satisfaction of Waco church it was the deposed minister who was guilty of wrong; then Marlin's course was calculated to encourage and confirm him in wrong rather than to promote repentance and confession.

In all these particulars Marlin has violated Gospel order, the sanctity of discipline, the comity acknowledged and observed by the Baptist churches, Christ's law of love and fellowship binding the churches, and has brought our form of church government into reproach in the presence of its enemies.

We therefore, respectfully and fraternally urge, that the Association now exercise its constitutional prerogative of "instituting inquiry concerning fellowship and order" in these matters, to the end that Marlin church may be vindicated if innocent, or led to repentance and confession if guilty; or if guilty, and failure of such repentance and confession, the Association may vindicate her own law by withdrawing from and disfellowshiping a delinquent and impenitent church.

B. H. Carroll, of the First Waco church, in accordance with the recommendations of the Committee of Nine, presented the matter against Marlin church before the Association, occupying one hour.

Adjourned till 2 p. m.

SECOND DAY—EVENING SESSION.

2 p. m. Devotional services by W. W. Finley, after which the Association re-assembled.

J. R. M. Touchstone's defense on behalf of Marlin church occupied one hour and fifteen minutes. He concluded by reading the following statement:

To the Waco Baptist Association, Convened at Lorena, Texas:

Dear Brethren—We have received a copy of the charges preferred against us, before your body, by the First Baptist church of Waco, concerning our several proceedings which culminated in the restoration of M. T. Martin to the ministry, who had been deposed by the Waco church.

After much reflection, we concede that these several proceedings of ours were calculated, under the circumstances to disturb the peace of the Association, and to be construed as a violation of our associational compact. We regret that our actions have been so construed.

We beg to assure you that it was not our intention to violate our associational compact, or in any way to inflict an injury upon a sister church. We voluntarily make this statement in the interest of peace.

We deplore the troubles and anxieties which have in any way resulted from our actions, and trust that this statement may be satisfactory to the Waco church and to your body, and that the old and pleasant relations may be restored.

Rejoinder by B. H. Carroll, thirty minutes.

The charges against Marlin were sustained by a vote of 77 to 7.

A point of order was raised by J. R. M. Touchstone, by which he insisted that a church could not be excluded except by a unanimous vote. The moderator ruled that a majority vote was sufficient. An appeal was taken and the chair sustained.

The following resolution was adopted by a vote of 77 to 14:

Resolved, That we withdraw fellowship from Marlin church.

The resignation of M. H. Curry, treasurer of the Association was accepted. H. T. Vaughn was chosen in his stead.

It was a sad time. Deacon M. H. Curry, of Marlin, wept long and sorely. Others wept.

The special committee appointed at last session of the Association on "One Hundred Years of Religious Liberty," reported a document (written by J. L. Walker) of which the following is a summary:

ONE HUNDRED YEARS OF RELIGIOUS LIBERTY.

1. Much is due to our Baptist fathers for the blessing of religious liberty in these United States.

2. At the beginning of this period, that is in 1790, there were in the United States 872 Baptist churches, with a membership of 64,975. The population in that year was 3,920,214. These figures show that we had one Baptist to every sixty of the population.

3. A grand revival began with soul freedom and continued for 22 years, during which time, the foundations were laid for our great mission and Sunday School work.

4. At the end of fifty years we had ten colleges and universities, besides four theological institutions. At that time (1840) we had increased to 7,787 churches and 572,122 members. Population of the country, 17,069,453. That is one Baptist to every twenty-nine of the population in 1840. Thirteen Baptist periodicals were circulating among the people before 1840.

5. We are still gaining on the population. We have now more than three millions of Baptists in the United States, about one to every twenty of the population. We have built a new college or theological institution every three years in the past 100 years, or one every two years the past seventy.

6. Our work in foreign fields had a feeble beginning seventy-seven years ago, and we then had one convert every six years. Now we are preaching in many countries and our converts average one every forty minutes. We have 140,506 members of Baptist churches in foreign fields, the result of the labors of American missionaries, nearly three times as many as we had in all the United States one hundred year ago.

On the first day of this session B. H. Carroll, J. R. M. Touchstone and J. S. Daugherty were appointed to report the action of the Southern Baptist Convention in regard to Sunday School literature. Their report sets forth approvingly the action of the Southern Baptist Convention at its recent session in Fort Worth, as substantially the following:

(a). The appointment of a Standing Publication Committee located at Louisville, Ky.

(b). This committee to be entrusted with our Sunday School interest, and required by annual report to bring the whole Sunday School work fully before the sessions of the Convention.

(c). This committee to be entrusted with the management of our Sunday School publication, known as Kind Word Series.

(d). That in its work it is to co-operate with State Sunday School and Colportage Boards.

(e). That the committee and its work be commended to the churches within our bounds for sympathy and prayers, and patronage, so far as may accord with their judgment.

The report, thus outlined, appears to your committee as having a very positive but not a proscriptive signification. It does positively establish and recommend a provision which places our whole Sunday School work and its literature under the management of a committee (practically a board) related to and responsible to the Southern Baptist Convention, just as the Richmond and Atlanta boards are so related and responsible. The trust with which this committee, or new board is charged, is as solemn, specific and obligatory as the Foreign Mission or Home Mission trust. Like them it must be executed in co-operation with State boards, and like them can not assume to compel patronage, but is to receive only such as may accord with the judgment of the churches.

While we find in this report no war-spirit, no antagonism to kindred agencies elsewhere, we do find that aggressive spirit essential to any Christian work, and that look and tendency toward future enlargement without which it ought not to exist.

We are now ready to answer the question: "What relation ought Waco Association to sustain to this policy of the Southern Baptist Convention?"

As this association is a direct constituent of that convention, sending to each annual session a delegate chosen by us according to the constitution of that body, and as we are and have been for years co-operating directly with that body in Home and Foreign Missions, it is the judgment and recommendation of your committee, that we, as an association, align ourselves also with the Sunday School policy of that Convention.

We also recommend that this Association respectfully urge our State Sunday School Board at Austin, to align itself by official action, with the Southern Baptist Convention on this point, and that they accept the appropriation tendered by the Atlanta Board, at the instance of the Louisville committee, and for which our Sunday School Convention applied at the late Tyler session.

In the way of practical application, we recommend to all the Sunday Schools of Waco Association:

1. The enlistment of their prayers, sympathy and patronage in behalf of the Kind Word Series, which intrinsically and richly merit them.

2. That all our churches and schools take up at least one collection annually for our Home Mission Board at Atlanta, just as we do for our Foreign Mission Board at Richmond.

3. That we notify the Louisville Committee, the Atlanta Board and the Austin Board of this, our action, and pledge them all our co-operation in their great work.

B. H. CARROLL, Chairman.

B. H. Carroll was appointed to prepare for publication, on the fly-leaf of this Minute, the necessary information with regard to the work of the Mission Board.

Board meetings were held during the past year at White Hall in November, at Caddo in December, at Durango in March, and at Geneva in June. At the first of these meetings the president, J. R. M. Touchstone, resigned and B. H. Carroll was chosen in his stead.

REPORT OF THE MISSION AND SUNDAY SCHOOL BOARD.

Submitted by B. H. Carroll, president.

It appears from last year's minutes that we began this year's work pledged as follows:

To State Missions	$600 00
To Sunday School Missions	150 00
To Associational Missions	300 00
To Foreign Missions	600 00
Total	$1,650 00

To meet the $750 for State and Sunday School Missions, we had pledges from the churches aggregating $516.50.

To meet the $300 for Associational Missions, we had pledged $65. For the rest no pledges.

Assuming that all pledges would be paid, the Board had imposed on it the onerous burden of raising outright $1,068.50 besides collecting the pledges.

Such an undertaking called for favorable conditions. But the conditions have not been favorable.

At the first board-meeting, the president, Rev. J. R. M. Touchstone, tendered his resignation, as he then expected, in a short time, to leave the Association for a Western field.

The new president had to adjust himself, abruptly, to a plan of work already matured for another's supervision.

Then, in the beginning of the year, the churches were disturbed and their minds diverted by the introduction of a trouble tending to mar the union, correspondence and fellowship of the body and to weakness and division in local church work. The peace and unity of more than one church have been seriously threatened thereby, while grave anxieties and perplexities have been excited among all the others. Such a state of affairs never before existed in our bounds.

Under the circumstances, it was more difficult than heretofore to secure harmony and power in mission work.

Moreover, the small-pox scare added no little to our embarrassments. One board meeting was practically broken up by a quarantine, and the meeting of the Association itself seriously threatened by an irrational panic.

The groundless fears on this account during the year, fed by giving credence and circulation to most monstrous lies, not only swept away all barriers of reason and common sense, but brought about great financial loss, commercial depression, disorganization of labor, and wrought a demoralization shameful to human nature, and most humiliating to a Christian people professing to believe in God and to be free from the bondage of the fear of death.

In addition to the duty of providing against obligations already incurred, the responsibility was forced upon the Board, at its second meeting, to increase the work and expense of Associational Missions by the employment of Rev. A. J. Shelton to supply destitution that seemed imperious in its call for help. It may be imagined, therefore, what a burden of toil and perplexity has been borne by the Board.

The pressure of the situation was relieved by increased volunteer contributions for the associational work, and by enlargement of the $5 Roll of Honor. Being still confronted with the inadequacy of salaries paid to brethren Gronde and Shelton, we allowed them to supplement salaries by special contributions on the field to a limited extent, and secured a small appropriation to each from the State Board on the co-operative plan. In this way their full time and undivided labor was utilized.

As worthy of special note, we call attention to our associational

GERMAN MISSIONS.

This theme called forth a stirring report last year, which culminated in the appointment of Rev. Joseph Gronde for his whole time, with instructions, however to give a part of his time to work among the Americans.

Our Association is to be congratulated on the wisdom of this work and the efficiency of the missionary. Bro. Gronde has brought to bear in this work a ripe experience, scholarship and pleasing address.

The few German Baptists of Waco were gathered together, and with the aid of Rev. R. C. Burleson and Rev. F. J. Gleiss, as a presbytery, were organized into a church, which presents a petitionary letter for membership to this body. No church in our bounds has displayed a more sacrificing mission spirit than this little church. They have, among themselves, raised for all purposes over $1,300. A valuable and eligible lot for chapel, with preacher's home has been secured.

He has not only visited and labored with the various German settlements in our bounds outside of Waco, but has preached sixty sermons to the Americans with good results. He asks additional help from our churches to enable him to build the much needed chapel for the Waco German church.

The following is a summary of his work: Months of labor, 11; stations supplied, 5; sermons and addresses, 193; received by letter and restoration, 9; churches organized, 1; prayer meetings and Sunday Schools organized, 1; Pages of tracts distributed, 5,000; religious visits, 540; church property secured, value $1,000; contributions on field to his work, $100; contributions on field for missions, $34; miles traveled, 1,400.

REV. A. J. SHELTON'S WORK.

This brother commenced his labors January 1, 1890. After surveying the field, his attention has been mainly given to the following places, viz: (1) Liberty Hill, between Mooresville and Deer Creek; (2) Blevins; (3) Gena and Willow Springs; (4) Rosebud and Lott, on the Aransas Pass Railroad, at both which places churches were organized; (5) Lone Elm; (6) Lang, half way between Lott and Rosebud; (7) Hope, twelve miles from Marlin, where a dead church was reorganized; (8) Pin Oak school house in the forks of Sandy and Big Creek; (9) Cedar Springs, near Viesca postoffice.

SUMMARY OF WORK.

Days labored, 259; stations supplied in whole or in part, 10; miles traveled, 2,435; sermons and addresses, 247; churches organized, 3; religious visits, 430; professed conversions, 67; baptized in connection with work, 48; received into mission churches, 52; pages of literature sold, 5,038; field collections for self, $101.50; for State Missions, $9.00.

SUNDAY SCHOOL MISSIONS.

We are in co-operation with State Sunday School Convention. That body recently had a harmonious and profitable session at Tyler. All past indebtedness was happily paid. The new board was located at Austin, Judge J. C. Townes, president. Bro. L. E. Peters, the superintendent, reported efficient work, in organizing, settling old scores and laying good foundations. His failing health, however, necessitated his resignation. (Bro. Friley, of Taylor, is his successor.)

In this connection we may state that Waco city missions, sustained by First Waco Church, has been a great success. Including missionary's salary, there has been collected and disbursed for all purposes in this work under the supervision of Rev. V. G. Cunningham, giving his whole time thereto, more than $2,500.

TOTALS FOR ALL PURPOSES.

State Missions	$1,142 01
S. S. Missions	149 43
Foreign Missions	601 48
German Mission Chapel	211 30
Home Missions, S. B. C.	47 00
City Missions (Waco)	2,570 00
Associational Missions	676 50
Orphans' Home	230 86
Aged Ministers	144 20
For Geronimo (Student)	16 00
Grand total	$5,787 78

These amounts fall far short of the facts, for S. S. Missions, Aged Ministers, Ministerial Education, and some other objects, because contributions have not been fully reported to the board. The amount for City Missions was collected and disbursed by First Church, Waco. The collection for Bro. Geronimo was paid to Bro. Puthuff to be disbursed by him in needed purchases for the beneficiary.

REMARKS ON FINANCIAL EXHIBIT.

The receipts from the churches for State Missions exceed the aggregate pledged by $45.20, without counting the $524.51 of voluntary contributions.

Seventeen churches paid the exact amount pledged; eleven churches exceeded the pledge; three fell below it; one paid nothing, and one pledged nothing but paid well.

The churches have not yet learned to report to the board funds sent to various objects, and hence complete statistics of work done are impossible. The minutes of district associations are the proper sources of correct statistics. It would be better if all funds to missions of every kind, to Orphans' Home, Ministerial Education, Aged Ministers' Relief, etc., were sent through the board. Then there would be fewer mistakes and more reliable statistics.

Twenty-five churches and one Sunday School have contributed to Foreign Missions.

The grand total of receipts for all purposes is perhaps the largest ever known in district associational work west of the Mississippi river.

RECOMMENDATIONS.

1. That we appropriate $600 to State Missions and continue co-operation with State Board.

2. That we pledge $400 to German Missions in the Association, re-employing Rev. Joseph Gronde at a salary of $600, two-thirds to be paid by us and one-third by State Board. Collections on the field divided pro-rata.

4. That we pledge $600 to Foreign Missions, in support of W. B. Bagby in Brazil.

5. That we pledge $200 to Sunday School work in connection with State S. S. Board at Austin, on condition that funds for this object contributed on our field be credited on this pledge. While for the collection of this fund we need no agent of the S. S. Board, yet he is invited cordially to visit us, hold institutes and to assist us in S. S. organization.

The report on Schools and Education was read. Pending the report, A. J. Holt secured for Baylor University, cash, $100; pledges, $200. The report on Schools and Education was adopted.

Sunday Schools in the Association at this time: Willow Springs, First Waco, Second Waco, McGregor, Reagan, Moody, Pleasant Grove, Eddy, East Waco, Goshen, Center, Chilton, Bold Springs, Caddo, (Baileyville), Durango, Marlin, Bosqueville, Rock Creek, Geneva, Lorena, White Hall, First German, Waco, Social Circle, Cottonwood German, Willow Springs, No. 2. Total, 25.

There may be others but they have not been reported. Of these 15 have reported the number of officers and teachers, and the number of pupils, and only 9 have made full reports.

From the meagre reports furnished we tabulate:

Number of Sunday Schools in Association, 25; officers and

teachers, 120; enrolled pupils, 794; baptized from school, 38; volumes in libraries, 185; contributions for all purposes, $570.86.

MEETING HOUSES.

At the close of this third decade there were in the Association meeting houses as follows:

1st Waco	$40,000	Bosqueville	$1,000
2d Waco	1,500	Rock Creek	1,000
East Waco	4,000	Oak Grove	500
Lorena	1,500	Geneva	1,500
Mastersville	1,000	Willow Springs	1,500
Eddy	1,500	Center	500
Moody	1,500	Liberty	500
McGregor	2,000	White Rock	1,500
White Hall	2,000	China Springs	300
Robinson	1,200	Waco (German)	1,000
Pretty Valley	1,000	Bold springs	1,500
Cottonwood, German	1,000	Olive Branch	600
Chilton	600	Social Circle	500
Deer Creek	600	Blue Ridge	800
Durango	600	Reagan	1,000
Beulah	500	Live Oak	800
Pleasant Grove	750	Speegleville	500
Caddo	500	Willow Springs, No. 2	300

Total value of church property in the Association.....$77,050

Total number of meetinghouses......36

BOARD MEETINGS.

B. H. Carroll was again elected president of the Board.

Meetings were appointed, districts arranged and vice presidents elected as follows:

1. With McGregor church, fifth Sunday in November.
2. With Waco Second church, fifth Sunday in March.
3. With Bold Springs, fifth Sunday in May.
4. With Deer Creek, fifth Sunday in July.

DISTRICTS AND VICE-PRESIDENTS.

District No. 1—H. H. Fort (McGregor) vice president, Oak

Grove, China Springs, Rock Creek, Bosqueville, Crawford, McGregor, Speegleville, Goshen, White Hall, Shiloh.

District No. 2—F. J. Gleiss (Lorena) vice president, Waco, Second Waco, Waco German, Moody, Lorena, Robinson, Pretty Valley, Cottonwood German.

District No. 3—W. D. Gaines (Chilton) vice president, Beulah, Chilton, Caddo, Cow Bayou, Deer Creek, Durango, Little Deer Creek, El Dorado, Live Oak, Pleasant Grove, Mastersville, Lott, Eddy, Rosebud.

District No. 4—H. T. Vaughn (Mart) vice president, Bold Springs, East Waco, Elm Grove, Geneva, Lone Oak, New Hope, Olive Branch, Social Circle, White Rock, Willow Springs, Concord, Cottonwood, Blue Ridge, Center, Liberty, Reagan.

RESUME.

On rolls in 1886, 35 churches.

On rolls at close of session at Lorena, 1890, 48 churches. The greatest number of churches at any one time in the history of the Association was 50 (next year).

Churches received in 1886, Durango and Prairie Hill; in 1887, Eldorado, China Springs and Lone Oak; in 1888, Caddo and Second Waco; in 1889, Cottonwood; in 1890, Shiloh, Moody.

McGregor, Crawford, Eddy (old church), came back); Cottonwood German, Lott, Waco German, Rosebud, Goshen, Oak Grove.

Churches dismissed: In 1887, Groesbeck; in 1889, Mount Calm, Mount Antioch and Prairie Hill; in 1890, New Hope (dissolved) and Marlin withdrawn from.

Baptized in five years, 1319; otherwise received, 1726. Total, 3035. Total dismissed, excluded and died 2985.

Membership in 1886, 3176.

Membership in 1891, 4141.

Total money for all purposes, $17,899.49.

CHAPTER VI.

SIX YEARS OF FOURTH DECADE.
1891–1896.

SESSION OF 1891 AT MOODY.

The thirty-second session was held at Moody. This is a growing little city in the heart of a grand country. It is on the Gulf, Colorado and Santa Fe railroad in the southwestern part of the county of McLennan, twenty miles from Waco. Moody has about 1,500 inhabitants. The Baptist church numbers nearly 300. They worship in a magnificent stone building worth about $12,000. Moody church had only been in the Association one year at the time of this meeting. The body met with a royal welcome.

On Friday at 10 o'clock a. m. the messengers from the churches assembled in the old Baptist meeting house. The new stone edifice has been erected since that time.

Devotional services were conducted by Elder J. B. Link, of Austin.

Moderator W. D. Gaines in the chair. Letters from the churches were read and statistics noted.

Two new churches were received, Harris Creek and Pleasant Grove (No. 2). These churches came to us with letters of dismission from McGregor Association (dissolved).

Harris Creek's place of meeting was at South Bosque, ten miles west of Waco, on the Cotton Belt railroad. This church first held membership in Leon River Association; joined the McGregor Association in 1886 (H. F. Clark, pastor). She came to us with twenty-two members (J. C. Johnson, pastor). She failed to represent next year; represented in 1893 with thirty-five members; never represented again and does not now exist. During the year 1895-6 South Bosque was supplied with preaching by Elder T. P. Walker, missionary of the Association. A number of people calling themselves "Free Thinkers" reside in the community. It is strictly missionary ground.

Pleasant Grove No. 2 was in the organization of McGregor Association in 1885, numbering at that time thirty-five members.

The church was organized by the late Elder J. F. Harris, of Eddy, Texas, who served the church till 1890. He died September 10, 1891.

This church owns a comfortable house near the North Cow Bayou Creek (on the south side), four miles from Lorena and seven from Moody. Elder G. W. North is the present pastor. She has never failed to represent in the Association. In 1895 the name was changed to Bethany. Present membership, 130.

In November, 1890, Reagan church formally withdrew from the Association, giving as a reason for such action, that she construed Art. VI, section 2, of the Constitution of the Association to grant that right to any church. The words of the Constitution referred to, read as follows: "This Association admits the right of any of her churches at any time to withdraw from her, and she claims the right to withdraw from and disfellowship any church which shall depart from the principles of this compact, or become heterodox in faith or disorderly in practice, and to this end she may institute inquiry concerning fellowship and order."

The Association decided by unanimous vote, (1) That the church was not correct in her construction, (2) that the language referred to should be construed to mean: "This Association admits the right of any of her churches to withdraw from her at any time when the Association is in session, the Association consenting to the same," etc.

Reagan church submitted cheerfully to the decision of the Association.

J. L. Walker was elected to represent the Association in the meeting of the Southern Baptist Convention at Atlanta, Ga., May, 1892.

The following letter was received from Marlin church:

"The Baptist church at Marlin, Texas, to the Waco Association, sends greeting:

"Dear Brethren—Last year at Lorena, charges were brought against Marlin Baptist church by the First Baptist church at Waco, for a violation of the Associational compact.

"We willingly concede that the Association sustained the

charges, and we cheerfully submit to the wisdom and decision of our brethren.

"We wish not to open the old question, argue the case, nor lay before you our complaints. But, on the contrary, we freely forgive all the wrong which we consider done to us; and we ask you to forgive all which you may consider we have done; that you bear with us for Christ's sake, and that you restore us to fellowship in your body.

"Trusting that the God of peace may be with you, and that brotherly love may abound, we are yours in Christ Jesus.

"Adopted by the church in regular conference, September 9, 1891. J. R. M. TOUCHSTONE, Moderator.
H. G. Houghton, Church Clerk."

Marlin church was restored to fellowship.

The right hand of fellowship was given by the moderator, to the delegates of Harris Creek, Pleasant Grove No. 2, and Marlin churches: Delegates seated and names enrolled.

The introductory sermon was preached by Elder J. M. Wright from 1 Cor. 3: 11, "For other foundations can no man lay than that is laid, which is Jesus Christ."

W. D. Gaines was elected moderator, J. L. Walker, clerk, and H. T. Vaughn, treasurer.

Churches and pastors: Blue Ridge, Center, Eldorado and Reagan, J. F. McLeod; Bold Springs, V. G. Cunningham; Bosqueville, S. L. Morris; Caddo, Chilton and Lott, J. L. Walker; China Springs, Shiloh and Crawford, J. M. Wright; Concord, T. C. Swafford; Cow Bayou and Deer Creek, G. G. Gibson; Cottonwood, J. J. Harris (died Sept. 10); Durango and Pleasant Grove, J. B. Reaves; Eddy, T. E. Muse; Elm Grove, and Mart (formerly Willow Springs), B. F. Tatum; Geneva and White Rock, Holmes Nichols; Goshen and Harris Creek, J. C. Johnson; Hillside (formerly Pretty Valley), W. W. Finley; Live Oak and Rosebud, W. B. White; Lorena, without pastor; Lone Oak, M. C. Bolton; Mastersville and Pleasant Grove No. 2, T. P. Walker; McGregor, without pastor; Moody, C. F. Maxwell; Oak Grove and White Hall. J. T. Gelispie; Olive Branch, R. C. A. Ashcraft; Robinson, C. P. Lumpkin; Rock Creek and Waco

German, Joseph Gronde; Speegleville, T. A. Mangum; East Waco and Second Waco, John Bateman; Social Circle, G. L. Jennings; First Waco, B. H. Carroll; Beulah and Marlin, J. R. M. Touchstone; Liberty, J. A. Sowders; Cottonwood German, F. J. Gleiss. Churches, 50; pastors, 29; present 121 messengers.

Rock Creek and Rosebud were not represented. Concord was represented by letter only.

During the preceding year the name of Willow Springs was changed to Mart and that of Pretty Valley was changed to Hillside.

During this session Marlin, Beulah, Eldorado, Liberty and Reagan, were dismissed by letter to form the Falls County Association.

Shortly after this meeting Cottonwood dissolved.

Lone Oak never represented again.

The largest number of messengers present at any session of the Association was at Lorena the preceding year, when the number reached 128.

At this meeting the following corresponding messengers were enrolled: Leon River Association, T. J. Tanner and N. A. Seal; Dallas County Association, J. T. S. Park.

Visitors were enrolled as follows: W. W. Finley, Navarro Association; D. H. Dobbs, Evergreen Association; Owen Miller and Jesse Welsh, Leon River Association; R. O. Dewberry, Blanco Association; A. M. Johnson, representing the Texas Baptist and Herald; J. M. Carroll, Lampasas, Texas, representing the Foreign Mission Board of the Southern Baptist Convention; R. R. White, Lockhart, Texas, representing the Home Mission Board of the Southern Baptist Convention; Miss Mina Everett, San Antonio, representing State Missionary Board of the Baptist General Convention of Texas, and both the Home and Foreign Mission Boards of the Southern Baptist Convention; J. B. Link, Austin Association, representing the Texas Historical and Biographical Magazine.

There were at this time Sunday Schools in the bounds of the Association, with superintendents as follows: Caddo, W. E. Bozeman; Blue Ridge, John Norman; Bold Springs, W. Harrison; Bosqueville, A. H. Rhodes; Center, F. A. Curry; Chilton, W. D. Gaines; Concord, L. Parish, Crawford, E. W. Thomas; Durango, J. M. Cooper; East Waco, J. W. Thompson; Geneva, Charles Ficklin; Lorena, H. A. Ingram; Mart, H. T. Vaughn; McGregor, H. L. King; Moody, W. F. Routh; Oak Grove, G. W. Brooks; Robinson, W. C. Crunk; White Hall, B. J. Kendrick; First Waco, W. H. Jenkins; Second Waco, J. C. Foulks; Waco German, E. Schneider; Marlin, M. H. Curry; Liberty (union school) J. S. Hays; Reagan, G. D. Robbins. The total number of officers and teachers was 164; scholars, 1884; contributions for all purposes, $726.99; conversions from schools, reported, 85. The largest school was at First Waco, 275 pupils; the second largest at Marlin, 150 pupils; the third at Moody, 128 pupils; the fourth at West (Bold Springs), 125 pupils.

Forty-six churches, all in the Association except Caddo, Harris Creek, White Rock and Liberty, reported accessions by baptisms. The whole number baptized was 594; the largest in one year in the history of the Association. The greatest number baptized by one church was 59 at the First Church, Waco, the second greatest number was 47 at Pleasant Grove No. 2.

The total membership in all the churches was 4749.

The Mission and Sunday School reported a successful year's work.

Board meetings "with varying success" were held at McGregor in November, at Second Waco in March, at Bold Springs in May and at Deer Creek in July.

GERMAN MISSIONS.

Bro. Joseph Gronde labored with gratifying success the whole year, supplying five stations, traveling 1000 miles, delivering 244 sermons and addresses (in German and English); aiding in the organization of one church and one Sunday school. He received into the Waco German church three by letter and six by baptism. This Mission church now numbers twenty members, whose liberality is exhibited in their payment of $100 for pastoral support, $42 for church and Sunday School expenses, $8 for ministerial education, $35.30 for various missions.

REV. A. J. SHELTON

labored for six months at the mission stations assigned him

and then being called to a western field resigned. He was succeeded by

REV. J. L. WALKER,

whose labors were confined to Lott Station. The following is a summary of his work: 81 sermons and addresses; received into Lott church 15 by baptism and 28 by letter and restoration; organized a prayer meeting and Sunday school, ordained two deacons; made 55 religious visits, distributed 8068 pages of religious literature and 60 Bibles and other books; collected for all purposes $196.30 on his field.

WACO CITY MISSIONS,

conducted under the auspices of the First church, by Rev. John G. Kendall, have prospered wonderfully. Bagby chapel has been built and furnished at a cost of $1,300. Many conversions have resulted from his labors. We note with pleasure that for next year the First church assumes all responsibility as to salary, raising it to $1,200.

To totals collected during the year for all purposes and from all sources were as follows: State and Associational Missions, $3,928.51; foreign missions, $954.02; home missions (Southern Baptist Convention), $181.82; Sunday school missionaries, $228.29; Orphans' Home, $443.53; aged ministers, $184.92. Grand total, $5,921.09.

The new Board organized in open session of the Association:

B. H. Carroll, Waco, president.

District No. 1.—Vice president, A. H. Rhodes, Bosqueville.

Churches—Oak Grove, China Springs, Rock Creek, Bosqueville, Crawford, McGregor, Speegleville, Goshen, White Hall, Shiloh, Harris Creek.

District No. 2.—Vice president, G. W. Stubblefield, Hillside.

Churches—Waco, Second Waco, Waco German, Moody, Lorena, Robinson, Hillside, Cottonwood German, Pleasant Grove No. 2.

District No. 3.—Vice president, W. D. Gaines, Chilton.

Churches—Chilton, Caddo, Cow Bayou, Deer Creek, Durango, Little Deer Creek, Live Oak, Pleasant Grove, Mastersville, Lott, Eddy, Rosebud, Center, Blue Ridge.

District No. 4.—Vice president, H. T. Vaughn, Mart.

Churches—Bold Springs, East Waco, Elm Grove, Geneva, Lone Oak, New Hope, Olive Branch, Social Circle, White Rock, Mart, Concord, Cottonwood.

There was an unhappy state of affairs in the church at Brandon in Hill county. It grew out of a business transaction, between two preachers. The church divided and one part was accepted by the Hill County Association as the true church; the other part made application for admission in the Waco Association. But the Association used her offices to restore peace and fellowship in that church. The party asking admittance were advised to withhold application or one year, and R. C. Burleson. B. J. Kendirck, Holmes Nichols and R. K. Vaughn were appointed to visit Brandon church and Hillsboro Association, with the purpose of restoring peace if possible. Their visit had the desired effect.

Appointed to represent the Association in the Baptist General Convention of Texas: L. Magee, J. C. West, C. F. Maxwell, Holmes Nichols, Homer Wells, J. L. Walker, G. G. Gibson, S. L. Morris, R. H. Hill, M. H. Curry, B. F. Tatum, J. Hansel Wood, W. H. Long, Sr., V. G. Cunningham, J. M. Wright, W. C. Edwards, J. C. F. Kyger, G. W. Stubblefield, A. M. Johnson, S. H. Abernathy, W. F. Routh, J. C. Isbell, E. F. Brock, P. J. Smith, G. W. Truett, T. E. Muse, J. F. McLeod, Henry Smilie, W. H. Jenkins.

The collections during the session were $23.47 for home missions, $110.10 for foreign missions, $50.46 for Orphans' Home and $115.05 for Baylor University; total $298.08.

Church property in the Association in 1891: Blue Ridge, $1,200; Bold Springs, $1,800; Bosqueville, $800; Caddo, $500; Chilton, $400; Concord, $100; Cow Bayou, $500, Deer Creek, $400; Durango, $600; East Waco, $4,000; Eddy, $1,500; Geneva, $1,000; Hillside, $1,000; Live Oak, $800; Lorena, $2,000; Lott, $1,000; Mart, $1,500; Mastersville, $1,500; McGregor, $2,00; Moody, $1,200; Oak Grove, $300; Olive Branch, $600; Pleasant Grove, $600; Robinson, $1,000; Rock Creek $1,000; Speegleville, $500; White Hall, $1,500; White Rock, $1,000; First Waco, $40,-

ooo; Second Waco $1,500; Beulah, $500; Liberty, $400; Marlin, $3,600; Reagan, $1,500. Total, $76,800.

September 10, 1891, was a sad day. On that day two ordained ministers of the Association, Elder J. J. Harris, of Mexia and Elder J. F. Harris, of Eddy, passed from their fields of labor to their reward. Not a shadow is on their memory. They lived and died pure, consecrated men of God.

SESSION OF 1892 AT DURANGO.

Durango is an ideal country village, in the western part of Falls county. The village is seven miles west of Lott. It is surrounded by rich, fertile lands and has a high type of citizenship. The Baptist people own an acre of land, and a commodious house of worship in the very heart of the town. The church at this time numbers 106, J. B. Reaves, pastor.

The thirty-third annual session was held with the church at Durango, beginning Friday and ending Saturday, September 23, 24, 1892. Moderator W. D. Gaines, in the chair.

Opening service was conducted by J. G. Kendall of Waco.

Thirty-five churches were present with letters and messengers; one, Rock Creek, was represented by letter, without messengers.

Blue Ridge, Crawford, Harris Creek, Lone Oak, Oak Grove and White Rock failed to represent.

Cottonwood had ceased to exist.

Nothwithstanding the fact that the Association, during her last sitting at Moody, had construed Article IV, Section 2, of her Constitution to mean: "This Association admits the right of any of her churches to withdraw from her at any time *when the Association is in session, the Association consenting to the same,*" etc., the Waco German church and the Cottonwood German church both joined the German Conference; it was done in the interval between the sessions of the Association. Of course, this was an infraction of the Associational compact; but it is probable that no wrong was intended by these German brethren. Another feature of the affair was displeasing to their brethren of the Association. It was this: The German churches had been nourished in their infancy by the Association, and now as soon as they are able to stand alone they join an organization fostered by the

Home Mission Society of New York. The German churches were dropped from the rolls. Our co-operation with them ceased September 1, 1892.

The name of Elm Grove appears changed to Kirk, and that of Social Circle to Battle.

A long and pointed report opposing "female delegates" was adopted by the Association at her meeting one year prior to this at Moody. Notwithstanding this action, Battle church sent a female delegate to this Durango meeting, and she was seated.

Churches and pastors: Blue Ridge, J. F. McLeod; Bold Springs, V. G. Cunningham; Bosqueville, S. L. Morris; Caddo, Chilton and Lott, J. L. Walker; China Springs and Shiloh, R. E. Smith; Concord, T. C. Swafford; Cow Bayou and Deer Creek, G. G. Gibson; Crawford, J. M. Wright; Durango, Pleasant Grove and White Hall, J. B. Reaves; East Waco and Second Waco, John Bateman; Eddy and Lorena, T. E. Muse; Geneva, Holmes Nichols; Goshen, T. A. Mangum; Kirk, Battle, Mart and White Rock, B. F. Tatum; Little Deer Creek, Reid Rector; Live Oak and Rosebud, W. B. White; Lone Oak, M. C. Bolton; Mastersville and Pleasant Grove No. 2, T. P. Walker; McGregor, J. H. Roberts; Moody, N. A. Seal; Olive Branch, R. C. A. Ashcraft; Hillside and Robinson, W. W. Finley; Rock Creek, Joseph Gronde; Speegleville, J. Kinchen; Waco, B. H. Carroll; Harris Creek and Oak Grove, without pastors.

The introductory sermon was preached by J. G. Kendall, from Matt. 4:8, "Again the devil taketh him up into an exceeding high mountain, and sheweth him all the kingdoms of the world and the glory of them."

The old officers were re-elected.

Thirty-six churches, all that were represented, reported additions by baptism. The largest number baptized at one place was 33 at Olive Branch; the second largest, 21 at Concord. Total baptisms reported, 361. Total membership, 3,410.

A special committee, consisting of B. H. Carroll, R. C. Burleson, and T. E. Muse, were appointed to recommend to the Association what course should be adopted with reference to the Centennial movement inaugurated by the Southern Baptist Convention at its recent session at Atlanta, Georgia. The committee reported favorably and recommended that the Association align itself with the movement, and that the Association endeavor to raise within its bounds $1,500.

Earnest endeavor to raise the $1,500 centennial fund failed. The amount raised was $1,355.95.

Corresponding messengers were received from the following associations: Meridian, J. W. Thomas; Hubbard City, W. T. Compere, representing the Texas Baptist and Herald; Hillsboro, J. M. Glass; Salado, St. Clair Lawrence and W. A. Clark; Falls County, J. R. M. Touchstone and J. F. McLeod.

Correspondence returned: Falls County Association, John Bateman, B. J. Kendrick, W. S. Huff, J. M. Freeman; Salado, T. E. Muse, Reid Rector; Little River, R. C. Burleson; Hubbard City, T. C. Swafford.

We would be glad to give the report of the Mission and Sunday School Board in full, as this is B. H. Carroll's last report; but space forbids.

We condense:

GERMAN MISSION.

Rev. Joseph Gronde had charge of the German Mission in Waco, aided by us, but after doing efficient work for three months he resigned to be succeeded by Bro. F. J. Gleiss, who in turn was succeeded by his son, Henry Gleiss. Our co-operation with this church closed Sept. 1. Our total appropriation to these three brethren was $120.80.

This church, which no longer applies for our help, is the product of our missionary labors.

SECOND CHURCH, WACO.

This church is the product of city missionary labor conducted by First Church at Waco.

Owing to the fact that a large per cent. of its members are factory operatives and others poor, our Board joined with the State Board in aiding them. Our appropriation was $100.

The pastor, Rev. John Bateman, reports most gratifying results.

He says they have been blessed with a gracious revival and a number of accessions by letter and baptism.

ROSEBUD.

The pastor, Rev. W. B. White, in order to leave their financial energies untaxed while building was preaching to them without compensation.

The Board appropriated $100 to Bro. White's salary.

LOTT STATION.

The situation here can be best expressed by a summary of Bro. J. L. Walker's report, which is as follows:

Days labored, 129; sermons and addresses, 137; baptized, 7; received by letter, 21; organized the prayer meeting and Sunday school; religious visits, 153; distributed 1,412 pages of religious literature and eight books.

Built a church house worth $1,500.

SUMMARY.

Total for State and Association missions	$2,574 40
Total for Home Board of S. B. C.	228 80
Total for Foreign missions	914 86
Total for S. S. missions	30 79
Total for Orphans' Home	354 49
Total for Aged ministers	155 10
Grand total for all purposes	$4,258 44

RECOMMENDATIONS.

1. That we appropriate $600 to State Missions.
2. That we appropriate $100 to the S. S. Convention, and that we heartily co-operate with Rev. W. C. Luther, and that we urge our Sunday schools to use the S. S. literature prepared by the S. S. Board of the B. S. C.
3. That we appropriate $150 to Lott mission, and request the State Board to continue co-operation with us at that point.
4. That we appropriate $75 to Second church at Waco.
5. That the application of Rosebud mission be referred to the Board with power to act.

RESIGNATION OF THE PRESIDENT.

After many years of arduous but pleasant service the President of the Board, on account of other and urgent responsibilities, tenders his resignation.

Most heartily does he thank the churches for their loving and trusting co-operation.

B. H. CARROLL,
President Board.

The President of the Mission Board tendered his resignation, which, on motion, was accepted with the thanks of the Association for the many years of hard labor he has given the work.

The organization of the new Associational Board was appointed to take place at 2 o'clock, in open session of the Association.

The New Associational Board was organized as follows:

OFFICERS OF THE BOARD.

President, J. L. Walker, Lott, Texas.
Secretary, T. C. Swofford, Waco, Texas.
Vice President, 1st District, B. J. Kendrick, Waco, Texas.
Vice President, 2nd District, J. M. Kendrick, Hillside, Texas.
Vice President, 3rd District, W. D. Gaines, Chilton, Texas.
Vice President, 4th District, H. T. Vaughn, Mart, Texas.

In this connection it is proper to give an exhibit of all funds received during Elder B. H. Carroll's incumbency as President of the Board. An exhibit of his first fourteen years has already been given. (See chapter on year 1888).

During the year from October 1, 1888, to October 1, 1889, J. R. M. Touchstone was president. Elder Touchstone continued one month in the new year, that is till November 2, 1889, when he resigned expecting to go to a western field. He did not go west, however.

His resignation was accepted by the Board assembled at White Hall, November 2, 1889.

Practically B. H. Carroll was President from October 1, 1889, to October 1, 1892. He lacked just one month of three years; and little, if anything, was done in this first month.

First, we reproduce in brief the amounts contributed to various objects during

PRESIDENT TOUCHSTONE'S INCUMBENCY.

The brethren who stood by President Touchstone with their personal contributions (additional to what they paid through their churches) were William McComb, $2.50; Henry Smilie, $2; M. H. Curry, $10; J. C. Lattimore, $5; E. M. Pace, $5; Miss Ermine Burk, $5; J. R. M. Touchstone, $15.50; A. C. McLeod, $5; J. F. McLeod, $9.50; Miss V. McLeod, $2; W. W. Mallett, $3.75; Ben Freeman, $2.50; J. Daffin, $5; M. F. Williams, $2; Carrie Whatley, $1; C. Daffin, $1; R. Grogan, $2; S. W. Chatham, $1; S. L. Perkins, $1. Total personal contributions, $81.75.

The amounts collected at all the Board meetings footed up $152.07.

Public collections at meetings of the Association at Marlin, $78.75.

Public collections at meetings of the Association at Marlin, Springs (not credited to churches), $535.44.

Following are the amounts paid by the churches for all purposes (exclusive of pastor's salary and home expenses) during President Touchstone's incumbency: Lorena, $22.60; First Waco, $500.15; Bold Springs (now West), $72.85; Marlin, $72.75; White Hall, $21.30; Bosqueville, $11.55; Caddo, $27.25; Durango, $13; Little Deer Creek, $6.10; Chilton, $27.36; Pleasant Grove, $7.50; Blue Ridge, $10; Center, $16.55; China Springs, $11.05; Concord, $1.30; Geneva, $12.35; Speegleville, $4.75; Eldorado, $5; East Waco, $32; Liberty, $10; Live Oak, $11.25; Mastersville, $10; Olive Branch, $4.65; Pretty Valley (now Hillside), $15.25; Rock Creek, $18; Reagan, $29.45; Social Circle (now Battle), $4.75; White Rock, $17.60; Willow Springs (now Mart), $31; Second Waco, $10. Total rom the churches, $1-037.36. Total rom all sources, $1,885.37.

PRESIDENT CARROLL'S INCUMBENCY.

B. H. Carroll's second administration embraced three years from November 2, 1889, to October 1, 1892.

The individuals contributing personally to the work during this period (in addition to contributions through their churches) were B. H. Carroll, Mrs. B. H. Carroll, G. W. Stubblefield, J. T. Battle, J. B. Scarborough, B. J. Kendrick, Henry Smiley, J. T. Everett, L. T. Ritchie, Homer Wells, Joseph Gronde, R. C. Burleson, L. P. Jennings, A. Goddard, J. E. Parker, S. L. Morris, G. W. Haynes, W. H. Bailey, Mrs. W. D. Gaines, A. J. Shelton, Mrs. Julia Askew, Mrs. McNeil (Baileyville), V. G. Cunningham, M. H. Curry, James Stewart, F. L. Carroll, W. H. Jenkins, D. M. Crenchaw.

The foregoing names were President Carroll's "Honor Roll" for the year 1889-90. Each of these paid $5.

For the year 1890-91 they were: H. J. Hudson, W. R. Kellum, C. Faulkner, N. J. Barton, C. A. Westbrook, J. S. Daugherty, C. H. Garrett, Homer Wells, Mrs. J. W. Davis, W. C. O'Bryan, Mrs. W. A. Dunklin, Mrs. Hallie Dunklin, Miss Kate Coleman, V. G. Cunnnigham, Samuel Johnson, F. L. Carroll, Henry Smilie, J. B. Scarborough, Joseph Gronde, J. C. West, J. T. Battle, B. H. Carroll, Mrs. B. H. Carroll, J. C. Lattimore, W. H. Smith, J. L. Walker, W. H. Jenkins, S. L. Morris, G. W. Stubblefield, B. J. Kendrick, E. C. Kellogg, H. T. Vaughn, J. A. McSpadden, W. D. Gaines, C. A. Mangum, J. N. Wright, Joe Flower, J. W. Patterson, W. L. Curry, W. E. Massey, J. C. Atwood, W. Harrison, A. D. Blackwell. These paid $5 each.

"Honor Roll" for 1891-2: B. H. Carroll, H. T. Vaughn, John Bateman, J. L. Walker, S. H. Carter, J. D. McPherson, W. D. Gaines, Henry Smilie, M. L. Davis, James E. Parker, J. T. Battle, W. H. Jenkins, H. W. Smith, A. Goddard, J. C. Lattimore, J. Hansell Wood, J. C. West, Joseph Gronde, Homer Wells, E. R. Nash, G. R. Trice, B. J. Kendrick, P. V. Thompson, J. B. Reaves. These paid $5 each.

The "Honor Roll" the first year numbered 28, the second year 44, the third year 24. There were other names on the "Honor Rolls," who paid less than $5.

All the "Honor Roll" money went to State and Association missions. Most of the "Honor Roll" members and many other liberal brethren contributed personally to other objects beside State and Association missions.

The personal contributions for all purposes the first year amounted to $741.26, the second year, $768.69; the third year, $699.89. Total, $2,209.84.

Some brethren contributed personally more than $100. R. H. Hill (of Hill's Business College) more than $200.

The public collections at Board meetings during these three years amounted to $527.55; at Associational meetings, $415.71. Total, $943.26.

During the same period the churches paid the following amounts: Beulah, $7; Blue Ridge, $65.17; Bold Springs, $283.55; Bosqueville, $65.10; China Springs, $25.90; Center, $51.80; Chilton, $101.85; Concord, $33.45; Cottonwood, $75.65; Caddo, $139.75; Cow Bayou, $51.05; Deer Creek, $83.65; Durango, $73.20; Eldorado, $10.50; East Waco, $383.65; Eddy, $84.25; Elm Grove, $48.45; Geneva, $38.10; Liberty, $20; Little Deer Creek, $22.05; Live Oak, $25.80; Lone Oak, $22; Lorena, $98.85; Marlin, $103.03; Mastersville, $57.97; Olive Branch, $47.90; Pretty Valley (Hillside), $30; Pleasant Grove, $25.35; Pleasant Grove No. 2 (Bethany), $7; Rock Creek, $78.55; Reagan, $49.55; Social Circle (Battle), $36.40; Speegleville, $35.65; Oak Grove, $30.15; White Hall, $113.80; Mart, $97.75; Second Waco, $89.55; First Waco, $4,164.61; Waco German, $134.50; White Rock, $23.25; Moody, $213.70; Goshen, $11.70; Robinson, $21; Rosebud, $3.20; Shiloh, $26.45; Crawford, $11.35; Lott, $36.60; McGregor, $50.20; Harris Creek, $5.

Total churches from October 1, 1889., to October 1, 1892, $7,219.11.

Not reckoned in the amounts here given are various other sums, collected by missionaries on the field, sums collected for mission chapels and contributions by parties living outside the Associational bounds, amounting to $5,596.10, which added make the grand total $15,968.31.

The funds raised by the Association for all purposes during the two terms of President Carroll's administration amount to $44,925.20.

This does not include contributions for minutes, pastor's salaries or home church expenses.

If any one is curious to know how much his church paid during both terms of Bro. Carroll's incumbency it will be easy to turn back to the amount given in the year 1888, and add to that given in this connection.

There were 26 Sunday Schools in this year (1892). Following are the names of the schools with superintendent's names: Blue Ridge, S. D. Durham; Bold Springs, V. G. Cunningham; Bosqueville, J. R. Conyers; Caddo, J. P. Greenlese; Center, F. A. Curry; Chilton, B. M. Lockard; Concord, J. N. Wolf; Cow Bayou, B. P. Roberts; Deer Creek, W. L. Bynum; East Waco, J. M. Thompson; Geneva, C. R. Battaile; Hillside, J. M. Kendrick; Kirk, J. O. Adams; Little Deer Creek, J. J. Jordan; Lorena, L. P. Jennings; Lott, R. E. Hamilton; Mastersville, D. C. Collins; Mart, H. T. Vaughn; McGregor, H. L. King; Moody, W. F. Routh; Olive Branch, J. C. Atwood; First Waco, W. H. Jenkins; Second Waco, J. C. Foulks; White Hall, B. J. Kendrick. Durango reported a school, but did not report the name of their superintendent. The schools at Kirk and Cow Bayou were union schools; the latter using Baptist literature, the former union.

The average attendance at First Waco was 750, at McGregor 150, at Second Waco 78, at Concord 75. The whole number of scholars enrolled was 2353, the general average attendance, 1859; the whole number of officers and teachers, 214. Contributions by all the schools for missions, $68.17; for Orphans' Home, $49.75; for school expenses, $571.24.

A large number of schools made no report of contributions.

In this work wherever estimates are made of contributions by churches the school contributions are included, except amounts for school expenses.

On the seventh day of May, 1892, a beloved, devoted young minister of the Association, Elder L. T. Richie, died at Waco after a lingering illness, "in great peace and bright prospects of heaven."

The following was adopted:

Resolved, That we appoint a standing committee on Obituaries.

The brethren appointed to represent the Association in the Baptist General Convention were Joseph Gronde, B. F. Tatum, C.

Faulkner, J. L. Walker, Jasper Howard, L. Bloxom, W. D. Gaines, J. R. Strange, C. C. Hawkins, J. H. Gilliam, B. J. Kendrick, Henry Johnson, Holmes Nichols, S. L. Morris, T. D. Johnson, W. W. Donaldson, John Bateman, S. T. Smith, L. B. Smyth and Park Carpenter.

SESSION OF 1893 AT GENEVA.

The pleasant country village, Elm Mott, is situated on the Missouri, Kansas and Texas Railroad, ten miles northeast from Waco.

The Geneva church meets at this place, Elder Holmes Nichols, pastor. Geneva church had at that time 84 members.

The thirty-fourth annual session of the Association was held with Geneva church Thursday, Friday and Saturday, September 21, 22 and 23, 1893.

Elder J. F. McLeod conducted devotional services.

Letters from the churches were read by Elders J. M. Carroll and J. C. F. Kyger.

Four new churches, Caledonia, Independence, Friendship and Flat Rock, were received at this session.

Caledonia meets in the northern part of McLennan county, three miles east of the Brazos river. She was first a member of Towash Association, afterwards of Hillsboro Association. She came to us with 84 members.

Independence is near West, in the northern part of McLennan county. This was a newly organized church, came into the Association with 43 members, and has now (February, 1897), 132.

Friendship meets five miles northwest from Lorena. She was but recently organized. When she united with the Association her membership numbered 21; in September, 1896, the number was 73.

Flat Rock worships on the Bosque river, five miles west from Bosqueville. She was newly organized and came into the Association with 27 members. In September, 1896, her membership was 64.

Churches and pastors: Blue Ridge, J. F. McLeod; Battle and Mart, B. F. Tatum; Bold Springs (West), I. Z. Kimbrough; Bosqueville, China Springs and Flat Rock, Joseph Gronde; Center,

Pleasant Grove and White Hall, J. B. Reaves; Caledonia and Oak Grove, S. R. Williams; Cow Bayou and Deer Creek, G. G. Gibson; Caddo and Mastersville, J. L. Walker; Chilton and Lott, J. E. McClerkin; Crawford, J. M. B. Gresham; Concord, Geneva and White Rock, Holmes Nichols; Eddy and Lorena, T. E. Muse; Friendship, Z. H. Reagan; Goshen and Harris Creek, T. A. Mangum; Hillside and Robinson, M. L. Davis; Independence, J. W. Thomas; Little Deer Creek, Reid Rector; Live Oak and Rosebud, W. B. White; Moody, N. A. Seale; Pleasant Grove No. 2, G. W. North; Rock Creek, V. G. Cunningham; Shiloh, R. E. Smith; Speegleville, J. P. Kinchen; First Waco, B. H. Carroll; Second Waco, John Bateman; East Waco, G. W. Truett; McGregor, J. H. Roberts; Kirk and Lone Oak without pastors. Durango (J. J. McBee, pastor), was not represented.

The Waco German church sent their pastor, F. A. Petereit, and E. Schneider as messengers to the Association asking financial assistance to the amount of $200, and asking further that the Association recommend to the State Board to make that church an additional grant of $200.

This petition was referred to the Associational Board and by the Board to a committee composed of B. J. Kendrick, J. T. Battle and T. E. Muse. The question was reported on and recommitted at two succeeding Board meetings, and was disposed of finally by adopting the following, April 28, 1894:

"*Resolved*, That the matter of assistance to the First German Baptist Church of Waco be referred to the Board of Directors of the General Convention with assurance of co-operation on our part in any measure of assistance they may adopt."

It is sufficient to state that the State Board (Board of Directors) never acted in the matter.

All the churches, save Friendship, Lott, White Rock and McGregor, reported additions by baptism.

The largest number baptized at one place was at Moody, where 90 souls followed Christ in immersion. Elder R. C. Pender of Denison, Texas, assisted the pastor, N. A. Seal, in the greatest revival in the history of that church.

The second largest number baptized at one place was 45 at

Rock Creek. This church also enjoyed the greatest revival in her history. The revival services were conducted by V. G. Cunningham and J. L. Walker.

While the Association was in session this year the First Waco church was in the midst of the greatest revival in her history. The preaching was all done by Pastor B. H. Carroll. The result was 108 additions by baptism, though not reported to the Association till next year.

The whole number baptized in the Association was 538. Total membership, 4,835.

Officers elected: B. J. Kendrick, moderator; Holmes Nichols, clerk; H. T. Vaughn, treasurer.

S. L. Morris was first chosen clerk. His eligibility was challenged, inasmuch as he was not a member of the Association.

The Association construed the constitution to mean that "no person is eligible to office who is not a member."

This act having passed, S. L. Morris resigned and J. L. Walker, the old clerk, resumed work in that capacity. The work already done by S. L. Morris as clerk was accepted and a vote of thanks tendered him by the Association. It was now the morning session of the second day. J. L. Walker refused re-election on the ground that he was president of the Board, and that duties in that capacity required much time and attention during the sessions. Elder Holmes Nichols was chosen clerk.

Correspondence seated: J. F. McLeod, Falls County Association; W. T. Compere, Hubbard City Association; E. W. Holeman, Austin Association.

Visitors seated: J. W. Staten, representing Baptist Observer and Sherman Institute; G. W. Given, Southern Baptist Theological Seminary; J. M. Carroll, General Convention Boards; A. J. Shelton, from Mastersville church.

Correspondence returned: Limestone County Association, J. H. Willingham; Leon River Association, T. A. Mangum.

J. L. Walker was elected messenger to the Southern Baptist Convention.

On motion of B. H. Carroll the following was adopted:

"*Resolved*, That a special committee of three be now appointed to prepare and present to this body for consideration at the special hour of 3 p. m., a report oh the gospel order of seeking to form or withdraw from associational relation."

B. H. Carroll, T. E. Muse and R. C. Burleson were appointed as provided for in the above resolution.

At the hour named that same afternoon (September 22) the committee presented the following report, which was adopted:

"REPORT OF COMMITTEE ON CHURCH ORDER IN SEEKING TO FORM AND WITHDRAW FROM ASSOCIATIONAL RELATIONS.

"The importance of this work is measured largely by the objects of such associations, the conditions of the membership therein and the reciprocal obligations incurred thereby.

"The nature and limitations of church sovereignty and the Christ required 'love of the brotherhood' at large also enter into the question.

"The common doctrinal basis of association and fellowship also modify the question.

"The objects of the Association are set forth in Article I, section 4; church sovereignty in Art. IV, Sec. 1; Associational powers in Art. IV, Sec. 2; limits those powers in Art. IV, Sec. 3; the conditions of membership in Art. V, Sec. 1; doctrinal basis in Art. V, Sec. 3; relation to the brotherhood in Art. V, Sec. 4.

"To enter, remain in or be regularly dismissed from this body, the church in its sovereignty by orderly methods must voluntarily petition for admission or dismission, must be orthodox in the faith according to the doctrinal basis, orderly in government and business and co-operative work. And now,

"*Whereas*, There seems to be a misconception with some as to what is church order in relation to associational fellowship, therefore to set such matters at rest, so far as our advisory judgment can go, and to put on record as information what is the mind of the Waco Baptist Association, be it now

"*Resolved* 1, That in seeking to form or withdraw from associational relations, it is good order according to Baptist usage from time immemorial for a church through its proper officers to give fair notice to all its members that such matter will be considered at a subsequent regular conference. The object of such notice grows out of the importance of the step to be taken, and to afford all members a privilege of being present so as to exercise their right of participation in the deliberations and particularly in the decision which has so much to do with the prosperity of the church. The unity and fellowship of the church can never be maintained, if by shrewd management of a few, or by any kind of snap judgment, a church is led to form or break associational relations.

"2. We count it as disorderly and unbrotherly for members of one association to seek to disturb the relations existing between another Association and its churches.

"3. In the formation of new Associations we express the following as gospel order:

"(a) A desire for such new organization and the perception of its necessity should come from the churches themselves, each one for herself, and not an article worked up by outsiders.

"(b) There can be no good co-operative work between church and Association unless something of permanency characterizes the bond which unites them. If this bond is to be shaken or broken every time a few discontented individuals are possessed with a restless desire for new things, then our great work of missions and education may be intermitted at any time to give space to agitators.

"(c) In a word, whenever a church in her own sovereignty and of her own motion, after proper gospel announcement and deliberation, wishes to dissolve her associational connections, her wishes in the matter should be regarded. But if it is in evidence that a petition for it is a result of disorderly agitation and without due notice given, so as to give it the appearance of being a fair, orderly and deliberate church action, the Association should advise the petitioning church to defer their request until the next meeting.

"(d) Particularly do we regard it as disorderly and contrary to the plainest scriptures when pastoral authority is disregarded and when to secure an end of this kind the pastor is undermined in his influence with his people. This becomes a graver offense when outsiders, desiring to work up a new Association, align themselves with a factional minority and virtually encourage their resistance to the will of the church and in their attempt to get rid of the pastor, so as thereby the more readily to work the church out of the Association. This offense becomes yet graver when the faction's minority are such by reason of false doctrines held by them.

"4. An association may properly decline to give a letter of dismission in fellowship to any church on fair constructive evidence that such letter is to be used as a leverage in further disturbing the relations of the churches which remain within; or if there be good reason to believe that such letter will be used in alignment with un-Baptistic doctrine.

"5. We hold it as contrary to the spirit of official obligation for an officer of an Association to seek, during his term of trust, to dismember the body which so honored him by trying to influence other churches than his own to separate from the body.

"B. H. CARROLL,
"R. C. BURLESON,
"T. E. MUSE."

The above report was discussed at length by B. H. Carroll, R. C. Burleson and J. H. Luther.

Dr. J. H. Luther was at this time theological teacher in Baylor University. The sum of $51 was collected at this sitting of the Association to pay him for his services.

Kirk, Little Deer Creek and Live Oak churches were dismissed by letter.

Lott church, through her messengers, called for a letter of dismission, but there being a protest from several members of Lott church requesting the messengers to not call for a letter of dismission from Waco Association, the following resolution was adopted:

Resolved, That we kindly, prayerfully and fraternally advise and request the messengers of Lott church to withdraw their petition for this time.

The petition was withdrawn by messengers J. L. Walker, I. H. Venable and H. Rector.

Chilton church called for a letter of dismission from this body and a motion and second was made asking that the letter be granted.

Whereupon the following substitute was offered by Jno. T. Battle:

"*Resolved*, that instead of granting the letter we kindly and lovingly and fraternally ask the church to withdraw their petition for letter for one year."

The substitute was adopted.

The total collections this year, October 1, 1892, to October 1, 1893, amounted to $7,162.50, the largest in the history of the Association.

Board meetings were held at West in October, at Moody in January, at Caddo in April and at Shiloh in July.

As had been the custom for many years, programs were prepared, printed and distributed among the churches for each of these meetings.

On the third day of the Association in the afternoon the report of the Mission Board was read by the president and adopted. Following is the report condensed:

J. L. Walker was sustained as missionary pastor at Lott. During this year nearly all the $400 debt on Lott house of worship was paid. Elder E. F. Brock did efficient and acceptable work, collecting funds for this debt. The Board paid the Lott pastor $150; the church paid him $100.

Elder John Bateman was missionary pastor of Second Waco. He reports good revivals and satisfactory work. The Board paid to this work $75.

Elder W. B. White was missionary pastor at Rosebud. The Baptists had at that time the only meeting house in the town. The Board paid W. B. White $100.

A committee was appointed at the West Board meeting in October, 1892, to secure a Sunday school missionary and colporteur. The committee consisted of B. J. Kendrick, Homer Wells and the president of the Board. Elder S. R. Williams was employed. The contract with him did not involve the Board. By an arrangement with S. L. Morris, editor of the Guardian, it was agreed that Bro. Williams should be compensated by profits on books sold, S. L. Morris to furnish the books. This arrangement was not satisfactory to Bro. Williams, and he resigned after forty days. However, he did some excellent work.

Elder T. P. Walker was employed at the Moody Board meeting, January 29, 1893. It was arranged with the Sunday school and colportage convention board that Bro. Walker was to be their missionary, but confine his labors to our bounds. This was a satisfactory arrangement as it did not involve our Board. All funds for Sunday school missions were turned over to the State S. S. and Corportage Board, and that board paid the salary of our missionary. He commenced work February 6, and continued till the meeting of the Association. Following is his report: Time labored, 7 months; days lost, 14; miles traveled, 1,400; visits, 500; Bibles sold, 90; Testaments sold, 156; Bibles given away, 25; Testaments given away, 21; books sold, 70; pages of tracts distributed, 3,800; sermons preached, 119; Sunday schools organized, 7; collected on field, $85.55; profits from sales, $63.05; books received from W. C. Luther, $125.65; cash received from W. C. Luther, $75.75; total salary, $350; total received, $350; conversions witnessed, 103. Bro. T. P. Walker resigns to go to the Seminary at Louisville, Ky.

SUMMARY.

Following is the summary of funds for all purposes:

State and Associational Missions	$2,822 92
Home missions	335 67
Foreign missions	1,115 94
Orphans' Home	851 05
Old Ministers' Relief Board	240 10
Sunday School missions	440 87
Centennial fund	1,355 95
Grand total	$7,162 50

RECOMMENDATIONS.

1. That we apropriate to Associational Missions $100, the amount pledged by the churches to that purpose.

2. That we appropriate $600 to State Missions.

3. That we co-operate with the State Board in sustaining the German Waco Mission, and designate for that object all funds for Associational Missions, not otherwise used.

4. That we continue co-operation with the State Sunday School Corportage Board in sustaining a colporter within our bounds, and that $300 be appropriated to that purpose.

5. That we appropriate $500 to Home Missions.

6. That we appropriate $1,500 to Foreign Missions.

Respectfully submitted,

J. L. WALKER, President Board.

The amount reported this year for all purposes, $7,162.50, is the largest in one year in the history of the Association.

The new Board organized by electing J. L. Walker president, and vice presidents as follows: First District, B. J. Kendrick; Second District, J. M. Kendrick; Third District, W. E. Bozeman; Fourth District, H. T. Vaughn.

Elder T. P. Walker, missionary, resigned, whereupon the following was adopted:

"*Whereas*, We learn that our young brother, T. P. Walker, who has been laboring as missionary in our bounds with great acceptance, is soon to leave us to enter the Southern Baptist Theological Seminary to better prepare himself for service in the Master's cause, be it hereby

"*Resolved*, That we heartily commend our young brother to the Christian confidence and esteem of our brethren at the seminary and our brethren and sisters everywhere. And may the blessing of Almighty God rest upon him and guide him in wisdom's ways, is our prayer."

A committee consisting of R. C. Burleson, T. E. Muse and V. G. Cunningham was appointed to draft resolutions expressing the sense of the Association on certain heresies. Following is an extract from their report which was adopted.

REPORT ON HERESY.

"*Whereas*, Several of our churches have been greatly disturbed for two or three years by a heresy familiarly known as 'Martinism,' which is in reality only a remodeling or conglomeration of the old heresies known as 'Hyper-Calvinism,' 'Two-Seedism,' and 'Campbellism,' yet this revamping of old and deadly heresies is so adroitly mixed up with and concealed under the dear old Bible doctrines of assurance, atonement and other doctrines of grace, that many good, unsuspecting Christians have been led astray to their great injury and to the disturbing of the peace of our Zion. Your committee therefore recommends that the Waco Association solemnly and emphatically advise and warn all good Christians and churches to beware of the fatal and delusive heresies of 'Martinism' on regeneration, repentance, faith, prayer and assurance. This last precious Bible doctrine of assurance Martinism confounds with presumption.

"We therefore advise all our churches and pastors to observe strictly the Bible rule: 'If any come to you and bring not this doctrine (the old time religion) receive him not into your houses, neither bid him God-speed, for he that biddeth him God-speed is partaker of his evil deeds.'"

A resolution was adopted changing the time of the annual meeting from Thursday till Saturday. The place appointed for next meeting was Mart.

The following were elected to represent the Association in the Baptist General Convention: R. C. Burleson, B. J. Kendrick, I. Z. Kimbrough, W. F. Routh, D. B. Bozeman.

SESSION OF 1894 AT MART.

Mart is at present on our extreme eastern border. It is in the heart of a fine large section of rich black land. The church was formerly known as Willow Springs. The membership at the time of this meeting was 221; it is now (February, 1897), 240. Elder B. F. Tatum was pastor. He was confined to his room during the session on account of a painful carbuncle on his neck. Mart church is composed of earnest, active, cultured and well informed people.

The thirty-fifth annual session of the Association convened in the Baptist meeting house at Mart September 22, 23 and 24 (Saturday, Sunday and Monday), 1894.

Letters from the churches were read by W. H. Jenkins and S. L. Morris.

Two new churches, Riesel and Downsville, were received.

These were both newly organized churches. Riesel is half way between Waco and Marlin on the Central railroad, and Downsville ten miles south from Waco, on the Aransas Pass railroad. The former came into the Association with 15 members, the latter with 75.

Churches and pastors: East Waco, G. W. Truett; Caledonia, S. R. Williams; Blue Ridge, J. F. McLeod; Shiloh, R. E. Smith; Oak Grove, Rock Creek, Olive Branch and China Springs, V. G. Cunningham; Downsville, A. J. Moore; Flat Rock and Bosqueville, Joseph Gronde; Goshen, M. Isbell; Robinson and Mastersville, J. L. Walker; Eddy, J. C. F. Kyger; White Rock, Geneva, Concord and Independence, Holmes Nichols; Crawford, J. M. B. Gresham; Caddo, S. B. McJunkin; Pleasant Grove, Center and White Hall, J. B. Reaves; Second Pleasant Grove, G. W. North; Bold Springs, I. Z. Kimbrough; Hillside and Speegleville, W. S. Huff; First Waco, B. H. Carroll; McGregor and Second Waco, J. H. Roberts; Battle and Mart, B. F. Tatum; Lott, J. E. McClerkin; Riesel, Cow Bayou, Rosebud, Friendship and Deer Creek were without pastors.

Blue Ridge, Lott and Chilton were dismissed by letter to go into Falls County Association.

B. J. Kendrick was elected moderator, Holmes Nichols, clerk, and H. T. Vaughn, treasurer.

Every church in the Association save Chilton and Riesel reported additions by baptism.

The largest number baptized was at Waco. This was perhaps the most precious revival ever enjoyed by the old First church; 108 were added by baptism, and a greater number by letter.

Next to Waco the largest number, 39, was baptized into the fellowship of the young church at Downsville. The total baptized was 592.

Brethren G. W. Truett, W. H. Jenkins and M. L. Davis were appointed a special committee on state missions. Following is an extract from their report:

"The work in Texas has made remarkable progress. Fifty-eight years ago there was not a Baptist church in Texas, and there were only two or three Baptist preachers. Now, including the colored people, we have about 4,000 churches, considerably over 3,000 preachers, and approximately 25,000 members. Yet, with all this great progress, the destitution in Texas is still enormous. Of 246 counties 72 are yet without a resident Baptist preacher. These counties nearly three years ago had an average population of about 2,500. About one-third of the other 174 counties are yet very poorly supplied with the gospel."

To an invitation from the moderator the following brethren responded and accepted seats in the body: T. P. Speakman, representing North Colorado Association; G. L. Jennings and D. J. Calvert of Limestone County Association, and E. J. Billington of Hubbard City Association.

Seated as visitors: W. T. Compere, representing the Texas Baptist and Herald (Dallas), and T. C. Boykin, representing the Sunday School and Colportage Convention.

Elder B. F. Tatum was elected messenger to the Southern Baptist Convention.

The introductory sermon was preached on Saturday night by Holmes Nichols. Text, Gen. 13:8. Theme: "A Plea for Peace."

Pending the report on Orphans' Home, a collection for that institution was taken amounting to $27.76.

On Sunday at 11 a. m. George W. Truett preached at the Baptist house and J. L. Walker at the Presbyterian house.

On Monday the report of the Associational Board was considered and adopted. Condensed, it is as follows:

REPORT OF THE ASSOCIATION BOARD.

"With gratitude to our beneficent heavenly Father we come before the Association with one of the hardest year's work in our history. It has been a year of financial pressure, but the God of missions has been with us.

"Our Board was instructed 'to continue co-operation with the State Sunday School and Colportage Board in sustaining a missionary in our bounds, and $300 were appropriated for that purpose. To continue to co-operate was interpreted to mean 'Go on as in the past year,' that is pay all our funds over to the State Sunday School and Colportage Board, that Board assuming the salary of our missionary, paying him in books and money. Accordingly, at our Bosqueville Board meeting October 29, 1893, Rev. C. D. Whitman was employed as our colporter and missionary. Rev. W. C. Luther of the State Sunday School and Colportage Board was advised and asked to co-operate. His reply was courteous, but he declined, except on the following terms: (1) All the $300 must be paid over to his board. (2) Our Board must pay the salary of our missionary. (3) To aid us in this $200 in books would be given us by his Board, payable quarterly. (4) Bibles, Testaments and tracts for free distribution would be furnished by his Board, amounting in all to 'about $50.'

"Our Board declined this proposition, and has sustained her missionary independently. Sent to W. C. Luther for State Sunday school work, $23.

Board meetings were held at Bosqueville in October, Mastersville in December, at Blue Ridge in April, and at White Rock in July, embracing fifth Sundays during the Associational year.

"Rev. C. D. Whitman began his labors November 1, 1893, and continued till July 28, 1894. He did acceptable work and was paid in full, $408.40.

All our obligations are over paid except home and foreign missions. We have fallen short on home missions $165.52, and on foreign missions $1,000.63, yet the total paid is nearly double the amount pledged.

SUMMARY.

Associational missions (including amount paid city missionary by Waco church and $23.00 sent W. C. Luther $2,033.68
State missions 2,002.20
Home missions 324.68
Foreign missions 499.37

Orphans' Home 600.05
Aged ministers 242.05

Total.... ....$5,702.03

Additional to the above are $10.45 collected for ministerial education.

RECOMMENDATIONS.

To be raised during the coming year:
For Association and S. S. missions...................$ 300
State missions 1,000
Home missions 400
Foreign missions 1,000

Respectfully submitted,

J. L. WALKER,
President of the Mission Board of Waco Association.

RESIGNATION OF THE PRESIDENT.

J. L. Walker tendered his resignation as president of the Board, which was accepted.

The following was adopted:

"*Whereas*, Our dearly beloved brother, J. L. Walker, has been president of our Board, and has been faithful and efficient, and now retires of his own voluntary motion, therefore be it

"*Resolved*, That we hereby extend to him our heartfelt thanks for his very faithful and efficient service in the past, and that we now and here assure him of our sympathy and prayers in whatever position of life he may occupy, and that these resolutions be spread on the minutes of Waco Association."

During the two years of the first term of J. L. Walker's incumbency as president of the Board of Waco Association the following brethren and sisters came to his help with their personal contributions. God bless them!

Miss Amanda Williams, V. G. Cunningham, Miss Charity Bush, Mrs. S. E. Whipkey, H. P. Tyra, B. Southard, Mrs. I. Z. Kimbrough, J. G. Martin, J. C. Denison, W. E. Bozeman, H. Smilie, J. B. McPherson, B. M. Lockard, Mrs. W. D. Gaines, J. C. Gibson, J. N. Bell, Mrs. S. M. Bryant, John Bateman, Mrs. L.

J. Evans, J. L. Walker, E. Schneider, Miss Mary Barton, H. T. Vaughn, B. F. Tatum, Park Carpenter, T. P. Walker, W. W. Donaldson, J. D. McSpadden, E. P. Kirkland, W. B. White, B. J. Kendrick, R. E. Smith, G. R. Trice, B. H. Carroll, J. B. Reaves, H. W. Smith, H. A. Covington, F. L. Carroll, W. H. Jenkins, J. T Battle, A. Goddard, J. C. West, H. J. Chamberlain, J. G. Kendall, M. H. Standifer, J. B. Cranfill, F. J. Gleiss, G. W. Truett, J. M. B. Gresham, R. C. Burleson, M. L. Davis, A. J. Shelton, J. S. Sligh, S. Cobb, J. H. Luther, Holmes Nichols, F. L. Kirkpatrick, F. O. Thomas, J. B. Scarborough, Mrs. C. A. Westbrook, J. C. Atwood, W. Home. Total personal contributions, $316.75.

The total realized during these two years from public contributions at Board and Associational meetings was $536.08.

The amounts paid by the churches during this period are the following:

Battle, $55; Blue Ridge, $62.95; Bold Springs, $217.76; Bosqueville, $54.10; Caddo, $186.55; Center, $43.71; Chilton, $71.10; China Springs, $23.75; Concord, $50.12; Cow Bayou, $18.10; Crawford, $17.35; Deer Creek, $62.05; Durango, $19.95; East Waco, $833.72; Eddy, $84.70; Flat Rock, $32.70; Geneva, $47.67; Goshen, $11.25; Hillside, $56.50; Kirk, $20; Little Deer Creek, $9.35; Live Oak, $11.50; Lorena, $36.35; Lott, $62.52; Mart, $106.49; Mastersville, $98.31; McGregor, $216.75; Moody, $281.90; Oak Grove, $8.20; Olive Branch, $96.55; First Pleasant Grove, $48.50; Second Pleasant Grove (Bethany), $36.20; Robinson, $73.26; Rock Creek, $52.95; Rosebud, $26.85; Shiloh, $30; Speegleville, $24.50; White Rock, $20; First Waco, $7,113.32; Second Waco, $127.35; White Hall, $116.05; Waco German $30; Cottonwood German, $25. Total from the churches, $10,639.87.

SUMMARY.

Individuals (not counted with churches)	$ 316 75
Public collections at Board and Associational meetings	536 08
Churches	10,639 87
Total	$11,492 70

In addition to this there were received from the American Baptist Publication Society, in books, collections on fields by missionaries, and received from various other sources, sums amounting to $1,371.38, making a grand total of $12,864.08 from all sources, and for all purposes.

NEW BOARD.

The new Board organized in open session of the Association, by electing B. J. Kendrick president, and the following brethren vice presidents: First district, J. M. Wright; Second district, J. M. Kendrick; Third district, W. E. Bozeman; Fourth district, H. T. Vaughn.

Board meetings were appointed, and work laid out for the new year.

There were at this time, in the Association, 30 Sunday Schools, with superintendents as follows: East Waco, L. L. Lusk; Caledonia, M. T. Presnall; Blue Ridge, S. D. Dunham; Shiloh, H. Lehman; Flat Rock, C. H. Creighton; Bosqueville, J. A. Moore; Robinson, J. L. Moore; Eddy, L. Amis; White Rock, W. H. Edwards; Moody, S. W. Miller; Rock Creek, R. B. Thomas; Geneva, C. R. Battaile; Mastersville, E. R. Tatum; Hillside, J. M. Kendrick; Caddo, W. E. Bozeman; Rosebud, J. P. Greenlese; Pleasant Grove, M. E. Brown; Second Pleasant Grove, W. J. Cook; Bold Springs, J. W. Patterson; White Hall, B. J. Kendrick; First Waco, W. H. Jenkins; Independence, W. T. Cobb; McGregor, T. D. Johnson; Battle, J. H. Gilliam; Mart, J. K. Dunn; Second Waco, J. W. Howard; Center, F. A. Curry; Olive Branch, T. A. Kirkland; Deer Creek, W. L. Bynum. The whole number of officers and teachers was 239, and the whole number of regular pupils 1,251. Twelve of these schools contributed to missions, viz: East Waco, Caledonia, Blue Ridge, Flat Rock, Robinson, Caddo, Bold Springs, McGregor, Mart, Waco, Second Waco and Olive Branch.

Ordained ministers: B. H. Carroll, J. B. Reaves, C. D. Whitman, T. E. Muse, W. D. Bowen, S. R. Williams, S. B. McJunkin, Geo. W. Truett, J. C. F. Kyger, John G. Kendall, R. C. Burleson, J. L. Ward, M. L. Davis, W. S. Huff, J. H. Roberts, R. J. Grant, S. L. Morris, V. G. Cunningham, J. B. Cranfill,

Joseph Gronde, F. A. Petereit, F. J. Gleiss, Waco; J. L. Walker, A. J. Shelton, G. W. North, Bruceville; N. A. Seale, Moody; John Witt, Eddy; I. Z. Kimbrough, W. C. Manning, West; J. H. Moore, Mt. Calm; G. G. Gibson, Mooreville; W. J. Pace, Peter S. Bruner, W. E. Self, Blevins; J. M. B. Gresham, J. M. Wright, Crawford; C. D. Lumpkin, McClanahan; T. P. Walker, Louisville, Ky.; R. E. Smith, W. F. Shumate, Ryan; E. F. Brock, Durango; J. F. Boynton, Bosqueville; A. J. Moore, Downsville; C. R. Osborne, M. Isbell, M. H. Curry, McGregor; B. F. Tatum, C. C. Hardwick, Mart; A. M. Harrington, Viesca; Holmes Nichols, Elm Mott.

SESSION OF 1895 AT McGREGOR.

McGregor church, organized as "Onion Creek," November 6, 1858, is two years older than the Waco Association. She united with the Association in September, 1890, with 235 members. The church is in the town of McGregor, on the Santa Fe and Cotton Belt railroads. The beloved and consecrated brother, H. D. Gilbert, was pastor in 1895.

It was with this church that the Association held her Thirty-sixth annual session, September 21, 22 and 23 (Saturday, Sunday and Monday), 1895.

Devotional services were conducted by Elder J. L. H. Hawkins.

Letters were read by J. L. Walker and G. W. Truett.

A beautiful address of welcome was delivered by Pastor H. D. Gilbert, and was responded to by G. W. Truett.

Two new churches, Hewitt and Axtell, were received into the fraternity of churches.

Hewitt meets in the town of Hewitt, eight miles south from Waco, and Axtell, in the town of Axtell, thirteen miles east from Waco. Each had 30 members, at the time of uniting with the Association.

Deer Creek was dismissed to unite with Falls County Association, and Olive Branch, to unite with Hubbard City Association. Second Pleasant Grove appears with name changed to Bethany.

Oak Grove, Rock Creek, Goshen, Caddo, Center, Durango and Riesel, not represented.

All the churches represented reported additions by baptism except Bosqueville, Caledonia, Crawford and Rosebud. Lorena reported the largest number baptized, 25; and Concord the second largest number, 22. The whole number baptized was 337. The total membership reported, 4,776.

The old officers were re-elected.

Correspondence received: W. T. Compere, Hubbard City Association; P. Nowlan and W. Hickerson, Meridian Association; Z. H. Reagan and W. A. Tippett, Leon River Association.

Visitors seated: J. C. Johnson, Meridian; W. J. Brown, Alvarado; J. M. Reynolds, Abilene; T. C. Boykin, Dallas; R. L. Stanley, Forest City, Ark., and R. G. Burnett, Monroe, La.

J. M. B. Gresham was elected messenger to the Southern Baptist Convention; H. D. Gilbert, alternate.

Elder J. M. Reynolds made an appeal in favor of his church at Clyde. This little frontier flock had just lost their house of worship in a cyclone. A collection was taken to aid them in re-building, amounting to $53.35.

J. L. Walker, John C. West and T. D. Johnson, were appointed a special committee on Sabbath desecration.

Following is their report, which was unanimously adopted:

SABBATH DESECRATION.

"God is Sovereign, and his laws must be obeyed. He can not be mocked, 'for whatsoever a man soweth, that shall he also reap.' The Divine law is, 'Remember the Sabbath day to keep it holy.' And kept in any other way than 'holy' means swift destruction, whether by individuals, corporations, municipalities, states or nations. Destroy the Sabbath, and falls the religion of Christ; destroy the Christian religion, and falls America; destroy America, and falls the world. Sunday excursions are a sin against God, and a powerful engine in the hand of Satan, for battering down the walls, both of our civil institutions and our holy religion. The same may be said of base ball contests and Sunday exhibitions.

"A sad time it is, when our young men, allured from the sanctuary of God, are carried away on God's holy day in a maddened stream of dissipation, and profanity. Sowing to the wind they can not fail to reap the whirlwind—a cyclone of destruction. Young Christians return from a Sabbath, spent in unholy devotion, to pleasure's shrine, with battered spirituality and battered morals, after having sacrificed both their self-respect and the respect of their fellows.

"1. We recommend, that discipline, swift and summary, be exercised by churches in every case of Sabbath desecration.

"2. We recommend, that preachers preach more against these giant evils; and we request and urge upon every member of this body and upon every Christian in our land, to strive more diligently to observe the Sabbath day, to keep it holy. All should pray God for help in this duty."

J. B. Cranfill occupied the pulpit on Saturday night. At the same hour, T. P. Walker preached in the Methodist house.

On Sabbath, G. W. Truett preached on State Missions, after which a cash collection was taken, amounting to $72.45. Elder J. G. Kendall preached in the Methodist house, and took a collection of $6.25. Total collected for State Missions, $78.70.

A Sunday School mass meeting was conducted on Sabbath afternoon, by T. C. Boykin, in his own inimitable way. A collection was taken for State Sunday School and Colportage work, amounting to $31.

On Sabbath night, R. C. Burleson preached in the Baptist meeting house, and G. W. Truett in the Methodist house.

On Monday morning, Elder M. D. Early, State Board corresponding secretary, addressed the Association, in the interest of foreign missions, and took a collection, amounting to $18.40.

Also during the day a collection of $15.60 was taken for Orphans' Home.

The report of the

ASSOCIATIONAL BOARD

showed a good average year's work. Following is a condensed statement:

"The Lord has enabled us to finish another year's labor. We

have sustained a Sunday School missionary in our bounds, as instructed, independently of the State Sunday School and Colportage Board. Besides sustaining our own missionary, our churches have contributed to the State Sunday School and Colportage Board.

"Elder T. P. Walker was employed at the meeting of committee appointed for that purpose, October 8, 1895, at $25 per month, in addition to what he could make on the field from the sale of books. At the meeting of the Board at Crawford, December 8, 1894, the contract with the missionary was changed to $50 per month, the Board to have the benefit of all funds raised on the field by sale of books or otherwise.

Sunday School Institute meetings have been held by our missionary at White Hall, Moody, Bruceville and East Waco.

"Elder T. P. Walker began his labors on October 12, 1894, and continued 'till September 22, 1895. Following is his report:

"Days labored, 323; lost, 23; visits, 340; miles traveled, 2,770; Bibles sold, 36; given away, 55; Testaments sold, 64; given away, 105; books sold, 38; given away, 2; pages of tracts distributed, 5,000; Sunday schools organized 15; institutes held, 4; churches visited, 33; Sunday school addresses, 26; sermons, 73; at school houses, 29; conversions, 34; baptisms, 16; letters and articles written, 210; families prayed with, 61.

Received for free distribution, (1) of Old Board of Association, Bibles 124, Testaments 194, tracts (pages) 1,200; (2) of American Baptist Publication Society, Testaments 25, tracts (pages), 936."

Summary of funds raised for all purposes:

Associational Missions	$1,753 02
State Missions	517 85
Home Missions	1,133 05
Foreign Missions	1,160 33
Orphans' Home	323 70
Aged Ministers	123 35
State S. S. Missions	74 75
Ministerial Education	126 35
Total	$5,212 40

RECOMMENDATIONS.

To be raised the coming year:
(1) For Associational and Sunday School Missions......$ 600
(2) State Missions 2,000
(3) Home Missions 1,000
(4) Foreign Missions 2,000
(5) Ministerial Education (Baylor University) 200

RESIGNATION OF THE PRESIDENT.

Deacon B. J. Kendrick tendered his resignation, which was accepted. He was paid $100 for his services.

The individuals contributing to the work during President Kendrick's incumbency were A. Goddard, J. M. Kendrick, A. J. Moore and J. H. Gilliam. The amount, $6.50.

The amount realized from public collections at Board meetings and at Association during this period was $268.25.

The churches contributed the following: Bethany, $21.20; Battle, $5.85; Bold Springs, $67.30; Bosqueville, $35.50; Caledonia, $32; Cow Bayou, $15.55; Caddo, $57.80; China Springs, $11.75; Crawford, $7.60; Concord, $18.60; Deer Creek, $30.13; Downsville, $7.50; Durango, $4.35; East Waco, $20; Eddy, $8.20; Flat Rock, $45.15; Friendship, $13.25; Geneva, $25; Goshen, $2; Hillside, $63.35; Lorena, $17.35; Mastersville, $27.60; Mart, $49.40; McGregor, $68.80; Moody, $134.06; Olive Branch, $16.75; Pleasant Grove, $57.05; Rosebud, $29.60; Robinson, $41.70; Rock Creek, $16.25; Shiloh, $25; White Rock, $16; White Hall, $56.45; First Waco, $3,736.03; Second Waco, $21. Total from the churches, $4,752.56.

SUMMARY.

Individual contributions..... ... .$ 6 50
Public collections at Board meetings and at Association....... ... . 268 25
Churches..... ... ... 4,752 56

Total..... ... ...$5,027 31

Add to this $237.44 realized from donations of books and

profits from sales of same, collections on field, etc., and we have a grand total of $5,264.75 collected from all sources and for all purposes.

NEW BOARD.

The new Board organized by electing J. L. Walker president, and the following brethren vice presidents: First District, B. J. Kendrick, Waco; Second District, Homer Wells, Waco; Third District, W. E. Bozeman, Baileyville; Fourth District, W. R. Thompson, West. Holmes Nichols was elected secretary.

Notwithstanding the fact that the Association had at former sittings expressed her judgment in unmistakable language on the heresy known as Martinism, yet at this session the following, introduced by Geo. W. Truett, was adopted:

MARTINISM.

"*Whereas*, In various portions of Texas Baptist churches are being divided and schismatic bodies organized in antagonism to Baptist churches by the advocates of the heresy known as Martinism, and,

"*Whereas*, At this time there seems to be a preconcerted plan aggressively to propagate Martinism in Texas,

"*Resolved*, Therefore, that the Waco Association declare non-fellowship for the doctrines and followers of M. T. Martin, and urge our Baptist bodies throughout the state to take similar action to the end that Baptist churches and principles may be protected and preserved."

The Baptist General Convention met in Belton two weeks after this and adopted a report (submitted by J. M. Robertson, R. C. Pender, J. H. Cason, J. D. Robnett and J. B. Riddle), of which the following is an extract:

"The fact that a man, presenting himself here for membership as a messenger, is known to believe and teach by speech or pen, the doctrine hereinbefore mentioned and commonly known as 'Martinism,' shall be sufficient cause for his rejection as a member." The convention, of course, left the matter of churches purging themselves of false teachers with the churches where it belongs.

It is now hoped that Martinism is dead in Texas forever.

The reports of standing committees adopted at this session of the Association were all well written, practical documents.

Extract from report on State Missions (written by A. Goddard): "Let us be loyal to our (State) Mission Board, loyal to Christ."

Extract from report on Ministerial Education (R. C. Burleson): "Learned Goliahs of infidelity and heresy, armed with 'philosophy, falsely, so called,' are defying the army of Israel, and ridiculing the pure gospel and the 'old time religion.' To meet these giants we need scores of young Davids, trained in Christian schools with gospel slings and smooth stones, gathered from the flowing brook of God's eternal truth."

Extract from report on Schools and Education: "The great Romish doctrine, 'Ignorance is the mother of religion,' under the benign touch of our holy religion, is made to read: 'Ignorance is the mother of superstition.' The patriotic cry, 'We must educate or we must perish,' is but a reproduction of the divine cry, 'My people perish for lack of knowledge.'"

Extract from report on Buckner Orphans' Home (G. R. Trice): "The comforts and equipments of the Home are growing better all the while, and the applications for admittance are more numerous than at any former date."

Extract from report on Foreign Missions: "(1) The obligation to give the gospel to the whole world rests on this generation. (2) The obligation to give the gospel to the whole world rests on the Baptists of this generation. (3) We believe that our God is able and willing to strengthen us for so great an undertaking."

Extract from report on Home Missions of S. B. C. (G. W. Truett): "The territory of this Board comprises a population of about 20,000,000. Of this population about 2,500,000 are Baptists; about 10,000,000 belong to other denominations, leaving probably one-third of this great population with no religion of any kind."

SESSION OF 1896 AT EAST WACO.

No church in the Waco Association is prospering more to-day than the East Waco church, under the pastoral care of Elder George W. Truett.

It was with this church that the Association held her thirty-seventh annual session, Saturday, Sunday and Monday, September 26, 27 and 28, 1896.

Elder Jno. G. Kendall led the congregation in devotional worship.

The old officers in their places, Brethren John G. Kendall and C. D. Whitman read the letters from the churches. Thirty-eight churches were represented by letter and delegates; one hundred delegates present.

Cottonwood, a new church, was received at this meeting, with 30 members. This church worships about two miles north of Mooreville, near the place where the old Cow Bayou held her services for more than thirty years.

Center and Crawford were not represented.

Following is the roll of churches and pastors: Axtell, J. S. Crossland; Bethany, G. W. North; Bosqueville, Concord; Eddy and Pleasant Grove, L. J. Mims; Battle, Riesel and Rock Creek, B. F. Tatum; Caddo, J. R. M. Touchstone; Cottonwood and Downsville, A. J. Moore; Durango, Hewitt, White Hall and Flat Rock, J. B. Reaves; Crawford, N. B. Brooks (began January, 1897); Caledonia, W. D. Bowen; Geneva, Holmes Nichols; Friendship and Goshen, E. B. Shope; Hillside and Robinson, H. R. Best; Independence, T. P. Speakman; Lorena and Speegleville, E. L. Compere; McGregor, J. B. Smith; Moody, R. C. Medaris; Mastersville, W. A. Hamlet (resigned January, 1897); Mart, J. L. Walker; China Springs, Shiloh and Oak Grove, R. E. Smith; Rosebud, C. D. Whitman, now D. P. Airhart; West, W. H. Park (began January, 1897); First Waco, B. H. Carroll; Second Waco and Cow Bayou, J. H. Roberts; East Waco, G. W. Truett.

The old officers were re-elected, viz: B. J. Kendrick, moderator; Holmes Nichols, clerk; H. T. Vaughn, treasurer.

Corresponding messengers present and welcomed to seats: W. T. Compere, representing Hubbard City Association; A. R. Watson, Salado Association; G. L. Jennings, Limestone Association; W. D. Gaines (former moderator of Waco Association), Falls County Association; C. E. Summers, Leon River Association.

There were several visitors present to whom was extended a cordial welcome, viz: S. E. Brooks, of Jacksboro Association; W. H. Parks of Ellis County Association; E. C. Rice, of Cherokee Association; J. O. Heath, of Montague Association; R. C. Burleson, representing Baylor University, Waco; J. M. Carroll, representing Baylor Female College, Belton; T. C. Boykin, representing the State Sunday School and Colportage Board; R. J. Grant, representing Baptist Standard, Waco; W. T. Compere, representing the Texas Baptist and Herald, Dallas; J. P. Aden, Brazil.

Corresponding messengers were appointed to represent the Waco Association in other bodies as follows: R. J. Grant and M. L. Davis to Meridian Association; Z. H. Reagan and T. A. Mangum to Leon River; S. B. McJunkin, C. P. Lumpkin and Holmes Nichols to Hubbard City; W. E. Bozeman and J. T. Glenn to Little River; Z. H. Reagan and R. J. Grant to Salado.

Messengers to the Baptist General Convention: Holmes Nichols, T. E. Muse, B. J. Kendrick, M. L. Davis, C. P. Lumpkin.

Elder John Bateman was elected messenger to the Southern Baptist Convention; John C. West and T. A. Mangum, alternates.

REPORT OF THE MISSION BOARD—(CONDENSED).

1. Missionary T. P. Walker was kept in the field the entire year; salary $553.33.

2. Board meetings were held at Lorena in December, at White Hall in March, at West in May, and at Caddo in August. All these meetings were fairly well attended except Caddo, where the attendance was small. The White Hall meeting" was made a "mission mass meeting." A "mission prayer meeting" was held at Mooresville in July.

3. "When our Board was organized in open session of the Association at McGregor J. L. Walker was elected president and $100 voted as compensation for his services. The burdensome duties of receiving and disbursing funds, keeping the accounts with all the churches, conducting the corespondence, etc., devolve on our president. * * * After adjournment of the Associa-

tion complaint was made in some quarters against the president's receiving compensation; he has therefore declined to receive pay."

The expenses ($39.83) were met by the liberality of generous individuals.

The amounts received and disbursed during the year were the following:

Expenses..	$ 39 83
Associational Missions..........................	557 51
State Missions..................................	1,553 28
Home Missions..................................	742 87
Foreign Missions................................	1,554 16
Aged Ministers..................................	153 40
State Sunday School Missions....................	156 09
Ministerial Education...........................	177 35
Paid City Missionary by First Waco Church.......	1,200 00
Collected for Miss Mary Vrazzle, Bohemian student, and paid same to J. C. Smith, who was managing her education.................................	7 00
Buckner Orphans' Home...........................	895 69
Total for all purposes......................	$7,037 18

This is the second time in the history of the Association that the total reached $7,000. The best year was 1893, when the total was $7,162.50.

RECOMMENDATIONS.

(1) That we employ a missionary in co-operation with the State Board to work among the foreign populations within our bounds at a salary of $600 per annum.

(2) That all funds, for whatever purpose, be sent the Board member or church treasurer to some Waco bank (to be chosen), both the depositor and the bank to notify the president of the Board of such deposit, whose duty it shall be to disburse the same by checks officially signed.

(3) That every church in the Association be requested to hold monthly mission prayer meetings.

(4) That the following amounts be raised:

For State Missions (including $600 for Associational missionary), $2,000; Home missions, $1,000; foreign missions, $2,000; ministerial education, Baylor University, $200."

The plan of depositing funds in the bank to be disbursed by check signed by the president of the Board has worked very satisfactorily. An arrangement was made with the First National Bank, Waco, by which an account is opened with the "Waco Associational Mission Fund." Funds thus deposited are far less burdensome to the president of the Board.

The new Board was organized in open session of the Association. J. L. Walker, against his earnest protest, was elected president of the Board.

We here present the district with churches and board members for 1896-1897:

First District—Vice President B. J. Kendrick, Waco, Texas.
Oak Grove—A. P. Smith, Greenock.
China Springs—W. R. McCants, China Springs.
Rock Creek—G. L. Robertson, Patrick.
Bosqueville—A. M. Woodard, Bosqueville.
Crawford—E. W. Thomas, Crawford.
McGregor—T. D. Johnson, McGregor.
Speegleville—F. Herring, Speegleville.
Joshen—E. Martin, McGregor.
White Hall—L. A. Trice, Waco.
Shiloh—J. P. Jones, Ocee.
Flat Rock—S. N. O'Neill, Bosqueville.
Hewitt—E. C. Kellogg, Hewitt.

Second District—Vice President John C. West, Waco.
First Waco—Homer Wells, Waco.
Second Waco—J. W. Howard, Waco.
Moody—J. C. Collier, Moody.
Lorena—Chas. W. Evans, Lorena.
Robinson—W. M. Brantley, Robinson.
Hillside—Harlan Matthews, Hillside.
Bethany—Hardy Hay, Bruceville.
Mastersville—A. J. Shelton, Bruceville.

Cow Bayou—P. M. Boten, Mooreville.
Eddy—J. H. Witt, Eddy.
Friendship—G. W. Cunningham, Moody.
Cottonwood—Robert Nix, Mooreville.
Downsville—T. B. Stovall, Downsville.

Third District—Vice President W. E. Bozeman, Baileyville.
Caddo—J. T. Whitehurst, Wilderville.
Pleasant Grove—J. T. Norris, Viesca.
Rosebud—J. T. Glenn, Rosebud.
Center—J. D. McPherson, Marlin.
Durango—I. H. Caudle, Durango.

Fourth District—Vice President W. R. Thompson, West.
West—Henry Johnson, West.
East Waco—C. Faulkner, Waco.
Geneva—J. J. Manley, Elm Mott.
White Rock—James Smith, Ross.
Mart—J. R. Lumpkin, Mart.
Concord—M. L. Bird, Waco.
Independence—W. R. Thompson, West.
Caledonia—A. J. Sparks, Gholson.
Riesel—W. D. Yates, Riesel.
Axtell—Davis St. Clair, Axtell.

At the March meeting, 1896, J. L. Walker submitted to the brethren the importance of organizing a "Texas Baptist Historical Society." This subject was given an hour's discussion at the next Board meeting in West, when the following was unanimously adopted:

"*Resolved*, That there ought to be formed in this state a 'Texas Baptist Historical Society.'"

J. L. Walker and G. W. Truett were appointed to "call the attention of the Association to this action and ask the endorsement of the Association." This was done, and the Association approved the plan. Whereupon a committee, consisting of J. L. Walker, G. W. Truett and I. P. Langley, were appointed to memorialize the Baptist General Convention on this subject.

The memorial was read before the convention in session in Houston, October 13, 1896.

The following was adopted by the convention:

"*Resolved*, That in response to the memorial of the Waco Association 1, That we deem the matter presented of great importance; and 2, that a committee of five be appointed by the chair with J. M. Carroll as chairman, to consider this question in all its phases and report at the next session of this body, and in the mean time using such means as they shall elect to collect and preserve documents." The president appointed as the committee provided for by this action J. M. Carroll, J. A. Shackleford, J. L. Walker, R. C. Burleson and S. J. Anderson.

Honorable and touching mention was made by the Association of the death of Elder J. M. Wright and Elder H. D. Gilbert, "two of our much loved ministers."

We give extracts from the very excellent reports adopted at this session of the Association.

Extract from report on State Missions: "The increase in our population by birth and immigration has greatly outstripped our mission extension. This ever increasing destitution should urge Christians to greater effort and larger liberality. * * * We console ourselves too much by considering the vast increase of the Baptist brotherhood in numbers. The population of Texas is outgrowing the increase of our membership. Our fathers laid foundation work and built wisely. They moved off grandly, but, brethren, are we accelerating the speed with which they started? * * * There is encouragement in the fact that some of our mission stations have not been chargeable to the Board since July, having reported self-supporting. * * * Our State Board reports 66 missionaries; white Americans, 57; Germans, 5; Mexican, 1; Swedes, 2; Chinese, 1. All these faithful men of God look to you to relieve their physical wants." This report was written by Andrew Goddard.

Extract from report on Sabbath Desecration: "Remember the Sabbath day to keep it holy. * * * No other commandment in the decalogue, not even the first, is introduced with the Father's uplifted hand, warning us to remember it. Reverence for the sanctuary with all the institutions of the Christian religion stand or fall, with obedience to this command."

Extract from report on Home Missions: "The Home Board, at Atlanta, Ga., is the backbone of the Southern Baptist Convention and the special benefactor of Texas. Its mission is to provide for all such destitution in the South as transcends the ability or willingness of state boards. To this is added the enormous work in Cuba. The states and territories west of the Mississippi are, none of them, able to cope with their local destitution. * * * We declare as an Association that gratitude for favors received, loyalty to our Savior and our own continued needs alike commend the work of this Board to the favor and co-operation of our churches; and we do now urge upon pastors and churches to see to it that all our congregations set apart a day especially for home missions." Geo. W. Truett.

All the pastors present promised to set apart a day to preach on Home Missions and take collections.

Extract from report on Ministerial Education: "While it is true that many uneducated men have been blessed of God in preaching his true gospel, yet this but emphasizes the fact that properly educated men could have done more and better service. In order that young men who, in the judgment of their churches, have been called to preach, may have the benefits of a literary course and proper training in Bible study, the Baptists of Texas founded Baylor University. In the Bible department, conducted by Dr. B. H. Carroll, they find ample opportunity for instruction in the study of the scriptures. We earnestly recommend that our people support this their own institution with their patronage, their prayers and their contributions." The Southern Baptist Theological Seminary, at Louisville, was also commended, but with special mention that "we are inclined to the opinion that Texas Baptists are against Dr. W. H. Whitsitt (president of the Seminary), both as to his facts of history and the manner and medium of their expression."—J. B. Scarborough.

Extracts from report on Temperance: "Believing prohibition to be the speediest and surest means of securing temperance, we declare in favor of prohibition in county, state and nation."—R. E. Smith.

Extract from report on Schools and Education: Higher education by the state is a modern idea. * * * Baylor University was a mighty power in the formative period of Texas history, when the state had no colleges. Baylor University originated the plan of a Bible department which teaches the Bible itself to both sexes and all classes. We are happy to note that several Southern Baptist colleges have followed this example. Baylor University has now a better corps of teachers and is doing better college work than ever before in its history."—Geo. W. Truett.

Extract from report on Foreign Missions: The term "Foreign," as used among Christians is borrowed from secular and mercantile vernacular, where it implies and refers to those living under different governments, and owing distinct allegiance each to his own recognized ruler, as distinguished from every other ruler and sovereign on earth. But Christians, as such, have but one Lord and King, to whom all on earth, everywhere, owe allegiance without regard to mercantile boundaries or civil jurisdiction. * * * We think there is no difference between our obligations, to give and to sympathize with both home and foreign missions. There will be neither life, nor health, nor strength, nor progress in either without our prayers and gifts."—Jno. C. West.

Extract from report on Buckner Orphan's Home: "This property is inalienable. Surely all Texas should feel proud of such a home, and especially so when we remember the fact that about 1,500, without father or mother, homeless and penniless, have found at this home a place to lay their little heads, clothed when cold, fed when hungry, and when sick nursed and provided for by loving hands and tender hearts."

Waco Association for sixteen years has taken special joy in contributing to this home.

The saddest night in the history of this home was the night of January 15, 1897. On that night the boys' home burned, and 18 children perished. It was a cold rainy night and almost without clothing more than 100 little motherless orphans scattered about over the prairie, frightened most out of their wits, while many of their companions perished in the flames.

Immediately and in abundance help came from many sources. The Waco Association was in the front in her benevolence. The

First Church, Waco, gave nearly $2,000 in cash and clothing.

Better buildings are to be erected; and may God grant that no such calamity will again befall the Orphans' Home.

During the period from October 1, 1895, to March 1, 1897, J. L. Walker's second incumbency, the churches paid for all purposes the amounts hereinafter stated. The second year of President Walker's second term will not end till the meeting of the Association at Hillside, September 25, 1897. But the amounts paid by the churches to March 1, 1897 (the date when this work goes to press), are here exhibited:

Public collections at Board meetings	79 68
Public collections at Association	102 55
Total	$182 23

Amounts from churches: Axtell, $40.70; Battle, $10; Bethany, $62.32; Bosqueville, $39.90; Caledonia, $45.30; Cow Bayou, $6.75; Caddo, $184.65; China Springs, $20.80; Crawford, $6.50; Concord, $25.25; Downsville, $11.95; Durango, $17.60; East Waco, $840.50; Eddy, $8; Flat Rock, $36.33; Friendship, $17.50; Geneva, $26; Goshen, $4; Hewitt, $35.70; Hillside, $79.55; Independence, $20; Lorena, $52.45; Mart, $243.20; Mastersville, 38.55; McGregor, $30.97; Moody, $155.75; Oak Grove, $10; Pleasant Grove, $5.70; Riesel, $3.30; Robinson, $84.65; Rock Creek, $16.50; Rosebud, $23.80; Shiloh, $13.75; Speegleville, $56.85; First Waco, $5,688.90; Second Waco, $47.10; West $82.50; White Hall, $52.75; White Rock, $17; Gerald (new church), $2.50. Total, $8,148.52.

Total from public collections	$ 182 23
Add to this profits realized from sales of books by missionary	106 57
Total	$8,437 32

The grand total for all denominational enterprises, and from all sources, during eighteen months of J. L. Walker's second administration (October 1, 1896, to March 1, 1897), was $8,437.32.

WACO BAPTIST ASSOCIATION.

GENERAL SUMMARY.

Before the organization of the Associational Mission Board in 1874 the amounts credited to churches (from 1860 to 1874) were as follows:

Antioch (Limestone), $7; Beulah, $550; Blue Ridge, $50; Bosqueville, $134.60; Bremond, $47.35; Concord, $15; Cow Bayou, $243.74; East Waco, $40.75; Greenwood, $18.90; Hope, $1.25; Marlin, $260.90; Mastersville, $46.80; New Hope, $152.45; Rock Creek, $9; Robinson, $70.75; Salem (Limestone), $25; White Hall, $26; White Rock, $24.35; First Waco, $1,871.16; West (Bold Springs), $39.60. Total, $3,634.60.

The amounts from all sources and for all purposes (denominational) and not credited to the churches (1860-1874) foot up $1,174.35. That is the whole amount raised in the Association for all purposes (not including money for minutes or home church expenses) from 1860 to 1874, is..............$ 4,809 35

Whole amount for all denominational purposes during B. H. Carroll's first administration as president of the Board (1874-1888)....... ....$28,956 89

Whole amount for all denominational purposes during J. R. M. Touchstone's administration (1888-1889)..... ... . 1,885 37

Whole amount for all denominational purposes during B. H. Carroll's second administration (1889-1892)..... .... 15,968 31

Whole amount for all denominational purposes during J. L. Walker's first administration (1892-1894).... .... 12,864 08

Whole amount for all denominational purposes during B. J. Kendrick's administration (1894-1895). 5,264 75

Whole amount for all denominational purposes during J. L. Walker's second administration from October 1, 1895, to March 1, 1897 (incomplete).. 8,437 32

Grand total for all denominational purposes from November 9, 1860, to March 1, 1897..............$78,186 07

This does not include sums for minutes, pastors' salaries or home church expenses.

All moneys have not been reported. Of course the figures here given relate only to sums reported to the Association.

The whole amounts paid by churches during their connection with the Association for denominational purposes are the following: Antioch (Bosque), —; Antioch (Limestone), $42.60; Axtell, $40.70; Battle, $103.70; Beulah, $431; Bethel, —; Bethany, $119.72; Blue Ridge, $488.94; Bosqueville, $751.25; Bremond, $160.35; Caddo, $629.65; Caledonia, $45.30; Carolina, $63.75; Center, $198.98; Chilton, $176.82; China Springs, $107.70; Concord, $236.17; Cottonwood, $75.65; Cottonwood German, $25; Cow Bayou, $511.75; Crawford, $42.80; Deer Creek, $244.81; Downsville, $11.95; Durango, $138.65; East Waco, $3,103.01; Ebenezer, —; Eddy, $267.15; Eldorado, $15.80; Flat Rock, $81.48; Friendship, $30.75; Geneva, $226.14; Golinda, $56.10; Goshen, $17.25; Greenwood, $45.60; Gerald not yet joined the Association), $2.50; Hillside, $322.62; Hewitt, $35.70; Hope, $75.05; Harris Creek, —; Independence, $20; Kirk, $99; Liberty, $175.04; Little Deer Creek, $67.15; Live Oak, $254.10; Lorena, $153.70; Lone Oak, $29.50; Lott, $62.52; Marlin, $833.65; Mart, $763; Mastersville, $388.43; Mexia, $85.25; Mount Antioch, $179.90; Mount Calm, $126.30; Mount Zion, $5; McGregor, $323.52; Moody, $571.71; New Hope, $119; New Zion, $45.35; Olive Branch, $299.12; Oak Grove, $41.65; Pleasant Grove, $194.90; Prairie Hill, $17.10; Reagan, $317.60; Riesel, $3.30; Robinson, $830.15; Rock Creek, $372.85; Rosebud, $125.45; Salem, $30.75; Searsville, $8; Shiloh, $68.75; Speegleville, $144.45; Union, $56.45; Union Springs, —; West, $887.65; White Hall, $756.90; White Rock, $310.08; First Waco, $33,684.71; Second Waco, $295; Waco German, $164.50.

The whole number baptized into all the churches during the first decade was 525; during the second decade, 1,758; during the third decade, 1,929; during the fourth decade, 3,273. The total baptisms reported from 1860 to 1896 are 7,585. These figures do not express the entire number of baptisms. Often churches were not represented, and in such cases no statistics were reported. There was no statistical table printed with the minutes of 1880. We have no means of finding the number baptized that year. If all the baptisms had been reported the figures would have approximated 8,000. The largest number baptized in one year was 594 in 1891.

The Baptist membership in the Association is at present near 4,300.

There are Sunday schools connected with most of the churches. The schools with superintendents are as follows: Bethany, G. M. Nix; Bosqueville, W. H. Gorham; Caledoma, J. P. Kenedy; Downsville, W. R. Smith; Durango, S. T. Belt; Flat Rock, C. H. Creighton; Geneva, G. M. Powers; Hillside, J. M. Kendrick; McGregor, T. D. Johnson; Moody, S. W. Miller; Mastersville, T. J. Mixon; Mart, H. T. Vaughn; Robinson, John Moore; Shiloh, John Roland; Speegleville, J. F. Dashner; White Hall, L. A. Trice; White Rock, W. H. Edwards; West, I. C. Bates; First Waco, W. H. Jenkins; Second Waco, Sam Stewart; East Waco, C. Faulkner.

Following are the ordained ministers of the Association, 1896-7: B. H. Carroll, J. B. Reaves, W. D. Bowen, T. E. Muse, S. R. Williams, G. W. Truett, J. C. F. Kyger, John G. Kendall, R. C. Burleson, M. L. Davis, S. L. Morris, R. J. Grant, S. B. McJunkin, W. E. Britton, J. L. H. Hawkins, J. H. Roberts, John Bateman, J. B. Cranfill, L. J. Mims, J. S. Crossland, E. L. Compere, H. R. Best, C. P. Lumpkin, J. H. H. Ellis, Waco; G. W. North, A. J. Shelton, Bruceville; T. P. Walker, Robinson; E. F. Brock, Durango; A. J. Moore, Downsville; J. L. Walker, B. F. Tatum, C. C. Hardwick, T. D. Suttle, Mart; M. Breeden, Lorena; John Witt, Eddy; G. G. Gibson, Mooreville; J. M. B. Gresham, Crawford; R. E. Smith, W. F. Shumate, Ryan; T. P. Speakman, W. H. Park, West; R C. Medaris, Moody; D. E. Adams, China Springs; J. M. Dean, Erath; C. R. Osborne, M. Isbel, M. H. Curry, S. I. Caldwell, J. B. Smith, McGregor.

The following churches own houses of worship: Bosqueville, $1,000; Bethany, $800; Cow Bayou, $1,000; Caledonia, $800; Crawford, $1,000; Downsville, $1,000; Eddy, $2,000; Geneva, $1,000; Hewitt, $1,500; Hillside, $1,500; Lorena, $1,500; McGregor, $1,800; Moody, $10,000; Mastersville, $2,000; Mart $1,200; Pleasant Grove, $600; Rosebud, $800; Robinson, $800; Speegleville, $600; Shiloh, $800; White Hall, $1,000; White Rock, $1,000; First Waco, $40,000; Second Waco, $1,000; East Waco, $8,000; Caddo, $1,000.

The Waco Association is not yet nearly so well organized for work as it should be. We believe, under the blessing of God, our people are abundantly able to pay $10,000 per annum toward carrying on the great work of evangelizing the world. Our prayers are that this figure may be reached in the near future, and that the Association shall go on ever increasing her work till Christ shall come.

APPENDIX.

HISTORY

OF

PARENT ASSOCIATIONS

AND

GENERAL BODIES,

FOLLOWED BY

HISTORICAL SKETCHES OF ALL THE CHURCHES

With Sketches of Many Prominent Individuals,
Pastors, Deacons, Leaders and
Foundation Builders.

EMBELLISHED WITH

A GREAT PROFUSION OF ELEGANT CUTS.

INTRODUCTORY.

BRIEF HISTORICAL VIEW OF PARENT ASSOCIATIONS AND GENERAL BODIES.

UNION ASSOCIATION.

The first Baptist Association in Texas was Union Association.

In October, 1840, at the little town of Travis, in Washington county, messengers from three churches met and organized Union Association. The first moderator was Elder T. W. Cox, who afterwards became a Campbellite. J. W. Collins was chosen clerk and R. E. B. Baylor corresponding secretary.

The three churches were Independence, which had at that time 17 members; Travis, with 13 members, and LaGrange with 15 members. The delegates from Independence were J. J. Davis, John McNeese and Thomas Tremmier, from Travis; W. H. Cleveland, J. W. Collins and James Hall, from LaGrange; T. W. Cox, R. E. B. Baylor, J. L. Davis and J. L. Lester.

Old Union Association has done a grand work for the Master. She still exists in South Texas, comprising most of the territory of Austin, Washington, Fort Bend, Brazoria, Harris, Grimes, Waller and Galveston counties. She has 39 churches, with a total membership of 1,402.

TRINITY RIVER ASSOCIATION

is the daughter of Union Association and the mother of Waco Association.

In 1835 in all that vast territory afterwards Trinity River Association there were not more than half a dozen Baptists. But one white family lived within the present limits of Leon county. Brother Robert Rogers, a Baptist, settled on Rogers' Prairie in the fall of 1835. He was the first. He died there July 18, 1871. Prior to building school houses, his rude log dwelling was often used as a place for preaching by any and all denominations who chanced to pass that way. Here Elder Z. N. Morrell at a very early day did some effectual preaching.

Later a few others located fifteen miles east. These settlers erected a small log house to be used for school and preaching purposes. Within the four walls of this log house was organized the first Baptist church in all that vast territory, Leona church. The early settlers at Leona were W. P. Evans (still living), Col. W. C. Fowler, Dr. J. C. Boggs, C. L. Dotson, Judge William Childress, Tom Davis, H. H. Hazeltine, John Beeming, —. Langham, Alexander Patrick, W. Carr, J. Copeland and J. J. Bell (still living). These were all heads of families. The country continued to settle at various points, as Springfield, Waco, Marlin, etc.

In the autumn of 1845 Eld. Z. N. Morrell received an appointment from the Domestic Mission Board at Marion, Ala., to travel as missionary over this territory at $250 per annum. He was then living in Milam county. From his home to Leona was sixty miles and three streams in the way, Brazos, Little Brazos and Navasota. The reader will remember there were no roads or bridge in this wilderness. From Leona his route lay through a trackless desert fifty miles north to Springfield; from Springfield fifty miles east to Navarro county, and from Navarro to his home 100 miles. This circuit he made each month for twelve months through a wilderness infested with wild beasts and savages, without missing a single appointment. He had no minister to co-operate with him except Elder N. T. Byars, who lived then on Richland creek, in Navarro county.

In July, 1848, messengers from six churches met with Providence church in Navarro county and organized Trinity River Association. Elder Z. N. Morrell was the first moderator, Alexander Patrick, secretary; N. T. Byars, corresponding secretary; C. B. Roberts, treasurer. The six original churches were Leona, Society Hill, Springfield, Union Hill, Corsicana and Providence. This Association grew, and in 1859 numbered 30 churches and a total membership of 1,009. Elder Michael Ross was at that time moderator and J. W. Speight clerk.

The Association had her school, Trinity River Classical, at Waco, a book depository at Waco, and another at Springfield.

At present she has but 28 churches, nearly all of them in Leon county. The present membership is 1,194.

BAPTIST STATE CONVENTION.

At the meeting of Union Association in 1847, when that body was seven years old, a committee was appointed to correspond with the churches of Texas and ascertain their wishes in regard to forming a state convention. Responses were favorable, and a call made to meet September 8, 1848, at Anderson, Grimes county. Delegates were present from 20 churches. Elder Z. N. Morrell preached the introductory sermon from Isa. 9:7, "Of the increase of his government and peace there shall be no end."

The convention organized by electing Henry L. Graves president; J. W. D. Creath, Hosea Garrett and J. W. Huckins, vice presidents: R. C. Burleson, corresponding secretary; J. G. Thomas, recording secretary, and J. W. Barnes, treasurer.

The convention at that time embraced all Texas. The whole number of missionaries employed by the convention from September 8, 1848, till the consolidation, June 29, 1886, was nearly 400. The total collections during the same period amount to nearly $200,000.

BAPTIST CONVENTION OF EASTERN TEXAS.

When the State Convention met at Marshall in 1852, the Baptists of Eastern Texas proposed to establish a female school at Tyler, and asked the patronage of the convention. The proposition did not meet with favor in that body. Because their proposition was pushed aside, discontent sprang up, which three years later culminated in the organization of the "Texas Baptist General Association," at Larissa, Cherokee county, in 1853. Elder I. H. Lane was made president. There was dissatisfaction all over Texas with the name. So an "adjourned meeting" convened at Tyler, May 24, 1855, dissolved, and then formed the "Eastern Texas Baptist Convention." There were messengers present from 24 churches. Elder W. H. Stokes was elected president and William Davenport secretary. This convention continued in existence till October 13, 1867, when in a "called meeting" at Tyler a motion prevailed unanimously to change the name to

"THE GENERAL ASSOCIATION OF TEXAS."

At this meeting when the Eastern Texas Convention resolved itself into the General Association there were delegates from the following associations: Waco, Rehoboth, Sister Grove, Richland, Elm Fork, Saline, Cherokee and Soda Lake; also from Ebenezer and Tyler churches.

General James E. Harrison was elected president; W. B. Featherstone, W. C. Buck and R. C. Burleson, vice presidents; J. A. Hand, recording secretary, and J. W. Speight, treasurer.

The revised constitution provided for three boards. They were located as follows: The Sunday school board at Marshall, the missionary board at Ladonia, and the Bible, Colportage and Educational board at Waco. R. C. Burleson resigned his office as vice president and was immediately elected corresponding secretary. He continued coresponding secretary five years and was seven years president. R. C. Buckner was president five years. The last president was L. L. Foster.

The Eastern Texas Convention employed in all 27 missionaries and collected a total of $5,692.23. The General Association, 1868-1886, employed 178 missionaries and collected $46,512.36.

THE EAST TEXAS CONVENTION.

Delegates from 19 churches met at Overton December 12, 1877, and again organized for the purpose of doing missionary work in East Texas, or as they expressed it: "Do our own work in our own way, as best we can. Elder E. A. Clemmons was elected president and George Yarbrough secretary.

A Board was appointed with W. O. Bailey as corresponding secretary. This convention continued to exist till 1884, and employed 46 missionaries all told. Their total collections amounted to $13,639.56. F. A. Whaley was coresponding secretary four years, Dock Pegues two years and Tully Choice the last year.

THE NORTH TEXAS CONVENTION.

This body was organized at Allen, October 19, 1879. Afterwards only four meetings were held. The presidents were W. L. Williams, J. K. Bumpass, I. M. Kimbro, W. E. Penn. No corresponding secretary was ever appointed. O. C. Pope was general agent two years. Missionaries, 14; collections, $1,825.55.

THE CENTRAL TEXAS ASSOCIATION.

The teritory occupied by this body was west of the Brazos, south of Clear Fork and north of Lampasas. It was organized November 12, 1880, at Doublin.

Seventeen churches were enrolled, one Association and nine brethren not appointed by churches. These formed themselves into a convention to advance mission and Sunday school interests. There were only four meetings after the organization. The corresponding secretaries were J. T. Harris, G. W. Clark, C. L. Graves and J. C. O'Bryan. Missionaries, 11; collections, $1,192.56.

The whole number of missionaries employed by all the general bodies prior to consolidation (1886) was 617, and the grand total collections, $255,698.30.

THE BAPTIST GENERAL CONVENTION

was the result of the consolidation of all general bodies into one in 1886, except the Sunday School and Colportage Convention. With the consolidation of these bodies came also the consolidation of Baylor University at Independence with Waco University. The consolidated University was located at Waco, and the Female College at Belton. Besides trustees for Baylor University and for Baylor College, two boards were appointed board of directors and ministers' relief board. The corresponding secretaries have been A. J. Holt, J. B. Cranfill, J. M. Carroll, M. D. Early and J. B. Gambrell. The presidents have been A. T. Spalding, L. L. Foster, R. C. Burleson and R. C.

Buckner. The board of directors has been located at Waco from the first.

The whole number of missionaries supported by the General Convention is 1,147; collections, $365,715.72. This added to the number of missionaries and amounts collected by all general bodies gives the following results of missionary effort by the Baptists of Texas from September, 1848, till March, 1897: missionaries, 1,764; and grand total collections $621,414.02. Of course these figures are below the real amount as they include only sums reported to the general bodies, and do not include work by the Sunday school and Colportage convention.

The ministers' relief board referred to above has been abolished and that work, with all mission interests, is now under the supervision of the board of directors.

This brief sketch of general bodies is given because that, in the consolidation the board was located at Waco and has been ever since in immediate touch with the Waco Association.

DEACON JAMES A. AKIN.

A native of Mississippi and an early emigrant to Texas, Deacon Akin, is a fine type of that generation of faithful Baptists, now fast passing away. He was born August 9, 1823. In 1850 he was buried in baptism by Elder U. H. Parker, and became a member of Shady Grove church, Bradley county, Arkansas. In 1854 he came to Robertson county, Texas, and united with Sterling church. He was married to Miss M. S. Woodward in 1859, and in 1865 was in the organization of Port Sullivan church, Milam county. By this church he was made deacon, Elders R. C. Burleson and T. M. Anderson acting as presbytery. He is now a member of Mart church.

In antebelum days Brother Akin was much prospered of the Lord in worldly possessions, but now he is poor in this world's goods, though rich in grace. He has been faithful to his church, his pastor and his Master. He led Elder C. P. Lumpkin down to the baptismal water in 1865, and has ever since been esteemed by Elder Lumpkin as a brother beloved of the Lord. His race is nearly run, he is waiting the Master's call.

ELDER JOHN SEABORN ALLEN.

Few men of his generation were truer or more consecrated than John S. Allen. He was born in Spartenburg District, S. C., July 9, 1830. He grew up in Calhoun county, Alabama, his parents having moved there in 1836. In early life he gave his heart to Christ and was laid in the baptismal grave by Elder Sterling G. Jenkins. A happy matrimonial alliance was formed

. ELD. JOHN S. ALLEN.

with Miss L. J. Park, November 4, 1852. Soon afterward they came to Texas and settled near Lexington in Lee county. Here Brother Allen engaged in farming and stock raising on an extensive scale.

Profoundly impressed with the duty of preaching the gospel of Christ, he was ordained to the office of New Testament bishop, by authority of Prospect Baptist church, Elders Hosea Garrett, R. C. Burleson, R. B. Burleson, J. G. Thomas and W. B.

Eaves serving as the presbytery. The Bible presented him by R. B. Burleson at his ordination as "the sword of the spirit," was his life-long weapon, and was used at his funeral, Waco, November 24, 1887.

As missionary of the Baptist State Convention he organized churches in Burleson, Bastrop, Bell, Coryell, Hamilton and McLennan counties, then the exposed frontier of Texas. He was much concerned about the education of his children, and moved to Waco for that purpose in 1873. Dr. Burleson said his removal to Waco located in that city "not less than $200,000 capital." After coming to Waco he became pastor of surrounding churches and was faithful as a pastor till the day of his death. His last work was with East Waco and Lorena churches. During his first year as pastor of White Hall he baptized 36. During his 14 years residence at Waco he was a leading spirit of the Waco Association. Much of the success of the Association is due to him. At the time of his death he was the Association's moderator. He was a member of the Board of Trustees of Baylor University at Waco, and of the building committee, where during 18 months he contributed most valuable services. He was a member of the Bible and Colportage Board of the General Association before the consolidation, and after the consolidation, a member of the Board of directors of the General Convention.

In the Historical and Biographical Magazine Dr. R. C. Burleson is quoted: "Bro. Allen had many pre-eminent virtues that all should admire and appreciate, especially young preachers. First, he had almost immaculate sincerity and purity of character, and a burning desire to maintain it spotless before God and man. Second, honesty and promptness in all matters of business. He observed the golden rule, 'Owe no man anything but love; pay as you go.' Third, his undying devotion to the cause of Christ. He was always watching and ever ready to seize the golden opportunity to do good. * * * Fourth, in tenderness and love he was a model father and husband, and no man was ever more blessed in his family. His sons and daughters are models of propriety—just what every preacher's children should be according to God's command to preachers. 1 Tim. 3:4."

In October, 1883, Bro. Allen sustained his heaviest stroke, which was the loss of his wife. "She had been a worthy, helping, sympathizing companion through all the toiling, trying years of his life. His second wife, Maggie Davis Allen, to whom he was married July, 1885, survives him, and is a member of the East Waco Baptist church. A tribute to Elder Allen, written by J. L. Walker, appears on the minutes of the Waco Association, 1888, from which we quote: "(1.) His first pastorate in Waco Association was with White Hall church, commencing here with six members, his eight years' work resulted in building a strong church of 120 members. The substantial church edifice at White Hall was built during his pastorate. (2.) His brief pastorate at Robinson was greatly blessed and appreciated. (3.) His noble work a East Waco, six years, greatly developed and strengthened the church, more than doubling her membership. (4) He died pastor of East Waco and Lorena. He is most tenderly and affectionately remembered. (5) His grand work as a member of the Board of Directors of the Baptist General Convention from its organization to the end of his life, appears when we state that he never failed to attend a meeting."

ELDER T. S. ALLEN.

This brother was born in Clark county, Ky., April, 1816, was born again in Howard county, Mo., 1838. He was baptized by Elder William Duncan, who was baptized by Elder James Ireland, while the latter was confined in Culpepper jail, Virginia, for religious opinions. Bro. Allen was married to a Christian young lady, Miss Malinda Balteton, Boone county, Mo., who remained a faithful Baptist till her death, March 26, 1891. He was ordained by the Baptist church at Brunswick, Mo., May, 1847. A book falling into his hands decided him to be a life colporter. Receiving an appointment as missionary of Mt. Pleasant Association in connection with the American Baptist Publication Society, he continued this work till 1864, during which time he baptized nearly 600 persons, and organized 50 churches. He came to Texas in the fall of 1864. He organized the First church, Dallas, and later was pastor of Macedonia and Caldwell churches in Burleson county, and other churches. He baptized Elder J. M. Carroll. He labored as an early pioneer over some of the territory now occupied by the Waco Association. He is now 81 years old, but is still doing work for the Master, as missionary of the Sunday School and Colportage Convention.

HON. JAS. M. ANDERSON

was born in Moulton, Ala., July 30, 1824. His father, Edward A., who was a native of Virginia, moved to Moulton, Tenn., and died, when his son was only two years old. The boy was educated at Corrick Academy, Winchester, Tenn., and at Cumberland University, Lebanon, Tenn. He afterwards taught school and studied law under Judge Nathan Greer, Chief Justice of Tennessee. When 24 years old he came to Rusk county, Texas, and practiced law 15 years, in partnership with Judge S. P. Donley. His business prospered. He was first married in Tennessee in 1849, to Miss Jane Buckhannan, who died in 1850. He was again married in Rusk, Texas, October 26, 1851, to Miss Winfrey Polk, daughter of Andrew Polk, who was cousin to President James K. Polk. Six children have blessed this union, who have all been well educated and who fill positions of honor and respect. Bro. Anderson united with the First Baptist church, Waco, in 1872, and continued a faithful and efficient member till his death, June 3, 1889. His death was a severe loss to his family, to Waco and to Texas. His manly bearing and fidelity to principle will ever be cherished by those who knew him best, as worthy of imitation. He was six feet, two and one-half inches high, and weighed 190 pounds. Once, supplying the place of Gov. R. B. Hubbard as speaker, he humorously opened by remarking, "Though Gov. Hubbard is absent, the audience may console themselves with the reflection that they have for speaker a man of higher standing, if not of equal weight.' His individuality was characterized by more than ordinary will power, firmness and independence. A beautiful poem, written by his daughter, Mrs. Lula Anderson Kimbrough, entitled, "In Memory of My Father, Col. James M. Anderson," begins thus:

" Once, in the long ago, a child came down
To dwell among the people here on earth.
He grew as other little children grow,
Playful at times and again at times self-willed,
Till at length he came to manhood's high estate.
Then as the days passed slowly into weeks,
The weeks to months, and months to slower years,
This man, who had appeared as other men,
Grew more and more into a noble man.
In learning and piety none lived that did excel him."

The poem closes sweetly:

"And yonder somewhere, somehow, he will know
How much we love him ere we tell him so."

ANTIOCH CHURCH No. 1.

This church came into the Association in October, 1862, with 20 members. It had at that time been but recently organized. It was in the northeast part of Bosque county. F. A. Mound, of Fort Graham, was pastor. The petitionary letter was borne by Elder W. A. Mason. The next year the Association met with Antioch. It was war times, and no church was represented save Antioch and Searsville. B. E. Lucas was pastor at this time, and the church reported a fine revival, with 20 additions by baptism. It is supposed that Antioch soon afterwards ceased to exist.

ANTIOCH CHURCH No. 2

was in the southern part of Limestone county, and was quite a strong church when it united with the Association in 1872, having at that time 51 members. This church was the result of some excellent work in that section by Elder R. F. Mattison, who was also its first pastor. It was organized about 1870. In 1872 the brethren enjoyed a fine revival, during which there were 15 additions by baptism. In 1873 the membership was 71. In 1875 Elder A. W. Middleton was pastor and W. C.

Manning in 1876-7. This church was dismissed in fellowship and order in 1877.

AXTELL CHURCH.

The town of Axtell is situated on Woodland ridge and on the Cotton Belt Railroad, 13 miles east of Waco. The church was constituted May 19, 1895. Six members entered into the covenant. The officiating presbytery were Elders V. G. Cunningham, J. W. A. Seale and Frank Marres. The articles of faith and church covenant found in Pendleton's Church Manual were adopted by the church. Elder Frank Marres accepted the call of the church till a permanent pastor could be secured. W. C. Morgan was chosen clerk.

August 24, 1895, Elder J. L. Ward was chosen pastor, and J. G. Blakely associational board member. The church paid $35 for missions and other benevolent objects. This was more than $1 per member. Perhaps not one church in a hundred, so young, has made a better record.

The church came into the Association at the McGregor meeting, September, 1895, with 30 members.

On July 25, Pastor J. L. Ward resigned and J. S. Crosslin was chosen pastor September 7, 1896. David St. Clair is the present clerk.

Axtell church is eligibly located in a prosperous community and flourishing little town. We bespeak for the church a career of great usefulness in the Master's service.

HON. T. P. AYCOCK.

Thomas Paulain Aycock was appointed as a delegate from the Marlin church, which was one of the constituent members of the Waco Association, but for some reason he failed to attend on that occasion. For many years after the Association was organized he gave it his hearty co-operation and support. He was born at Herman, Clark county, Georgia, May 25, 1830; was eldest son of R. M. Aycock and Ann W. Aycock. In his infancy his parents moved from middle Georgia, to La-Fayette, Walker county—then "Cherokee country"—in the extreme northern tier of counties of that state. Here his education was begun, and at quite an early age, he gave promise of a more than ordinary mind. He was sent to school at Cave Springs, Whitfield county, Georgia, and was a boarder in the household of Rev. Zachariah Gordon, a prominent Baptist divine of that day, and who was General John B. Gordon's father. At Cave Springs he advanced rapidly, and was prepared to enter

REV. T. P. AYCOCK.

the junior class at the East Tennessee University, Knoxville, where he graduated with the class of 1850, winning the distinction of delivering the valedictory. While at Knoxville, Tenn., he was converted, and joined the Baptist church, making glad the hearts of his parents and friends. Returning to LaFayette, he did not stay long at home, though very young, but went almost immediately to Houston, Chickasaw county, Miss. Here teaching school, and reading law by turns, he prepared himself, and was in 1851 admitted to the bar. May 6, 1852, he married Miss Mary Jane Steele, daughter of Capt. R. G. Steele, of Houston, Miss. In 1854 they migrated to Texas, and settled at Marlin, Falls county. Here he began his professional life, with flattering prospects, and soon his forensic powers attracted attention, and he received the confidence and the patronage of a goodly clientage. In 1856 he was elected to the lower house of the Texas legislature. While in the legislature, among other useful measures he warmly espoused the "University Bill," and saw the fulfillment of its rich endowment in land, but did not live to see its consummation in granite, nor its generous enrollment of Texas youths.

As one of the members of the Marlin Baptist church (having been enrolled among the first of this band of pioneer Baptists), he was ever afterwards identified with them, and in 1857, for his zeal and aptitude in the Scriptures, was by his brethren licensed to preach.

He was full of the eloquent fervor of a true leader of Zion, and before the war it was his intention to quit the law and enter fully into the ministry, but his secular affairs interrupted, and soon afterwards the war disarranged his plans. Notwithstanding this, he did much preaching. At Calvert in 1873, among his neighbors, a notable revival, participated in by him, took place, when many of Calvert's business men made profession of religion. His private life and example always exerted a marked effect for good.

Having in 1873, lost his life's companion, he from this time began to fail in health, and left his five children at Calvert, and went direct to Los Angeles, Cal., in the hope of regaining his health. From this time—the winter of 1875—only a few short months remained for him on earth. Two thousand miles from his soon to be orphaned children, he spent the few more days alloted him. But into them were crowded years of agonized suspense. In a letter to his aged mother, he wrote, that he was prepared, and that he longed for the rest he knew awaited him. On the 1st day of April, A. D. 1876, he passed away. The Masonic lodge at Los Angeles, Cal., buried his remains in their cemetery.

BAYLOR UNIVERSITY

is the oldest educational institution in Texas. It was first located at Independence, Texas, 1845, and was removed to Waco in 1886, and consolidated with Waco University. It has matriculated over 8,000 students, and graduated 534. It is the pioneer co-educational school in the South, and second in America, and the third in the world. It is the property of the Baptist General Convention of Texas, representing 273,000 Baptists.

Baylor University was founded in the stormy days of the Republic of Texas, after the Fall of the Alamo and before

BAYLOR UNIVERSITY AT WACO.

the annexation of the Republic of Texas to the United States. While the chaos of a bloody revolution reigned over nine-tenths of her territory, while there was not a railroad nor a telegraph line, our Baptist fathers, few, poor and widely scattered, laid the foundation of this great institution.

In 1842, six years after the battle of San Jacinto, the Union Association, in session on Clear Creek, Fayette county, resolved to found a great Baptist University. Among the leading spirits in that enterprise, were Rev. Wm. M. Tryon, a native of New York; Rev. Jas. Huckins, a native of New Hampshire, and the

Hon. R. E. B. Baylor, a native of Kentucky, eminent as a United States Congressman, a learned jurist and a Baptist preacher. These illustrious men, with their co-laborers, formed a Texas Baptist Educational Society, in order to develop and concentrate the best talent of the infant Republic on the contemplated University. In 1845 this society procured the charter and located the institution at Independence, Washington county, then near the center of population, and a village noted for beautiful scenery, fertile soil and highly cultured people. Among the early trustees were such eminent men as Judge R. E. B. Baylor, after whom the University was named, Wm. M. Tryon, Jas. Huckins, Hon. A. S. Lipscomb, Supreme Judge, Gov. A. C. Horton, Albert G. Haynes and Rev. Hosea Garrett.

The infant University was what Jefferson called the University of Virginia in his day, "*Universitas in Ovo.*" But from that "*ovo*" was to come the young eagle that should soar aloft above the clouds and storms of adversity, and bask in the sunlight of usefulness and glory.

In the same year (1845) Professor Henry F. Gillett was elected the first teacher, and the Preparatory School was opened in a two-story building, 30x50 feet, at that time quite an imposing structure for Texas, which was soon crowded to overflowing. Military drill was also inaugurated. In 1847, Rev. Henry L. Graves, a graduate of the University of North Carolina, and also of Madison University, New York, was elected President. In 1850, a second building was erected, 50x65 feet. But at the close of the annual examination of 1851, unfortunate complications and divisions having arisen, the President and all the teachers resigned. Fortunately, the morning after the resignation, the Baptist Convention, which had in the meantime adopted the institution, met at Independence, and, after two days of earnest prayer and deliberation, Rev. Rufus C. Burleson was chosen as the successor of Dr. Graves. Dr. Burleson was then 28 years old, having spent seven years preparing for his life work in Nashville University, in teaching a select school in Mississippi, and in the Theological Seminary of Covington, Ky. This "*Universitas in Ovo,*" with its young President, opened September 1, 1851, with three professors and two female teachers; with fifty-three students, thirty male and twenty-three female. The first regular College Class graduated in 1856. Dr. Burleson conducted the affairs of Baylor University for ten years, conferring in the meantime twenty-eight diplomas in the Literary and twenty-nine in the Law Department. The Law Department was organized in 1857, with a faculty of pre-eminent ability, composed of Hon. R. T. Wheeler, Supreme Judge, Hon. R. E. B Baylor, Gen. Wm. P. Rodgers and Hon. John Sayles.

At this juncture the educational stream divided. The citizens of Independence and Washington refused to co-operate with the Houston and Texas Central Railroad in running their Austin branch through Washington and Independence. Dr. Burleson and his associates, seeing that Independence would become isolated and inaccessible, resigned and laid the foundation of Waco University at Waco. The dear old College at Independence struggled on from 1861 to 1885. Rev. G. W. Baines served as President one year, and conferred one diploma. In 1862, Dr. Wm. Carey Crane became President, and labored with great fidelity and unsurpassed ability until his death, a period of twenty-three years, during which time he conferred fifty-six diplomas. On the death of Dr. Crane, Rev. Dr. Reddin Andrews was elected President and presided one year, conferring one diploma. There were in all, during a period of forty-one years, eighty-six diplomas conferred in the Literary Department and twenty-nine in the Law Department at Independence. In the meantime, from 1861 to 1886, Dr. Burleson was President of Waco University, during which time he conferred two hundred and twenty-six diplomas at Waco.

This institution was at first organically connected with the Trinity River Baptist Association; then with Waco Association, and was afterward organically connected with the Baptist General Association, which had been organized in 1868 and whose territory lay mainly in Central and North Texas, while the Baptist State Convention occupied mainly South Texas.

In 1885, the number of students in Baylor University had been reduced to twenty-eight, and there was a general desire for a consolidation of Baylor and Waco Universities. In 1886, after long and prayerful deliberation, the two institutions were united under the name of Baylor University at Waco, with Dr. Burleson as President. One party conceding the name and the other the locality.

Thus the long parted educational streams were reunited and mingled their waters as of old. In the meantime the two general bodies, the Baptist State Convention and Baptist General Association, were consolidated under the name of the Baptist General Convention of Texas. We thus clearly see that from the beginning the Baptists of Texas have been committed in their whole history by solemn resolutions and liberal donations to the great cause of Christian education. To-day the denomination stands pledged by one thousand holy memories, and by express resolutions and great sacrifices, to build up and endow Baylor University, and make it equal to any institution between the oceans.

The Baptist family in Texas number over 273,000 communicants, extending from the Red River to the Gulf and from the Sabine to the Rio Grande, and nothing is wanting but holy enthusiasm and concentration of effort to make Baylor University the peer of any institution on the continent. The past glorious history of Baylor University should fire the hearts of the whole Baptist family of Texas. It is the only institution in Texas that has survived the storms and perils of the last half a hundred years, during which time over 8,000 students have been instructed and over 500 graduated. It is a glorious fact that a very small per cent. of her students have left her halls unconverted. The great majority of them have gone forth not only thoroughly drilled in intellect, but with hearts full of love to Jesus and humanity. Over 260 young ministers have been educated in Baylor University, many of whom have become bright and shining lights in our Zion. It is also a glorious fact that Baylor students have everywhere attained to positions of great distinction, profit and usefulness, while her daughters have brightened and beautified so many homes in Texas. It is a glorious fact that Baylor University is the pioneer co-education college in the South, and that the greatest Universities in Europe and

America are now gladly adopting this practical and glorious development of our educational systems.

Why should the people of Texas, especially Baptists, patronize this school?

1. Because of the splendid facilities offered, the thoroughness of its course, the scholarship of its faculty; the moral and Christian atmosphere surrounding and pervading the institution, the splendid buildings and beautiful grounds in a city of refinement and culture with all modern advantages.

2. Dr. Burleson, the pioneer of Baptist education in Texas, with his ripe experience and vast store of information, presides, assisted by as able a corps of teachers as was ever assembled in any Southern institution—all Christian men and women, thoroughly imbued with the importance of the work committed to them by the Baptists of Texas, and fully abreast with the times, and keenly alive to the fact that in well developed manhood and womanhood the mental, moral, and physical natures must each in turn receive due attention. Aside from its being the best school in the South, it is the property of Texas Baptists, founded by the fathers, built up and made grand in its proportion by worthy sons of noble sires. It is the heritage of the Baptist children of Texas, blessed of God for their benefit in becoming educated Christians, grand in what has been accomplished and glorious in its future usefulness and greatness.

3. Without endowment these grand accomplishments in the future must depend upon your exertions and patronage. With one-fourth of the annual attendance beneficiaries either (young ministers or ministers' children), it requires the utmost economy and skill to maintain a faculty of such high standing. Will you aid by exerting yourself in its behalf? It requires the united effort of the trustees, faculty, patrons, alumni and friends to maintain and carry forward this great work. Are you aiding in it.—*Baylor Literary.*

ELDER JOHN BATEMAN.

Elder Bateman is a native of Rockingham county, North Carolina; was born August 10, 1822. The family moved to Carroll county, Tenn., in 1825. Young John had an insatiable thirst for knowledge, devoured books as he could find them. He gave himself to Christ and received baptism at the hands of Elder John Martin in 1837, uniting with Mount Comfort Baptist church. His inquiry, "Lord, what wilt thou have me to do," was answered by burning impressions to preach Christ to dying men and women. Mount Comfort church said he must preach, and John Martin and English Autry set him apart to that work

ELDER JOHN BATEMAN, M. D.
(Photo by Jackson, Waco, Texas.)

March 24, 1844. He entered the classical school at Denmark, Tenn., and took charge of the Big Black church near that place. His teacher, Dr. Wm. Slack, was a scholarly Presbyterian preacher. Together they studied the Greek New Testament; and as they did so Dr. Slack became convinced that the Greek verb, baptizo, could in no instance mean "sprinkle" or "pour." Accordingly the doctor presented himself to Big Black church for membership, and the teacher was baptized by the pupil.

Bro. Bateman spent a short while in Georgetown College, Kentucky. Returned to Tennessee, married Miss Emily J. Roberts, daughter of Elder L. C. Roberts, November 15, 1848. He graduated in medicine at Memphis, Tenn., and practiced medicine in Memphis a short time after the war, though he did not quit preaching. While in Tennessee he served Beal Street church, Memphis, and many country churches.

In 1884 he moved with his family to Coryell county, Texas. He was missionary of Leon Baptist Association one year, and afterwards pastor of several churches. He was pastor of East Waco church four and one-half years, and was two years the Associational missionary pastor of Second Waco church. After this he served the Second church, Galveston, fourteen months. His health was good and his work prospering, when one evening, alighting from a street car, he was thrown violently to the ground and sustained serious injuries. He was compelled to resign. He returned to his home in Waco and at this writing has been confined to his bed two months. Hopes are entertained that he is slowly recovering. Sister Bateman writes: "During his long illness he has been completely happy, rejoicing amid the most excruciating pain, perfectly resigned to the will of God." His life has been one of meek submission and consecration to his Savior.

ELDER A. E. BATEN.

Alabama has given Texas many noble men. It takes a good degree of courage to leave the old neighborhood, with its thousand dear associations. For this reason usually the most energetic families emigrate. This is why Texas is 50 years in advance of the old states.

Elder A. E. Baten was born in Coffee county, Alabama, October 5, 1855. When he was six years old, his parents moved to Louisiana. In 1876 he came to Texas. He was licensed to preach in 1881. He was educated partly in Louisiana, and partly in Waco (now Baylor) University. In 1884 he left the University and entered the pastorate of the Marlin Baptist church. In 1885 he became pastor of the Baptist church in Brenham, and remained there a little more than three years. He was a year and a half at Navasota, during which time the elegant stone meeting house was built. During his pastorate at Brenham and Navasota he was corresponding secretary of Union Association. In 1890 he became pastor of the Broadway Baptist church, Fort Worth, remaining there nearly four years. It was during this pastorate that he preached a series of sermons on "Municipal Meanness," which brought about some important reforms in the administration of municipal affairs. After spending a year at

ELDER A. E. BATEN.

McKinney, he was called to the care of the First Baptist church of Brownwood in 1894, which position he now holds. He is also director of the Bible School, connected with Howard Payne College. In 1889 he was elected one of the recording secretaries of the Baptist General Convention of Texas, and has been re-elected to the same position at each annual session of that body. In June, 1891, he wrote the call for the first Baptist Young Peoples' Union Convention to convene with Broadway church, Ft. Worth, of which he was, at the time, pastor. This call was published in the denominational papers; in response to which messengers from 25 or 26 churches assembled in Broadway church, September 9 and 10 following, and organized the Baptist Young Peoples' Union of Texas. Brother Baten was elected corresponding secretary of this body, and held the position for three years. He was afterwards president of the body one year.

BATTLE CHURCH

was at first called Social Circle. The name first appears on our minutes in 1884. It was organized by Elder T. D. Suttle, a short time previous to joining the Association. At that time T. D. Suttle was pastor, and G. W. Punchard, clark; membership 35. The name was changed to Battle in 1892. The pastors have been T. D. Suttle, five years; W. D. G. Anderson, one year; G. L. Jennings, one year; B. F. Tatum, present pastor, four years. Battle church worships in the town of Battle, 15 miles southeast from Waco, and counts among her members many consecrated and spiritual brethren and sisters. The present membership is 91. This church is strategetically located, and has a promising future.

DEACON JOHN T. BATTLE.

John T. Battle was born in Wilkes county, Georgia, and at the age of 23 years joined the church at Washington, Ga., of which Dr. H. A. Tupper was pastor. In 1872 moved to Waco, Texas, and united with the First Baptist church, since which time he has worked continuously in the church and Sunday school. After some years he was ordained deacon by the First church, and is the only deacon of that church by her ordained. At the meeting of the Baptist General Convention of Texas, held with the church at Houston in 1890, he was elected treasurer of the Convention, and has been re-elected each year since. He is secretary of the Board of Trustees of Baylor University at Waco, Texas. Bro. Battle has given much time, labor and means to this institution, and to the cause of Christian education. This beloved brother says the recollection of his first meeting with Waco Association will be always to him most precious; for there he met such brethren as Jno. S. Allen, J. J. Ridle, S. F.

Sparks, B. J. Kendrick, W. D. Gaines and others. While all these years Bro. Battle has been an active business man, taking an interest in all the affairs of his city and state, still he finds time to think of, pray for, and work in the Master's cause.

JOHN T. BATTLE.
(Photo by Deane, Waco, Texas.)

ELDER W. H. BAYLISS.

Colonel Bayliss was a lawyer in early life and had a large practice. He was born in Augusta, Georgia, in 1806, and at the age of 36 he professed faith in Christ and became a Baptist preacher of great zeal and power. He succeeded Dr. R. C Howell as pastor of Nashville, Tenn., where the sainted J. R. Graves and A. C. Dayton held membership. He was called to a large church in New York City, with salary of $5,000 offered, but declined because of his southern principles. He held pastorates in Arkansas, Mississippi and Louisiana, and afterwards, through the influence of Dr. R. C. Burleson, came to Waco, Texas. He was pastor at Waco in 1860, when the Association was organized, and though appointed by his church as delegate, for some reason, was not present. He was pastor at Waco in 1861 and 1862. He wrote the report on literature and periodicals, adopted by the Association in 1861. He went from Waco to Marshall, Texas, and after the war became pastor of Coliseum Place church, New Orleans, where he remained till his death, June 13, 1867. He died at Amite City, La., where he had gone for his health. He was loved and honored by all who knew him.

ELDER R. E. B. BAYLOR.

This eminent pioneer, preacher, scholar, lawyer and statesman, was born in Bourbon county Kentucky, May 10, 1791. He studied law in his native state, then moved to Alabama and practiced his profession at Cahaba and Tuscaloosa. He was a member of United States congress two terms. He was converted in 1838, and came to Texas as a licentiate preacher. He became at once identified with Texas and her interests. He was in the Plum Creek fight in 1840, and participated in the struggle against the Mexicans and Indians in 1842-4. He was a member of the Texas congress, for 25 years was judge of Circuit Court, embracing Washington, Fayette and other counties, and was at one time on the Supreme bench. He was a preacher of power and eloquence, and would often hold court in the day and preach at night. It is said that Judge Baylor preached the first sermon in Waco, while holding District Court. He preached in Captain Shapley Ross' hotel on Bridge street. The last ten years of his life were spent chiefly in attending religious meetings. He died Dec. 30, 1873. His remains sleep at Independence. He was a man of fine appearance, of noble bearing and grand preacher.

He was the first president of the "Texas Baptist Educational Society," and was the first president of the Board of Trustees of Baylor University, which Institution was named for him. He gave to the Institution its first $1,000, at a time when money was exceedingly scarce. His memory is sacred to all Texas.

ELDER H. R. BEST.

"For ye see your calling, brethren, how that not many wise men after the flesh, not many mighty, not many noble, are called."

Bro. Best's mother died when he was small. She was a Christian. But he was deprived of that choicest of heaven's blessings, a mother's Christian counsel.

He was born in the Ozark mountains in Southwest Missouri, Nov. 5, 1872. His father spent much time in traveling and carried the boy with him. But when eleven years old, he found himself almost alone in the big world, and thrown upon his own resources.

At the age of 18 years he came to Eastland county, Texas, and began work on a farm. Soon afterward he met a lovely, Christian girl, Miss Lena L. Kinnison. The reader need not be told the rest.

Like many other boys, whom the Lord calls to preach, young Best tried his *best* to be an Infidel. But his young Christian wife and the recollection of his mother under God's blessings, won him from skepticism, and to the Lord Jesus. After struggling with impression for a year, he decided to preach, and on the advice of Dr. B. H. Carroll, entered Baylor University Sept., 1895. He is now pastor of Robinson and Hillside, two of our best churches, half time with each. He is a young man of pleasing address and an acceptable preacher.

BETHEL CHURCH

was in Bosque county, near Valley Mills; came into the Association in 1868 with J. A. Land as pastor, and with 13 members. In 1870 Sam Lacy was pastor, in 1871 J. Sandifer. The church never represented after 1871. The membership at that time was 17.

BETHLEHEM

was at first called Pleasant Grove. She came to the Waco Assotiation in 1892 with a letter of dismission from McGregor Association, and had been in existence several years at that time. The first pastor was J. F. Harris. At the time when McGregor Association was organized in 1885, Pleasant Grove had 35 members.

The name was changed to Bethany in 1895. The pastors have been J. F. Harris, T. P. Walker and G. W. North. Bro. North has been pastor since 1893. The church owns a good house, four miles west of Lorena, has a fine Sunday school (which at one time gained the Associational banner) and has a membership of 130.

BEULAH CHURCH

worships five miles west of Marlin. First came into the Association in 1864. The petitioning letter was borne by Frank Stallsworth and L. Magee. The church had then 38 members. Calvin Magee was pastor many years. In 1880 S. L. Morris was pastor, in 1881-2 A. J. Shelton was pastor. After Bro. Shelton the church was several years without a pastor. J. R. M. Touchstone accepted the care in 1887. After that for years she did not represent in the Association. She was for a time in a disorganized state. Her membership is now in Falls county Association.

ELDER E. J. BILLINGTON.

Every state in the Union has helped to people Texas, and usually the best citizens are contributed. This time it was Kentucky. Elder Billington was born in Bedford county, Tenn., Jan. 11, 1826, but moved with his parents to Ballard county, Ky., in 1830, where he grew up. In his eighteenth year he was baptized into the Lovelaceville Baptist church by Elder Willis White. In 1847 Elder Billington was married to Miss Kittie Ann Rosco. They came to Texas in 1854 and settled in Limestone county. Here they found a sparsely settled population, many of them very kind and hospitable. There were some Baptists. The Trinity River Association had been organized six years, and was doing active work. Bro. Billington collected $25 and bought a log house in which to worship. He then rode 25 miles to get Elder W. J. Bowden to aid in the organization of Mt. Antioch church. Bro. Bowden lived near where the town of Groesbeck now stands. Bro. Billington was recognized as deacon of the church. He lived in the Mt. Antioch church 34 years. By this church he was ordained to the gospel ministry in 1862. In 1869 he organized a church on Christmas Creek, seven miles north of Horn Hill, and organized the Horn Hill church in a log school house, with 7 members. At one time he baptized 17 into this church. Among them the beloved Hon. L. L. Foster. In 1869 Bro. Billington was pastor of Clover Dale church (now Hubbard City), continuing two years. These were years of prosperity at Clover Dale. Bro. Billington lost his first wife March 30, 1864. This sad affliction made it necessary for him to give up three churches and remain at home with his six children.

ELDER E. J. BILLINGTON.

On June 4, 1865, he was married to Mrs. Amanda A. Stokes, and on April 24, 1874, this lady died.

On Feb. 24, 1875, he married Miss Louisa Jane Polk. Three children are the result of this last marriage.

In the early days of Bro. Billington's ministry they had no fine houses. On one occasion he preached in a grove and the sun burned his bald head so badly that the skin peeled off. He fell asleep in Jesus Aug. 5, 1896. He knew his time had come and asked his children to sing, "We shall meet beyond the river," and "Death is only a dream." The town Billington perpetuates his memory.

BLEVINS CHURCH,

formerly, Deer Creek, was organized April, 1875, by Elder B. J. Bassel. Their place of meeting was 20 miles west of Marlin, in Falls county, at a place called Barron, in honor of Thos. H. Barron, the first settler. The original members were Uriah Gibson, Matilda Gibson, G. G. Gibson, F. M. Griggs and Sarah Griggs. They took the name of "Deer Creek," and adopted the articles and church covenant found in Pendleton's Church Manual. In August following, Deer Creek was received into the Association and continued in good standing and co-operation till September, 1895, when she was dismissed by letter to join Falls County. The following have served Deer Creek as pastors: B. J. Bassel, T. A. Mangum, John Witt, G. G. Gibson, Thos. Burrows, A. A. Hensler, J. M. Mizzell, J. R. M. Touchstone and W. E. Self. The largest ingatherings have been in 1888, 1894, and 1896. Present membership, 118. The church has ordained the following preachers: T. P. Walker, 1891; W. J. Pace and W. E. Self in 1894. The following ordained ministers hold membership at Blevins: L. A. Hays, G. G. Gibson, W. E. Self, W. J. Pace and Peter S. Bruner. The first clerk was R. C. Barron; present clerk, Peter S. Bruner.

BLUE RIDGE CHURCH

was constituted in 1859 by Elders W. B. Eaves and William Clark. Original members—David Barclay, A. H. Chamberlain, A. S. Trigg, C. T. Barclay, A. M. Smith, D. B. Barclay, Eliza Harlan, Susan Ross, Emily Harlan, Tempie Chamberlain, Louisa M. Morrell, Laura A. Trigg. First pastor, W. B. Eaves; first deacon, A. H. Chamberlain. Their first house, built in 1850, cost $550. Held membership first in Trinity River Association. Elder Z. N. Morrell and A. S. Trigg were delegates from Blue Ridge to the convention in 1860, when Waco Association was organized. Z. N. Morrell was pastor during the war. Since then the pastors have been C. W. Wright, C. B. Kinnard, C. W. Kinnard,

J. J. Davis, J. V. Wright, J. L. Lattimore, S. L. Morris, B. H. Beal, L. W. Duke, J. F. McLeod. Blue Ridge was dismissed from Waco Association in 1844 in fellowship and order with 106 members. She now belongs to Falls county.

ELDER W. G. BOONE, A. M.

Short, spiritual, sunshiny. Such was the beautiful life of Elder Boone. A son of Heard county, Georgia, he was born April 18, 1837. August. 19, 1849, he was baptized by Elder Robert Fleming into Bethel church of his native county. He graduated from Mercer University, at Penfield, Georgia, in 1859, and was ordained at Penfield, May 29, 1859, by the following eminent ministers: T. D. Martin, A. M., Drs. N. M. Crawford, W. Williams and H. H. Tucker. He was married November 7, 1859, to Miss Mary E. Watson, Elder S. R. Hood officiating. His pastorate at Gadsden, Ala., though brief, was fruitful of good. From Gadsden he went to Bayou De Glaze, Louisiana, where he was pastor three years. From this place he was called to become professor of languages in Mount Lebanon University. He was chairman of the faculty and at the same time served as pastor of the churches at Mount Lebanon and Mount Gilead. In 1862 he accepted the invitation to take charge of the church and the college at Homer, where he remained eight months. The institution at Evergreen was the next scene of his labor. Here he remained two years, teaching and preaching. He served as pastor of Big Cane church sixteen months. In 1867 he came to Texas and spent one year in teaching. In 1870 he became pastor of Bremond church, then an infant flock. It was under his care that the church first united with the Waco Association, August, 1870. After a happy and prosperous pastorate of three years at Bremond the Lord took him November 13, 1873.

A resolution adopted by the Association in 1874 at Bremond says, "In the death of Elder W. C. Boone our Association has lost an eminent scholar and an able expounder and defender of God's word."

Though eminent for his scholarship, his modesty was remarkable. His nature was retiring. He loved his home and his flock. He died universally beloved and mourned.

BOSQUEVILLE CHURCH,

located at Bosqueville, six miles from Waco, was constituted by Elder Solomon G. O'Bryan on the fifth Sabbath in November, 1854. There were only eight persons, six males and two females. The church first joined Trinity River Association, was in the organization of Waco Association in 1860. The delegates were: A. H. Rhodes and H. Rodgers. S. G. O'Bryan was the first pastor. He was succeeded by N. W. Crain.

Since then the pastors have been R. C. Burleson, T. F. Lockett, V. G. Cunningham, J. J. Riddle, R. B. Burleson, W. S. Huff, J. L. Walker, S. L. Morris, Joseph Gronde, J. B. Reaves, and L. J. Mims, in the order named. This church has done vast good, and has from the first been loyal to all our denominational interests. Present membership, 71.

The greatest revival was in 1876.

The first meeting-house was erected 1887. This building cost $1,500, and was burned down soon after completion. The present house was built in 1895, and is valued at $1,000. They have a good Sunday School and Ladies' Missionary Society.

DEACON W. E. BOZEMAN.

This dear brother is a cousin of Hon. J. M. McKenney, of Milam county; was born in Loundes county, Ala., March 23, 1841; was raised in Coosa county. He volunteered in the first company that left Coosa county for the Confederate service. He spent four years in the war, mostly in Virginia, and much of the time under "Stonewall" Jackson. He was wounded in the battle of Cedar Creek, October 19, 1864, and obtained a furlough and was never again in the army. On December 29, 1864, he was married to Miss Sallie A. Pilant, a lady of culture, and one who for more than 30 years has been a true help-meet to her husband.

Bro. Bozeman moved to Texas in 1866, and lived one year in Red River county. In 1868 he settled in Milam county, near Caddo church, where he has ever since lived.

In 1870 he was converted, and the next year was baptized into the fellowship of Caddo by Pastor A. E. Vandivere. His membership remains there till this day. In 1872, W. E. Bozeman and

J. M. Killen were ordained to the deaconship by Elders A. E. Vandivere and W. J. Glazener. In all her joys and sorrows, bright days and dark hours, Bro. B. has never ceased to be a faithful supporter of his church, nor has he lost faith in her ultimate triumph. For many years he has been superintendent of the Caddo Sunday School.

Sister Bozeman, his noble wife, was born in Coosa county, Ala. She was converted in early life, and was the instrument in God's hand in leading her husband to Christ. They have a happy family of six bright girls, all church members but the youngest. As in the past may God continue to bless them.

Brother Bozeman has long been one of the honored vice presidents of the mission board of Waco Association.

BREMOND CHURCH.

Under the leadership of Pastor W. C. Boone, Bremond church united with the Waco Association in 1869. A. H. Jackson, S. Durham, R. P. Snelling, J. F. Jackson and J. J. Trost were the bearers of the petitionary letter. She remained with us till 1880. In 1879 her membership was 148. C. C. Lee was pastor at that date, and had succeeded L. R. Scruggs, whose predecessor was was C. E. Stephens. Bremond is a prosperous church at this day.

ELDER PETER S. BRUNER

was born March 7, 1842, in Breckenridge county, Ky. His grand parents came from Germany at an early day. When but six years old emigrated to Schuyler county, Ill., in boyhood to Macon county, Mo., and in 1860 to Perry county, Mo., where his father departed this life in 1862, his mother following in 1868. Elder Bruner was married October 12, 1862, to Lydia Jane, daughter of James Preston. Six children were born to them, two of whom are living and professed Christians. He was married a second time to Nancy Catharine, daughter of Elder R. Moore, Oakwoods, Texas. Eleven heirs have brightened their home, four of whom survive. Under the preaching of Elder Joseph R. Rutler, a missionary Baptist in Perry county, Mo., in September, 1863, Brother Bruner professed faith in Christ, and was baptized into Boise Brule Baptist church. Soon he was ordained a deacon. December 31, 1870, he was licensed to preach, and preached his first sermon Jan. 15, 1871, from Eph. 4:29-30. Came to Texas in 1875, and joined Salem church, now Mastersville. Joined the Carolina church in 1880. Dr. T. J. Drane, pastor, passed an encomium on the Bruner family (whom he had known

ELDER PETER S. BRUNER.

in Kentucky), and expressed the hope that this one was "a chip off the old block." Brother Bruner was ordained by Carolina church, January, 1882. Presbytery: T. J. Drane, R. Moore and G. G. Gibson. He is grateful to God that he has been permitted to preach Christ in Missouri, Illinois, Tennessee and Texas.

NANCY MOORE BRUNER.

This lady, whose portrait we give, was born in Hardin county, Tenn., June 5, 1853, and the same year moved to St. Genevieve county, Mo. At a protracted meeting in July, 1873, held by the pastor of Macedonia Baptist church, in Dent county, Mo., this sister was brought to Christ and through baptism (by Elder Adams) into said church. Returned to Hardin county, Tenn., in 1874, and on September 24, same year, united in marriage

MRS. PETER S. BRUNER.

with Elder Peter S. Bruner, in Perry county, Mo., and came immediately to Texas. From that day her life and labors have been joined with his.

ELDER WILLIAM CALMES BUCK.

No grander man than Brother Buck ever came to Texas. The great Baptists at an early day gravitated to Texas and Waco. This brother was raised by a well-to-do Virginia farmer. His father was Charles Buck, who gave the son good educational advantages for those days. He was born in Shenandoah county (now Warren), August 23, 1790. As he advanced toward manhood his thirst for knowledge became insatiable. He read all the good books he could find, all the volumes of the "British Encyclopedia," and many other volumes of a public library. He pursued his studies until acquainted with the Greek and Hebrew languages. He became a member of the Water Lick Baptist church, Virginia, in 1807, and after farming some years gave himself wholly to the ministry. In 1812 he was ordained and became pastor of the church of which he was a member. He was a lieutenant in the United States army in the war of 1812. From 1820 to 1836 he was pastor of several churches in Kentucky, and became pastor of the First church, Louisville, in 1836. He organized the East church, Louisville. While in Louisville he edited the Western Pioneer and Baptist Banner. Was secretary of the Bible Board of the Southern Baptist Convention at Nashville, Tenn., from May, 1851, till March, 1854, when he became pastor at Columbus, Miss., remaining three years. In 1857 he was pastor at Greenborough, Ala., in 1858 at Selma, and in 1859 he moved to Marion, Ala., and began the publication of the Baptist Correspondent. The war put an end to this enterprise, and Elder Buck went to the Confederate army as a missionary. In 1866 he came to Texas. Those of us who remember his grand sermon at Bold Springs on the "church" in 1868 will always thank God. His brethren were wont to call him "Father Buck" because of his fatherly appearance. He died at Waco, 1872. He was the author of "The Baptist Hymn Book, "The Philosophy of Religion," and the "Science of Life."

ELDER RUFUS C. BURLESON.

Elder Rufus C. Burleson, D. D., LL. D., is one of the most successful and widely known preachers and educators in the South. Only Dr. F. Wayland and E. Knott have held the office of college president as long as he has. He has preached in every old town in Texas, and held protracted meetings in all the great cities. He is the son of Jonathan Burleson, a wealthy farmer, was born near Decatur, Ala., August 7, 1823. He was trained to habits of industry on the farm, and was early instructed in a good preparatory school. He was converted April 2, 1839, joined the old Mt. Pisgah church, and was baptized by Rev. W. H. Holcomb. He gave up his desire to become a lawyer, and under a profound sense of "Woe is me if I preach not the gospel," and while a student of Nashville University, he was licensed to preach, No-

R. C. BURLESON, D. D. LL. D.
(Photo by Deane, Waco, Texas.)

vember 12, 1840, by the First Baptist church of Nashville, under the care of the great and good Dr. R. B. C. Howell. Intense application to study day and night, and neglecting all exercise, fearfully impaired his health, and he was wrapped up in blankets and sent home to die. But God in mercy restored him to reasonable health, and after spending a year on the farm he found it necessary to enter the great University of Common Sense and Practical Wisdom, physicians assuring his father it would be certain death to send him back to college. His father offered him the beautiful plantation and five negroes to work, and urged him to marry a pious girl and become a farmer preacher. But he replied: "The Lord has farmer Baptist preachers enough for a hundred years. And on my knees I have vowed to put the Baptists, and especially Baptist preachers, on a higher plane of intelligence and piety or die in the struggle." By consent of his father at nineteen years old he went to the state of Mississippi, and by teaching school three and a half years he put a thousand and fifty dollars in bank. During these three and a half years he preached every Sunday. He was called by three country churches and was ordained June 10, 1845, by W. H. Holcomb, J. C. Keeny, Wm. Carey Crane and Andrew McGowen. He then entered the splendidly endowed but ill fated theological institute at Covington, Ky. He graduated with distinguished honor June 10, 1847. He spent seven months studying prayerfully and profoundly the lives of Romulus, Alfred the Great, Peter the Great, Roger Williams, John Calvin, Martin Luther, John Wesley and his own great ancestor, Sir William Byrd, the founder of Richmond and Lynchburg, Va. He was elected pastor of Houston Baptist church to fill the place of the great and good Dr. Wm. M. Tryon, who died of yellow fever November 20, 1847. He landed at Galveston January 5, 1848, and that night kneeling down on the strand prayed, "Oh God, give me Texas for Jesus and His church, or I die. Spare my life to preach the gospel in every town in Texas. Spare my life to see a Baptist church and Sunday school in every neighborhood." God has enabled him to see the little disorganized band of 1,900 Baptists, overshadowed by 10,000 Methodists and 3,500 Catholics, become a grand organized army of 273,000 Baptists, excelling every other denomination in Texas. He has lived to see Texas the greatest Baptist state in America, except one. He was a prominent actor in the organization of the Baptist State Convention at Anderson in 1848, and was its corresponding secretary for seven years. He also took a prominent part in the organization of the General Association at Tyler in 1867. He introduced the resolution in the convention at Anderson in 1848 to commence as early as practicable a Texas Baptist paper. His national reputation is based on his great success as an educator. Baylor University is the only institution in Texas that has survived the storms of half a hundred years, and Baylor University was going down in 1851 when such eminent trustees as Hon. R. E. B. Baylor, Gov. A. C. Horton, Rev. Hosea Garret and others came to him and said: "Unless you go aboard and take charge of the sinking ship, all will be lost for this generation." It was a fearful struggle to give up his beloved church in Houston. But after a day and night spent in prayer and fasting, he was profoundly penetrated with the conviction that a great Baptist University was indispensable to the highest success of the Baptist cause of Texas. He therefore said to the trustees: "I will accept on these conditions: First, the trustees of the University must never go in debt. Second, an endowment of $10,000 in cash and interest bearing notes be raised during this convention or before the next meeting, and that $10,000 be added every ten years till the endowment amounts to $50,000. Third, the duties of the trustees and professors must be clearly defined so as not to conflict as heretofore." During that convention $5,300 were raised in cash and notes. His first session as president opened September, 1851. Fifty-two students, thirty-two in the male and twenty in the female department, entered the first day. Since 1851 he has instructed over 8,500 students, male and female. Over 250 of whom are preachers, such as D. B. Morrill, H. B. Renfro, Pinkney Harris, W. W. (Spurgeon) Harris, and Dr. B. H. Carroll. His students have filled the offices of Governor, Lieutenant Governor, Supreme Judge, Circuit Judge and many of the most important positions in the state, as lawyers, doctors, merchants, stock kings and queens of heart and home. In 1893, the next year, twenty-seven professors and teachers were employed and 859 students matriculated.

Dr. Burleson served as president of Baylor University at Independence till June 27, 1861, when he resigned and moved to Waco. The Classical High School at Waco was immediately chartered as the Waco University, and Dr. B. was elected president. Rev. G. W. Baines was elected president of Baylor University at Independence, and served the institution in that capacity until January 1, 1863, when Dr. Wm. Carey Crane became president. Dr. Crane continued till his death in February, 1885. Rev. Reddin Andrews succeeded Dr. Crane, and was president of Baylor till the consolidation with Waco University, October 6, 1886.

All this time Waco University was a grand school, with Dr. Burleson as president. When Baylor University was consolidated with Waco University, Dr. Burleson was elected president of the consolidated institution.

Dr. Burleson is the pioneer of co-education in the South. Baylor (Waco) University is the second co-educational school in America, and the third in the world. He is also the pioneer in organizing summer schools which, like co-education, have now extended over the continent. During his arduous labors as president of Baylor University he has been indefatigable as a preacher. Over 4,000 persons have been converted at meetings he has conducted. Among them such eminent persons as A. S. Lipscomb and A. W. Donnell, Supreme Judges; Gen. James Davis and his brother, Judge Wm. E. Davis, Col. James M. Anderson, etc.

He has buried in holy baptism such persons as Gen. Sam Houston, the hero of San Jacinto, the heroine of the Alamo, Col. Jas. M. Anderson, Judge J. B. Berry, and scores and hundreds of others, not only of the illustrious, but the humble and the poor, white and black. His success he attributes to divine guidance. But as a means which God has so gloriously blessed, we suggest the following causes of his success for the study and imitation of young preachers:

First—His fixedness to one life purpose. For fifty-seven years he has had but one purpose and that was to place the Baptists, and especially Baptist preachers, upon a higher, grander plane of intelligence, piety and zeal. Second—His thorough and profound preparation for his life work. Third—His courage is heaven born and never falters. In the yellow fever scourge at Houston in 1848, and the cholera in 1849, 565 persons died. Some of the preachers and many of the people fled, and urged him to do so. But he said, "Nay, I will die at my post if need be." Fourth—His great gentleness. Little children will fondle on his knee and the poorest people approach him familiarly as a spiritual father and friend. His mottoes have been these: "Love God with all thy heart, soul, mind and strength, and thy neighbor as thyself." "Honor thy father and thy mother." "Be ever willing and ready to die for my country." "Never hear, tell, read or do anything that I would blush to tell my mother." "Death and debt are almost synonymous." "A resolute mind is omnipotent." "Have one grand life purpose." "Eternal vigilance, untiring energy, unfaltering courage, under God, will remove mountains of difficulty and erect monuments of usefulness and glory." "Never get mad, never get scared. Always be swift to hear, slow to speak, slow to wrath." "Never ride the fence. Be neutral in nothing, independent in all things." "Luck is a fool. Pluck, providence and right are omnipotent." "In firmness take Andrew Jackson for my model. In courage and integrity take Fabricius. In piety, zeal and courage, take Paul and Athenacious. Take Christ as my model in all things."

His health has been remarkable. He says he has not had headache for over fifty years. Amid all the toil and exposures in Texas for forty-nine years, he has not had ten days sickness except from yellow fever, cholera and dengue, contracted when pastor at Houston from waiting on the sick and dying.

He is profoundly convinced with the great Dr. Silliman, the father of natural science in American colleges, that the human frame was made and wound up to run eighty years. He writes: "I confidently expect to outlive this century and look down upon the twentieth, or millennial century, and see Texas one of the grandest states on the planet, and Baylor University, with all her buildings, apparatus, telescope, botonical gardens, fitted out splendidly with five hundred thousand dollars endowment, and sixty-four professors in the literary, law, medical, theological and commercial departments, with 1,500 students. Then I will be ready to say, 'Now, Lord, let thy servant depart in peace, for mine eyes have seen the consummation of my great life purpose.'"

He was several times moderator of the Waco Association, and has often been called to serve on important committees.

ELDER RICHARD BYRD BURLESON, A. M., LL. D.

This distinguished divine and educator was truly one of the fathers of Waco Association. He was of the same Burleson family whose name is so honorably linked with the early history of Texas, and his mother, Elizabeth Byrd, was the grand-daughter of Sir William Byrd, who founded Richmond and Lynchburg, Virginia.

ELDER R. B. BURLESON, A. M., LL. D.

He was born near Decatur, Ala., January 1, 1822. He was educated in the University of Nashville, Tenn., graduating in 1843. He was converted April 18, 1839, and was baptized three days afterwards into the fellowship of Mount Pisgah church by Rev. W. H. Holcomb.

He was licensed to preach in 1841 by the First Baptist church at Nashville, under the pastorate of Rev. Dr. R. B. C. Howell.

He was ordained November, 1842, by the Athens church, two

years later accepted the call of the church at Tuscumbia, Ala., and continued till 1849, when he became president of Moulton Female Institute, Ala., remaining six years. In December, 1855, he came to Texas and opened the female school at Austin, and became pastor of the Baptist church in that city.

He was chosen professor of natural science in Baylor University at Independence in 1857. He labored in this important position with characteristic zeal, ability and fidelity. In 1861 he was chosen vice president of Waco University and professor of natural sciences. He adorned this position for eighteen years, till the day of his death, December 21, 1879. He was a power, both in Baylor University at Independence and Waco University at Waco. He labored much to organize churches in destitute places and build up feeble churches in the bounds of Waco Association. His only failing was too great modesty, something almost unknown in these degenerate days. He was pastor at different times of the following churches: Sunset, near Marlin; Pleasant Grove, Greenwood and Robinson. He and his brother, Rufus Burleson, in order to have a clear division of labor, agreed that Richard Burleson should devote all his time and energy that could be spared from Waco University to building up Waco Association, while his brother Rufus C. was to take a broader field, the whole state of Texas, and visit all the Associations and all the great cities. However, after having done a glorious work, his health becoming feeble, he found it important to confine his whole labor to Waco University. In 1874, the whole state of Texas felt that her geological resources had been shamefully overlooked, and at the earnest request of Governor Coke and other distinguished Texans, he consented to become state geologist. But finding he was so much needed in the University, and having located the vast beds of coal and marble of Texas, he resigned after one year. On December 21, 1879, this eminent servant of God and of Texas passed away. He endured his long and patient illness with eminent Christian resignation. He spent his last hours with his family and his devoted brother Rufus.

On the day he died he had his brother read to him the words of our blessed Savior, where he says: "I am the resurrection and the life," and also the 23d Psalm, "The Lord is my shepherd," etc. He asked his brother to pray that every cloud might pass away, and that by faith he might stand on Pisgah's top and view the promised land with no cloud intervening. And while all were kneeling by his bedside praying, he exclaimed: 'Praise the Lord; every cloud has disappeared, and I stand on the Mount and see the glory world. I hear my blessed Savior saying: 'I will be with you.'" And when the last moment came, with heaven beaming on his countenance, without a moan or struggle, he passed away. His pastor, Rev. B. H. Carroll, conducted the funeral services, and afterwards penned these words:

"Thus lived, and toiled, and suffered and prayed and died, one of the noblest, purest, greatest and best men Texas ever knew. May thousands rise up to call him blessed, and imitate his resplendent virtues. May the cries of his orphan children and lonely widow never be disregarded, and from the jasper walls of the eternal city may his redeemed spirit behold the ever widening influence and increasing glory of the churches and the University for which he toiled and for which he died, and may his beloved wife and children all be fully prepared to meet him in that world that is brighter than day."

ELDER N. T. BYARS.

This brother, who helped mould Texas, was born in South Carolina, May 17, 1808; was raised by pious parents; was converted at 16. His educational advantages were limited. He moved to Georgia, and later, about 1835, to Washington, Texas. He was a blacksmith, and rendered General Houston's army valuable service in that capacity. In March, 1836, the Declaration of Texas Independence was written in his house. He was one of the members of the missionary Baptist church, organized at Washington in 1837. He served the senate of the republic as sergeant-at-arms in 1837-1842. In 1838 he married and moved to Bastrop. He was associate judge for the county of Austin, and was re-elected but resigned, under profound conviction that it was his duty to preach. He was ordained October 16, 1841, by Z. N. Morrell and John Woodruff. President Lamar and some of his cabinet were present. Afterwards he was missionary of the Southern Baptist Convention, and labored along the Trinity river and in Navarro county. He was the first missionary of the Baptist State Convention, and labored as such ten years, till his health failed. He organized the First church at Waco, and was its first pastor. He organized sixty churches. He sleeps at Brownwood.

DEACON J. D. BUTTS.

This good brother was born in Alabama, May 21, 1834. His parents died when he was a child. He grew up in Butler county.

J. D. BUTTS.

In 1869 he joined the Mt. Zion Baptist church, Butler county; was ordained to the deaconship in 1870. He came to Texas in 1873 and settled in the southern part of Falls county, two miles west of the Brazos river. He still lives on the little home where he first settled. He was in the organization of Pleasant Grove church in 1878, and has ever since been an active deacon in the church. He has always been true to his church and to Baptist faith.

CADDO BAPTIST CHURCH

was constituted in 1854. Presbytery: Elders Z. N. Morrell, J. J. Haggard and — Langston. It was organized at Caddo Springs in the northeast corner of Milam county, near the Brazos river. The following went into the organization: Deacon John Knight and wife, Elizabeth Knight, Wm. Pruitt, Jacob Pruitt, Mrs. Elizabeth Lewis, Miss Sarah Lewis and Mrs. Malinda J. Walker, all gone to their reward. Brother Knight was self sacrificing, and during the war greatly endeared himself to mothers whose husbands were in the Confederate army, by repeated acts of kindness. The church moved one and one-half miles to its present place of meeting in 1858.

Had pastors as follows: J. J. Haggard till 1856. Then W. B. Eaves, J. W. McHorse, J. J. Sledge, A. E. Vandivere, W. J. Glazener, S. B. McJunkin, J. T. Shannon, J. W. Crosby, L. W. Duke, J. L. Walker, J. R. M. Touchstone, present pastor. The greatest ingathering was in August, 1876, during a revival conducted by Elder S. B. McJunkin, when the church was much revived, receiving forty by experience and baptism, and forty by letter.

From the time of organization till about 1882 or 1883 the neighborhood was in a formative condition. The church usually had large additions in the summer, and lost in the fall by removals. Since 1883 the community has been more settled, and there has been less variation of the membership. She has at present a membership of 116, active and "zealous of good works." The contributions to missions and other denominational objects average one dollar per capita, compared with other churches, not a bad showing.

The church has a prosperous Sunday school, of which Deacon W. E. Bozeman is the efficient superintendent. In this school he has with him a few faithful co-workers and about sixty pupils. Average attendance about fifty.

The deacons are W. E. Bozeman, J. H. Taylor and S. R. Whitehurst. This last named brother is also a licentiate minister, keeping up regular appointments.

Deacon J. H. Taylor was born in North Carolina, October 22, 1830, moved with his father to Mississippi in 1845, and to Texas in 1856. He settled in the neighborhood of Caddo church, and has lived there continuously ever since. He was baptized in 1881 by Pastor S. B. McJunkin; was ordained deacon during pastorate of L. W. Duke.

Bro. W. H. Bailey, who is now living in the added years beyond his three score and ten, is a native of Virginia. He came to Texas early in the fifties, and settled first at Independence, the site of Baylor University. In 1856 he came to Caddo neighborhood, when neighbors were "few and far between." He was converted in early youth, and was baptized by the sainted Jeremiah Bell Jeter. The town of Baileyville was named for him.

Bro. Henry Smilie, a leader in the church, was born in Alabama. Coming to Texas when a young man, he settled first in Robertson county, but has been living in the Caddo neighborhood for 35 years. For many years he lived a man of the world. But when he surrendered to Christ, he surrendered his whole heart. His power and influence is felt in the neighborhood and church.

Bro. J. T. Whitehurst, born in Louisiana, moved to Texas in 1875, has long been a member of the Mission Board of Waco Association. He was baptized into the fellowship of Caddo church in 1876 by pastor S. B. McJunkin. His faithful work as board member has caused him to be widely known and greatly loved throughout the Association.

Sister A. E. Bozeman ("Grandma"), wife of Col. Dave Bozeman, deceased, was born in Green county, Ga., in 1817. She moved to Alabama when quite young, married young, was baptized in 1833, was mother of a large family, six of whom lived to be grown. She moved to Texas in 1869, settling near, and uniting with, Caddo church. Three of her sons with their wives, and quite a large number of her grandchildren, are members of Caddo church.

Elder L. P. Eaves was born in Virginia in 1795, moved to South Carolina when a boy, was a soldier in the war of 1812, moved to Georgia when a young man, was converted in 1828, and was ordained before 1837. He was an able minister, and had the care of many churches in Georgia. He was much associated with Elder Jesse Mercer in revival and Associational meetings. About 1848 or 50 he moved to Alabama, and labored extensively in pastoral and revival work. He constituted many churches in Alabama. He raised a large family, nearly all of whom became members of Baptist churches during his life. His eldest, Sister McGee, is 79 years old, and a devoted member of Caddo. Bro. Eaves came to Texas in 1870, and made a crop, preaching as opportunity offered; though 75 years old, returned to Alabama on horseback. Came again in 1876, settling in the neighborhood of Caddo church, and joining the church by letter in 1877. He was an active worker and a safe counsellor. He died at Wilderville in 1890, being 94 years old.

Caddo church first joined Trinity River Association, and went from that into the organization of Waco Association in 1860 at the town of Waco. Later the church requested a letter of dismission, which was granted, and the next year she joined Little River Association. After remaining with Little River some years she again united with Waco, where she continues till this day.

The church now occupies her third meeting-house. The first was a log structure, and was built by the pioneer fathers with their own hands. The next house was a large, roomy box building, which answered the purposes of the brethren many years. It was a veritable tabernacle, and many precious outpourings of blessing did the saints enjoy within its ample walls. The present house, a beautiful plain, modern frame, neatly finished, was erected in 1892, during the pastorate of J. L. Walker.

CALEDONIA CHURCH

began to exist Sept. 1, 1872. The original members were: Jno. Dunn, W. F. Umberson, H. S. Dunn, J. C. Minix, P. H. Philips, Sisters M. E. Minix, Nancy E. Dunn, Elizabeth Umberson, Delia E. Dunn, Paulina C. Worrell. The only known survivor of this original little band is Deacon W. F. Umberson, who is still a member of this church. This church has had a gradual, harmonious growth. Her present membership is 80. Caledonia first joined Towash Association, and after the consolidation of Towash with Hill county, was a member of the consolidated body known as Hillsboro Association. United with the Waco Association at Geneva in 1893. This church was organized by Elders Jno. Dunn and W. W. Smith. The pastors have been Thos. Hooker, B. F. Tatum, J. W. Anderson, H. N. Reese, T. P. Speakman, Holmes Nichols, H. P. Tyra, S. R. Williams, C. D. Whitman, W. D. Bowen, present pastor. Bro. Bowman is a consecrated, amiable young man, and one of our most promising young preachers. They met for worship in the Kellum school house for several years. This school house was 15 miles north of Waco and one mile east of the Brazos river. The new house is one mile east of the old site.

DEACON WILLIAM FRANK UMBERSON

was born in Winston county, Miss., May 11, 1837. Moved to Texas in 1855, and has lived near Waco ever since. He was baptized in August, 1855, by Elder G. L. Jennings. Held membership in the First church, Waco, in 1857, and afterwards in East Waco. Was in the organization of Caledonia in 1872 as above narrated. Brother Umberson is a nephew of the late merchant prince, Deacon W. R. Kellum, of East Waco. Elder J. L. Walker's first wife was a step-daughter of W. F. Umberson.

ELDER THOS. HOOKER,

the first pastor of Caledonia church, was a native of Georgia; was a well-educated and faithful Baptist preacher. He still lives, near 80 years old, at Duffau, in Erath county, Texas. He sold whisky at an early day, but when the light of God's grace shined into his heart he emptied several barrels of spirits—his entire stock—in the streets, and has been an enemy to liquor ever since. A few years ago he was a powerful preacher, and served several churches in McLennan and Hill counties. His home was on a farm in the southern portion of Hill, near Patten's Mills.

CALVERT CHURCH

first appears on the minutes of the Association in 1870. There were then 40 members. A. E. Vandivere was pastor. The church was represented by Chas. H. Fisher. In 1871 she was not represented; in 1872 H. Ball was clerk, but no pastor. In 1873 W. H. Dodson was pastor. The membership this year is reported 38. After 1873 Calvert appears no more on our minutes. The church still exists, a member of Little Brazos Association, with the beloved J. C. Burkett as pastor.

ELDER S. I. CALDWELL.

This venerable servant of God, now 80 years old, is living in the town of McGregor, McLennan county, Texas. He was born in Mecklenburg county, N. C., 1817. Was the son of Samuel P. Caldwell, a Presbyterian minister. He was educated at Hall's Seminary, N. C., and Center College, at Danville, Ky. Professed faith in Christ in 1833, and united with the Presbyterians at Statesville, N. C.; moved to Mississippi in 1840, soon after which he united with the Antioch Baptist church, near Vicksburg, Miss. In 1841 began preaching the gospel. Was ordained to the full work of the gospel ministry in 1842. The ordaining council consisted of Rev. D. B. Crawford and Rev. W. H. Taylor. He served as pastor of the following churches: Flower Hill, Yazoo City, Jackson, Canton and Society Ridge, Miss. Owing to a throat disease, he was compelled to give up preaching for a long time, but his heart yearned within him to, in some way, render service for his Lord, hence he devoted himself to the subject of ministerial education, which resulted in founding Clinton College in Mississippi.

He came to Texas in 1853, and settled in Fayette county, where he was pastor of LaGrange and Navadad churches. In 1856 moved to Williamson county, and engaged in stock raising, as the return of throat trouble compelled him to give up preaching. Later he moved to Coryell county, where he spent twenty-five years farming and preaching, as opportunity offered, and as his health would allow. In this way he has done much gratuitous service, striving to do what he could for the advancement of the Master's kingdom. At a meeting of the old Union Association in 1865, Bro. Caldwell made suggestions and exerted influences which led materially to the organization of the Sunday school and Colportage Convention of Texas. It was also largely through his suggestions and influence in several Associations that Sunday school institutes were organized and made very helpful in the development of our work.

He has rendered much and valuable service to the church and to the cause in a general way in McGregor and the surrounding country.

Even now that he has passed his four score years, he finds his chief delight in the preaching and prayer meeting services of his church. This dear old brother has a remarkably patriarchal appearance, and seems as one standing on the shores of time waiting the summon to come over to the land of never withering flowers; and ere this book is printed he may have joined the ransomed host on the other shore.

CAROLINA CHURCH.

This church, now extinct, was organized in the Presbyterian meeting house near Durango, in Falls county, in 1875, with 16 members. W. D. Gaines and wife, J. J. Jordan and wife, Andrew Daffin and wife, Ben Freeman and son, Ben O. Freeman and three daughters, Kate Jackson and others, were the original members. The church was organized by Elder Calvin Magee, who, for a time, served them as supply. Elder T. D. Suttle was chosen pastor in 1877 and served acceptably till 1880. During his pastorate, 1879, the Association convened with Carolina church. During Brother Suttle's time the church was moved three miles to Union school house. The little flock, under Brother Suttle, quadrupled her membership. He left them in 1880 with 96 members. Elder T. J. Drane succeeded, and was the last pastor. The church was moved to Durango in Brother Drane's time. It represented in the Association regularly till 1883, and soon after ceased to exist. On the ruins of Carolina was built Durango church, in 1885. The old Carolina graveyard still exists.

ELDER B. H. CARROLL, D. D.
(Photo by Deane, Waco, Texas.)

ELDER B. H. CARROLL, D. D.

(Condensed from sketch in volume of Dr. Carroll's Sermons, compiled by J. B. Cranfill.)

There are not many genuinely great men. To be gifted is a great endowment; but gifts are not graces. Some of the most gifted men have possessed none of the elements of real greatness. It is only where depth of intellect and breadth of attainments are combined with greatness of heart and gentleness of spirit, that there is real greatness.

Elder B. H. Carroll is, in the highest, broadest and best sense, a genuinely great man. In gifts he towers a very giant above his fellows, while in breadth of learning and research he ranks with the profoundest scholars of the age. But crowning all is his great heart power, his gentleness and humility, and his consideration for the feelings of others. These graces, so unobtrusive, yet conspicuous to his nearest friends, emphasize his likeness to that disciple whom Jesus loved. All who read his sermons are impressed with the further fact that Brother Carroll is a theologian. His theological views are clear, and ring out with sharp distinctness. On a theological proposition he is as sound and as strong as any of the great writers of our denomination, and these have been among the greatest. However great Dr. Carroll's gifts, learning, eloquence, let it not be forgotten, that he is greater in his home life, in his loyalty to principle, in his whole-hearted support of our organized work, and in his fidelity to his friends, than in all other things combined.

Dr. Carroll is of Irish descent, his great grandfather, Jesse Carroll, having come over from Ireland, and, after a short stay in Virginia, settled finally in what is now called Sampson county, North Carolina. He had three sons, John, Thomas and Joseph. One of these, John, was B. H. Carroll's grandfather. His father, Rev. Benajah Carroll, married Miss Mary Eliza Mallard. He was the rover of the family. He first moved to Carroll county, Miss., subsequently to Drew county, Ark., and finally, in December, 1858, to Burleson county, Texas. Benajah Harvey Carroll was born near Carrollton, Carroll county, Miss., December 27, 1843. Of his father's family of twelve children, Elder J. M. Carroll and himself alone survive. Another of his brothers, Francis Wayland, was likewise a Baptist preacher. He also has three cousins, J. L. Carroll of North Carolina, E. B. Carroll of Georgia, and C. V. Carroll of San Saba, Texas, who are Baptist preachers. His eldest son, B. H. Carroll, Jr., now 22 years old, is also a Baptist preacher of great power; is pastor of Colorado Baptist church. Another son, Charley, gives promise of becoming a preacher of usefulness.

Brother Carroll's home was in Burleson county till 1869, when he moved to Waco, Texas. He was educated at old Baylor University at Independence, Texas. When a schoolboy he helped to raise the last star-spangled banner that floated on a Texas breeze before the civil war, and made one of the grandest speeches of his life. It was delivered from a dry goods box on the streets of Independence in the presence of an immense and incensed crowd of secessionists. In eloquence it was a flame of fire, in logic a ponderous trip-hammer. It showed the folly and predicted the failure and ruin of secession in the South; closed with the famous words of Cutter, paraphrasing the words of Henry Clay in his Bunker Hill oration:

"You asked me when I'd send the scroll our fathers' names are written o'er,
When I could see our flag unroll its mingled stars and stripes no more;
When with a worse than felon hand or felon counsels I would sever
The union of this glorious land, I answer, never! never!"

Notwithstanding his deep convictions on preserving the Union, yet when the secession convention, which carried Texas out of the Union, called for a regiment of rangers to protect the frontier, he mustered into the Confederate service at San Antonio, April 15, 1861. His service as a Texas ranger covered a period of a year, which was filled with thrilling adventure and many exposures to danger. Western Texas was at that time a wilderness, infested with wild animals and savage Indians; but with characteristic courage and manliness, he did his duty faithfully, and won the esteem and plaudits of his comrades and superiors. In the spring of 1862 he joined the Seventeenth Regiment of

Texas Infantry at Austin, of which R. T. P. Allen was commanding colonel. The regiment was attached to McCullough's Brigade, Walker's Division. Soon after mustering into service, he delivered a speech at Monticello, Ark., on the "Delusions of the South." These delusions were set forth as (1) speedy victory of the Confederate armies, (2) cowardice of Northern troops, (3) reliance on Northern democrats, (4) reliance on European intervention. Later, in a negative reply to a speech on the fall of Vicksburg, his exordium commenced: "The stars in their courses fought against Sisera; so the Fourth of July fights against us. In one disastrous day it gives us Lee's repulse at Gettysburg, Holmes' repulse at Helena, and the downfall of Vicksburg. The Confederacy is as much divided as if the father of waters were a river of fire. All the Trans-Mississippi department is eliminated from the conflict. We can witness, but not relieve, the dying agonies of the states beyond the river." In another reply to a speech charging that "Grant is no general," the exordium of Brother Carroll's speech commenced: " 'Whom the gods would destroy, they first make mad.' It is madness to underestimate the talents and resources of an enemy. Fort Donelson, Vicksburg and Chattanooga are witnesses to Grant's generalship, whose testimony is unanswerable and ineffable. The campaign resulting in the investment of Vicksburg will rank in generalship and strategy with the most brilliant achievements of Bonaparte in Italy. Another witness testifies, 'He is a great general who attracts to himself, or who develops great subordinates.' Sherman, Logan, McPherson, Sheridan and Thomas cluster around Grant. My friends, I dread this man's cool, self-poised, everlasting bulldog persistence." These are diamond flashes from some of his "camp-fire debates." He served through the war, being severely wounded in the battle of Mansfield, La.

He was converted in 1865 at a Methodist campmeeting in Burleson county. In June, 1866, was married to Miss Helen Bell, who had recently moved from Starkville, Miss., to Burleson county. His marriage was of God. There are few women possessed of the good sense, tact, energy and industry of Mrs. Carroll. She is indeed her husband's helpmeet. Soon after his marriage, Brother Carroll was ordained to the gospel ministry. He preached and taught school in Burleson county till the fall of 1869.

Coming to Waco in 1869 he held one of the greatest revivals of his life at old New Hope church, assisted by Elder B. Walker. In January, 1870, he became assistant pastor, and in January, 1871, pastor of First Baptist church, Waco, where he has continued for more than 26 years. His pastorate at Waco stretching over more than a quarter of a century, is one of the most brilliant chapters in Texas Baptist history. When he began, this church numbered 200, now 1,000. No church in the state, and few, if any, in America have developed like the Waco church.

When the legislature of Texas submitted the prohibition amendment to a vote of the people, Dr. Carroll was elected chairman of the State Prohibition Executive Committee. He entered vigorously into the campaign with tongue and pen. On July 4, of that year (1887), he held his memorable debate with Roger Q. Mills, who championed the anti-Prohibition cause.

The next notable campaign in which B. H. Carroll engaged, was the one for the payment of the harrassing debt on Baylor University at Waco. He was released by his church for three months, and, together with Elder G. W. Truett, raised in cash in a short time the entire debt of the school, amounting to more than $80,000.

He was in another campaign. The debt of the State Mission Board had grown to $7,000. It was in the year of 1894, one of the hardest years known in Texas. Disaster threatened our organized work in Texas. All eyes again turned to Brother Carroll, and again he was released by his church. He entered the field, and the debt disappeared.

Brother Carroll has always been in active co-operation with all our organized work. He has been several years president of the Board of Trustees of Baylor University at Waco, and was president of the Board of Directors of the Baptist General Convention for some years. He held positions of trust and honor in the General Association before the consolidation. His grand work while fourteen years president of Waco Association he characterizes as "the most joyful and perhaps the most successful service of his life." He is loved and honored throughout America.

DEACON F. L. CARROLL.

This princely giver was born in Dallas county, Alabama, May 25, 1831. When he was 17 years old moved with his parents to

DEACON F. L. CARROLL.
(Photo by Jackson, Waco, Texas.)

De Soto Parish, La. He was converted and baptized in October, 1853. Miss Sarah Long became one with him for life December 23, 1853. He was ordained deacon in 1869. He moved to Beaumont, Texas, in 1873, and in 1882 to Waco. In 1888 he was elected treasurer of Baylor University, which position he now holds. For nine years he has kept the finances of the University in excellent condition, and has given more money to the institution than any other person in Texas.

Deacon Carroll is president of the Beaumont Lumber Company, one of the largest lumber manufacturing enterprises in the South.

He has several times been elected as a member of the Board of Directors of the Baptist General Convention of Texas. He is a noble Christian brother.

CENTER CHURCH.

During the time of the first settlements, Rev. John Fortune and others preached occasionally at residences.

The first Baptist revival in this community was held in the year 1871 by Revs. C. P. Lumpkin and Cain, at the residence of Mr. J. M. Taylor, whose wife with her father and mother, were Methodists. At this revival a great many professed Christ, and 15 were baptized and organized as Hope church. After a short time the church was moved to six miles northeast. Some of the members went to Marlin church.

Hope church being six miles northeast, and Marlin six miles southwest, it was deemed expedient to organize another church. The following is copied from the church records:

"This is to certify that on Thursday night, September 6, 1883, the following brethren and sisters, to-wit: Brothers F. A. Curry and G. W. Morris, and Sisters Cornelia L. Curry, Mary Curry, C. E. Curry, Easter Barton, Sarah Carroll, N. J. Wilsford and Mary E. Morris. who had drawn their letters from the churches at Marlin and Hope, Falls county, Texas, came together at the schoolhouse known by the name of Center * * * and were constituted into a missionary Baptist church of Christ by Elder B. H. Beal, missionary of Little Brazos Association. On motion adopted the church covenant found in Hiscox Directory. On motion adopted Articles of Faith, found in Encyclopedia of Religious Knowledge. On motion adopted the name of Center for church, followed by Brother Beal, the missionary, giving the hand of recognition as a church."

Center church first united with Little Brazos Association, joined Waco Association in 1884. The pastors have been B. H. Beal, A. E. Baten, J. F. McLeod, J. B. Reaves, J. C. Smith, In September, 1895, J. C. Smith held a meeting of days with the church, which resulted in a precious revival, adding 36 to the membership.

The total membership is now 124. The average contributions for all missionary purposes is about $25 per annum. They have a good Sunday school, with library worth $30. Their new meeting house, costing $1,000, was dedicated December 9, 1894.

J. R. M'CLANAHAN,

son of Peter and Sarah McClanahan, was born in Lownds county, Miss., June 1, 1832. His parents were Baptists. J. R. came to

MR. AND MRS. McCLANAHAN.

Anderson county, Texas, 1850, was married to Miss Kate Smith in 1858. They moved to Falls county in 1860, were among the first in the neighborhood, and Mrs. Mc. was among the earliest members of Center church. Of their three children only Mrs. Alice Barton is living. Mr. McClanahan is not a church member, but says he is a Baptist. He is afflicted, yet no member of Center church attends services better or pays more money than he to the cause.

GEORGE MORRIS, SR.,

was the first Baptist settler in Center community; was born in Mississippi in 1826; was baptized into Big Sandy church, Sabine county, Texas, by Elder Sam Lacy, in 1863; moved to Falls county in 1863, and was in the organization of both Hope and Center churches. He died in Trinity county, Texas, in 1891.

DEACON PRESTON JEROME SMITH

was born in Washita parish, La., August 16, 1855. He was the son of Samuel N. and Sarah C. Smith, Methodists. Left an

PRESTON JEROME SMITH.

orphan at 11 he was carried by his Baptist uncle to Alabama. The Baptist Sunday school, Baptist preaching, with careful study of God's word, made him a Baptist. He was baptized into Beulah church, Falls county, Texas, in 1875, by Elder Calvin Magee. December 31, 1879, he was married to Miss Laura Manly, who had previously been baptized by Rev. F. W. Carroll at Independence, Texas. Brother S. is now deacon of Center church, having been ordained July 1, 1888, by Elders J. F. McLeod and J. R. M. Touchstone. He has been clerk of Center church eight years. His only child, Jodie, has been twelve years a member of Center church.

DEACON J. D. M'PHERSON,

a sound Baptist brother, and several years board member of his church, was born in Conecuh county, Ala., August, 1849; moved

J. D. McPherson.

to Texas with his Presbyterian parents in 1866. He was baptized into Hope church in September, 1879; joined Center church in August, 1885, and was ordained deacon by J. F. McLeod and J. R. M. Touchstone, July 1, 1888.

Brethren J. Saxon and J. F. Hickman are also deacons of Center church, spiritual, consecrated men.

DEACON HARVEY JUDSON CHAMBERLIN, LL. B.

We take the following from "Biographical Sketches of the Class of 1858, Dartmouth College," published in 1884: Harvey Judson Chamberlin, LL. B., the son of Chauncey Milton and Fannie (Tolles) Chamberlin, was born at Weathersford, Vt., September 18, 1834. His father was a farmer. Preparatory studies at the academies of Ludlow, Townshend and Thetford, Vt.;

DEACON HARVEY JUDSON CHAMBERLIN, LL. D.
(Photo by Jackson, Waco, Texas.

joined the class at the beginning of middle year. After graduating read law and was graduated at Albany Law School in May, 1859. Admitted to the bar the same month. After practicing about a year in Vermont went to Texas. His health prevented him from confinement to office duties and so in Bell and Milam counties he engaged in stock raising, with banking and mercantile interests. He was postmaster at Belton, Texas, under two presidential administrations. He has taken a prominent part in educational and religious enterprises in his adopted state. * * * Married December 30, 1863, Mary Ferris, daughter of Mark Harmon and Emaline (Catlin) Pike. Children: Charlie Milton, born January 20, 1865, died December 20, 1866; David Tolles, born September 19, 1871, died October 5, 1875; Chauncey Milton, born February 26, 1873, died October 17, 1875."

While a student of Dartmouth, H. J. Chamberlin was converted, and soon after baptized and received in the Baptist church at Perkinsville, Vt. During the last seven years of his college life, three months were spent each year in teaching. The effect of the change from active farm life of boyhood to the sedentary life of student and teacher resulted in breaking down a not very strong constitution. Hoping that a change of climate and habits might be beneficial, he came to Texas, arriving in Belton, November, 1860. Engaged in stock raising, which with several other enterprises claimed his attention till 1888, when, debilitated by bronchial and lung troubles, he disposed of his interests and again sought a change of climate. After residing one year at Boone, Iowa, and three years at Chicago, he returned to Texas and became connected with the Texas Baptist Standard, uniting with the First Baptist church, Waco. On Brother Chamberlin's first arrival in Texas in 1860 he became identified with the work of the Baptist denomination. There were then very few Sunday schools in Texas. He felt the importance of this work, and interested himself actively in the work of organizing schools. He has been a zealous laborer in Sunday schools ever since, and has always taken a deep interest in the work of his church and the missions connected with it. In the early days of the First Baptist church at Salado Brother Chamberlin held membership with W. W. Harris as pastor. Soon afterward he moved to Milam county and went into the organization of the Baptist church at Davilla, with Geo. W. Baines, Sr., pastor. On July 4, 1868, he was ordained deacon at Davilla. The same year he became clerk of Leon River Association, and served till the organization of Salado Association in 1874. He was then made corresponding secretary of Salado Association, and was the next year elected moderator, and re-elected each year until his removal from the state. While living in Belton Brother Chamberlin was instrumental in securing the removal of the late M. V. Smith to that place. Brethren M. V. Smith and H. J. Chamberlin organized the first Sunday school institute in Texas, and perhaps the first in the world, in 1875. Though this dear brother has been for more than twenty years in active business, and much of the time in very feeble health, he has been one of the laymen who has found time and strength to attend to his church duties, and very seldom ever failed to attend any of its services. As business manager of the Baptist Standard at Waco he is giving his denomination noble service.

CHILTON CHURCH.

The town of Chilton is on the Aransas Pass railroad, twenty miles south of Waco, in Falls county. It is in a fine country and in a most excellent community. At the local option election, held Tuesday, October 27, 1896, the vote stood: "For Prohibition, 110;" "against Prohibition, 4." The Chilton church was constituted March 24, 1883, with 15 members. At a meeting of the Association in September they reported 32. The presbytery was composed of Deacon W. D. Gaines and Elder J. T. Crawford. At the April conference Elder L. H. Ewing was chosen pastor. In January, 1884, T. D. Suttle became pastor, and was succeeded after four months by J. R. M. Touchstone. This year the church enjoyed a most gracious revival, swelling her membership to 92. Brother Touchstone's pastorate terminated September, 1886—"an era of peace and prosperity." A. A. Hensler served as pastor from September, 1886, to November, 1887. From November, 1887, to March, 1888, the church was without a pastor. From March, 1888, to July, 1890, J. F. McLeod was pastor—"another era of prosperity." In the summer of 1889 the church had a precious revival season. The number baptized was 30. We quote from Brother J. M. Freeman, clerk: "Fourth Saturday in July, 1890, J. L. Walker became pastor, resigned second Saturday in July, 1893—a successful pastorate." In September, 1893, J. E. McClerkin was chosen, who served till January, 1895. In March, 1895, B. J. Skinner was chosen and served nearly two years. During the pastorate of Brother Skinner, the church built and paid for a comfortable and elegant house of worship.

The clerks have been W. D. Gaines, W. D. Thomas, W. A. Powell and J. M. Freeman.

The deacons have been Samuel Thomas, W. D. Gaines, J. C. Nunn, B. M. Lockard, W. C. Bolton and D. H. Hyden. W. D. Gaines, whose sketch appears elsewhere in this book, has always taken an active part in the affairs of this church and Association.

Almost from the very beginning of its existence the church, under the lead of W. D. Gaines, has kept up a Sunday school and prayer meeting. The Lord continue with them in the future as in the past.

CHINA SPRINGS CHURCH.

China Springs is in the northwestern part of McLennan county. It is on one of the highest points in the county. The China Springs church was organized in a school house in the town of China Springs March 13, 1887, by J. L. Walker. Brother W. B. McCants was chosen clerk at the time of the organization.

The following names were enrolled: J. Willoughby, Richard Tolbert, J. F. Kirkpatrick, James Rice, W. R. McCants, Sisters L. C. Kirkpatrick, M. S. Rice and Willie F. McCants.

Brethren J. Willoughby, Richard Tolbert and W. R. McCants were elected deacons. They were ordained the first Sabbath in May following, the presbytery composed of Elders J. L. Walker and W. F. Shumate and Deacons B. T. Dehay and W. J. Harrell.

Elder J. T. Boynton was the first pastor. Brother Boynton served the church two years. Elder P. W. Eldridge followed, serving one year.

The church was received into the Association at the East Waco session in September, 1887, with 19 members.

Brother J. M. Wright was chosen pastor in 1890, and served one year.

Elder R. E. Smith became pastor in 1891, served one year; Joseph Gronde in 1892, and served one year. He was succeeded by V. G. Cunningham, who served till 1894. R. E. Smith is the present pastor.

A bright future is before this little flock. We believe a rich harvest of usefulness and divine blessing is theirs.

CONCORD CHURCH.

Concord, first called "Tehuacana," was organized in the spring of 1867. The first pastor was Elder Benjamin Walker. The church united with the Association in August, 1867, at the Marlin meeting, with 22 members. The name was changed to Concord in 1874. From 1879 to 1889 the church was in a somewhat disorganized state. The present membership is 55. The place of meeting is six miles east from Waco. The pastors have been Benjamin Walker, A. W. Ellege, N. W. Crain, V. G. Cunningham, J. B. Parrack, B. F. Tatum, L. T. Ritchie, M. L. Davis, T. C. Swafford, Holmes Nichols, W. A. Garrett and L. J. Mims. This church has been advancing during the past few years.

COTTONWOOD CHURCH

existed only a little more than three years. It was in Limestone county, five miles from Mart. It united with the Association in 1889. L. B. Smyth, now a member of Mart church, bore the petitionary letter. Elder J. J. Harris was the pastor till he died September 10, 1891. He was a good man, and well educated. The church dissolved soon after Elder Harris' death.

COTTONWOOD NO. 2.

This church was organized in 1896 with 30 members. The pastor is A. J. Moore. Their place of meeting is one mile north of Cow Bayou creek and two miles north of Mooreville, in Falls county. They meet on the spot where Cow Bayou church met for more than thirty years.

COTTONWOOD GERMAN CHURCH.

In 1884 Elder J. C. Grimmell was general secretary of the German work for America. This brother gathered a few German Baptists into a church near Mooreville, Tex. Elder A. A.

Hensler assisted in the organization. The way was dark. They could not speak English, and American ministers could not serve them. But a higher power kept them alive. In June, 1887, Elder F. J. Gleiss became pastor. The six years of his pastorate were years of prosperity. Brother Gleiss resigned in 1893 on account of declining age. The church then had 66 members. For about a year Elder F. A. Petereit gave half of his time to this church. In 1894 Elder C. H. Keller took up the work, and remained until January, 1896. Elder H. Brukman is now pastor. The church is in a prosperous condition. They have a prosperous Sunday school, a woman's mission society, and live young people's society. They own their house of worship, but are expected to build a larger house soon. The membership now numbers about 100. This church cooperated with the Waco Association for some years, but is now connected with the German Conference.

COW BAYOU CHURCH,

one of the nine original churches of the Association, was organized about 1859, by Elders John McClain and W. A. Mason. The delegate in the organization of Waco Association in November, 1860, was Robert Moore. The church at that time numbered 19 members. In 1861 N. W. Crain was pastor. Since then the pastors have been John McClain, C. Magee, J. M. Gambrell, T. A. Mangum, S. L. Morris, L. H. Ewing, A. J. Shelton, J. W. Roberts, G. G. Gibson, J. B. Reaves, Z. H. Reagan, J. H. Roberts. Present membership, 170. The Cow Bayou church met for a third of a century two miles north of the town of Mooreville. Meets now in a new house in Mooreville. The town was named for Robert Moore, the first deacon of Cow Bayou church.

ELDER NEWELL W. CRAIN

was a native of Tennessee. His father moved to Texas in 1833 or 1834, and settled in San Augustine county. He moved to Nacogdoches county in 1837. Newel received some schooling in San Augustine, though his education was limited. He was a hard student, both before and after entering the ministry. He was converted and joined Union church, in Nacogdoches county, about 1840, and was by this church ordained. Came to McLennan county in 1854. He was a delegate from Waco church in the organization of the Waco Association in 1860. He served on the committee that framed the constitution; was at that time pastor of Bosqueville church. After the war he moved to Mexico and died there. He was a consecrated, pioneer worker, and is remembered with much pleasure by the older brethren.

ELDER J. S. CROSSLIN.

This promising young brother was born near the quiet little town of Manchester, Tenn., October 21, 1864. His father was

ELDER J. S. CROSSLIN.
(Photo by Jackson, Waco, Texas.)

H. B. and his mother Eliza Jane (Jolly) Crosslin. The family moved to Laurence county, Ala., in 1873. At the tender age of 11 years, young J. S. professed a hope in Christ and joined Liberty Baptist church at Town Creek, Ala. In 1881 he went to Mississippi, and won the heart and hand of Miss Fannie Conger, daughter of a wealthy farmer, Eli Conger. With his young wife he moved to Arkansas, but he returned to Mississippi and lived for several years in the little town of Arkabutta.

At the age of 27 he yielded to the impressions which had followed him from his conversion, to preach the gospel, and he was licensed by the Hopewell Baptist church in December, 1891.

He entered Mississippi College at Clinton and spent two years. Failing health admonished him to seek a new locality. So with a letter of introduction from his beloved president, R. A. Venable, to the Baptist brotherhood of Texas, he turned his eyes toward the setting sun, crossed the great father of waters, and was soon in the little town of Omaha, Texas. Here he taught school for a little while. On September 11, 1894, he and his little daughter, Nina, entered Baylor University, where he is still a student. He was ordained by the First Baptist church, Waco, October 3, 1896, and immediately became pastor of Axtell church, and soon afterward of Gerald church, a newly organized body.

CRAWFORD CHURCH.

Organized August 3, 1878. Original members: A. F. Damon, A. H. Meredith, Lucinda Meredith, A. E. Hedrick, J. F. Wicks, S. E. Wicks, D. N. Wicks, Ellen E. Norman, D. H. Temples, Susan Temples, Martha Temples. The presbytery consisted of Elders P. O'Keeffe and W. R. Bowden. P. O'Keeffe was the first pastor, and A. F. Damon and Phil Nolan the first deacons. J. M. Wright succeeded to the pastorate in October, 1879. In 1880 the church united with Leon River Association. M. Isbell became pastor in December, 1882. J. M. Wright in December, 1886. J. M. B. Gresham was called in January, 1893. During his pastorate the meeting house was built. He was overseer of the work. He was at that time pastor of three other churches, but he would work on this house all the week till just time to get to his appointment, and he continued to do so till the house was completed. Crawford is on the Santa Fe railroad, in the western part of McLennan county, and in the midst of a fine community.

In September, 1887, Crawford church went into the McGregor

Association, and after the dissolution of that body came into Waco Association in 1890. Four of the original members are still with the church, viz: Brother Damon, Brother and Sister Meredith and Sister Hedrick. The church is now in a prosperous condition. The lot, house, etc., costing $1,400, are all paid for. The membership is now more than 100, with Elder —. Brooks, pastor.

ELDER VIRGIL GILBERT CUNNINGHAM,

son of Elder J. H. Cunningham, was born near Greenwood, Caddo parish, La., October 10, 1844. Professed religion in

ELDER V. G. CUNNINGHAM.

1863, while a Confederate prisoner of war on parole. He was a Confederate soldier four years; took part in much hard fighting, and was wounded three times. In 1865 he studied in Mt. Lebanon University. In 1867 took charge of the church in Caldwell, Texas. Was married to Miss Mary Pilgrim of Gonzales in

March, 1868, and was ordained the same year. His father preached the ordination sermon. Ordaining elders: Jesse Thomas, Jno. S. Allen, M. Cole, J. G. Gage, J. H. Cunningham and B. H. Carroll. The last named alone survives. Brother Cunningham's ministry has been given to Natchitoches, La., and Waco, Texas, and neighboring points. He graduated at Baylor University in 1871, while his wife was a teacher in charge of the primary and art departments of the University, and thus was enabled to aid him. His wife was a woman of fine education, of devout and consecrated life. After having her to stand by him for twenty-one years, he gathered their four surviving children, Berta, Mamie, Courtland and Carey, around her dying bed, and held their last family worship. His present wife was Mrs. E. M. Huff, a most excellent Christian lady. With her three children, Nannie, Gussie and Willie, and his four, he claims a preacher's family of the standard size. The prisoner in jail or camp or public work, and the poor and outcast members of society, have received a brother's attention at his hand. He is entirely free from that patronizing air which at once erects a rock wall between the poor and his visitor. He has devoted himself mainly to pastoral work, which he feels is his strong point. He has always evinced a spirit of brotherly love for his brother preachers. His uniform good health has encouraged him in the indulgence of a humorous vein. This has occasioned him some anxiety and regret. Being untrained in business management and receiving an inheritance of a few thousand dollars later in life, and the unwise investment of it in stocks and lands, and the immediate depreciation in values, so occupied him in trying to come out honorably, that his preacher's life for years became overshadowed. While he has lost largely, he has acted honorably, and has a good home and the love of his brethren, and a wide field of labor yet left. He was the first city missionary Waco ever had. He labored in that sphere four years with success. He took an active part in all the early work in the development of Waco Association as a strong missionary body.

He has been liberal with his means in university and mission work, and has done a splendid work by scattering our best books over his whole field of labor. When he is dead, we will all feel that the loss was that of a friend and brother indeed. He has recently moved to Northwest Texas and is followed by our prayers and best wishes.

LIFE SKETCH OF J. B. CRANFILL.

Rev. J. B. Cranfill, M. D., editor of the Texas Baptist Standard, was born in Parker county, Texas, September 12, 1858. His parents came from Kentucky to Texas in 1849. His father, Rev. E. A. Cranfill, is a Baptist preacher, and is living at Gatesville, being now in his 68th year. His mother was Martha Jane Galloway, and was descended from Welsh stock. The subject of this sketch spent his childhood and youth as a farmer boy, and later as a cow boy. In July, 1876, he was converted in a meeting held by Rev. M. Ray, on Hog creek, Coryell county, four miles from Turnersville. He joined the Hardshell Baptists, of which his father and mother were then members, and was by them licensed to preach in the winter of 1876. He, however, preached but little, having found himself out of harmony with his church on both Sunday schools and missions. In March, 1877, he moved to Crawford, McLennan county, and later the same year taught the Crawford school. He preached his last sermon as a Hardshell preacher during the summer of 1877 at the old Crawford schoolhouse, and deeming himself unworthy to be a preacher, he laid aside his license and decided, so far as in him lay, that he would never again enter the pulpit. It was not until July, 1886—ten years after his conversion—that he finally yielded to his convictions and took up his cross as a minister of the gospel. From 1877 to 1882 he kept the church letter given him by the Hardshells in his trunk, and was for the most part in a cold and backslidden condition. On September 1, 1878, at a Methodist camp meeting at Patton, McLennan county, he was married to Miss Ollie Allen, daughter of A. D. Allen, of Crawford. In February, 1879, having completed a course of study in medicine, which he had been pursu-

J. B. CRANFILL.

ing for several years, he moved to Turnersville, Coryell county, and began his work as a physician. As a doctor he met with good success, but in 1881 his natural bent for newspaper work led him to start a monthly paper—a two-column folio—called the "Turnersville Effort," with a subscription price of 25 cents a year. Meantime he had, through the generous help of John B. Nichols, now of Crawford, Texas, opened a general store, and his little paper was utilized as a means of advertising his merchandise. In June, 1882, the Cotton Belt railroad having been graded to Gatesville, he moved to that point to engage in the publication of the Gatesville Advance, a six-column, four page weekly paper. His merchandise business was soon closed out, and all his energies were devoted to his paper. The enterprise was successful from the beginning, and at once took the lead in that growing section. In June, 1882, a few months before he moved from Turnersville, and during a great revival there, he resurrected his Hardshell letter, and was received on it into the fellowship of the Turnersville Missionary Baptist church. After his removal to Gatesville, he joined that church and was a member there until his removal to Waco in December, 1886. In July, 1886, after having buried his baby boy, who died at the age of two and a half years, he was, by the grace of God, made willing to preach the gospel, and was licensed the same summer by the Gatesville church. In the meantime Dr. Cranfill's paper had taken a prominent position as an advocate of the temperance reform. The interest in Prohibition had grown constantly, and in September, 1886, under a call made by him, the first party Prohibition convention that ever met in Texas convened at Dallas. He was made chairman of the state executive committee, and has since then been an attendant at every state and national convention of the party. In December, 1886, he moved his paper to Waco, and it was issued until 1888 as the Waco Advance. In August, 1888, he sold the paper to W. D. Knowles, of Dallas. Meantime the great campaign for constitutional prohibition was fought and Dr. Cranfill's paper was the leading organ of the reform, while he was one of its chief exponents on the stump. In 1892, when the national Prohibition convention met at Cincinnati, Ohio, he was nominated for vice president of the United States, and with John Bidwell at the head of the ticket, polled 250,000 votes—the largest vote ever polled by that party. He is still a member of the national Prohibition committee, and active in all the counsels of the party. On the first Sunday in January, 1887, Dr. Cranfill joined the First Baptist church, Waco, of which he is still a member. During all that time, except the time when he was in the traveling work, he has been a teacher in the Sunday school and an active Sunday school worker. In January, 1889, he was elected by the trustees financial secretary of Baylor University, which position he held until October of the same year, when he resigned to take the position of superintendent of Texas missions, to which the Baptist General Convention had elected him. This position he held until March, 1892, when he resigned to engage with Rev. M. V. Smith in the publication of the Texas Baptist Standard. As superintendent of missions he did a great work— the greatest ever recorded in the history of mission work in Texas, or any other state. In February, 1893, Rev. M. V. Smith died, and since then Dr. Cranfill has been sole proprietor of the Texas Baptist Standard at Waco. From a circulation of 6,000 in 1892 the paper has grown until now it has 22,000 subscribers, and enjoys the largest circulation of any Baptist paper in the Southern States. In 1895 Dr. Cranfill brought out a volume of Dr. B. H. Carroll's sermons, which is a most valuable contribution to Baptist literature. He is now at work on a book to be issued this fall entitled,"Sheaves of Gold, or Sunday Morning Thoughts." This will be a large volume, and will be sold by subscription. Dr. Cranfill is still a young man, having not yet reached 39,and if it is the Lord's will to spare his life,it is his ambition to do great things for his fellow men and for the glory of his God.

DEACON M. H. CURRY

was treasurer of the Waco Association from September, 1878, till September, 1883, and was one of the vice presidents of the Mission Board from September, 1885, till September, 1890. He was truly one of the "old guard" of the Association. After his church went into Falls County Association, he was an active worker till his death, which occurred at his home in Marlin, Texas, September 21, 1895. He was born in Sumpter county, Ala., January 21, 1835. Was married to Miss Julia A. Logan, who knew how to fill the delicate position of deacon's wife. In 1865 Brother Curry came to Falls county, Texas, from Mississippi, to which state he had previously moved. Marlin church owes much of her development to Deacon Curry. For more than twenty years he was superintendent of Marlin Sunday school.

REV. M. L. DAVIS,

son of Mead L. and Mary L. Davis, was born in Cherokee county, Ga., Nev. 1, 1856. When two years old his parents moved to Oconee county, S. C., where young M. L. was brought up. He was raised on the farm where he was taught to do all kinds of farm work. Having no early school privileges, he learned to read in a Sunday school at the age of 13. When about 17 years old he professed faith in Christ, and united with the Methodist church. Subsequently he became disturbed on the subject of baptism, which lead him to a thorough investigation of the scriptures, upon that subject, and resulted in his uniting with the Westminster Baptist church, South Carolina. Soon after this, Brother Davis made the mistake of his life in refusing the proffered help of this church to enable him to acquire an education. When 20 years old, without any means of support, yet with a burning desire for an education, he started to a country school, and continued going to school and teaching, alternately, until he succeeded in completing a three years' course in Furman University, Greenville, S. C. In 1885 he came to Peoria, Hill county, Texas, where lived his maternal grandfather, William Bell. Here he engaged in school teaching for two years, during which time he met, wooed and won the hand and heart of Miss Nannie L. Edney, daughter of Newton J. and Elizabeth Edney, of Brenham, Texas, to whom he was most happily married. After this he taught school one year in Kopperl, Tex., and then moved to Louisville, Ky., where he attended the S. B. T. Seminary one and one-half sessions, spending the summer vacations as missionary in Louisiana, under the appointment of the State Mission Board.

He returned to Texas in January, 1890, and located in Waco, and since that time has been connected with the interests and work of Waco Association. Here he started and managed the Baptist Book Depository for three years, under the auspices of the Baptist State Sunday School Board. He voluntarily resigned this position to enter the pastorate. After more than ten years experience as a licensed preacher, he was called to and submitted to ordination and on the 9th day of April, 1893, he was set apart to the full work of the gospel ministry, after which he accepted the pastoral care of the Robinson Baptist church. Since then he has served some time as an efficient agent for the Texas Baptist Standard. Brother Davis is a man of Christian piety, loved and honored by all who know him, and still resides in Waco, Texas.

ELDER RICHARD OSWALD DEWBERRY

was born near Manningham, Butler county, Ala., December 25, 1868. When only four years of age, his father removed to Falls county, Texas. His parents were both devout Baptists, and were in the organization of the Pleasant Grove church. He was converted August 8, 1879, and on the 10th day of the same month united with the Pleasant Grove Baptist church, and was baptized in the Brazos river by Rev. J. McA. Black. Before he had reached the age of 16, he felt divinely called to enter the ministry. His ordination having been called for by a church which desired his services as pastor, he was ordained September 16, 1888. He immediately took charge of the Durango Baptist church, serving it faithfully for two years. During a part of this time he served as pastor Pleasant Grove (his home church) and Little Deer Creek. He attended Baylor University two sessions—1888-90. He was pastor of Corpus Christi in 1890-1. During a pastorate of one year the membership was exactly doubled. He was recalled by a unanimous vote, but on account of a case of discipline, in which the church failed to take the stand he thought it ought, declined to accept. It was here he met Miss Ethel L. Phillips, whom he led to the marriage altar December 16, 1891. She was the daughter of one of the leading members of the church. She stood lovingly by her husband's side till God called him home. During two years—1891-3, he was pastor of Athens, Bazette, Kerens and Blooming Grove. During these two years he welcomed into his Athens church 186 members, 99 being by baptism. In the fall of 1893 he attended the Southern Baptist Theological Seminary at Louisville, Ky. During the summer of 1894 he "supplied" for Rev. Jeff D. Ray, pastor at Huntsville, and chaplain of the State Penitentiary, lo-

ELDER RICHARD OSWALD DEWBERRY.

cated at that place. The satisfaction given may be expressed by saying, that when Bro. Ray resigned the care of the church in June of 1895, Bro. Dewberry was called to the pastorate. In the meantime, or from October, 1894, to September, 1895, he was pastor at Jacksonville, Noonday and Pine Springs churches. On September 15, 1895, entered upon his work at Huntsville, and while there 67 were added to the church roll, 19 by baptism. In 1890, Bro. Dewberry preached the associational sermon at the meeting of the Association at Lorena. In September, 1896, Bro. Dewberry was taken sick; he lingered several weeks and died October 26, 1896. Touching resolutions were passed by the Huntsville church with reference to his death. To all who knew him his memory is precious.

C. L. DOTSON,

a pioneer Baptist in Texas, was a native of Williamson county, Tenn. Moved to Pickens county, Ala., in 1832; received a common school education; was married to Miss Mary Childress; was baptized in 1837 by Elder W. W. Nash into Oakridge Baptist church, and came to Texas in 1840. He afterward moved to Roger's Prairie, and was in the organization of Sand Prairie church. His death occurred on Saturday, October 8, 1864. This was the regular conference day of Sand Prairie church. After the service his pastor, Elder Thomas Eaton, knowing of his sickness, called at his bedside. The dying saint asked: "Is that matter satisfactorily arranged?" referring to a case of discipline touching the fellowship of some members. When informed that all was settled, he replied: "I am glad; it is well," and then passed to his home beyond.

J. J. DOTSON, ESQ.

This brother, to whom we are indebted for much valuable data, is a native Texan, having been born in Austin colony, in the Republic of Texas, July 26, 1842. He is the eldest son of C. L. and Mary Dotson, who came to Texas from Mississippi in 1840. J. J. Dotson attended the first school taught in the first school house erected in Leon county. This house was of logs, with dirt floor; was at Leona. The school was taught by William Keigwin. Bro. Dotson remembers with peculiar pleasure the early visits to his father's house of Z. N. Morrell, who preached the first sermon he ever heard. Elder Morrell awakened in him a thirst for Biblical and religious knowledge. He professed conversion in the summer of 1856, and was buried with Christ in baptism by Elder Gabriel Nash. When about 20 years old, he was married to Miss Miranda Greer Rogers, daughter of Robert Rogers, the first settler in Leon county. Their nine children are living in Leon county, the youngest being 11 years old. He served during the war in the Confederate army, Gould's Battalion, Walker's Division. He was a member of the Confederate States army church, organized by the late M. V. Smith, and remained a member till the war closed. At the close of the war he chose the profession of law, and has made it a success. He now resides at Jewett, and is a member of the Baptist church at that place.

DOWNSVILLE CHURCH.

Elder A. J. Moore began work some years ago in a country heretofore almost entirely neglected. That country is the section about Downsville. This place is near the Brazos river and ten miles south from Waco, on the Aransas Pass railroad. A few well-to-do families live in the community. But the farm lands are tilled largely by tenants, mostly negroes. In the early spring of 1894 a little colony of 24 brethren and sisters took letters from Robinson church, and in May of that year were organized into Downsville church by Elders A. J. Moore and S. R. Williams. Elder A. J. Moore was chosen pastor, and continues in that position. During the summer of 1894 Downsville church enjoyed a precious revival, and 39 were added by baptism. She united with the Association in September, 1894. The petitionary letter was borne by A. J. Moore, J. W. Stripling and Thomas Adams. The church had at that time 75 members. J. W. Stripling was their board member and continued in that capacity till September, 1896, when T. B. Stovall was chosen. The whole number received into this church by baptism is 62. The Downsville brethren have built a good house of worship at a cost of $1,000. She has paid to denominational work $40.35, and to the poor $26. They keep up a good Sunday school, use the literature of the Southern Baptist Convention. The superintendent is W. R. Smith, formerly was W. S. Moore.

ELDER L. W. DUKE

was born in Monroe county, Ala., April 25, 1843. Professed religion and joined the Concord Baptist church at Buena Vista, Ala., in 1858. Baptized by Rev. L. W. Lindsey. Entered the Confederate army in 1861 at 18 years of age. His regiment, the Fifth Alabama Infantry, was sent to Virginia in June, 1861; was on advanced picket line, and was among the first to open fire on the enemy at Farrar's Crossroads, near Alexandria, a few days previous to the first battle of Manassas. Was in nearly all the hard battles in Virginia. Was seriously wounded at the battle of Gaines' Mills. Was taken prisoner at the battle of the Wilderness on May 5, 1864, and remained a prisoner till the war closed. Ordained by the Concord church in 1870. Preached at Buena Vista, Burnt Corn, Monroeville, Claiborne and other points in Monroe, Wilcox and Conecuh counties for twelve years. Was pastor at Claiborne nearly ten years. Came to Texas in December, 1882; settled at Reagan, in Falls county. Was elected moderator of the Association in 1889. Became pastor of the Baptist church at Calvert in 1889, and in 1891 was called by the Mexia church. He resigned in his seventh year as pastor of Mexia. At the beginning of this pastorate there were but 120 names on church book; at the end, 276. Married twice; first in Alabama in 1867, to Mrs. S. E. Owen. Six children were the fruit of this union, five of whom are living and have all been students either of Baylor University or Baylor College. The second marrage was to Miss Sue Granberry.

ELDER JAMES FRANKLIN DUNCAN.

Perhaps the most sturdy and active of all the American families are the Scotch-Irish. Of such family, James F. Duncan is descended. His ancestors settled in South Carolina long before the American revolution. He was born in Alexander City, Ala.; in 1867 the family came to Texas, and located at Clarksville. He joined Shamrock Baptist church, near Clarksville, in September, 1870, being baptized by the pastor, Nelson Sansing. At 19 years of age, September, 1871, he was licensed to preach and immediately entered Sylvan Academy, near Paris. He entered Baylor University October, 1873, graduating June 21, 1877. He was ordained by the Clarksville church December 26, 1876. During his senior year in college he served as pastor the Olive Branch, Mooreville and Golinda churches. After graduating he became principal of the Mount Calm Masonic Institute for one session, serving as pastor at the same time the Olive Branch, Pin Oak and Mount Antioch churches. He then served as missionary for Waco Association from May to September, 1878. During this time he held many precious meetings. August 22, 1878, he was married to Miss Annie B. Vesey of Waco. He practiced medicine at Wolf City, Corsicana, Baird and Savoy, preaching to churches all the while. He organized the church at Wolf City, and became its first pastor in 1882. In 1886 he entered the Southern Baptist Theological Seminary and graduated May, 1888. Soon after entering the seminary he was called to the pastoral care of the Cable Street Baptist church, Louisville; afterwards Franklin Street church. This church prospered during his pastorate, increasing in membership, and more than doubling in financial strength. During this period the church made the exchange of an old frame building in an undesirable locality, for a handsome and commodious brick in a desirable community. January 1, 1889, he was pastor of the First Baptist church, Baton Rouge, La. He served as chaplain of the State Penitentiary two years, and one term as chaplain of the Louisiana legislature, taking an active part in encouraging the passage of the law that ousted the Louisiana lottery from the state and nation. He was pastor of the First Baptist church, Bonham, Texas, one year. April, 1893, he became pastor of the First Baptist church, at Navasota. He is now editing the South Texas Baptist.

DURANGO CHURCH

is in the western part of Falls county. The first settler in the community was J. M. Jackson (Uncle Joe), a pioneer stock raiser and farmer. "Uncle Joe" is a Baptist—now very feeble with age. The first sermon at Durango was prached by Solomon G. O'Brian. Miss Mollie Bohanner taught the first school. The Durango church was organized in 1885. Previously, Carolina church had been moved to Durango, but had ceased to exist. The original members were P. V. Thompson, Sister M. W. Tompson, Sister E. Wright, J. J. Jenkins, Sister C. C. Jenkins, J. L. Collier, Sister M. E. Collier, E. L. Brewer, S. A. Brewer, S. M. Bryant, Sister F. T. Bowlin, Lizzie Fleming, Lizzie High. The presbytery were Elders G. W. Green, A. A. Hensler, A. A. Murry and J. A. Lea (licentrate). The pastors have been A. A. Hensler, R. O. Dewberry, A. P. Collins, J. B. Reaves, J. J. McBee, J. R. M. Touchstone, and again J. B. Reaves, the present pastor. Among those who have greatly endeared themselves to the church for their piety and liberality, the names of J. M. Jackson, P. V. Thompson and wife, E. L. Brewer and wife and Sister S. M. Bryant deserve to be especially mentioned. The church first united with the Salado Association, and continued there one year. In 1886 she united with Waco, reporting a membership of 84. The church has enjoyed some gracious revivals, notably in 1885, Pastor A. A. Hensler, assisted by G. W. Green; in 1887, Pastor Hensler, assisted by J. R. M. Touchstone; in 1889, Pastor R. O. Dewberry, assisted by B. H. Carroll. The deacons of Durango have been J. E. Bailey, E. L. Brewer, J. N. Bell, F. M. Reaves, John Stanley. The present deacon is J. W. Boyd. They have kept up a Sunday school almost from the beginning. The church owns a comfortable house of worship, with one acre of land, located in the center of the village.

EAST WACO CHURCH.

"In the earlier part of the year 1867, Elders R. C. and R. B. Burleson, aided by their teachers and students of Waco University, began to hold religious services in a log house near the factory in East Waco." The factory at that time was running, and the services were attended mostly by the employees. "In October of the same year, at the same place, Elder B. Walker conducted a revival meeting, which resulted in a large number of conversions. Concord church was then in existence, six miles east. It was not convenient for all the converts to go so far in order to unite with the church. Some of the Concord members were then living in East Waco. At the regular meeting of Concord church, November 1867, an act was passed extending an 'arm' of that church to East Waco, with authority to receive and baptize the new converts. This 'arm,' which consisted of East Waco members and such others as chose to attend, met, heard several of the new converts relate their Christian experience, and authorized their baptism. They were then in full membership with Concord church, though meeting in East Waco as an 'arm.' These meetings were held monthly during the latter months of 1867 and early months of 1868. During the early part of 1868 a meeting house was erected three-fourths of a mile from

EAST WACO BAPTIST CHURCH.
(Photo by Sanders, Waco, Texas.)

the river, on the Corsicana road; and on May 9, 1868, the East Waco church was organized. The members of the 'arm' of Concord obtained letters and went into the new organization."

The following are the original members: Elder B. Walker, Mrs. Rachel L. Walker, J. L. Walker, J. A. Marley, Mrs. Frances Marley, J. B. Chestnut, Mrs. Mary E. Chestnut, W. R. Kellum, Mrs. K. H. Kellum, S. F. Sparks, Mrs. Jane Sparks, Mrs.

L. M. Brown, Mrs. C. Newlin, Mrs. Sarah Newlin, Mrs. Mary Lucky, Louis Rusin, Mrs. N. Rusin, John Puckett, Mrs. E. Puckett; W. R. Kellum and S. F. Sparks were recognized as deacons. The new organization called Elder B. Walker to the pastorate, which position he held till his death, April 2, 1870. The presbytery that organized the church consisted of Elders W. C. Buck, S. E. Brooks and T. F. Lockett. Almost immediately the pastor, Elder B. Walker, organized the East Waco Sunday school, which has never suspended or gone into winter quarters. "Thus began the East Waco Baptist church. Its beginning was a favorable one, for its membership, though small, comprised some of the most godly and influential men and women ever given to a church or community. The new brick house was erected in 1878. In this house the services were held till December 24, 1895. On that date the first service was held in the splendid modern house in which the body now meets. The pastors have been B. Walker, M. B. Hardin, N. W. Crain, R. C. Burleson, G. L. Jennings, V. G. Cunningham, J. G. Nash, B. F. Tatum, J. S. Allen, W. W. Finley, John Bateman, G. W. Truett. Of these B. Walker, M. B. Hardin, N. W. Crain and J. S. Allen have gone to their long home. Deacons: W. R. Kellum, T. J. Powers, S. F. Sparks, D. W. Davis, S. T. Crossland, J. Whitaker, C. J. George, E. G. P. Kellum, W. R. Turner, W. N. Steed, C. Faulkner, W. H. Deaton, O. I. Halbert. The present deacons are the four last named. East Waco church united with the Association in 1868 with 44 members. B. Walker and J. B. Chestnut were the bearers of the petitionary letter. Next to First Waco, East Waco is the most prosperous church in the Association. Present membership, 297.

ELDER THOMAS EATON.

While we believe in an educated ministry, we rejoice in the fact that in all the ages, the world has been turned upside down by men who knew naught but to preach Christ and Him crucified. Such a man was Elder Thos. Eaton. His early education was neglected. Yet by giving himself to prayer and study of God's eternal truth, he became a most powerful preacher of the cross.

He was born December 6, 1817, and died January 6, 1888. Early in the "fifties" he was converted and joined Shiloh Baptist church, Robertson county. The change was complete. If he had been active in the service of Satan, ever afterward he was zealous in the service of his new Master, Jesus Christ. On December 9, 1854, by request of Shiloh church, he was set apart to the full work of the gospel ministry. The names of the grand

ELDER THOMAS EATON.

old pioneers, William W. Walker, B. Clark and William Clark, appear on his credentials as presbytery. To say that Elder Eaton was a great preacher of his day, is to put it mildly. Bro. J. J. Dotson, Jewett, Texas, who remembers him well, writes: "While he often terribly mutilated 'the king's English,' yet few men possessed greater power in the pulpit. He was verily a preacher to the common people. Eternity alone will reveal the work of this old veteran." In 1858 and 1859 he was missionary of Trinity River Association. A great part of his life was spent in the pastorate, mostly in Robertson county. The churches of Shiloh, Sand Prairie, Bethel (Leon county), Leona and a number of others, enjoyed seasons of prosperity while under the care of this faithful Shepherd. In church and associational meetings he did no useless talking, but never failed to come boldly to the front with all the power he could command when the Baptist cause was involved. His love for a friend was remarkable. Among those he loved best was the pioneer Baptist, C. L. Dotson. Bro. Dotson was buried by the Masonic fraternity. Elder Eaton was present and lead in prayer at the funeral. Many people were there, and it was the universal verdict that here was offered the most powerful prayer ever heard by this audience. A third of a century has passed since that time, and till this day the old people talk of the deep and touching effect of that prayer. Bro. Eaton died as he lived, a faithful minister of the cross. He had faith in God's word, and God blessed his ministry. His work is done. Beloved brother, farewell. Walk in peace the golden streets. Year by year will the coming ages harvest the fruits of thy seed-sowing. Beloved brother, farewell!

ELDER W. B. EAVES,

a warm-hearted preacher and indefatigable worker, was born in Montgomery county, Alabama, November 19, 1819. He was baptized by Elder Levy Parks, in Perry county, Alabama, in the year 1843. He was made deacon by the Memphis church, in Pickens county, in 1846. In 1852 he came to Burleson county, Texas, and united with Providence church. He was ordained to the gospel ministry October 30, 1853, by a presbytery composed of R. E. B. Baylor, David Fisher, J. G. Thomas and S. G. O'Bryan. He had but very little education, and he struggled with his convictions for quite a while before entering the ministry. His brethren in Alabama had a habit of putting him forward, and he came to Texas to escape. But he found it no better here. We quote from Link's Magazine: "His first effort was in a log cabin in the post oaks, where he thought no Christian was present. He preached at 11 o'clock, and was induced to make another appointment at night, when several were converted. This gave him encouragement. The meeting was continued, and thirty-seven professed conversion. Elder David Fisher was sent for to baptize them. They were organized into a church, which called for the ordaination of Bro. Eaves." Elder Eaves was in the organization of Waco Association, as a delegate from Marlin church, and served on the committee that had under consideration the Articles of Faith. He was several years pastor of Marlin church, and held many precious revivals there and elsewhere. He was a mechanic, a real genius, and his own hands ministered to his necessities. He lived to a ripe old age, and then went home to live with Jesus.

EBENEZER CHURCH

came to Waco Association from Trinity River in 1867, with 41 members. J. W. Kinnard was pastor. In 1869 trouble arose, and two parties presented themselves, asking to be seated in the Association. Both were denied seats, and a few moments spent in special prayer for the fellowship, union, peace and harmony of Ebenezer church; and thereafter the moderator announced the following committee to visit and labor with said church, to-wit: Z. N. Morrell, Irvin Brown, J. P. Brown, R. M. Turner, Harrison Bryan and J. V. Wright. The next year, 1870, the committee reported the church "still in disorder," and she was "excluded from representation." By the time of the meeting of the Association in 1871 harmony was restored, and the Association adopted the following resolution:

"*Resolved*, That we rejoice with them, and most cordially receive their messengers, and invite them to participate with us in all our labors for the glory of God, and the good of souls."

Ebenezer was at this meeting dismissed by letter. W. T. Wright, pastor. Membership, 91. The church still exists in Little Brazos Association, and has a membership of 210.

EDDY CHURCH NO. 1.

This church was organized as "Sage Chapel," in July, 1875, in McLennan county, about two miles west of where the town of Eddy now stands. Original members: J. H. McGlockin, M.

J. McGlockin, Wm. McGlockin, Polly McGlockin, G. M. Nix, Samantha Nix, John Pool, Francis Pool, L. Smith and M. F. Smith. The Articles of Faith and Covenant in Pendleton's Manuel were adopted. T. A. Mangum was the first pastor, and served seven years. The next pastor was John Witt. In June, 1882, the church convened at Eddy, on the M., K. & T. railroad. The next year there were dissensions, and an effort by some to dissolve the church. The vote to dissolve was taken at a called conference in 1883, but at a subsequent conference, of which M. F. Whatley was moderator pro tem., and Peter S. Bruner clerk, the act of dissolution was declared illegal, and was rescinded. The church was afterward consolidated with Deer Creek (now Blevins) church.

EDDY CHURCH NO. 2.

About 1883 a church was organized at Eddy, while Sage Chapel was still in existence. This church went into the McGregor Association in 1885 with 40 members. Elder B. Wright was pastor. The next year this church reported 56 members. In 1890 T. E. Muse was pastor. In September of this year she came to the Waco Association with a letter from McGregor, and 96 members. T. E. Muse continued to serve the church till 1894, when he was succeeded by J. C. F. Kyger. After Bro. Kyger, L. J. Mims, the present pastor, was called. Eddy has a good Sunday school, and her present membership is 140.

ELDORADO CHURCH.

Eldorado church is in Falls county, 15 miles southwest from Marlin, and five east from Rosebud. The first settler in this community was the pioneer Baptist, W. A. Woolie. Others came later, and soon the necessity for a church began to be discussed. The Baptists were compelled to go several miles to Pleasant Grove and other points for church accommodations. The Eldorado church was constituted June 11, 1887. The first members were Brethren George Hale, David Castleman, W. A. Woolie, T. R. Flood, James McKim, J. T. Daniel, Wm. Romans; Sisters Bettie Stallworth, Mary Romans, Lucy Castleman, Dora Flood. The presbytery was composed of Elders Geo. S. Harris,

—. Jackson, J. Daffin and J. R. M. Touchstone. W. A. Woolie was called away to his heavenly home in the spring of 1891. Bro. Castleman, a prominent deacon, has moved to Schackleford county. The pastors have been Geo. S. Harris, J. W. Roberts, J. F. McLeod and J. R. M. Touchstone. Elder J. L. Stuckey was ordained by, and holds membership with, this church. The deacons are R. G. Boyd and J. W. Murphy. The greatest revival was held in 1891 by Pastor J. W. Roberts, assisted by J. R. M. Touchstone. The church first joined the Waco Association, withdrew and in 1891 was in the organization of Falls County Association. In 1891 the church paid $50 for missions; has averaged $40 per year since. The first house was small and inconvenient. Recently she has built a house, and now worships under her own roof. The house first used was 14x20 feet. The present house is 28x48. From time of organization to present the church has received nearly 100 by baptism and letter. The year of greatest increase, 1891; the year of greatest loss, 1890. Present membership (June, 1896), 80. The clerks have been J. F. Daniel, W. S. Farrar, R. J. Flood, J. A. Atkins. A live Sunday school, presided over by Elder J. L. Stuckey, is under the supervision of this church.

ELDER W. A. ELLEGE

was missionary of the Waco Association from September 6, 1871, to May 14, 1872. He did much hard, active service during this period; received by baptism and letter 60 members, and organizing three churches. Gen. J. E. Harrison said: "Bro. Ellege was an industrious, efficient missionary." He was born in East Tennessee December 23, 1809, of poor parents, and grew up without an education. He was married to Miss Mary Cherry, and soon afterward was converted and became a Baptist preacher. It was his custom to take his Bible and hymn book with him to the field and, while resting, study the text and memorize the hymn for the next Sunday's service. He moved to Mississippi before 1850, and held many precious protracted meetings. He would preach the truth, let it hurt whom it would. He was coarse and uncouth in both manner and language. It is said that on one occasion he arrived on the ground after the protracted meeting had commenced and was dragging slowly along. He took a seat by himself. The congregation whispered, "Who is that?" A brother went to him and asked: "Are you a preacher?" "Well, I try to preach sometimes about home, where they know me." He was introduced to the preachers and invited to preach. He consented to *try*. He opened the service in a most awkard manner, and drawled out his text and began to drawl out his thoughts till the congregation felt humiliated. "When he saw that all had decided him a failure, he straightened up and began to preach with such eloquence and pathos that he soon had the congregation in tears, and before he closed some where shouting. The revival commenced."

A "Hardshell" preacher in Mississippi, named Jerry Pearcell, once preached a sermon in which he said there were "three calls" to the ministry: "One class God called," who preached for the good of souls. Another class money called, who would not preach without pay; and yet another class, the devil called, who preached from education and for popularity. Ellege circulated an appointment to reply to Pearcell's sermon. A large crowd came out. Ellege took for his text, "By their fruits ye shall know them." "I grant," said he, "that there are 'three calls,' as the gentleman stated: 1. Those who are called of God to preach the gospel to sinners, and many are converted and saved. This fruit belongs to all, who are called of God, for 'by their fruits ye shall know them.' But this does not apply to Mr. Pearcell, therefore, he is not called of God. He is not called of money, for he would scorn to take money for his preaching. Therefore, if he has any call at all, it is of the devil." It is said the "Hardshells" never got over this in that community. He came to Texas in 1852, and preached much over Southern and Middle Texas. He rode as a missionary of different Associations, organized many churches, and was pastor of many. He died July 8, 1884. He sleeps at Clear Creek church, Lampasas county.

FLAT ROCK CHURCH

worships near the Bosque river, nine miles northwest from Waco. It is only four years old; is in the midst of a populous community, and has a mission for good. The church had 27 members when she united with the Association, in 1894. Joseph Gronde was pastor. The membership is now 64, and among them some noble, godly, consecrated men and women. Elder J. B. Reaves is the present pastor. An ordained minister, J. M. Dean, holds membership in this church. S. N. O'Neill is Board member.

FRIENDSHIP CHURCH.

This little flock worships about 10 miles southwest from Waco. They are a consecrated, spiritual band, alive to all our mission interests and loyal to all our organized work. They were organized in 1893, and reported 21 members to the Association that year. The pastors have been Z. H. Reagan, H. D. Gilbert and E. B. Shope. The present membership is 73.

JOHN FLOWER.

John Flower was born in England, August 7, 1818, and died at his home near Waco November 19, 1890. The family came to America and settled in New York in 1840, afterwards in Madison county, Ill. It was here that John was converted. At the age of 24, he, with his sister, Hannah Flower, were baptized in Silver creek, Madison county, Ill. Soon afterward he was married to Miss Nancy Renfro. Bro. Flower first settled in Texas, near Hillsboro, where he lost his wife. He was the first sheriff of Hill county, afterward county surveyor of that county. He was married the second time to Mrs. Almorinda (Bennett) Moore. After a happy union of about 18 years, death claimed this companion. Nearly five years later, he was married to Miss Merritt, who also died soon afterward. Bro. Flower was a devoted companion and father, a true Christian and patriot. It was the rule of his life to hold family worship every night before retiring. His Christian children remember this habit of their father with much joy.

DEACON W. H. FRANCIS.

was born in Bertie county, North Carolina, February 9, 1841. His parents and grand parents were Baptists. His father was a deacon. Bro. Francis became a Christian when he was about 15 years old, and was baptized into the fellowship of Capart church, in his native county, by Elder John N. Hogwood. He afterward united with Coldrain church, North Carolina, and brought a letter from that church to Texas, in 1872. After coming to Texas, he joined the New Hope church, and was by that church ordained deacon in the fall of 1876. Was in the organization of Mart church April 28, 1878, and has been an active deacon of that church ever since. His life has been consistent and a benediction to his church and community. He is the only male member of Mart that was in the organization. His moral character is of a high order. True to his convictions, and withal co-operating fully with his pastor and church. Brother Francis is one of the very best men known to this writer. He has only pleasant smiles and good words for all.

DEACON W. D. GAINES.

This brother was born in Escamambia county, territory of Florida, October 11, 1824. He was the eldest of 11 children, born to Jacob and Lucinda (McDavid) Gaines, only three of whom are now living: Reuben R., Paris, Texas, chief justice of Supreme Court of Texas; G. W., druggist, Houston, and the subject of this sketch. In 1836 the family moved to Sumpter county, Ala. Young W. D., before his majority, was associated with his father in a merchantile business. He obtained a fair education in the common schools of the country, and has been all his life a close reader. For 8 years, after reaching his majority, he was overseer on a farm, part of the time managing two farms, 18 miles apart. November 27, 1847, he married Miss Elizabeth M. Spinks, Washington (now Choctaw) county, Ala. In 1854 he moved to Mt. Sterling, and carried on a farming interest on the Bigbee river. At the close of the war (1866) he came, with his family, to Rock Dam, Falls county, Texas, purchasing 250 acres of Brazos bottom land. He sold out at Rock Dam in 1874, and purchased land on Deer Creek (adjoining the present town site of Chilton), where he still lives. There have been born to W. D. and Elizabeth Gaines 11 children. Of these 8 are living, 3 died young. Bro. Gaines and wife joined the Baptist church October, 1852, in Choctaw county, Ala. They were baptized in Clear creek, by Eld. Noah Slay, and became members of Clear Creek church. Moving their membership to Mt. Sterling in 1856, Bro. Gaines was ordained deacon. There being no church in the vicinity of Rock Dam, they attached themselves to Robinson church, 14 miles from home, in 1868. In 1874 they united with Cow Bayou church, near Mooreville. They were in the constitution of Carolina church, near Durango, in 1875. The country now rapidly settled up, and it became necessary to organize a church between Cow bayou and Deer creek. New Zion church was formed, but the location was a mistake. After six years, this church dissolved, and the brethren organized at Chilton, in 1883. Bro. Gaines was in both organizations. Chilton church has prospered from the first. For twenty years Deacon Gaines was in the front rank of workers of Waco Association. He was one of the vice-presidents of the Mission and Sunday School Board for 16 years. For 18 years he was in all the meetings of the Association except one, and for 16 years he met all the fifth Sunday appointments except four. He was moderator of the Association four years. He has represented the Association in the Southern Baptist Convention, and several times in the State Convention.

GENEVA CHURCH.

The unpretentious little village of Elm Mott nestles ten miles north from Waco, where the forests lying along the Brazos river meet the great, broad, fertile prairies. It is an ideal place, pleasant and inviting. When it was a new country, the red deer might be seen galloping about the untenanted woodland and on the grassy glades with the wildest freedom. Our early pioneer preachers followed up every new settlement in Central Texas, and in most instances without the knowledge of any missionary board. Elder Thomas Hooker, now at a very ripe old age, living at Duffau, was among the first preachers to hunt up the fragments of the old first Union Grove settlement. A few Baptists were found, and July 17, 1879, fixed as the date to organize a church. Elders Thomas Hooker, J. F. Duncan and W.

M. Garrett were invited to be present and assist in the organization. The following brethren and sisters had their names enrolled: J. B. Teat and wife, W. J. Miller, Sister Grose and two daughters, G. W. Moore and wife, and W. M. Garrett. These solemnly covenanted together as a church of Christ, July 17, 1879. The Articles of Faith, as found in the Encyclopedia of Religious Knowledge, were adopted (New Hampshire Declaration), and the little family began keeping house. The church was constituted in the old Union Grove schoolhouse. The new church took the name of Union Grove. The name was changed to Geneva in 1886. Elder Thomas Hooker was the first pastor, and continued till 1882, when he was succeeded by W. B. Brantley. In 1885 Bro. T. E. Muse was pastor, and continued till 1889. It was during his pastorate that the meeting house in which the church now worships, was erected, at a cost of $1,200. Bro. Muse was followed by T. P. Speakman. Next came the brilliant eight years' pastorate of Elder Holmes Nichols. The church united with Waco Association in 1879, joining with 28 members. Moderator J. J. Riddle extended the right hand of Associational fellowship to her messengers, J. B. Teat, J. W. Miller and S. T. Christian. In 1882 the church represented in the Association (at Mart) by letter only; at all other meetings till this day, by letter and messengers. The whole number baptized into this church from its beginning to the present time is 75. The present membership is 84. From the first she has had a steady growth.

GERALD CHURCH

has been very recently organized; is five miles northeast of Geneva. She has not yet joined any association. Our young brother, J. S. Crosslin, is pastor. This little flock has already shown signs of missionary life, having sent in contributions for the Master's work.

ELDER F. J. GLEISS.

Elder F. J. Gleiss was born in Prussia, Germany, September 19, 1826. In 1854 he came to Texas, and was converted in February, 1856, among the Methodists, who licensed him to preach in

1860. Having been thrown into the company of some Baptists, he became convinced that infant baptism was unscriptural, and after a personal search of the Scriptures, he declared that he could sprinkle no more babies; that he did not believe in falling from grace, and that the Episcopal church government was unscriptural. He applied for membership in the small German

ELDER F. J. GLEISS.
(Photo by Jackson, Waco, Texas.)

Baptist church at Greenvine, Washington county, Texas, and he and his consecrated wife were baptized in 1868 by Rev. F. Kiefer. He was at once called to the pastorate of this little flock, thus becoming the first German Baptist pastor in Texas, Dr. Kiefer spending his time in evangelistic work and studying medicine. After serving this church very acceptably for about seven years, in which time he built up this church and organized two others, he resigned and took up work in Gonzales county. Here he labored as pastor and missionary till 1885, and organized one more church. From 1885 till 1887 he was missionary in Brenham, Washington county, and from 1887 till 1893, pastor of Cottonwood church, Falls county, near Mooresville. Since 1893 he has been living at Waco, the most of this time acting as pastor of the German Baptist church of Waco. Our brother has been permitted to see 16 German Baptist churches spring up in Texas, with 14 ministers.

ELDER G. G. GIBSON

was one of the pioneer settlers on Deer creek, in the neighborhood of Blevins. He was in the organization of Deer Creek (now Blevins) church. His education is limited, but he has done some good work as a minister in that country. He is sound in the faith and a man of influence. He has served several churches as pastor, and has assisted in the ordination of a number of preachers and deacons.

ANDREW GODDARD, A. M., M. D.,

president of the Sunday School Institute of Waco Association, was born January 8, 1831, on Crooked Fork of Emory's river, in a deep cove of the Cumberland mountains, Morgan county, Tenn. Little things often indicate the state of mind, even in a child, so this incident is related: A poor woman, a fortune teller, passed and called for something to eat. She was fed from the kitchen table. After eating, as if in compensation, she turned the coffee cup over in the saucer and, after the grounds had run down the side of the cup, she began: "The father and mother shall both die young, and most of the children; but one of the boys shall become a great scholar." Young "Andy" sprang up, saying, "Me him! me him!"

His father and mother, Joseph and Rachel Goddard, provided for their children the best means of education in their power. Together with a neighbor, they engaged a teacher, who inspired his pupils with a thirst for knowledge. By the time young Andy had reached the age of 15 years, he had finished the studies taught in that school. His teacher, John Farmer, advised that he should go to college. He entered the University of East Tennessee in 1847, finished the curriculum, and graduated to the degree of A. B. in 1853, and two years later received the degree of A. M. He never prayed for wealth nor fame, but ten thousand times has he prayed for the privilege to be a wiser and better boy, a wiser and better man. His prayer still is, "Lord, make me to know." He claims to-day to be a student in God's Great University. His whole life has been a student's life, and he feels sure that death shall not make a

ANDREW GODDARD, A. M., M. D.

break in his studies. When a boy he went to mill. Later he taught school, practiced medicine, worked on a farm and surveyed land. Such occupations he regards as incidental and subordinate. He believes that the whole aim of our being should be to present ourselves at last, a piece of workmanship worthy of the hand that created it, fit for a place in the everlasting habitations, well pleasing to God. In the fall of 1849 he was baptized by Elder Alfred Agee, in the beautiful water of the Beech Fork of Emory's river. He was a member of the First Baptist church of Knoxville, Tenn., Mat Hillsman, pastor, and of the Union Baptist church, Coosa county, Ala., Platt Stout, pastor, who baptized Mrs. N. E. Goddard. Dr. Goddard held the chair of Greek and Latin in the Central Institute. At the close of the Civil war, in which he served as a private soldier, he became principal of the Byar's Institute in Chambers county, Texas, and was in the organization of Cedar Bayou church. After leaving the University, he was principal of Robertsonville Academy, in Anderson county, Tenn., and while there was chosen superintendent of a Presbyterian Sunday school, there being no Baptist church in the village. He had no controversy with the elders; but three years after he had gone away, a large number of those Presbyterian children were converted and became Baptists. The result was a large Baptist church. In 1880 Dr. Goddard was elected president of the Sunday School Institute of Waco Association, which position he has held till the present time, with the exception of three years of bad health. He and his companion, Sister Goddard, are among the very best Christians in Waco, are members of Dr. Carroll's church. Their residence is No. 1904 South Seventh street. Dr. Goddard has for years been county surveyor of McLennan county. He and his wife are the parents of nine boys and six girls.

GOLINDA CHURCH.

The village of Golinda is 12 miles south of Waco, on the west side of the Brazos. Golinda church was organized in 1875 or 76. Came into the Association at the Blue Ridge meeting, August, 1876. The messenger was J. E. Brown. R. C. Burleson was pastor. The membership numbered 21. The next pastor was J. F. Duncan, who was followed by J. B. Parrock, T. P. Speakman and S. L. Morris. This church last represented in 1881. The membership was 38, at that time. Soon after this Golinda dissolved.

GOSHEN CHURCH

was organized September, 1890. Original members: E. Martin, M. C. Martin, S. E. Upchurch, David Connally, Martha

Connally, Hattie Boykin, Cora Boykin, G. T. Cain, Martha Cain, E. Cain, J. M. Boatwright, W. L. Baits, P. L. Baits, J. M. Brazill, M. A. Brazill, J. E. Brazill, J. M. McGhee, Martha McGhee, W. J. Peacock, M. E. McKever, J. N. McKever, H. H. Fort, Helen Fort, W. R. Wood, Jose McGhee, Missouri McGhee, J. M. Boykin. It will be seen that this church started off with 31 names. The organizing presbytery consisted of J. S. Daugherty, J. M. Wright and T. A. Mangum. They enjoyed a fine revival in 1892. The church came into the Association in 1890. The pastors have been W. O. Millican, J. C. Johnson, T. A. Mangum, M. Isbel, H. F. Curry and E. B. Shope, present pastor. Goshen meets 4 miles south of McGregor, on the east side of the Santa Fe railroad. Present membership, 46.

GREENWOOD CHURCH

was organized about 1869. Their place of meeting was 10 miles west of Waco and one mile south of North Bosque river, and near the residence of L. P. Standifer, who was one of the leading members. The church united with the Association in 1870, with 23 members. R. B. Burleson was pastor till 1874, when J. J. Riddle was chosen and served one year. The next pastor was J. H. Harrison, and the last T. P. Speakman. Greenwood ceased to exist about 1883. Such men as L. P. Standifer, B. T. DeHay, W. H. Long, S. A. C. Kilgore have held membership in this church.

ELDER J. M. B. GRESHAM

was born in Polk county, Ga., June 18, 1856. His father died in 1865, and on this account his early education was neglected. He was baptized at 15 years of age, and was married very young. He was a licentiate preacher four years. He was ordained at Lafayette, Ga., by Elders F. S. Moore and J. C. Camp. He preached for various churches in Georgia. Came to Texas in 1889, and has resided since in Moody and Crawford. Since coming to Texas he has served Stampede, Coryell, Eagle Springs, Crawford, Patton and Oglesby churches. His work at Crawford has been told in the history of that church.

During his pastorate, houses of worship have been built at Eagle Springs, Crawford and Patton. His home is at Crawford.

GROESBECK CHURCH.

The records of Groesbeck have been lost, and her early history can not be written. This church came into Waco Association in 1876, with 20 members. Elder G. L. Jennings was pastor. J. A. Aikin was the messenger. Bro. Jennings served till 1880. In 1881 G. A. Coulson was pastor, in '82 H. W. Watson, in '83 G. L. Jennings, in '84 J. J. Harris, who continued till 1886, when the church ceased to belong to Waco Association. At that time the membership was 35. The messengers were J. J. Harris and W. P. Brown. In 1881 the Association was held at Groesbeck. This church now has 175 members, and is one of the most prosperous in Limestone Association.

ELDER MARTIN B. HARDIN

was one of the best preachers we had in the early days of Waco Association. He was the youngest of seven children, was born in Florida, September 23, 1836. The family moved from Florida to Columbus, Ga., about 1841. Young Martin had excellent educational advantages, and enjoyed the pulpit ministrations of Dr. John E. Dawson. He was converted under the ministry of Dr. J. H. DeVotie, and by him baptized. He was ordained February, 1859, by presbytery composed of Elders C. C. Willis, Joseph Walker, T. B. Shade, James Whitten, J. M. Watt, John E. Dawson and J. H. De Votie. He succeeded Dr. W. Williams to the pastorate of Auburn church, Ala. Unanimously called by the church at Waco, Texas, he came from Auburn to Waco early in 1869, and was pastor at Waco that year. He remained in Texas two years; was corresponding secretary of the Bible and Colportage Board, and assisted in the organization of the General Association. In July, 1871, he returned to Georgia, and accepted the pastorate of the church at LaGrange, where he continued till he died. He was a clear, forcible and earnest preacher, universally honored and beloved.

ELDER W. W. HARRIS.

(Condensed from J. B. Link's Magazine.)

Elder W. W. Harris was the son of Moses and Mary Ann Harris, and was born in Russell county, Ky., in 1836. His maternal grandfather was Achilles Jasper, of Pulaski county, Ky., a man of prominence, and for several years a member of the legislature. Moses Harris died in Missouri in 1845, leaving a widowed mother with two little boys, of whom W. W. was the eldest. The mother and children were destitute, but were cared for by Mr. A. J. Jasper, who was uncle to the boys, and who afterwards brought them to Texas, and placed the eldest in school. Another uncle of the boys was a preacher of the reformation, inaugurated by A. Campbell. On one occasion W. W. asked his uncle, A. J., for a horse to ride about ten miles to be baptized and join a congregation of that order. He was refused. Soon afterwards he attended a protracted meeting at Bear Creek church, in Tarrant county, where he professed religion and joined the Bear Creek Baptist church. He was then about 17 years of age. He began almost immediately to exercise in public, and it was not long before the church gave him license to preach. He was an exceedingly awkward, gawky boy, but had a musical voice. He had great power in prayer. At a meeting of the West Fork Association a contribution was made, and he was placed in Baylor University, at Independence. He was now about 21 years old. While at Baylor he began to be spoken of as the "Spurgeon of Texas." A brother came to Independence and asked for a preacher to fill an appointment at his church. He wanted a "good preacher, pious, of godly walk and conversation." He was told they had a good preacher, pious, but of "most ungodly walk." The reference was to the winding gait of young Harris. But when "Spurgeon" Harris looked into the faces of his congregation, and delivered his powerful discourses of omnipotent truth, people forgot the awkward, absent-minded habits of the preacher. His logic, his eloquence, his vivid descriptions, his powerful and burning appeals, were not without effect. He was the greatest revival preacher in his day in the state. He baptized large numbers, among them some of our best preachers as B. H. Carroll and C. P. Lumpkin, of

Waco, Tex. In 1871, he was missionary of the Waco Association. He would sometimes accept calls from churches, but would not remain with them. He would go into another part of the state, engage in protracted meetings, and possibly never return to his church. He seemed not to care for money; never accumulated anything. He considered his uncle's home, in Dallas county, his own home. He was never married. He died near Del Rio, in Southwest Texas, August 21, 1880. His remains sleep in the cemetery in that town.

HARRIS CREEK CHURCH

held its meetings near South Bosque, in McLennan county; was first in Leon River Association; went from Leon River, into McGregor Association, in 1886; came into Waco Association in 1891; had at that time 22 members. T. A. Mangum was pastor in 1893, when the membership was 35. The church never represented in the Association after 1893. In the spring of 1896 Elder T. P. Walker, missionary, visited and preached for them. They have ceased to meet.

GENERAL JAMES E. HARRISON.

Few men in America have been more honorably connected than General Harrison. His great grandfather was Carter Henry, a brother of President William H. Harrison, and a son of Governor Benjamin Harrison, of Virginia, one of the signers of the Declaration of Independence. His grandfather, James Harrison, was an officer in the revolutionary war. His grandmother Harrison was a sister of General Wade Hampton, of revolutionary fame. Fourteen children blessed his grand parents, James and Elizabeth Harrison. Their seat was in Greenville District, South Carolina. Among their sons was Isham, who married Harriett Kelly, daughter of a noble Irish family, distinguished before crossing the water. Isham and Harriett first settled in South Carolina; afterwards moved to Alabama, and in 1833 to Monroe county, Miss. There came to them six daughters and seven sons, among them James E. Harrison. James E. married Miss Mary Evans. Of their ten children only five are living, John H., postmaster at Waco; Mrs. Mary E. Abbott, Richard H. and Mrs. Eliza E. Bollinger. James E. Harrison obtained a hope in Christ at 16 years of age, and united with a Baptist church. General Harrison married a second wife, Mrs. Carter, sister of Rev. M. B. Hardin, once pastor at Waco. She is still living in Waco. He was a member of the state senate of Mississippi in 1857-8. While in that position he placed in nomination the name of Jefferson Davis for United States senator, and

GEN. JAMES E. HARRISON.

secured his election. He came to McLennan county, Texas, in 1859 in search of health, and settled near the Brazos, a few miles east of Waco. The town of Harrison, on the Waco branch of the Central railroad, commemorates the locality of his settlement. During the late war his Southern patriotism called him to the front. He was a delegate to the Secession Convention at Austin, and was the "Patrick Henry of the occasion." He was chairman of the commission appointed by Governor Clark to treat with the

Choctaw, Chickasaw, Cherokee and Creek Indians. The result was, those tribes cast their lot with the South. He went to the army as lieutenant, but active, skillful service secured his promotion, first to lieutenant colonel, then colonel, and finally to brigadier general. His last promotion was in answer to a petition from officers in General Polignac's brigade. General Kirby Smith endorsed the petition with honorable mention of Colonel Harrison's "distinguished skill and bravery upon many battle fields." President Davis gave the petition his most hearty approval. Jeff Davis remembered the man who put his name in nomination in the Mississippi legislature for United States senator, and he was a life long friend of General Harrison. General Harrison was a man of principle, and a Baptist of convictions. He was a delegate from the Waco church in the organization of the Waco Association in 1860. He was a member of the Board of Directors of Waco University, and was the first president of the Baptist General Association of Texas. He was moderator of the Waco Association in 1871 and 1872, and in the formative period of those early years he was a leading spirit of the Association. Brother Harrison was a liberal contributor to all our work. He believed that one great, central university of learning was absolutely essential to the best interests of Texas Baptists, and he cherished the hope that Waco University would one day grow to be equal to any institution on the continent. He was a firm friend of ministerial education, and did much toward helping young ministers. New Hope was his church, and was prosperous during his life time.

HEWITT CHURCH

was organized in the spring of 1895, of brethren who had held membership at White Hall and other points. The church came into the Association at the McGregor meeting, 1895. Membership at that time, 30; present membership, 55. Elder J. B. Reaves has been the pastor from the first. Hewitt is nine miles from Waco, on the Katy railroad. They have a splendid house.

ELDER JOHN A. HELD.

In the life of this young brother we have an example of how

courage wins, as well as one on whom God has bestowed abundant grace. In Czernowitz, Austria, 1869, was born John A. Held, whose parents were devout Catholics. When but one year old his father died. Leaving home at an early age, his young life was spent as a shepherd's boy among the European hills. It was during this time that a lady who had escaped from Catholicism led our young brother to the Messiah. He came to Amer-

ELDER JOHN A. HELD.
(Photo by Deane, Waco, Texas.)

ica, surmounted difficulties higher than his native hills, and has obtained a first-class education, having graduated from Baylor University in 1896. He is a true Baptist, and a minister of the gospel. He is now financial agent of Howard Payne College.

HILLSIDE CHURCH,

formerly known as Pretty Valley. This church began to exist in the spring of 1883; was organized by Elder C. P. Lumpkin. In 1884, united with the Association with 56 members. The pastors have been T. P. Speakman, 4 years; W. W. Finley, 5 years; M. L. Davis, 1 year; W. S. Huff, 2 years, and H. R. Best, 1 year. Membership (1897), 101. Hillside is in a densely populated and prosperous section. Some of the noblest men in the Association hold membership here, as J. M. Kendrick, W. R. Lawson, etc. The church has a splendid house of worship, and is in every way in a most prosperous condition; has done and is doing great good.

ELDER THOS. HOOKER

now lives at Duffau, and is very old. He was a grand preacher in earlier days. Organized Geneva church, served Geneva, Caledonia, Bold Springs, Olive Branch, and other churches. He is now retired.

HOPE CHURCH.

In 1871 a fine revival was held by Elders C. P. Lumkin and Elder Cain at the residence of Mr. J. M. Taylor, six miles northeast of Marlin, in Falls county. Mr. Taylor's wife and father and mother were Methodists. At this revival quite a number professed religion, and 15 were baptized. These were organized into a church called Hope, at a small schoolhouse on Little Sandy creek. After a short time the church was moved six miles to the northeast. In August, 1873, the church joined the Waco Association with 11 members. The delegates bearing the petitionary letter were G. W. Morris, John Taylor and John M. Seay. G. W. Morris was clerk. The church had no pastor. G. W. Morris withdrew next year and joined Center church.

In 1873 Hope, with Elder J. J. Davis as pastor, enjoyed the best revival in her history, adding 35 by baptism and 18 by letter to her membership. G. W. Morris was now returned to the church and was her clerk. In 1874 one was baptized and three received by letter. J. J. Davis and G. W. Morris, pastor and clerk. In 1875-6 J. L. Lattimore was pastor and A. P. Daugherty, clerk. The church withdrew from Waco Association by letter in 1877. In 1891 went into the organization of Falls County Association with 44 members; J. J. Davis, pastor. In 1895 she had 50 members; J. R. J. Russell, pastor.

ELDER THOMAS HORSELEY

formerly lived on a farm, about ten miles west of Huntsville, on the road leading to Anderson. His education was limited, but piety and goodness of heart gave him influence. He made it a rule of life to be useful in the Master's cause. In 1844 he assisted Elder Z. N. Morrell in organizing Anderson church. In those early days he preached to small churches in remote comminutes, and did much gratuitous preaching in neighborhoods where there were no churches. He was one of the earliest settlers in the neighborhood of Bold Springs (West) church, and as a delegate from that church was in the organization of Waco Association in 1860. He was a member of the committee that framed the constitution of the Association. He was a noble, good man, plain and unassuming in his manner, and of a retiring disposition. He has been many years in heaven.

DEACON JASPER HOWARD.

Brother Howard was born in Shelby county, Alabama, September 31, 1835; came to Texas in 1844. His parents, who were anti-mission Baptists, settled in Nacogdoches county, Texas, in that year. Jasper H. was born from above in 1862, and was baptized into the fellowship of Galveston church. Brother Howard moved to Parker county, Texas, in 1865, and united with Bethel church. From Parker county he moved to Falls, from Falls to Limestone. He was ordained deacon by Horn Hill church in 1877. From Horn Hill he moved to Groesbeck, and from Groesbeck to Mart. He became a member and deacon of Mart church in May, 1883. He is still an honored deacon of Mart. He is a man of strong convictions, and he has the courage to express them. He is a zealous supporter of his church, and he believes in carrying the gospel into all the world. The "good degree and great boldness in the faith" are his reward.

ELDER WILLIAM SCOTT HUFF

was a native of Saline county, Mo. His parents emigrated from Tennessee. W. S. Huff was born November 22, 1840. At the age of 12 gave himself to Christ, and was baptized into Good

Hope church by Elder W. M. Bell, who has been pastor of that church 49 years. Educated at William Jewell College. Ordained at Waconda church, Carroll county, Mo., October 13, 1866, by Elders G. L. Black and Curtis Bullock. We quote from

ELDER W. S. HUFF.

an article signed, "J. Calla," in a recent issue of the Central Baptist: "It is a singular and touching incident that the same presbytery, 29 years later, on the ninth day of last September, 1896, again laid their hands in blessing upon him, and just three days after he had delivered his last sermon, thus unconsciously setting him apart for death, as they had previously done for the ministry." On October 3, 1867, Elder Huff and Miss Mary C. Fisher were joined in holy matrimony. It was a sweet, blessed, union. Sister Huff writes: "I can say he never spoke a short word to me, much less a cross one. We were so happy together. I feel as if I never can rally from this, the greatest grief of my life." His first work in Texas was at Rockwall, where he was pastor one year. In 1878 Brother Huff moved to Waco, Texas, where he lived till he fell asleep in Jesus, November 2, 1896. From September, 1878, till June, 1879, Brother Huff was an honored missionary of the Waco Baptist Association. During this period he instructed 140 anxious inquirers, organized three Sunday schools and four prayer meetings, and made 600 family visits. He preached the introductory sermon at the meeting of the Association at White Rock in 1878, and also at the Robinson meeting of the Association in 1884. The Waco Association was the scene of his labors for nearly 20 years. During this time he served several country churches. His mother, R. D. (Hampton) Huff, was an eminently pious woman, and left her impress on the son. She preceded him a few years to the home of the blessed. Elder Huff's old pastor in Missouri (who baptized him), has sent Sister Huff a beautiful poem, of which the following is an extract:

"Farewell, earth, with all thy charms,
   Farewell to sorrows, too,
Jesus holds out loving arms,
   He calls and I must go.

"Farewell, wife and children, dear,
   Farewell, friends and neighbors, too;
Angel bands are waiting near,
   They call and I must go."

Brother Huff kept a diary of his work, with record of every sermon, etc. He preached 3,564 sermons, baptized over 800 converts. He was a pulpit orator of more than ordinary ability, and a genial, good-humored companion. His devoted wife, two noble sons, and many friends mourn his loss. His death occurred after nearly two months of fever. When the old ship of Zion, bearing the soul of her husband, was nearly into the port, Sister Huff's mind caught and found comfort in the lines:

> "God holds the key of all unknown,
>   And I am glad;
> If other hands should hold the key,
> Or if he trusted it to me,
>   I might be sad."

PROFESSOR R. H. HILL,

president and founder of Hill's Business College, is a member of the First Baptist church of Waco, having been baptized by Pastor Carroll into its fellowship. Prof. Hill is one of those men who began life's struggle at the bottom, but by industry, pluck and energetic application to business, has achieved great success. He is a liberal contributor to all of our denominational interests. His Christian life has been spent in the bounds of Waco Association. Prof. Robert H. Hill was born in Alabama, April, 1856. He resided on a farm, and the only educational advantages he obtained were those afforded by the country schools in the vicinity of his home. In 1876 he came to Texas, where he entered college and remained for four years, making his expenses by teaching penmanship for one hour each day. He took both a literary and business course, and afterward went North, where he thoroughly prepared himself in one of the best institutions for the work of his subsequent career. In 1880 he returned to Waco, Texas, and with only $65 to his credit, opened Hill's Business College. He began with one student, but the institution steadily advanced under his efficient direction, and the attendance is now about 500 pupils annually. This college ranks with the first of its kind in the United States, having overshadowed all similar institutions in its own state, and is now attracting a continual increase of patronage from many of the older states. Brother Hill is thoroughly up with the times in all the work of his profession. His success is only an illustration of what a man can do by correct habits of life and diligent application to business.

INDEPENDENCE CHURCH

was organized on May 21, 1893. The following visiting brethren were present: From West, I. Z. Kimbrough, H. P. Tyra and R. Y. Vaughn; from Waco, J. W. Thomas and J. M. Hunt; from Battle, R. F. Gilliam. These brethren composed the presbytery. The following went into the organization: W. R. Thompson, Sister N. J. Thompson, W. P. Cobb, Sister Tressi Cobb, A. A. Lawson, Sister N. P. Lawson, D. H. Cobb, Sister A. R. Cobb, P. F. Dameron, Sister Georgia Cobb, J. H. Cobb. J. W. Thomas was the first pastor. The church united with the Association in September following with 24 members. A revival in the summer of 1893 added 11 by baptism and several by letter. Holmes Nichols was the next pastor, and served till September, 1896, when T. P. Speakman took the oversight. This church has had a steady growth, and numbers at this writng more than sixty members. Their territory is the populous district lying between White Rock and Bold Springs churches.

W. R. THOMPSON

was born in Belfast, Ireland, September 16, 1844. Came with his parents to America in 1844; served in the Federal army during the civil war; after the war moved from Pennsylvania to Tennessee; was married to Miss S. E. M. Walker, January 19, 1871. His wife was a Presbyterian and his father a Methodist exhorter. Mrs. Thompson afterwards joined the Baptist church at Poplar Grove, Gibson county, Tenn. Brother Thompson professed religion at a Methodist revival, and was baptized by Elder V. G. Cunningham into the church at West. In May, 1887, his wife died, leaving him with seven children. He was married a second time to Mrs. N. J. Dameron, in October, 1892. He was in the organization of Independence church, and has been her Board member ever since. He is now vice president of the Associational Board, which comprises all the churches on the west side of the Brazos.

A. S. GRAHAM

was born in Van Buren county, Ark.; married very young; moved to California; from there to Oregon, then to Idaho; from Idaho back to Oregon; from there to British America, then back to California; from there to Arizona, then to Utah, then to Kansas, and from Kansas back to Van Buren county, Ark. After two years he came to McLennan county, Texas, and settled on the head of White Rock creek. And (would you believe it?) he has lived there 27 years. He professed faith in Christ at a meeting held by the late beloved "Maj." W. E. Penn, and united with White Rock church. After the organization of Independence he joined that church. He has been many years a faithful church member.

ELDER G. L. JENNINGS

was born in Edgefield county, S. C., September 19, 1830; surrendered to his Savior in 1843; moved with his father, Osborne Jennings, to Chickasaw county, Miss., November, 1844. He was baptized by Elder Gideon Woodruff July 30, 1845, and on August 28, 1851, was married to Miss Susan Griffis, who has shared his labors and pleasures for nearly half a century, and to whom he is indebted largely for his success as a minister of the gospel and for their pleasant home in the evening of life. God has given them eight children; two died in infancy; their eldest son, G. G. Jennings, died March 21, 1893. The others are all living. They have a good home one mile east of the town of Kirk, in Limestone county, Texas. G. L. Jennings was ordained September 19, 1859. He immediately entered upon pastoral duties, but in March, 1862, enlisted in the Confederate army, and served as captain of Company H, Thirty-first Mississippi Volunteers, till January, 1864, when, in consequence of failing health, he resigned. He was with John C. Breckenridge in the defense of Vicksburg in 1862, and has a vivid recollection of the heavy bombardment of that city, especially on the night when the "Arkansaw Ram" (gunboat) ran through the Federal fleet and into the city. Brother Jennings was in the fight at Baton Rouge, La., when Lieutenant Todd, on Helm's staff, was killed, and talked to him in his dying moments. Lieutenant Todd was brother-in-law to both Abraham Lincoln and General Helm, these gentlemen having married his sisters. When General Helm was shot, Brother Jennings was near and held him on his horse till borne to the rear. He did much preaching in the army, and held some successful revivals among the soldiers. After the war he preached to churches in Mississippi till 1873, when he came to Texas. He lived in Bryan two years, and then came to Limestone county, where he has since resided. He has had the care of churches 33 years of the 36 since his ordination, and has baptized about 1,500 persons. He had the

ELDER G. R. JENNINGS.

bishopric of East Waco in 1874 and 1875. This was his first church in Texas. He was moderator of the Zion Association in Mississippi four years; moderator of Prairie Grove Association in Texas ten years, and is now moderator of Limestone County Association. He attended all the meetings of Prairie Grove and of Limestone save one. He is now (March, 1896), pastor of Kirk church, and he has sufficient means for the evening of life.

DEACON W. H. JENKINS.

This consecrated and honored brother is the son of James R. Jenkins, of Alabama, who came to Texas at an early day. James R. was one of that little band, found by Z. N. Morrell, in the old town of Washington, Texas, in 1837, and whom he organized into a prayer meeting and later into the first missionary Baptist church west of the Brazos river. The Baptists in and around Washing-

JUDGE W. H. JENKINS.
(Photo by Sanders, Waco, Texas.)

ton held a consultation meeting in 1837, and appointed Elder Z. N. Morrell, James R. Jenkins, A. Buffington and H. R. Cartmell to prepare and publish an appeal to the Baptists of the old states, for aid in the evangelization of the new Republic of Texas. Jas. R. Jenkins wrote the appeal. This appeal stirred the great heart and purse of Jesse Mercer, of Georgia, and moved the hearts of the beloved Wm. M. Tryon and James Huckins to come to Texas as missionaries. Judge W. H. Jenkins was born in Washington county, Texas, November 14, 1848. His mother, Harriett Jenkins, was a woman of strong common sense and superior piety. His father died when young W. H. was but two years old. The influence of his mother shaped the boy's destiny. At the age of ten years he entered Baylor University, at Independence, and when the faculty of the male department moved to Waco, young Jenkins followed, and entered Waco University. In June, 1863, before he was 15 years old, he joined the Confederate army, and served till the close of the war. Again in September, 1865, he entered Waco University, and continued one year. He then accepted a place in a dry goods store, in which position he continued till he began the study of law in the fall of 1867. In 1868 he was converted, and joined the First Baptist church at Waco, where he has ever since held membership. He was admitted to the bar and began the practice of law in Waco, in April, 1869. He was happily married April 27, 1871, to Miss Jessie Speight, daughter of General J. W. Speight, of Waco. He was clerk of the Waco Association in 1878. The same year he was elected clerk of the First Baptist church of Waco, and has served the church continuously in that capacity till this day. For 15 years he has been the superintendent of the First Baptist Sunday school. There is no better Sunday school superintendent in the state. His pastor says that for ten years he prayed the Lord for a superintendent. W. H. Jenkins is the answer to that prayer. Bro. Jenkins was elected county judge of McLennan county in 1888, and served four successive terms—eight years. For ten years he has been a member of the Board of Directors of the Baptist General Convention, and for the past two years he has been president of that Board. He was a member of the Bible and Colportage Board of the General Association before the General Convention was organized. Brother Jenkins has three rules which have done much toward shaping his religious life. (1) Labor by precept and example to extend the mission spirit. (2) Make it the supreme principle of life to glorify Christ through the church. (3) Make religion the chief concern, and subordinate everything to Christian duty. He rejoices that God has greatly blessed him in his family. He and his wife, in the prime and vigor of middle life, have around them their nine children, all of whom he looks upon as God-given. Six of these have given their hearts to the Savior, and are members of the church. He counts it one of his choice blessings that God spared to him his venerable and venerated mother till her 86th year, January 4, 1895. The Lord spare to us this precious brother many years.

DEACON W. R. KELLUM.

William Riley Kellum came to Texas from Mississippi. He was born in Alabama, December 27, 1817. When a youth his parents moved to Tishmingo county, Miss. He grew up in that county, identified himself with the Baptist church, and married Miss N. J. Cooper, in 1843. In 1854 he came, with his own and his father's family, to Waco, Texas, where he resided till his death, October 23, 1890. His wife died soon after coming to Texas, and he was married again to Miss M. E. Jurney. Six children, one the child of the first wife, and five presented by his second wife, survive. He was in the organization of the East Waco Baptist church, and had his membership there till God took him. He was one of the earliest members of the First Baptist church at Waco. He was successful in business and accumulated large property. His home was two miles north of Waco, where he owned 900 acres of Brazos valley land. He was many years the senior partner of the firm of Kellum & Rotan, wholesale grocers. His devotion to his church and the Sunday school, of which he was many years the superintendent, deserves special mention. He never failed to attend when not providentially hindered. He was a liberal contributor. He was a deacon at the time the East Waco church was organized, and served the church in that capacity till his death. He was elected a member of the Board of Trustees of Baylor University in 1867. He was a firm friend of the University, and contributed largely to its success.

ELDER J. R. KELLEY.

Elder Kelley was born in Warren county, Ky., in July, 1847. His parents brought their church letters to Texas in 1854, and joined Five Mile church, in Dallas county. They had no Sunday school, but had preaching occasionally. His mother died in

1861, and father died in the Confederate army in 1863. In August, 1864, J. R. Kelley was baptized into Five Mile church by J. W. Mitchell. He moved to Johnson county in 1867, and united with Alvarado church, where he was ordained July 7, 1872. His first pastorate was at Alvarado. He attended the Cleburne Institute, presided over by the beloved J. R. Clark and W. B. Featherston. In 1882 he was appointed missionary of the Waco Association to the Texas frontier. He entered the field September 21, 1882. His work was at Baird and Abilene, and adjoining territory. Elder L. S. Knight, missionary of Alvarado Association, was on this field a few weeks earlier, and rendered valuable aid to Brother Kelley in planning the work. The country was new and sparsely settled, which made the work difficult and laborious. The few Baptists at Abilene were mostly from South Texas, and were prejudiced against the work of the General Association. However, fourteen of them were induced to unite with the church. He held a meeting in June, 1893, at Abilene, at the close of which $1,700 were subscribed to build a house of worship, and soon thereafter Elder Bennett Hatcher was settled as pastor. The Abilene church has since been prosperous. Bro. Kelley continued to preach at Baird and other points till J. F. Duncan, under appointment of the General Association, succeeded him, when he retired from the mission work. Waco Association paid Elder Kelley $75 per month, and kept him in the field two years. After retiring from the employ of our Board, he remained in that country ten years, preaching to weak churches. While in the employ of our Association he delivered 464 sermons and addresses, organized two churches, traveled 7,058 miles, and baptized 28 persons. He now resides at Alvarado, Texas.

DEACON B. J. KENDRICK,

the present moderator of the Waco Association, was born in Middle Georgia, September 23, 1824; was born again in 1858, and was baptized into the fellowship of Cave Creek church before he was 14 years old. He came to Texas immediately after the war. In 1868 he was ordained deacon. Judge R. E. B. Baylor preached the ordination sermon. In 1870 Bro. K. became a member of the First Baptist church, Waco, but the next year went into the organization of White Hall church, of which he is now a member and senior deacon. He has been an active worker in the Waco Association ever since coming among us. He has labored to advance her interests, and has contributed liberally to the calls of his church and the Association. It has been the rule of his life to stand by and co-operate with his pastor. His house has been "the preachers' home." He has ever kept himself well

DEACON B. J. KENDRICK.

posted on denominational affairs, in which he takes a keen interest. In 1893 he was elected moderator of the Waco Association, which position he still holds with credit to himself. He has during many years served the Mission Board of the Association as vice president of his district, and was one year, from October 1, 1893, to October 1, 1894, president of the Board. He has been connected with Sunday schools from early childhood, and has filled the position of superintendent of schools for a quarter of a century. He loves the Sunday school to-day as dearly as he did when a small boy. He is strong and hale at 73 years of age. The ideal "green old age" finds in Deacon Kendrick its happy illustration. His children are among McLennan county's best citizens —all of them Baptists. May his declining years be full of comfort and his sun go down in a clear sky.

ELDER JOHN G. KENDALL.

He was born in Carroll county, Miss., October 2, 1846. His father, J. W. Kendall (who is still living, aged 87 years), and his mother, Margaret Gray Kendall, were both native Kentuckians, and they removed to their native state when John G. was only 3 years old. So he grew to manhood in Kentucky. When only 13 years old he was converted and joined the Graysville Baptist church, and was baptized November 29, 1859, by the pastor, Elder S. A. Holland. He was educated at Shelby College, Kentucky. In 1868 he entered the Southern Baptist Theological Seminary, at Greenville, S. C., and remained there two sessions, becoming an English graduate of that institution. He was ordained to the full work of the ministry by the Graysville church, Todd county, Ky., May 30, 1870. (This church soon afterward removed to Guthrie, Ky.) Elder W. W. Gardner, of Russellville, Ky., preached the sermon on the occasion of his ordination. In October, of 1870, he moved to Bayou Sara, La. After preaching there for a few months, he, in February, 1871, accepted the call of the church at Verona, Miss., and thus began his regular ministry in his native state. In January, 1873, he became pastor of the church in Washington, Ark., where he remained for one year. In October, 1873, he was married to Miss Mattie Bell, at Forrest City, Ark., and shortly afterward returned to Kentucky, and in January, 1874, became pastor at Elkton, the county seat of the county (Todd), in which he was raised. He remained with this church six years, and during this time the substantial brick house still occupied by the church, was built and dedicated. He remained in Kentucky preaching as pastor for a number of the churches of old Bethel Association until 1890. In November, 1890, he removed to Waco, Texas, and became city missionary under appointment of the First Baptist church of

Waco, which position he still holds. Since he took this work three neat chapels have ben erected in different parts of the city. Bro. Kendall has four children, two boys and two girls. The oldest son (William) is now (1897) attending the Theological Seminary in Louisville, Ky., preparing for the gospel ministry. He is a man of deep piety, earnestness and thorough consecration to his Master's work. Bro. Kendall has done a splendid work in Waco, and is deeply entrenched in the hearts of the people.

ELDER C. W. KINNARD

came to this state from Louisiana. He was ordained in Arkansas, and both in that state and Louisiana made full proof of his ministry. His name first appears on the minutes of Waco Association as pastor of Blue Ridge church, in 1866. For some years after that he was a leading pastor and worker in the Association. His death occurred about 1875. The Association, after his departure, declared that he had been "an unobtrusive, unassuming, quiet, persistent, continuously indefatigable worker in the Lord's vineyard." Glorious record.

KIRK CHURCH.

Kirk church worships in the beautiful country town of Kirk, in the western part of Limestone county. The church was formerly called Elm Grove, and was organized April 1, 1883, by Elders A. Price and G. L. Jennings. The original members were Elder A. Price, J. L. Griffis, G. W. Carpenter, Wm. Carpenter, R. H. Swain, W. H. H. Little, J. E. Riddle, J. B. Gayden, J. B. Reed; Sisters, Eliza Price, Susan Griffis, Rachel Swain, E. Little, Kittie Carpenter and Julia A. Riddle. All the sisters were married. The following brethren have served the church as pastors in the order named: G. L. Jennings, J. J. Harris, H. J. E. Williams, W. C. Manning, B. F. Tatum, J. L. Milstead, J. C. White. The present pastor is G. L. Jennings. J. E. Riddle, H. Swain, B. F. Pearce and F. W. Reed. The clerks have been organization until recently, when J. E. Riddle and J. L. Griffis were released at their own request. The present deacons are: R. H. Swain, B. F. Pearce and F. W. Reed. The clerks have been P. W. Wheelis, G. G. Jennings and W. E. Riddle, present clerk.

WACO BAPTIST ASSOCIATION. 333

The name was changed to Kirk in 1892. This church became a member of the Waco Association in 1883. W. E. Riddle and P. W. Wheelis bore the petitionary letter. She was dismissed from the Association in order and fellowship in 1893, with 77 members. Her present associational membership is with Limestone county. Kirk church now has 91 members. Her future is cloudless.

ELDER JOHN C. F. KYGER

is of German descent, the son of Adam Kyger, and was born April 26, 1860, near Hermitage, Hickory county; Mo. He is next to the youngest of eight children. His parents spent five years at Danville, Ill.; thence returned to their old home in Missouri. John's youth was spent in attending school and laboring on his father's farm. In 1874 he taught school in Rome, Mo. In 1887 he came to Texas, and soon afterward entered Savoy College, in Fannin county. After one year in Savoy and one year in Dallas College, he took charge of the Basin Springs Academy, Granger county, Texas. This school increased from 35 pupils to 335, and he continued here six years. In 1887 he was married to Miss Emma Hightower, of Basin Springs, Texas. To them one son was born, but the death of Mrs. Kyger cut short this happy union. He was ordained to the gospel ministry in 1888, and then entered Baylor University, graduating with the degree of A. B. in June, 1888. While in his senior year he was elected principal of the commercial college of Baylor University; held that position till 1892, when he resigned and founded the "Youth's Southland," a literary and religious magazine of worth. The circulation ran up to 15,000. During 1893-4 he preached to churches, but resigned in June, 1895, and entered the field as an evangelist. He has succeeded in this work, the Lord blessing his labors. He is well qualified for evangelistic work, being consecrated and well educated. He sets forth the plan of salvation with clearness, and never courts popular favor by dodging denominational peculiarities. He has gained some distinction as a writer. His first work was, "Elocution Simplified; or, How to Read and Speak," published in 1884. In 1885 he published "Texas Gems," a compilation of prose and poetry by Texas

REV. JOHN C. F. KYGER.
(Photo by Deane, Waco, Texas.)

authors. In 1890 he gave to the world "Eighty Lessons in Penmanship." In 1894 followed "Sunday School and Young People's Song Book." "Bells of Heaven" is his greatest work, a collection of 500 hymns and tunes, many of them entirely new. Already 12,000 copies of this work have been sold and it is prophesied that the sales will reach 100,000. In 1889 he was happily married to Miss Ennie E. Bryan, of Lake Charles, La. They have three bright children by this union.

ELDER J. L. LATTIMORE

was born in Benton county, Miss., March 2, 1836. His father, S. S. Lattimore, was a well known minister in Mississippi for many years. His maternal grandfather, Rev. Lee Compere, was one of the early English missionaries to the Indies. J. L. Lattimore was educated at Georgetown, Ky., and Marion, Ala. He afterward taught school at Enterprise, Miss. He was ordained in October, 1861, by Elders D. P. Bester and N. L. Clark. He entered the Confederate army the second year of the war and continued till the surrender. A part of the time he was in the ranks as a private soldier and part of the time chaplain. He baptized many soldiers. After the war he taught school and labored as pastor in Mississippi, in Alabama, and finally in Texas. He came to Falls county, Texas, about 1874, and for several years preached for churches. Hope, Liberty, Blue Ridge, Marlin and Union enjoyed his ministerial labors. He died after a long illness, while on his way to Florida in search of health, December 12, 1887. Mrs. Lattimore writes: "He was earnest, faithful, devoted and self-denying."

ELDER ISAM P. LANGLEY

was born September 2, 1851, near Arkadelphia, Ark. He was born again September 2, 1867, and joined Pleasant Hill Baptist church. His parents held membership in this church. He was ordained November 6, 1870. Three months prior to his ordination he was married to Miss Martha A. Freeman. Their family consist of one son and four daughters, all living and all Baptists. He was a successful newspaper man and lawyer, but gave up these interests to accept the call of the First Baptist church at Poplar Bluff, Mo., in January, 1891. Prior to this he had preached for several churches in his native state. His four and a half years at Poplar Bluff resulted in doubling the membership, and a good, modern house was built during this time. He began work as pastor of the West Baptist church, in the Waco Association, April 1, 1894. On account of his wife's ill health he re-

ELDER I. P. LANGLEY.

signed at West after eight months and accepted the care of a church in Texarkana. Bro. Langley is a man of commanding appearance and uniform habits of life. His social qualities are fine, and his preaching ability above the average.

LIBERTY CHURCH.

The name first appears on the minutes of Waco Association in 1879. The church then had 105 members. J. L. Lattimore was pastor, and continued till 1882. In 1879 W. T. Rogers was clerk and W. C. Berry Board member. W. C. Berry was afterward clerk and Board member for several years. James Newman was the next pastor, and was succeeded in 1883 by W. S. Huff. In 1884 L. W. Duke was pastor, R. J. Garrett, clerk, and Wm. Griggers, Board member. L. W. Duke served till 1887. In 1889 J. A. Sowders was pastor, T. J. Hair, clerk, and R. J. Garrett, Board member. In 1891 Liberty was dismissed by letter from Waco Association, J. A. Sowders, pastor. The church still exists in Falls county Association. Their territory is in the eastern part of Falls county.

LITTLE DEER CREEK CHURCH.

This church is named for the creek in the neighborhood. It was constituted the third Sabbath in June, 1885, Elders A. J. Shelton, Robert Moore and G. G. Gibson, acting as presbytery. The following went into the organization: Brethren J. J. Jordan, James McMillan, A. Hamilton, John Moore, Z. A. McMillan, May McMillan, I. H. Venable, R. E. Hamilton; Sisters M. Moore, Amanda Jordan, Rosa Jordan, Lula Hamilton, Mary Pelt, Valeria McMillan, Hortense McMillan, W. C. Venable, Susan Hamilton. A. J. Shelton suggested the name "Little Deer Creek." Brethren J. J. Jordan and James McMillan were recognized as deacons. Elder Robert Moore was the first pastor. Elder A. A. Hensler served from September, 1880, to January, 1888. Eld. J. Daffin followed, serving eight months, when Bro. A. A. Hensler again became the shepherd, and continued till June, 1889. Elder R. O. Dewberry supplied during the summer of 1889. Bro. T. P. Walker was next called, and not being ordained, the church petitioned Deer Creek to set him apart to the full work of the ministry. He was ordained, became the pastor, and served till October, 1891. Bro. Walker was succeeded by Bro. Reed Rector, October, 1891. Under the labors of Bro. Rector the church has had a steady growth. This brother is in the hearts of his people. The church united with Waco Association in 1885, and remained in active co-operation till 1893, when she obtained a letter and joined Falls County Association. The church worshiped in Busby schoolhouse till 1894, when she built a Baptist house, 28x40 feet.

ROLEN SCOTT,

a member of Little Deer Creek, was born in Bartow county, Ga., October 16, 1861. His father moved to Texas in 1869, settling in Falls county. In 1882 he was converted and baptized into the fellowship of Pleasant Grove Baptist church. In the year 1892 he became a member by letter of Little Deer Creek. In 1893 he married Miss Ella Henderson. Being gifted in music, he is a power in the church for good.

DEACON JAMES M'MILLAN.

This brother was born in Thomas county, Ga., December 15, 1826. Was converted when a boy, but did not unite with the church. In 1849 at the age of 23 he came to Texas. In May, 1862, he entered the Confederate service, and continued till the war closed. Under the preaching of the late M. V. Smith he was made to see his error, and was baptized by Bro. Smith. In the spring of 1866, a church was organized four miles north of Cotton Gin. Bro. McMillan first united with this church, and was by it ordained deacon. Moved to Falls county in 1884.

DEACON WILLIAM MOORE

was born in Clark county, Ala., in 1854. In 1873 he moved to Choctaw county. In 1874 he was converted and baptized. Came to Grimes county, Texas, in 1875. In 1882 he was married. He united with Little Deer Creek church in 1890, and was ordained to the deaconship next year.

DEACON J. J. JORDAN.

Deacon Jordan was born in Washington county, Ga., Nov. 4, 1823. He came to Freestone county, Texas, in 1849, and in 1858 united with Tehuacana Baptist church. He was baptized by the lamented Elder W. B. Eaves. He was married to Miss Amanda T. Hodges of Denton county, Texas, in 1859. He served in the Confederate army two and a half years. In 1870 he settled in Falls county, Texas, and in 1877 he was ordained to the office of deacon by Carolina church, Elders Calvin, Magee and T. D. Suttle officiating.

LIVE OAK CHURCH

united with the Waco Association in 1876. It had then been organized only a short time. N. C. Curfam and W. M. Vaughn bore the petitionary letter. The membership was 19. They had no pastor. W. C. Golding was clerk. The next year C. Magee was pastor; membership, 20. S. S. Johnson was pastor in 1878 and 1879. In 1881 J. T. Crawford was pastor; membership, 67. T. D. Suttle was pastor in 1882, M. F. Whatley in 1883 and 1884, J. R. M. Touchstone in 1885, A. A. Hensler in 1886 and 1887. The church was without a pastor in 1888-9. In 1890 W. B. White was pastor. Live Oak withdrew from the Waco Association in 1891 with 32 members. It still exists in Falls County Association. The Live Oak meeting house is five miles southwest of the town of Lott. Elder J. Daffin was for years a pillar of this church.

ELDER JACKSON DAFFIN

was born in Clark county, Ala., June 18, 1804. Baptized into Paron Baptist church in 1832. Ordained by Grove Hill church in 1870. Served several churches in Alabama, and in 1889 Little Deer Creek church, in Falls county, Texas. In 1878 came to Texas, and settled in Live Oak neighborhood; was a member of Live Oak Baptist church till November, 1894, when he joined the church at Lott. Bro. Daffin's habits have been exemplary. He never used ardent spirits, never swore, never used tobacco, or gambled. He is waiting the Master's call.

ELDER T. F. LOCKETT,

a native of Prince Edwards county, Va., was born July 30, 1826. He still lives at Morgan, Texas. In youth he attended a Methodist Sunday school and also a Presbyterian Sunday school. He was baptized in 1842. He was four years a student at Richmond College. In 1848 he went to Cole county, Mo., joined the Osage church, and was by that church ordained. The names of James Suggett, Levy Roark, Noah Flood, Elias George and Snelling Johnson appear on his credentials, which document bears date of September 18, 1848. He established an academy in 1848, and in that academy a Bible school, which resulted in the conversion and baptism of about 60 of his pupils. When William Jewell College was founded, Elder Lockett was elected professor of natural sciences, January, 1850. To enable the church at Liberty to pay off a distressing debt Elders Lockett and E. S. Dulin, professors in William Jewell, filled the pulpit for one year without charge. Overwork undermined Bro. Lockett's health, and he was compelled to resign his chair in the college. He afterward did grand work as pastor of churches. He was for a time pastor at Jefferson City, during which God enabled him to infuse new life into the church. At the commencement of the war he was pastor at Jefferson City and chaplain of the state penitentiary. The last year of the war he came to Washington, Texas, and in 1866 to Bosqueville, near Waco. He was immediately elected to take charge of the Bosqueville College, then a flourishing school. He soon afterward became pastor of Bosqueville and Bold Springs churches. Later he was financial agent of Waco University, and raised and paid off $10,000 of the floating debt. He has preached much over Texas, held many important pastorates, and has baptized large numbers. Much preaching in the open air brought on bronchial troubles, and he cannot now preach regularly. He was missionary pastor at Laredo, Texas, in 1893 and 1894, which was his last regular work. He is waiting for the bid to come up higher.

LONE OAK CHURCH.

About the year 1887 a church was constituted on Snake creek, near the line of McLennan and Hill counties. This church was named Lone Oak. It joined the Association in 1887 and ceased to represent in 1892. The pastors have been T. P. Speakman, Holmes Nichols and M. C. Bolton. In 1887 the membership was 72; in 1882, 78. The church of late years maintains only a nominal existence. J. W. Hartsfield was the first Board member and first clerk.

LORENA CHURCH.

Lorena is one of the nicest little railroad towns in Texas. It is 14 miles southwest from Waco, on the Missouri, Kansas and

Texas railroad, and in the beautiful valley of the North Cow Bayou creek. The railroad reached this place in 1882, and in September, of the same year, Lorena church was organized. The town and church were named for Miss Lorena Westbrook, daughter of Captain and Mrs. C. A. (Whitsitt) Westbrook. The original members of Lorena church were J. H. McBrayer, C. A. Westbrook, Mrs. C. A. Westbrook, A. J. Shelton, Mrs. Mollie Shelton, John F. Shelton, Mrs. Ann Shelton, J. T. Shelton, Loula and Callie Shelton, Joseph Crook, Mrs. Georgia Crook, Joe Shelton, Abb Ponder, Mrs. Abb Ponder, Samuel Bartlett and John H. Miller. The church was organized by Elder John S. Allen, of blessed memory, who was the first pastor. He was followed by W. S. Huff, C. D. Daniel, S. B. McJunkin, T. E. Muse, J. L. Walker, W. A. Garrett and E. L. Compere, the present pastor. The church has kept up a good Sunday school and prayer meeting from the first. They have a well finished frame house and membership of 120. The first clerk was J. R. Shelton, after him J. W. Brightwell, then J. W. Whitsitt, the present clerk. Brother Whitsitt has been clerk ten years. Lorena church joined the Association in 1883 at Rock Creek. The petitionary letter was borne by Deacon H. B. Sherman. This church has a magnificent prospect before her. Lorena is a live town and has a "twin artesian well," one stream of pure freestone water and the other white sulphur water. Bro. J. W. Whitsitt writes, "the healthiest place in Texas."

LOTT CHURCH.

This church was organized at Lott, Falls county, Texas, May 18, 1890, with eight members. The presbytery consisted of Elders A. J. Shelton and R. O. Dewberry. The Articles of Faith and Church Covenant in Pendleton's Manual, were adopted. A. J. Shelton, missionary of Waco Association, was the first pastor; D. J. Barnes, the first clerk; R. E. Busby, the first Board member. In May, 1891, J. L. Walker became pastor, and served the church two and a half years. During his pastorate the membership increased from 15 to 70, and the splendid house in which the church now meets was built. The Waco Association at first assisted the church in paying the pastor's salary. In September,

1893, J. E. McClerkin became pastor, and served one year. In August, 1894, J. R. M. Touchstone was called and began work in October following. During his time the church increased in membership and made some improvements on the meeting house. In September, 1894, Lott was dismissed from Waco Association by letter, and has since then been in Falls County Association. They have had a good Sunday school from the first. J. R. Strange, who was ordained deacon while J. L. Walker was pastor, has been superintendent of the school much of the time since its commencement. He is one of the pillars of the church. The other deacons are R. E. Hamilton, J. C. Calvert and J. N. Bell. The outlook for Lott is most encouraging.

DEACON JOHN R. LUMPKIN

is descended from John and Lucy Lumpkin, one of the earliest and most prominent families of Georgia. John Lumpkin was very probably one of three brothers who came over from England in the early settlement of the colonies. He was the father of Governor Wilson Lumpkin, of Rev. John Lumpkin and of Judge Joseph Henry Lumpkin. Deacon John R. Lumpkin, the son of George and Lucinda Lumpkin, was born in Newton county, Ga., September 7, 1827. His father moved to Floyd county, Ga., in 1836, where young John R. grew up. His mother was of Irish descent. In 1849 he married Miss Evaline Cornutt, daughter of David Cornutt, formerly of Virginia. In 1852 he, with his wife and one child (now Elder C. P. Lumpkin), moved to Milam county, Texas, and located at old Port Sullivan, on the west bank of the Brazos river, where his six children were raised. In December, 1879, he moved to Limestone county, near Mart, where he now lives. He is the father of nine children, three of whom died in early childhood. Those surviving are Elder C. P. Lumpkin, Waco; J. C. Lumpkin, Hearne; L. B. Lumpkin, Cameron; Mrs. Bettie Stodghill, Waco; Mrs. Ida Guinn and H. P. Lumpkin, of Mart. Brother Lumpkin ad wife professed faith in Christ, and united with the Little River church, at the noted Blackhouse Springs meeting, in Milam county, 1855. He was baptized by Eld. Z. N. Morrell, and his wife by Elder W. B. Eaves. Went into the organization of Port Sullivan Baptist church in 1865, and was ordained deacon by that church soon after its organization. He has served the Lord in that office in a humble way for 32 years. His educational advantages were limited, but nature has endowed him with more than an ordinary degree of common sense. By industry and diligent attention to business, coupled with a vast amount of hard work in his early days, he has succeeded in providing things honest in the sight of men, and in fortifying himself

DEACON JOHN R. LUMPKIN.

against over-anxiety in the evening of life. He is most grateful for what the grace of God has done for him in saving his soul from sin, and permitting him in some humble way to render service to the dear Lord. One special cause of gratitude to God is that all his children, save one, the youngest, are partakers with him of the grace of salvation, and are now members of Baptist churches. Brother Lumpkin has always been a liberal contributor to the religious and public interests of his church and community.

ELDER C. P. LUMPKIN.

The subject of this sketch is the son of J. R. and Evaline Lumpkin, and was born in Rome, Ga., May 28, 1850. He is the oldest child, having three brothers and two sisters. The father and mother, with their infant son, moved to Texas in 1852, and located at Port Sullivan, in Milam county, where he was raised

ELDER C. P. LUMPKIN.

and received a liberal English education in Port Sullivan College. In October, 1865, he was converted to Christ and united with the Port Sullivan Baptist church, and was baptized by Elder W. W. Harris. In his seventeenth year he was deeply impressed that God was calling him to preach the gospel of Christ, but he being very timid and his education being limited, he made no confession of this impression to any one until he was 19 years old. He was at that time very intimately associated with Elder W. S. Lackey, a man of deep piety and earnest sympathy for young preachers, and to him he confessed his deep and long left impression. He has ever felt that Bro. Lackey's influence over him was a benediction from God. It was this brother who made the motion that he be liberated to exercise his gift in public. He was united in marriage to Miss Florence A. McKinney on the 13th day of December, 1871. He was called to ordination by the Port Sullivan Baptist church, and was regularly set apart to the full work of the gospel ministry January 7, 1872, the ordination council consisting of Elders R. C. Burleson, S. D. Kendall and T. M. Anderson. He served as pastor of the Port Sullivan church eight years, and of Cameron church, in Milam county, five years; he also served some other churches in Milam and Burleson counties. November 29, 1873, the dark-winged angel of death visited his happy family, and bore away to heaven the lovely, young Christian wife and mother, and left him with his 1-year-old daughter, Florence B. (now Mrs. W. H. Long, Jr.), wrapt in a mantle of sorrow. He was united a second time in marriage to Miss Helen J. Middleton, only child of Capt. H. H. Middleton, of Milam county, March 25, 1875. Five children, three sons and two daughters, blessed this union. In March, 1882, the Robinson Baptist church, McLennan county, called him to her pastorate. During his three years' pastorate there, the church was greatly prospered. It was during this time that he organized the Pretty Valley (now Hillside church). He was called to the care of the Moody church in 1885, and served that church three years. This pastorate was greatly blessed, he having baptized more than one hundred into that church. The Stampede Valley church was organized by him while pastor of the Moody church. He moved to Hubbard City in 1885, and was called to the care of that church, which he served for nine years very acceptably. The church was prospered and built up. Their splendid house of worship was built under his pastorate. He served for a part of his time the Mt. Calm church three years, the Dawson church six years, the Armour church four years, and the Mart church three years. It was largely through the influence of Bro. Lumpkin and Bro. W. T. Compere that the Hubbard City Association was organized, Bro. Lumpkin serving as moderator from its organization until he moved to Waco, in 1894, to educate his children. He has ever been in full sympathy with all our Baptist work, true to his convictions, speaking out in very decided terms on all points of doctrine and denominational interest.

MISS HELEN EVA LUMPKIN.

This brilliant young lady was born at Port Sullivan, Milam county, Texas. She is the daughter of Rev. C. P. Lumpkin,

Miss Helen Eva Lumpkin.

Waco, and granddaughter of Deacon J. R. Lumpkin, and also of Capt. H. H. Middleton. She was converted at Hubbard City in August, 1887, under the ministry of her father, and was baptized by him into the fellowship of Hubbard City Baptist church. She is a beautiful writer. The popularity of "Agnes Lamont" and "Rescued," continued romances in the Guardian of Waco, sufficiently attest her genius. She is a member of the graduating class of Baylor University of 1897. But owing to ill health, she has been compelled to stop school for the present. There is a rosy future for Miss Eva, and we confidently look forward to the day when she will wear laurels. The sweet hymn, "Going Home to Live Forever," recently published by Prof. J. Edmond Thomas, was written by Miss Lumpkin.

ELDER B. E. LUCAS.

This faithful servant of God, whose labors have been so abundant in Texas, and whose name appears frequently in the minutes of the Waco Association, having once been appointed as its missionary, was born in Pennsylvania, in 1808; was the son of Governor Lucas, of Ohio. His father having moved to Ohio, the subject of this sketch grew up there, and at the age of 16 went to Lexington, Ky., where he made a profession of religion when he was 20 years old, and united with the Methodist Episcopal church. At the age of 21 he was ordained by Bishop Capers as a minister of that denomination. In 1832 he moved to Nashville, Tenn. In 1833 he was united in marriage to Miss Louisa Barber. He lived and labored a few years in Georgia and Alabama. In 1844 he came to Texas, and settled in Sabine county. In 1847 his religious views underwent an entire change, and he united with a missionary Baptist church; was baptized by Elder Britton at Hamilton, Shelby county, Texas, and was soon after ordained to the full work of the gospel ministry, Elders J. W. D. Creath and Jesse Witt serving as presbytery. Soon after he received an appointment under the Home Mission Board, then of Marion, Ala., as missionary for Texas, under which appointment he rendered faithful and efficient service in the following counties: Shelby, Sabine, San Augustine, Nacogdoches, Rusk, Panola and Cherokee. During this term of service he organized and built up many churches, some of which are still in existence as monuments of his labor. He also ordained several preachers. In 1862 he moved to Bosque county, where he rendered extensive and efficient service, preaching in the following counties: Bosque, Johnson, Erath, Coleman, Dallas, Collin, Kaufman, Hunt, Van Zandt, Coryell, McLennan, Falls, Limestone and Hill. He organized the church at Armour, Limestone county; also the Pin Oak church (now Hubbard City). In 1874 he moved to Fayette county, where he rendered very efficient service, preaching the gospel nearly all over that country. He served as pastor at Flatonia, Weimar, Elgin, Plum Grove and another church near where Muldoon is now located. Brother Lucas was a man of limited education, but nature had bestowed upon him some superior gifts. He was possessed of strong mental faculties, and was a forcible speaker, and withal was a Baptist to the core. He was indeed a foundation builder, and his power for good was felt wherever he went. He suddenly and peacefully fell asleep in the arms of his Lord, on the last morning of December, 1884, while sitting in his chair. Several of his children survive him, one of whom, Deacon P. F. M. Lucas, of Hubbard City, the writer, has every reason to regard as well deserving of mention in connection with this sketch of his illustrious father. Deacon Lucas was indeed and in truth one of the warmest and closest friends the writer ever had. The last sermon that this man of God ever preached was from the text: "There remaineth therefore a rest unto the people of God." "Servant of God well done, rest from thy loved employ."—C. P. L.

ELDER CALVIN MAGEE,

son of Fleet Magee, was born June 7, 1808, in Pike county, Miss., and was the first white child born in that county. He professed faith in Christ and joined the new Zion Baptist church when quite young. He married Mrs. Catharine McAlpin about 1830. Ten children were the fruit. His first wife died in 1850. In 1859 he was again married to Mrs. Mary Young, by whom he had one child. All of his first family of children are dead but one. He began preaching soon after his first marriage, and devoted all his time to the ministry while in Mississippi. Came to Texas in 1863; spent one year in Limestone county, then went to Falls, and settled west of the Brazos river, opposite Marlin, where he spent the rest of his days preaching and farming. His name first appears on the minutes of Waco Association as pastor of Beulah church, in 1864. In 1865 he wrote the report on temperance in which occur these words: "The use of ardent spirits as a beverage is intemperance." He continued pastor of Beulah church till near the time of his death, which occurred December 16, 1882.

He also served the churches at Live Oak, Carolina and Cow Bayou. He did great good in the western part of Falls county in laying foundation work. Till time shall be no more the good work which he began will not cease.

DEACON LEONARD MAGEE.

Mr. Fleet Magee, the father of L. Magee, was a native of South Carolina. Magee's creek, in the southern part of that

DEACON LEONARD MAGEE.
(Photo by Sanders, Waco, Texas.)

state, was named for Fleet Magee. He was in the war of 1812, was a staunch Baptist, and died about the year 1845, in Marion county, Miss. Leonard Magee was born January 15, 1823, in Marion county, Miss.; grew up in that county and was educated partly under an Irish teacher named Henry Burke, and partly at Columbia Academy under Prof. Robert Cochran. Brother Magee was converted when about 16 years of age; tried to get his own consent to unite with the Presbyterians. Failing in this, he was baptized into the fellowship of New Zion church by Elder Jesse Crawford. He spent the summer of 1856 in Texas, and moved to Marlin January, 1857. At that time the Marlin church was in a cold, inactive state; but in the summer of 1858 Elder W. B. Eaves, missionary of the State Convention, held a meeting in Marlin, which resulted in the church taking on new life. A large number was baptized. Bro. Magee had united with the Marlin church previously to this meeting, and had been ordained deacon by Elder W. B. Eaves. He was in the organization of Waco Association as a delegate from Marlin church in 1860, and served on the committee with J. W. Speight and Elder Z. N. Morrell, that framed the constitution of the Association. He was the first treasurer of the Association. In 1864-5 he was again treasurer, when $1,296 Confederate notes and county warrants died in his hands. Bro. Magee has always been in the front in all of the Master's work. He was prominent in the Association for many years, and was a member of the Trinity River Association two years before the Waco Association was organized. He was in the organization of the McGregor Association as a delegate from Eddy church, at McGregor, in 1886, and remained with that Association till its dissolution in 1890. He served the Confederate cause in important positions of trust, as courier in Mississippi, as shipper, nearly a year, in which time he shipped more than 17,000 head of cattle, and as assistant in commissary department. At Marlin he was assistant commissary under Judge Oltorf. He was clerk of the court in Mississippi, and in Falls county, Texas, he served as justice of the peace. He has kept posted in denominational affairs, and has been a liberal contributor to the cause of education and missions. He still lives in his elegant home in Waco, and has a competency.

ELDER T. A. MANGUM

has done much excellent work in the Waco Association. He was a pastor in the Association as early as 1876, serving at that time Cow Bayou and Sage Chapel. In 1877 he was pastor of Cow Bayou and Deer creek. Other churches have enjoyed the benefits of his ministerial labors. In May, 1893, he represented the Association in the Southern Baptist Convention. He has done much work outside of the Association, and has held many precious revivals. He is considerate, sound in the faith, and an acceptable preacher and pastor. His home is at McGregor.

MARLIN CHURCH.

Marlin is the county seat of Falls county. The 640 acres on which the town now stands were donated by Edward Hanrick. The town was laid out in 1851. In 1871 the Waco branch of the Houston and Texas Central railroad reached Marlin. Falls county was originally a part of the municipality of Viesca. The settlement began in 1834, at Viesca, on a high bluff on the west side of the Brazos, just below the historic falls. When Santa Anna invaded Texas in 1835-6, all the available men were called to the front, leaving Viesca (Milam) defenseless. After the fall of Fort Parker, in Limestone, the town was evacuated. After the battle of San Jacinto Fort Marlin was built, near the town of Marlin. The Indians were unfriendly, and on June 9, 1839, the Morgan family was massacred six miles above Marlin. The battle of Morgan Point was fought, and the Indians repulsed. Settlers came, and the country filled up. Marlin Baptist church was organized April 10, 1852, by Elder Z. N. Morrell. The original members were A. B. Ewing, L. B. Barton, Nancy Dobbs, Margay Morgan, —. Prewitt, wife and servant—7. The pastors have been S. G. O'Bryan, W. J. Bowden, W. B. Eaves, W. M. Gough, R. B. Burleson, S. King, J. L. Lattimore, J. V. Wright, J. J. Riddle, T. J. Drane, S. L. Morris, A. E. Baten, J. R. M. Touchstone, M. K. Thornton. In 1852 Marlin had seven members; in 1860, 113 members; in 1870, 61 members; in 1880, 107 members; in 1890, 162 members. Marlin first united with Trinity River Association. The church was in a disorganized condition for a short time before the great revival in 1858, conducted by W. B. Eaves. During that revival 23 were added by baptism. Another revival, held by Pastor W. B. Eaves, in 1859, added 7 by baptism and 10 by letter, increasing the membership to 94. In 1864 W. B. Eaves held another grand revival meeting, in which 30 were baptized. Brother Eaves ceased to be pastor in 1865. Before the war, the deacons were L. Magee and John A. Fortune,

Jr. During the same period the clerks were L. B. Barton, A. W. Ewing and A. G. Perry. Marlin church was in the organization of the Waco Association in 1860. Her messengers on that occasion were W. B. Eaves, L. Magee and W. A. Mason. Marlin withdrew from Waco Association in 1891 with 173 members, and went into the organization of Falls County Association. In October, 1895, the membership was 184. The fifth Sunday in August, 1896, about 60 of the Marlin members withdrew from the First church and organized the Second church. The First church is prospering under their faithful shepherd, M. K. Thornton. The Second church, led by Pastor R. R. White, also shows signs of prosperity.

JESSE ALBERT MARLEY

was born in Chatham county, N. C., September 27, 1824. His father, Benjamin Marley, was born and raised in the same county. The family moved to Green county, Mo. (now Christian), in 1841, and settled in three miles of Ozark. Benjamin Marley was a staunch missionary Baptist. He owned quite a large number of slaves. During the war he was brutally murdered while sick in bed in the presence of his wife and daughters by a set of ruffians, calling themselves "home guards." At that time all of his four sons were away from home in the Confederate army. Jesse A. Marley saw four years of hard war service. He was in 18 states and 37 hard battles. Was never touched by a bullet. Was captured at Bellfont, Ark., and was six months a prisoner of war at St. Louis, Mo., and Alton, Ill. He has for a much longer time been engaged in another war. We mean the Christian warfare. This conflict has been going on for 45 years, and instead of 37 battles, the fights with the enemy of souls have been more than the number of days in which the long struggle has been going on. He was baptized into the fellowship of Prospect church, Missouri, in 1852, by Elder Ephram Wray; coming to Texas after the close of the civil war with his family, he spent one year in Grayson county, and in 1867 moved to Waco; ever since he has lived in McLennan county. Has held membership in East Waco, Caledonia, Rock Creek and Battle churches. Resides at present near Battle, where he is an honored member. On October 4, 1896, he buried his aged wife. For many long years she had been the comfort and companion of his life. Bro. Marley has ever been true to his principles, his church and his God. He is now in his seventies, patiently waiting the Master's call.

ELDER WILEY ALLEN MASON.

W. A. Mason was born in Smith county, Tenn., in 1828. His parents, Wiley Mason and Nancy Simms, were married in 1824,

ELDER W. A. MASON.

and emigrated from North Carolina in 1826. They were devoted, consecrated Christians, and members of Peyton's Creek Baptist church, in Smith county, Tenn. They died in the faith. Bro. Mason's mother died when he was but 5 years old. After that sad event, he became the constant companion of his pious father. At the age of 13, professed faith in Christ, and was baptized into Peyton Creek church by Elder E. B. Haney, 1842. His father died next year. After the death of his father, he left the old homestead for McKindree College, Lebanon, Ill. Here for two years he worked his way, and kept up with his classes. Failing health compelled him to leave school, and he returned to Tennessee. Afterward taught school in Alabama, and at the same time studied law by pine knot lights. At the breaking out of the Mexican war, in 1847, he joined the army as a volunteer, "for five years, or during the war," was discharged at Mobile in 1848. In 1849 he was married to Miss Chilton of Alabama. In 1854 came to Texas and taught school. He joined the Shiloh Baptist church, Williamson county, in 1855, and was by that church licensed to preach. His ordination being called for by the San Gabriel church, Milam county, he was set apart to the work of the ministry by authority of the Shiloh church, Nov. 23, 1856. Elders J. S. Allen, J. C. Mundine and W. B. Eaves composed the presbytery. Bro. Mason assisted in the organization of the Leon River Association, and was its first missionary, at a salary of $400. In 1858 was missionary of Richland Association, serving in that capacity two years at a salary of $600. He assisted in the organization of Elm Grove church (Salado), Cow Bayou, Meridian, Cedar Creek (near Temple), Speegleville, Cleburne, Waxahachie, Mesquite (Kopperl), Bowie, Bellview, and about 50 others. He aided in the organization of Little River Association, Leon River, Waco and others. At the organization of Waco Association he was chairman of the committee on Articles of Faith. His membership was at that time with Marlin church. In 1866 Elder Mason reorganized the Alvarado Association, and he was for years its moderator. He has been moderator of Shiloh Association of Montague, of Stevens county, and of Cisco. During the war Bro. Mason was sent as a missionary to the Confederate army by the State Convention. The service rendered was in General Gano's command, Walker's Division. He was also one year missionary of Little River Association to Walker's Division, and was brigade chaplain to Waterhouse's Brigade. A regular Baptist church was organized in the army, of which Chaplain Mason was pastor. After the war he served the State Convention two years as assistant financial agent with Elder J. W. D. Creath, of precious memory. As agent of the Aged Ministers' Relief Board of the Baptist General Convention from 1886 to 1889 (33 months),

Bro. Mason raised in cash and bonds nearly $20,000. He has served quite a large number of churches, and baptized many hundreds of converts. His longest pastorate was four years at Towash. He is now 68 years old; is pastor (March, 1897) of the church at Putnam, Callahan county. He writes: "I wish to fall with the armor on, contending for the faith once delivered to the saints. I am for maintaining Bible principles, first, last and always." The Lord be with you, brother.

DEACON E. MARTIN,

a pillar in the Goshen church, was born in Missouri in 1843. In the year 1868 he was baptized by Elder John McClain. During the war he was a soldier on the Texas frontier about three years. He has been Board member of his church from its organization to the present time. His home is near McGregor, on South Bosque.

MART CHURCH.

The town of Mart is in the southeastern portion of McLennan county, and in the heart of one of the most fertile sections of black land in Texas. W. H. Criswell, the first settler, located there in 1877. The first Baptist settler was W. H. Francis, who is now an active deacon of Mart church. This church was organized April 28, 1878, under a large elm tree, which is still standing in the Baptist cemetery. The presbytery consisted of Elders C. C. Hardwick and T. D. Suttle. The following brethren and sisters went into the organization: W. H. Francis and wife, L. R. Francis, W. C. Gates and wife, N. C. Gates, A. J. Breland and wife, M. A. Breland, Jane Breland, W. B. Stodghill, J. A. Flower and wife, Sallie Flower, Jacob Weaver and wife, Mattie Weaver, H. P. Whitman and wife, M. J. Whitman, J. M. Cancelor, Isabella Douglass, Corene Frasel and Rebecca Shelton—18 members. W. H. Francis was a deacon, and so recognized. J. M. Cancelor was ordained deacon soon afterward. The first pastor was T. D. Suttle. Bro. Suttle served till July, 1883. He was followed by H. R. Puryear, who was pastor, till October, 1884. G. L. Jennings was the next pastor, and continued one year. After Bro. Jennings came C. P. Lumpkin, who took charge of the church in April, 1886, and served till September, 1888. W. C. Manning accepted the care of the church in December, 1888, and continued till June, 1889. C. C. Hardwick served the church as supply from June, 1889, till 1890, when B. F. Tatum was called and accepted. Bro. Tatum served six years. J. L. Walker accepted the church in January, 1896, and is the present pastor. The following brethren have served the church as deacons: W. H. Francis, J. M. Cancelor, J. R. Lumpkin, J. H. Gilliam, R. W.

MART BAPTIST CHURCH.

Dennis, Jasper Howard, E. A. Chatman, A. P. Smyth, J. D. Pearce, Uriah Smith, J. M. Akin. Brethren Cancelor, Gilliam, Chatman have been lettered out. The other brethren named above are still members. The church was at first called Willow Springs; the name was changed to Mart in 1891. The present house was built in 1893, at a cost of $950. The church has among her members many cultured and consecrated people. She supports a pastor for his full time, has one of the best Sunday schools in Texas, under Superintendent H. T. Vaughn.

MASTERSVILLE CHURCH,

first called Salem, was organized near the town of Bruceville, about 1870. C. A. Westbrook, Mrs. Jennie Westbrook, A. D. Blackwell, Mrs. Blackwell, J. M. Harris and Littleton Smith were among the original members. When Salem united with the Association in 1871, the membership aggregated 39. John McClain was the first pastor, and had the oversight eight years, during which time the membership more than doubled. A. P. Scofield was pastor in 1879, and in 1881, A. J. Shelton. The next pastor was L. H. Ewing. The name was changed to Mastersville in 1884. The village of Bruceville was at first called Mastersville, in honor of Jacob Masters, an old veteran and an early settler. W. S. Huff was pastor in 1884; in 1885 A. J. Shelton was again pastor. D. M. Ayres followed in 1886, and in 1887 J. A. Lea supplied. Next came J. L. Walker, three and a half years; then T. P. Walker. The greatest revival in the history of the church was conducted by Pastor T. P. Walker, in 1891. J. L. Walker followed T. P. Walker, and had the oversight till January 1, 1896. Holmes Nichols served from January 1, 1896, till September, 1896. Soon after this W. A. Hamlet was ordained pastor, but resigned to attend the Theological Seminary at Louisville. The church is now (March, 1897) without a pastor. For many years Mastersville church had a half interest in the house now owned by the Methodists. In the spring of 1896 this church erected a new, modern house, the best between Waco and Temple.

ELDER JOHN M'CLAIN,

one of the pioneers of Waco Association, was born in Knox county, Tenn., November 26, 1826. His early life was spent in Illinois, where he was converted, in March, 1852, and was baptized the same year. He was licensed to preach by Barry church, in 1854. In the same year he came o Texas and settled at old Perry, in McLennan county, twenty miles southwest of Waco. He was in the organization of Perry (now Moody) church in March, 1855. He was ordained at Owl Creek, Coryell county, at the request of Perry church, August 9, 1857. The presbytery consisted of the sainted R. E. B. Baylor and W. B. Eaves. He assisted in the organization of Cow Bayou church, McGregor (then Onion Creek), and many other churches. He was the first pastor of Cow Bayou. "Uncle John McClain" still lives at Eagle Springs, Coryell county, Texas, full of years and honor. The Lord give him a cloudless sunset.

ELDER J. M. M'CRAW.

Elder McCraw was a licentiate minister, and a member of Ebenezer church, in Walker county, Texas, before the war. He entered the army at the beginning of the war as a private soldier, in General Walker's Division. As a private soldier he did much preaching, and won the confidence and esteem of his comrades. During the war the Board of the Eastern Texas Convention, located at Tyler, appointed him missionary in the army. He was assigned to do duty as chaplain. Many were converted under his preaching. Not being ordained, he had to ask other ministers in the army to baptize for him. His home church, Ebenezer, heard of this, and authorized any ministers in the army to ordain him. Accordingly, a presbytery composed of Elders M. V. Smith, A. L. May and W. A. Mason, set him apart to the holy office of New Testament bishop. After this, he baptized large numbers of his fellow soldiers, and "continued in the faithful performance of his duties till the close of the war." (See Flowers and Fruits, p. 337-8). After the war Elder McCraw was employed as a missionary of the Waco Association from November 17, 1866, till August 24, 1867. During this time he preached in many destitute neighborhoods, and organized two churches. He traveled 2,405 miles over our territory. He afterward went to Arkansas, and continued a faithful minister till God called him up higher.

M'GREGOR CHURCH.

The town of McGregor enjoys the distinction of being the only railroad junction outside of Waco, in McLennan county. It is 20 miles west of Waco, at the junction of the Santa Fe and Cotton Belt railroads. It is beautifully situated on a high prairie, near the head of the South Bosque creek, and has about 1,500 inhabitants. It has the best school building in the county outside the corporate limits of Waco. McGregor church was first organized at Onion Creek (now Eagle Springs), Coryell county, November 6, 1858, by Elder John McClain. It was moved to McGregor after the town began to build. The original members were J. H. Estep, Nancy Estep, E. A. Culpepper, Tabitha Culpepper, Wyatt Hall, Naoma Hall, Serepta Hall, F. M. Grimes, Elmira Grimes, Mary A. Grimes and Daniel Jones. The pastors have been John McClain, J. M. Wright, S. I. Caldwell, T. A. Mangum, M. Isbell, W. S. Huff, G. W. Clark, J. S. Daugherty, J. H. Roberts, H. D. Gilbert and J. B. Smith, who is the present pastor (March, 1897). The church first held membership in Leon River Association, afterward McGregor Association. The house was built in 1886. When McGregor church came into Waco Association (1890) J. S. Daugherty was pastor. At that time the membership aggregated 235. The membership is now (March, 1897,) more than 300. Their Sunday school numbers more than 200. J. B. Smith is making an efficient pastor. T. D. Johnson is Sunday school superintendent and Board member. McGregor church owns property worth more than $3,000. She counts among her membership several ordained ministers: C. R. Osborne, M. Isbell, M. H. Curry, S. I. Caldwell, J. B. Smith.

ELDER SAMUEL BROOKS M'JUNKIN,

son of John S. and Eliza Ann Morrow McJunkin, was born in Stewart (now Webster) county, Ga., December 23, 1838. He professed Christ in baptism September, 1859, and was ordained July 30, 1861, in Pike county, Ala. Elder B. Hardin, once pastor at Waco, was one of the presbytery. He served in the Confederate army till the second battle of Manassas, when he received two severe wounds, on account of which he was discharged from the service. He remained with the army from that time as a missionary. During the last year of the war he baptized nearly five hundred soldiers, being known to thousands only as the "boy preacher." After the war he returned to his native state, where he had previously married Miss Rosaline L. Thorp. With her and one child he moved to Texas. His first Texas pastorate was in Huntsville, where he buried his wife. He married Mrs. Leah A. Storey, his present wife, January 14, 1875, in Grimes county, Texas. More than five thousand persons have professed faith in Christ under his preaching, nearly three thousand of whom he baptized. From choice he has served country churches principally, but has served as pastor in the cities of Cold Springs, Moscow, Calvert, Waco, Rockport and Cuero. He is now (1897) pastor at Mount Calm. His brethren have often put him in positions of trust and honor. He has served as moderator the Nav-

ELDER S. B. McJUNKIN.
(Photo by Sanders, Waco, Texas.)

asota River, Little Brazos, Blanco and Colorado Associations. He is still active, full of vigor, and is an able preacher. May the Lord add yet many years to his useful life.

ELDER JAMES FRANKLIN M'LEOD,

the son of a Baptist deacon, was many years pastor in Falls county, Texas. Was born near Roonske, Ala., October 11, 1853. At the age of 9 years he suffered the loss of his mother, a saintly woman. But she made lasting impressions for good upon her first born and only son. Being made a "new creature" at 16, he was baptized into Bethel church, Chambers county, Ala., by Elder John Cumbee. He was early trained in piety, and applied himself to books, especially the Bible. He took an active part in Sunday schools and prayer meetings, and it was whispered that

ELDER J. F. McLEOD.

"Jimmie" would preach. Soon he was "liberated." For educational reasons, James protested against the action of the church, but to no effect. Soon afterward the Bethel church called for his ordination, and he was set apart for the ministry, Elds. John Cumbee, J. C. Burden, R. A. J. Cumbee and Dr. J. P. Shaffer acting as presbytery. During this time he was married to Miss Augusta C. Jordan. The fruits of his union are three daughters and two sons. The oldest and youngest, both girls, are dead. The first years of his ministry were spent in his native state. In October, 1884, he resigned all work there and came to Falls county, Texas, at that time all in the Waco Association. Here, as before, he found an open door. He was a member of the Waco Association till the fall of 1892, and was faithful to attend all its meetings. Has always been in sympathy and co-operation with the general work of the state. He has served some of the most prominent churches in his county, and God has greatly blessed his labors. He has baptized nearly 1,000 persons. "Nothing too hard for God" has been his motto. Modesty, temperance and piety are among his characteristics. He says: "The Lord called him to the ministry to show what He (God) could make of nothing." The pastorate is his field, and he has served one church successively for 12 years.

ELDER L. J. MIMS,

one of our most promising young preachers, is pastor (1897) of four churches in the Waco Association, viz: Bosqueville, Concord, Eddy and Pleasant Grove. He makes a circuit of 200 miles each month in attending these churches. He is fairly well educated, an attractive speaker, has good social qualities, and is a close student of the Bible. We bespeak for him a useful life in the Master's service.

ELDER ROBERT CUMMINGS MEDARIS,

pastor at Moody, is a native of Eagle Bend, Anderson county, Tenn., where he was born November 23 1858. He was educated at Clinton, Tenn., and the Southern Baptist Theological Seminary, at Louisville, Ky. On March 23, 1884, he was ordained by the Baptist church at Clinton, Tenn. Elder Medaris taught school four years. He has held over fifty revival meetings in Tennessee, Indiana, Kentucky and Arkansas; has witnessed over 2,000 conversions, and has received more than 2,500 into churches where he has labored. He has served churches in Tennessee, Indiana and Kentucky, and has organized churches at various points. For three years he edited the "Mountain Baptist," at Williamsburg, Ky., an influential paper in that part of the state. He founded Williamsburg Institute, a Baptist college, Williamsburg, Ky., and had the pleasure of seeing it on a firm basis, with building and grounds worth $35,000, and $45,000 endowment. For six years he had charge of the mission work in

Eastern Kentucky, and during this time organized two associations, and led six others into active co-operation. Being elected secretary and evangelist of the Arkansas Sunday School and Bible Board, he moved to Arkansas in May, 1893, and continued in the

ELDER R. C. MEDARIS.

service of that Board till its consolidation with the State Mission Board. He was then elected state evangelist of the Mission Board, and served for a time. He was called to the church at Moody, in the Waco Association, March 26, 1896. He is secretary of the Associational Mission Board. We rejoice and thank God that he has come into our midst.

MEXIA CHURCH.

The Mexia Baptist church was organized on the second Sunday in May, 1873, by Elder W. H. Parks, D. D. Fifteen persons went into the organization, five males and ten females, viz: Dr. J. J. Kirksey, who was elected clerk; J. J. Ligon, H. W. Grey, L. L. Robertson, T. J. Gibson, Mrs. M. G. Kirksey, Mrs. Maggie Grey, Mrs. Fannie McDonald, Mrs. Lucy McDonald, Mrs. Emma Ligon, Mrs. A. V. Archer, Misses Mattie Campbell, Mary A. Campbell, Susie L. Campbell and Lizzie Campbell. The pastors have been W. H. Parks, J. R. Malone, R. W. Priest (returned missionary from Africa), H. W. Watson, J. H. Rowland, B. B. Williams, W. I. Feasell, C. F. Maxwell, L. W. Duke, the present pastor. The church united with the Waco Association in 1882, when A. H. Watson was pastor. Elders A. H. Watson and J. T. S. Park bore the petitionary letter. The memberships at that time numbered 37. R. H. Keeling was clerk. In 1885 the church withdrew from Waco Association and went into the organization of Prairie Grove Association; withdrew from Prairie Grove in 1892, and went into the organization of Limestone County Association. At the last meeting of Limestone this church reported 275 members. It is the strongest and most liberal church in that Association. The Mexia brethren are free from internal troubles, and the church enjoys a reasonable degree of prosperity.

MOODY CHURCH.

The town of Moody is in the southwestern part of McLennan county, on the Santa Fe railroad. It is in a good country, and contains about 1,500 inhabitants. It is steadily growing. William Hancock, a Baptist, settled there in 1852 or 1853. He was the first settler. The McClain family followed in the fall of 1853. The next year Miss Jane Leach taught the first school. She was the first white person to die in the settlement. She sleeps in old Perry cemetery. Rev. Herbert, a Methodist, preached the first sermon at the house of Mr. Clemmons, in 1854. During the autumn of the same year, S. G. O'Bryan preached the first Baptist sermon. About the first of March, 1855, the Perry church (now Moody) was organized in the house of Daniel McClain, by Elder S. G. O'Bryan and Deacon Isaac McClain, with eleven members.

MOODY BAPTIST CHURCH.

Following is a partial list of them: Isaac McClain, E. W. McClain, Daniel McClain, John McClain, Moses Ogden, William McClain, and Sisters Meriam McClain, Susan McClain, Polly Ogden and Josephine McClain. S. G. O'Bryan was immediately elected pastor. Isaac McClain was the first deacon, and E. W. McClain the first clerk. The first house of worship was built in the fall of 1855. It was of hewn oak foundation, hewn cedar framing, with weatherboarding of dressed clapboards. The seats were of pine lumber, hauled on wagons from Houston, Texas. Soon after organizing, the church became a member of Trinity River Association. About 1857 Elder O'Bryan resigned the pastorate, and was followed by Elder John McClain. Later Elder W. B. Eaves assisted Pastor McClain in a series of meetings, which resulted in about 50 additions to the church, 37 by baptism. In 1859 Perry church joined Leon River Association. The church prospered till the war, when it was much disorganized. The membership scattered. Some of them moved north, and among others E. W. McClain, who carried the church records to Kansas, where they were lost or destroyed. There are no records prior to 1870. From 1861 to 1870 the church had preaching at intervals, and occasionally prayer and song service. On the first Sunday in January, 1870, Elder R. C. Burleson preached, after which several new members were received, and A. G. G. Perkins was chosen pastor. In October, same year, Elder Perkins resigned. The church was without a pastor from October, 1870, till July, 1875, but during this period Elders J. M. Gambrel and T. A. Mangum became members, and preached occasionally. Regular conferences were kept up. In July, 1875, John McClain was chosen pastor. In July, 1880, Elder T. A. Mangum became pastor. The new house was completed in the fall of 1883; was frame, 32x48 feet. The name of the church was changed to Moody, in July, 1883. In August, 1883, John McClain succeeded T. A. Mangum in the pastorate. In January, 1885, Elder C. P. Lumpkin was chosen pastor. The church this year, August 22-September 6—enjoyed one of the best revivals in her history, resulting in 69 additions, 41 by baptism. Two deacons, C. G. Branham and W. W. Donaldson, were ordained Aug. 6, 1886; presbytery, C. P. Lumpkin and J. M. Gambrel, assisted by the deacons of the church. Pastor C. P. Lumpkin resigned Dec. 6, 1886, and six days afterward G. W. Capps was chosen, who served till September, 1888. From October 24, to December, 1888, C. H. Coltharp was pastor. In February, 1889, C. P.

Lumpkin was again called. In March following J. A. McSpadden and J. C. Collier were ordained deacons; presbytery, Elders C. P. Lumpkin and J. M. Gresham, assisted by the deacons of the church. In February, 1891, C. F. Maxwell was elected pastor, C. P. Lumpkin having resigned two months previously. Bro. Maxwell was succeeded by N. A. Seal, January 1, 1892. During the summer of this year (1892) Pastor Seal, assisted by Elder R. C. Pender, of Denison, Texas, held one of the best revivals ever witnessed in Texas, adding 100 new members, 86 by experience and baptism. In October, following, committees were appointed to secure means and make preparations to build the splendid stone edifice in which the church now worships. This building, with seating capacity for 800, was completed (except basement) in April, 1895, at a cost of $10,000. The property has been incorporated for the term of 50 years. At this time the name was changed to "First Baptist Church at Moody." After the resignation of Bro. Seal (February, 1895), the church was without a pastor for about a year and a half. During the latter half of the year 1895, Elder R. R. White supplied two Sundays in each month. On March 26, 1896, the present pastor, R. C. Medaris, was chosen. He is a noble, good man, and gives his entire time to the church. Moody church became a member of the Waco Association in 1890, during the pastorate of Elder C. P. Lumpkin. The membership at that date was 235. She had been previously connected with Trinity River, Leon River and McGregor Associations. With Pastor Medaris as leader, and with a membership of nearly 300, she is to-day one of the very best and strongest churches in the Waco Association. Clerk S. W. Miller writes: "It has now been 42 years since this church was organized, and though it has passed through some trials we have many reasons to thank God and take courage. He has ever been with us, and has given us almost continued prosperity. We have now a membership of 285, two weekly prayer meetings, an interesting Baptist Young People's Union, which meets weekly, and a large and interesting Sunday school."

MOODY SUNDAY SCHOOL

was organized March 29, 1885, with R. W. Witt, superintendent;

D. C. Jones, secretary; Mrs. Nannie Clay, treasurer, and with the following teachers: J. M. Gambrel, Mrs. R. W. Routh, Mrs. Nannie Clay and Miss Lula Hunter. It numbered 53. From that day it has been a steady growth. The superintendents have been R. W. Witt, one year; J. C. Collier, 14 months; J. A. McSpadden, one year; W. S. Sidall, one year; W. F. Routh, five years; S. W. Miller (present incumbent), three years. The school now has 143 members. At the meeting of the Sunday School Institute of Waco Association, at Cow Bayou, June, 1895, on motion of J. L. Walker it was resolved to have a splendid banner made to be awarded at each fifth Sunday meeting to the school sending the best report. The banner was made. The schools meriting it have been White Hall, Bethany, Caddo, Mart and Moody. Moody holds the banner at the time this book goes to press.

ELDER Z. N. MORRELL,

the author of that remarkable book, "Flowers and Fruits," and the fourth Baptist preacher in Texas, was born in South Carolina, January 17, 1803. His early education was neglected, but he was naturally endowed with a grasping intellect, a quick intuition, and a vast deal of courage and common sense. He came to Tennessee in early life, where he was converted and entered the ministry. He moved to Mississippi in 1835, in search of health, and made himself felt in the organization of the new Association at Troy, on the Yallabusha river. The Hardshells were endeavoring to capture the new organization. His influence and persistence saved the body to the missionaries. His old physician and several other friends from Tennessee came through Mississippi on their way to Texas, and Bro. Morrell joined them. The company then consisted of two lawyers, two Baptist deacons and one Baptist preacher. The trip was made on horseback. At that time there was a camp of 40 Tennesseeans prospecting on Little River. Indians were hostile, but the journey was safely made, and the Tennessee camp reached December 30, 1835. All sorts of game was in abundance. Elder Morrell preached that night to the Tennessee campers. He returned to Mississippi, sold his lands, and moved to Texas. And no grander man ever came. He hunted buffalo, fought Indians and preached the gospel all over Southern and Middle Texas for many years. He organized at Washington, in 1837, the first missionary Baptist church west of the Brazos river. Trackless deserts, wild beasts, savage foes, and swollen streams had no terrors for him. He plunged into sparsely settled districts, sought out the scattered Baptists, organized them into churches and associations, till 50,000 square miles of wilderness "blossomed as the rose." He first settled at the Falls of the Brazos, later at Washington, on the Brazos. In 1838 he went far southwest to Corpus Christi, spying out the country. In 1839 he held a meeting at Plum Grove. He organized Plum Grove church March, 1839. He organized the church at Gonzales in 1841, and settled two miles above Gonzales. The year 1842 was spent in working in a blacksmith shop, working on a farm, and preaching. The war cloud hanging in the west, admonished the Gonzales people to fall back to the Colorado, which they did. Woll came on with his Mexicans. The awful "Mesquite battle" was fought, and Captain Nicholas M. Dawson and 34 of his comrades lay dead. A. H. Morrell, son of Z. N. Morrell, was a prisoner with the Mexicans. The Texans, under General Mayfield, followed and overtook Woll's rear guard at Hondo. "Z. N. Morrell's soul was fired as never before." He led the charge against the Mexicans. Many were killed, but the rest escaped with the prisoners. Young Morrell and others were two years prisoners in Mexico. In 1846 Bro. Morrell was missionary of the Marion Board, in that vast territory lying between the Brazos and Trinity. The result of his work was the Trinity River Association. In 1848 Elders Z. N. Morrell and N. T. Byars organized the Trinity River Association at Providence church, in Navarro county. At the time of the organization of Waco Association, Z. N. Morrell lived on Blue Ridge, in Falls county, and as a delegate from Blue Ridge church took part in the organization. He was chairman of the convention which met at Waco November 9, 1860, to organize the Association, and he was the first moderator of Waco Association. He served on the committee that framed the best associational constitution in the state—that of the Waco Association. After the war Bro. Morrell went to British Honduras, but returned to

Texas after 18 months. In 1872 he went to work to produce the most readable book ever published by a Texas author. We refer to "Flowers and Fruits." It has passed through the third edition. It was written at the home of the late M. V. Smith, in Brenham, to whom Texas is indebted for its racy, readable style. Elder Morrell died at the home of his granddaughter, near Kyle, Texas, December 10, 1883, at the ripe old age of 84. Coming generations to the end of time will gather the "flowers and fruits" of his sowing from the pleasant fields of our beloved Texas paradise.

ELDER S. L. MORRIS

was born in Rankin county, Miss., July 31, 1854. Later the family moved to Winn parish, La. Silas L. was the eldest of eight children. He was ambitious to secure a classical education and gave his spare moments to study. He was sent to school continuously till 12 years old. At 17 years of age he attended school three months, and again the next year three months. These two terms were well improved, and a place was given him as teacher in the public school. Though earnestly desiring to complete his education, every cent earned during his minority was turned over to his father. In the fall of 1876 he entered Mississippi College. He afterward attended Sule's Business College, in New Orleans, and in June, 1878, came to Texas. In 1879 he married Miss Mary J. Davis, of Robertson county. She lived but a short time. In 1881 he entered the senior class of Waco University, deferred his graduation, but was unanimously elected an alumnus of the University. He was converted at the age of 16, and was ordained before his majority. He was pastor of a large church in Louisiana before coming to Texas. He became pastor of Marlin church in 1882. Earlier than this he served Cow Bayou, Beulah and New Zion churches. While pastor at Marlin, in 1883, he was chosen to raise $60,000 endowment for Waco University. This was a gigantic undertaking. But he bravely undertook the difficult task. He succeeded in raising the amount in cash and notes. On April 30, 1885, he was married to Miss Hallie Byrd Burleson, daughter of Dr. R. C. Burleson. He was for one year co-editor and joint proprietor of the "Home and

Sunday School," a religious paper, that enjoyed a good patronage. In 1886 he purchased the Guardian, then with 24 pages, and circulation of 250. With characteristic persistence and energy, aided by his versatile, accomplished and talented wife, he has brought it up to take position among the leading magazines of the South. Bro. Morris claims to know more men than any other man in Texas. It is conceded that he is without a peer as a solicitor,

REV. S. L. MORRIS.
(Photo by Sanders, Waco, Texas.)

and it is this extraordinary talent that has given the Guardian its success. He was for many years clerk of the Waco Association, and did his work well. He contributed much toward the development of the Association, often conducting the collections. As a preacher his views are clear, his voice pleasant, and his bearing graceful.

MRS. HALLIE B. BURLESON-MORRIS.

Mrs. Morris, wife of S. L. Morris, is the only daughter of Dr. R. C. Burleson and Mrs. Georgia Burleson. She was born September 3, 1865, in Waco, Texas. At 13 years of age she became a member of Christ and his church (First Baptist), at Waco. Since then she has been a faithful and devoted Christian, and has done much efficient work in the Sunday school. She has always

MRS. HALLIE B. BURLESON-MORRIS.
(Photo by Sanders, Waco, Texas.)

had a class, and it has been few Sundays that, for any reason, she has been kept away from her class. In 1883 she graduated at Waco University, thus completing her university course, begun in early childhood and directed by the tender, skillful hand of her father, the prince of Texas educators. Ever pure and conscientious, her delicate and refining impress has been left upon many students and classmates of her historic alma mater. April 30,

1885, she was married to Rev. S. L. Morris, and thenceforth two distinct streams of human existence harmoniously blended into one. In wifehood, as in girlhood, her example is worthy of emulation. Her accurate information and rare acomplishments are brought to bear in giving tone and fragrance to the "Guardian."

MT. ANTIOCH CHURCH.

In 1855 E. J. Billington raised $25 and purchased a log house in which to worship. In this log house the Mt. Antioch church was constituted, Sabbath, July 21, same year. The following went into the organization: Penuel Billington and wife, Nancy; Haughton Hughes and wife, Midian; E. J. Billington and wife, Kitty Ann, and M. J. Billington—seven in all. Bro. E. J. Billington, then deacon, entered upon the duties of that office. Elder W. J. Bowden was the first pastor, and served till 1857. In 1857 Dr. J. J. Riddle joined Mt. Antioch church, and was by that church ordained pastor. Bro. Riddle was a good physician and an excellent preacher. He preached for Mt. Antioch nine years, and was again called in 1879. Texas never had a safer preacher. Healing the body and preaching for the good of the soul, this brother's life was the delight of Baptists and the glory of God. It is remarkable that Bro. Riddle preached his first and last sermon at Mt. Antioch. His last sermon was delivered in tears and much love. He seemed to be well, but returned home to die. Mt. Antioch has ordained four preachers, Dr. J. J. Riddle, 1857; E. J. Billington, 1862; A. C. Graves and J. M. Wright, 1867. Three churches have gone out from Mt. Antioch: Mt. Calm, Prairie Hill and Antioch, at Billington. In 1855 Mt. Antioch joined Trinity River Association. In 1858 E. J. Billington and Dr. J. J. Riddle were appointed messengers of this church to meet in convention with Dresden church, in Navarro county, for the purpose of organizing the Richland Association. The messengers attended and were in the organization. Mt. Antioch joined Waco Association in 1882, continuing till 1888, when she joined Hubbard City. The church is now 42 years old. The first pastor, W. J. Bowden, continued till 1857. He died in 1859. The following illustrious names have been the shepherds:

W. J. Bowden, J. J. Riddle, H. R. Puryear, T. H. Compere, T. D. Suttle, A. C. Graves, J. M. McDonald, J. R. Malone, S. R. Williams, W. A. Scott, C. L. Harris, J. C. Smith, who is her present pastor. Three noble brothers, T. H. Holloway, J. V. Holloway and G. W. Holloway, have all been deacons; also D. W. Davis. The present deacons are C. D. Shilling and J. V. Holloway. T. B. Wharton was the faithful clerk for maney years. The beloved C. B. Shead and his son, W. R., were once pillars in this church.

MOUNT CALM CHURCH

was ten years a member of the Waco Association, from 1878 to 1888. The church had only been organized a short time when she joined the Association in 1878. It was originally organized principally of Mt. Antioch members. G. L. Jennings was pastor in 1878-9. At the time of joining the Association in 1878 the membership aggregated 33. While Mt. Calm was in Waco Association the pastors were G. L. Jennings, T. L. M. Duncan, Jas. Scarborough, R. S. Taylor and C. P. Lumpkin. The membership numbered 65 at the time the church withdrew from Waco Association. In 1888 Mt. Calm joined Hubbard Association. S. B. McJunkin is the present pastor, and the membership aggregates 196. Mt. Calm is on the Cotton Belt railroad, 20 miles east from Waco.

MOUNT PISGAH CHURCH.

Mount Pisgah united with the Association in 1873. It was a new church at that time, and had but 15 members. Though but recently organized, it counted among its membership some of the best men in Texas. E. F. Russing, C. W. Kinnard, Z. N. Morrell, Jesse Tubb, J. Williams and W. J. Keeling were among the original members. C. E. Stephen was the first pastor. He was followed by C. W. Kinnard the next year. The church was either dissolved or merged into Reagan in 1876, most probably the latter.

ELDER T. E. MUSE

was born near Winchester, Franklin county, Tenn., June 30, 1844. His parents were "Primitive" Baptists, devoted and prominent in church relations. Was baptized into Bethpage

Missionary Baptist church in 1858. Served in the Confederate army and was wounded at the battle of Missionary Ridge. Married to Edna E. Johnson January 3, 1867. Ordained to the ministry in May, 1869, the presbytery consisting of Elders A. D. Trimble, pastor; D. B. Stamps, M. B. Clements and J. G. Nash. Moved to Louisiana in December, 1870, and in January, 1872, became pastor of the church at Evergreen, La. In 1876, with

ELDER T. E. MUSE.
(Photo by Jackson, Waco, Texas.)

his family, moved to Texas, reaching Hill county March 4, of that year. For years served in various pastorates in Hill and Ellis counties. In January, 1885, moved from Hillsboro to Waco for the educational advantages of Waco Baylor University. With the exception of four years' residence in the pastorate at Eddy, has remained and yet resides in Waco. His pastorates have been successful. A number of church houses have been erected in connection with his labors. In doctrine and polity he is a Landmark Baptist. Was never in a trouble with a church or at material variance with brethren, but in many instances instrumental in relieving and helping others. Has kept a diary of his ministerial life, and from his books can locate the place of preaching every Sabbath since January, 1872, with the text and notes of sermon. Also a record of every candidate baptized. A devoted Christian companion has largely strengthened his efforts, and fully borne the burdens, and shared the trials allotted to the preacher's wife. Five grown children live to be the comfort and satisfaction and the hope and stay of their future years. Bro. Muse has now passed his meridian, yet his strength is unabated and his zeal and labors are not lessened. Not a moral or doctrinal shadow has ever darkened his life. He is truly one of the Lord's noblemen.

NEW HOPE CHURCH

was organized in 1869. S. Wright, J. H. Shelton, S. W. Punchard, S. Adams and J. Modawell were among the original members. This church resulted from a revival meeting held in the neighborhood by Elders B. H. Carroll and B. Walker. The place of meeting was ten miles from Waco, near the town of Harrison. New Hope prospered for several years. The pastors were R. C. Burleson, M. B. Hardin, R. B. Burleson, J. B. Parrack, S. King, J. H. Harrison, T. D. Suttle and A. P. Scofield. New Hope ceased to exist about 1885. It was received into the Waco Association 1869 with 49 members. The number was 49 in 1879. The following brethren held membership in New Hope at different times: P. S. Scofield, J. W. Freeman, W. H. Thompson, D. Lacy, F. M. Dunklin, J. M. Yeates, T. D. Suttle, W. H. Francis, J. H. Harrison T. B. Mothershead, J. E. Ware, M. Warner, and J. E. Harrison.

NEW ZION CHURCH.

The New Zion church was organized in 1877 by Elder Calvin Magee. W. D. Gaines, P. D. Wall, J. H. Livingston and Leonard Magee were among the original members. The church first represented in the Association in 1878, at which time Elder T. D.

Suttle was pastor, and A. O. Gaines, clerk. A gracious revival in 1878 resulted in 28 baptisms. In 1881 S. L. Morris was pastor and W. D. Gaines clerk; sixty-four reported. In 1882 A. J. Shelton was pastor; membership, 57. On February 24, 1883, the church dissolved. The house of worship was purchased by the new body constituted at Chilton one month later.

ELDER HOLMES NICHOLS,

son of M. P. and Eliza Holmes Nichols, was born in Waco, Texas, April 3, 1859. His youth was spent on his uncle's farm, in McLennan county, his parents having died when he was a child. His father was a lawyer, and was at one time tax assessor of McLennan county. Prior to her marriage, his mother supported herself and her aged mother by teaching in Waco and Bosqueville. At the age of 20 Bro. Nichols left his uncle and engaged in railroad bridge building in Texas, Tennessee, Arkansas and Mississippi. Returned to his boyhood home in 1884. In speaking of his railroad life, he says: "I quit the work a total wreck; robbed of character by the wine cup, and a helpless, cowering slave to drink, with a craving and an increasing mania for the gambling table. I returned to the home of my youth to reform, but instead I repented of my sins, trusted Christ as my Savior; was washed in His blood, and now, by the grace of God, 'I am what I am,' a sinner, having the imputed righteousness of Jesus Christ." Bro. Nichols was educated in country schools, and at Baylor University. He is a great lover of books, and is a close student. On his return to Texas, he was elected president of McLennan County Farmers' Alliance, in August, 1885; was also lecturer of State Alliance. He was tendered the nomination of "floater" of the Seventeenth Representative District by the Union Labor party and by the Knights of Labor in 1886, but declined the nomination and accepted the position of deputy tax assessor of McLennan county in January, 1887. Bro. Nichols was ordained a minister by Bold Springs Baptist church at West, Tex., April 7, 1888, the presbytery consisting of Revs. T. P. Speakman, under whose ministry he was converted, in 1886, V. G. Cunningham and W. W. Finley. Since his ordination he has given himself "wholly to the work of the ministry," and has had more calls to churches than he could accept. He was elected clerk of Waco Baptist Association in 1893, which position he continues to fill with acceptance. He was married to Miss Edna A. McDonald in March, 1890, Rev. J. B. Cranfill officiating. It has been our pleasure to assist Bro. Nichols in meetings at his home church, and to spend some time with his interesting little family, and we do not hesitate to say that our dear brother

ELDER HOLMES NICHOLS.

made a wise choice in selecting a companion, and that she is a "help meet" in word and deed. Bro. Nichols has served the following churches as pastor: Lone Oak, Caledonia, White Rock, Aquilla, Leon, Concord and Mastersville, at Bruceville. The fact that he has baptized over four hundred people into the fellowship of these churches, and that he has been instrumental in developing in them the mission spirit, is evidence that he has adhered to the injunction: "Preach the word," and that he is making "full proof of his ministry." He is at present pastor of Elm Mott, his eighth year, and at Blooming Grove, his present home. In referring to his locating in Blooming Grove, and to the reception given him by the Baptist church on his arrival, the Blooming Grove Rustler pays to Bro. Nichols a most brilliant compliment. And Dr. J. B. Cranfill, editor of the Texas Baptist Standard, who has known him long and intimately, says in the editorial columns of his paper: "Rev. Holmes Nichols, so long the clerk of Waco Association, is a loyal, earnest, able preacher, and our brethren in Navarro county will find in him a great accession to their ranks." Bro. Nichols is an occasional contributor to our denominational papers. His strongest articles being, "Campbellism vs. the Word of God," which appeared in the Texas Baptist and Herald; "The New Version," a piece of irony, which appeared in the Western Baptist; "The Selection of a Pastor," "Is a Limited Pastorate Scriptural?" ordered published in leaflet form by the mission board of Waco Association; "A Serious Question Settled," "My Martinite," being a denunciation of Elder L. W. Davis, and which resulted in his expulsion from Comanche County Association. "Comparisons are not odious," all of which appeared in the Texas Baptist Standard, and "B. H. Carroll Vindicated," which appeared in the Texas Baptist and Herald in the beginning of recent mission troubles.

OAK GROVE CHURCH

was organized in 1874. S. F. Sparks, O. Barrett, Isaac Parker, J. B. Dagley and W. B. Jenkins were among the original members. Oak Grove is the picturesque country north of Childers creek, and near the Brazos, in McLennan county. It first joined Towash Association at the first annual session of that body in 1874. Elder Sam Lacy was the first pastor. When the church went into Towash Association in 1874 there were 37 members, six of whom had been but recently received by baptism. Dr. Hatchett was pastor in 1876. From 1876 to 1880 the church was without a pastor. In that year T. P. Speakman took the oversight. The membership was reduced to 17. The church built up under the ministrations of Bro. Speakman. When B. F. Tatum took charge in 1882, the number was 43. Bro. Tatum served till 1885; when J. L. Walker accepted, the number was then 39. J. L. Walker served two years. For many years after this, Oak Grove was somewhat disorganized. In 1890 it came into Waco Association and had at that time 34 members. L. T. Ritchie was pastor. Since then the pastors have been J. T. Gelispie, S. R. Williams, V. G. Cunningham and the present pastor, R. E. Smith. In September, 1896, there were 29 members.

ELDER SOLOMON GREEN O'BRYAN

came to Texas from North Carolina by way of Alabama. He was born in Warren county, N. C., January 22, 1821. Was baptized into Brown's Baptist church in 1843, by Elder W. Hudgins. He was educated at Wake Forest College, graduating from that institution June, 1849. During the autumn of that year left his native state; spent two years in Alabama, teaching at Sumpterville and preaching for the churches at Sumpterville and Gainesville. In February, 1854, he began his six years' pastorate at Waco, Texas. Waco was then a rude, frontier town, with but few inhabitants. During his six years 67 were received by baptism and 121 by letter. He preached much in Central Texas during this period, served many churches and organized many. The old first brick house of worship in Waco was erected while he was pastor. In 1858 he was corresponding secretary of Trinity River Association, and in 1859 was moderator of that body. It was mainly through his influence that the Trinity River Classical School was located at Waco, which was the foundation of Waco University and Baylor University at Waco. He was the first president of the Trinity River Classical School. During the war he was president of Bosqueville College two years, and he organized the Bosqueville church. In 1860 he took the oversight of the church at Huntsville. In 1867 he settled near Port Sullivan, in Milam county, and accepted the churches at Cameron, Port Sullivan and Little River. This same year his Master called him to rest September 26, 1867. He preached his last sermon on the night of September 24, from the text: "Take ye away the stone." It was said to be one of his best efforts. Sixteen came forward for prayer. He was twice married. His first wife was Miss L. E. Swan. She died in 1852. She left no children. His second wife was Miss Sarah Ann Chandler, daughter of Elder P. B. Chandler, of Fayette county, Texas. His second marriage was in February, 1854. He left three sons and one daughter. The oldest, W. C. O'Bryan, at McGregor, was but 11 years old. These all grew up and became church members. Two are now dead. S. G. O'Bryan was well educated, and a grand preacher. He could have filled any pulpit in the South. He chose the frontier wilderness instead. We reap the fruits of his labors.

OLIVE BRANCH CHURCH

was organized about 1874. This church was the result of the missionary work of V. G. Cunningham. There were 16 members when the church joined the Association in 1874. V. G. Cunningham was the first pastor. He was succeeded by J. B. Parrack. The pastors have been V. G. Cunningham, J. B. Parrack, J. F. Duncan, Thos. Hooker, Jas. Scarborough, A. A. Hensler, T. P. Speakman, W. S. Huff, M. L. Davis, R. C. A. Ashcraft. Olive Branch withdrew by letter from Waco Association in 1895, and united with Hubbard City. The membership was 30 at that time. The church has a good house of worship and some wealthy members. Their place of meeting is five miles north of Axtell.

ELDER W. H. PARKS, D. D.,

came from Alabama to Texas with his father at the age of 14 years. He was born in Monroe county Ga., August 2, 1836. His father, Isaac Parks, moved to Chambers county, Ala., in 1844, and in 1853 to Anderson, Grimes county, Texas. W. H. Parks professed faith in Christ in August, 1850, and was baptized by Elder Willis Jones. He entered Baylor University at Independence, in the spring of 1854, and graduated in June, 1856. Returning home, became superintendent of his father's farm, and at the same time read law. At the opening of the first law school of Baylor University in 1857, he entered as a student, and graduated in a class of thirteen in 1858. He was licensed to practice law by the district court of Washington county at its fall term, 1857, Hon. R. E. B. Baylor, presiding. In 1859 opened a law office in Bonham, Fannin county, Texas. He there met Miss Josephine Drake of Dallas, student of the Bonham high school. They were married June 11, 1861. He entered the Confederate service in the fall of the same year, and served under General Tom Green till the death of that officer; then under Gen-

ELDER W. H. PARKS, D. D.

eral J. P. Majors to the close of the war. In 1865 his ever helpful wife taught school in Collin county. From the day of his baptism he had felt it his duty to preach, but his aspirations in another direction smothered back his impressions of duty. His sense of duty grew till at length, August 3, 1867, he submitted to ordination, and was, by the Spring Creek Baptist church, set apart to the responsible office of New Testament bishop. After preaching nearly two years for churches in Collin and Dallas counties, he accepted an appointment as missionary of the Trinity River Association, with headquarters at Fairfield. He declined re-appointment and accepted the care of Fairfield church and three other churches, where he labored three years, after which, in January, 1873, he moved to Mexia. He organized Mexia church in May, same year, and preached for it six years. He also served Ennis church three years of this period. Under his pastorate Ennis built two meeting houses, the first being destroyed in a cyclone. In January, 1879, he became pastor of the Denison church, and in the fall of that year conducted a nine weeks' meeting, doing all the preaching except four sermons. The membership of the church was about doubled during this meeting. In the winter of 1879-80 a division occurred in the First church of Dallas, and in April, 1880, Bro. Parks accepted the care of one of these parties. In this relation he was associated with his old time and intimate friend, the beloved R. C. Buckner. In October, 1881, he resigned his Dallas flock, leaving them prosperous and in a new house. He then settled in Bosque county, near Morgan, and preached to small churches, supporting himself and family mainly from his flocks of fine sheep. In the fall of 1884 he assisted in the organization of Meridian Association. And he was moderator of this body six years, a period of uninterrupted peace and prosperity. In 1891 he responded to a call from the church at Seymour, and his eleven months' pastorate at that place resulted in 45 or 50 additions to the church. He resigned at Seymour, to accept a call at Ennis. This church soon became united, and entered on an era of prosperity. The next year his son, Elder J. D. Parks, returning from the seminary, held a glorious revival meeting at Ennis. During his four years at Ennis, the membership increased nearly three-fold, a splendid new house was erected and paid for and a chapel built. But his wife's health gave way, and he resigned. Sister Parks was thought to have consumption, but the fresh mountain air of Bosque county measurably restored her to health. Bro. Parks and family joined the East Waco church in September, 1896. He is now pastor of West church. In 1856 Bro. Park received from Baylor University the degree of A. B., two years later the degree of LL. B., afterward the degree of A. M., and in 1880 the honorary degree of D. D. Bro. Parks is a man of eminent piety, and is a warm hearted preacher. His influence is felt all over Texas, and the good he has done will only be revealed at the last day. He is the author of the "Texas Baptist Pulpit," a volume that has attained a wide circulation.

PEORIA CHURCH

was organized about 1866, at Peoria, in Hill county. T. J. Sparkman was the first pastor. T. J. Sparkman, Thos. R. Johnson, S. A. Johnson and A. C. Bragg were among the original members. When this church united with the Association in August, 1867, their number was 34. The next year N. C. Brooks, C. Brooks, J. Bookout and J. W. Leatherwood were members, and it is probable that they were in the organization. In 1868 J. A. Land was pastor. In 1869 W. K. Posey became a member. It is possible that he was a member earlier. W. K. Posey was a grand man, and was afterward several years moderator of Towash Association. S. E. Brooks, one of the best educated men in Central Texas, was pastor in 1869. Peoria church did not represent in the Waco Association after 1869. In 1872 the church went into the organization of Towash Association. It still exists in the town of Peoria, Hill county, and belongs to Hillsboro Association. The present membership is about 60. This church has been a blessing to a large section of the surrounding country.

PLEASANT GROVE CHORCH.

Nestling in a beautiful, shady grove in southern Falls county, is the quaint old country meeting house of Pleasant Grove Baptist church. The house is two miles from the Brazos (west side), and 18 from Marlin. Pleasant Grove church was organized in 1878, one mile west of its present site, by Elders T. J. Shannon, C. P. Lumpkin and W. J. Glazener. Pastors in the following order: —. Johnson, W. J. Glazener, M. H. Whatley, J. F. McLeod, Robert Moore, J. W. Roberts, J. B. Reaves, C. D. Whitman, L. J. Mims. The clerks have been J. L. Pomphrey, Morgan Pomphrey, J. F. Dewberry, E. J. Wilcox, —. Jones. Two deacons, R. G. Boyd and C. M. Dewberry, have been ordained by this church. One of the best preachers of this state was baptized and ordained by Pleasant Grove church. We refer to the late R. O. Dewberry, who died pastor at Huntsville, Texas. Elder J. L. Stuckey, of Eldorado church, was first liberated by Pleasant Grove. The church united with Waco Association in 1879, and has never belonged anywhere else. She is small in membership, but has distinguished herself for soundness of doctrine and fidelity of co-operation. The grand old deacon, J. D. Butts, deserves much credit for the steadfastness in doctrine and practice of Pleasant Grove. Adverse winds have come more than once, yet this little vine continues to grow. May the sunshine of Divine love, dews of Divine blessing, and soft, balmy breezes of Divine help, be her portion; and may the husbandman receive fruit year by year till earth's sun shall set to rise no more.

PRAIRIE HILL CHURCH,

in the beautiful country, in the northwest part of Limestone county, was organized October 18, 1885, by Elder T. D. Suttle. The following went into the organization: Sam Ellison, Betty Hughes, L. C. Hughes, D. E. Person, E. H. Person, P. F. Person, W. L. Davis, J. M. Davis, Lucy P. Davis, J. A. Downs, P. P. Downs, Hugh Davis, H. R. Dyer, R. J. Dyer, M. V. Baker—15 in all. G. L. Jennings was pastor from the organization till December, 1887. T. D. Suttle followed, serving two years. The next pastor was W. D. G. Anderson, from December, 1889, till September, 1890. J. J. Harris succeeded, and had the oversight from September 1890, till August, 1891. G. L. Jennings was then called and held the pastorate three years, till November, 1894. Then followed S. B. McJunkin, from November, 1894, to October, 1896, when the present incumbent, J. C. Smith, was installed. The deacons are G. W. Morris, M. V. Baker. Prairie Hill church became a member of the Waco Association at the session of 1886. L. C. Hughes, Jas. Davis, S. C. Foster, Baker were bearers of the petitionary letter. The membership was 33 at that date. Was dismissed by letter September, 1888, in fellowship and order, with 42 members. After four years' connection with Hubbard City, this church went into the organization of Limestone

County Association, Nov. 11, 1892. Prairie Hill has at this time 157 members, and is the largest church but three in Limestone Association. They have a flourishing Sunday school of 50 scholars, with R. H. Ferguson as superintendent. The obliging clerk of Prairie Hill church is D. J. Calvery.

ELDER H. R. PURYEAR,

the subject of this sketch, was born in Halifax county, Virginia, August 7, 1817. His father, Wm. Puryear, removed from Vir-

ELDER H. R. PURYEAR.

ginia to Graves county, Ky., where H. R. Puryear grew up to young manhood. After his conversion he joined the Baptist church, and being impressed that it was his duty to preach the gospel, he was liberated, and was afterward ordained to the work of the gospel ministry. That he might the better discharge his ministerial labors, he decided to take a collegiate course in Georgetown College, Kentucky, from which institution he graduated when about 30 years of age. Two years later he married Miss Caroline V. Adams, of Ballard county, Ky. Seven children were born to them. Four of the children and the noble, Christian companion, preceded him to the better land. In 1857, or in 1858, he and his brother, Deacon S. H. Puryear, now of Parker county, Texas, removed with their families to this state. Elder Puryear settled in Navarro county, and for twenty years was prominent and active in all Baptist work in that part of Texas. For seven years in succession he was pastor at Corsicana; he served many years as moderator of Richland Association; was pastor at Hopewell, Providence, Rehoboth, Richland and of many other churches during this time. He engaged in many revival meetings, witnessed many conversions, and baptized large numbers. In 1877 he lost his faithful companion by death. He was married again to Mrs. Elizabeth Cole of Waxahachie, Texas, in 1882. In 1883 he removed to Mount Calm, Texas, where he served as pastor for some time. After this he also preached to a number of the churches of Waco Association, serving as pastor at Mart, White Rock, Geneva and perhaps at other points. He was always a friend to the cause of missions, education and religious progress. He was gentle in disposition, but a bold defender of the truth as understood by Baptists. Vigorous in body and mind, he "fought a good fight," having preached faithfully in Texas for at least thirty years. After a brief illness at his home, near Mount Calm, he passed to his reward January 12, 1888. A modest monument in the Mount Calm cemetery, erected by his three surviving children, Wm. P. and Mary Ellen Puryear, and Mrs. W. H. Pool, marks his last resting place. "Blessed are the dead who die in the Lord."

ELDER E. A. PUTHUFF,

the subject of this sketch, is a mixture of German and Irish extraction; Irish on the mother's side, and German on the father's. The grand parents on both sides were among the first settlers of Kentucky, and located at an early day in what is now known as the City of Lexington. E. A. Puthuff was born in Franklin county, Ky., August 26, 1850, and was left to the care of a widowed mother, together with five other children, he being the youngest, and only 11 months old at the time of his father's death. He was led to trust in Christ as his personal Savior in 1861. In 1874 he joined the Baptist church, in Greenville, Hunt county, Texas, and was baptized by Elder J. E. Sligh. He entered upon the ministry in 1882, and was called to ordination by Sulphur Springs church in 1884, Dr. R. C. Burleson, S. J. Anderson, J. H. Boyett, Elder James Christian and Elder W. I. Feazell acting as presbytery. During his course as a student in Baylor University, at Waco, he preached regularly on Saturdays and Sundays to country churches, and spent his vacations in protracted meetings, mainly in the bounds of Waco Association, his labors being abundantly blessed in leading many precious souls to Christ. His first work as pastor was with Union Grove church, in McLennan county, Tex. In 1885 he resigned his pastorate to accept an appointment under the F. M. Board at Richmond, Va., as foreign missionary to Brazil. He was married to Miss Emma Fox, of Slate Springs, Miss., November 25, 1885, and the following day left with his wife for Richmond, Va., where they joined Elder C. D. Daniel and wife en route for Brazil. On December 5, the company ran down to Newport News and the same day, about 7 p. m., on board the steamship "Finance," they loosed from the moorings and steamed out for South America, Bro. Daniel locating in Bahia, Bro. Puthuff in Rio de Janeiro. Yellow fever was prevailing in Rio at the time, and it was thought best by the friends in the mission for Bro. Puthuff and wife to go to the city of Sao Paulo, about 300 miles interior, and study the Portuguese language. After remaining in Sao Paulo about one year, they were instructed by the Board to move to Estacao de Santa Barbara, where there was an English colony, and also a small English-speaking church. Here they established a mission school, erecting a commodious brick building for school and church purposes at their own expense, gathered in and taught the Brazilian and American children, and organized the first native Baptist church in the Province of Sao Paulo. They remained upon this field three years, when Sister Puthuff was advised by her physicians to return to the United States for medical treatment, Bro. Puthuff continuing nine months in the work.

He then also returned, and about six months later resigned his work as foreign missionary, and accepted the pastorate of Bold Springs church, at West, McLennan county, Texas, in Waco Association. Here his labors were graciously blessed of God, as the record of that church will show. From this church he was called as pastor by the Sunset church, San Antonio, where he remained about a year, when, by advice of physicians, in quest of health for his wife, he traveled and preached in 17 counties in Western Texas. He then again located as pastor, this time in Dallas county, at Seagoville, on the Trunk railroad, where he remained two years. Here his labors were greatly blessed in building a house of worship and organizing the church for more efficient work, baptizing over 40 into the fellowship of the church. Having been importuned at various times for more than three years by the brethren of Trinity River Association to act as general missionary for that body, he left Seagoville and began that work in October, 1894, and labored two years within the bounds of that Association, traveled on dirt road 5,608 miles, visited 1,152 families, preached 448 sermons, delivered 103 religious addresses, held 468 prayer services, baptized 53, received 44 by letter, sold and gave away 1,490 Bibles, and other books, distributed 29,240 pages of tracts, and left the Association identified with every interest fostered by our denomination, as shown by the minutes of 1896, in pledges from the different churches for the various objects. At the close of the last associational year, Bro. Puthuff accepted the call of Fairfield church, where he is now located.

REAGAN CHURCH

is most probably old Mt. Pisgah, with the name changed. Mt. Pisgah united with the Association in 1873 with 15 members. The sainted Z. N. Morrell and Jesse Tubb held membership in Mt. Pisgah in 1875. The same brethren were members of Reagan in 1876. Mt. Pisgah appears in the associational minutes last in 1875, with 34 members. Reagan appears first in 1876, not as a new church, but as having reported 34 members the previous year. Reagan exists till this day, and is one of the most prosperous churches in Falls county, thoroughly in sympathy with all our work. The total number in fellowship in 1895 was 136. The whole amount paid by the church that year outside of pastor's salary and home expenses, was $72.30; more than 50 cents per member. The pastors (since name was changed to Reagan) have been Jesse Tubb, J. V. Wright, W. S. Huff, L. W. Duke, J. H. Rowland, J. F. McLeod and B. J. Skinner. S. E. Whipkey is the pastor now. In 1891 Reagan church was granted a letter of admission from Waco Association. On November 14, 1891, eight churches met at Reagan and organized Falls County Association. Reagan church went into the organization. The churches were Beulah, El Dorado, Hope, Liberty, Marlin, New Hope, Reagan and Rocky. Falls County Association occupies territory once in the Waco Association, and is composed of churches mostly from the Waco Association. Reagan had 100 members at the time Falls County Association was formed, and has had a steady growth ever since. The town of Reagan is 10 miles southwest of Marlin, having the historic prairies of Blue Ridge on the north and east, and the great, wide alluvial valley of the Brazos river on the west and southwest. This valley, lying contiguous to the town of Reagan, contains near 20 square miles of land of unsurpassed fertility. Reagan is rapidly growing in population and wealth, and will continue to do so for many years to come. The church has a mission to inspire this coming population with the spirit of Christ.

ELDER JAMES BAILEY REAVES

was born near Pine Bluff, in Jefferson county, Ark., June 2, 1859. He was the second son of his parents, Thomas and Mary Reaves, who moved to Saline (now Grant county). When he was 3 years old his mother died. His father was killed at the battle of Corinth, leaving the children to be brought up by their grandfather, Elder Jesse Reaves, a Baptist preacher. J. B. Reaves came to Collin county, Texas, in 1876; was converted there in August, 1877. In 1878 he went to Bosque county, and was baptized into Spring Creek Baptist church in March, 1879, by Elder J. W. Staton, now pastor at Kingston, Texas. In the spring of 1881 he was married to Miss Esther Jordan, who was also a member of the Baptist church, and daughter of a Baptist deacon.

Bro. Reaves was ordained a deacon of the Spring Creek church in 1884, and licensed to preach by the same church July, 1885. Moved to Coleman county in 1886. Here he was ordained to the full work of the ministry, and called as their pastor by the Camp Creek Baptist church, in March, 1888, Elders J. W. Stanton, A. R. Watson and C. H. Featherstone forming the presbytery. Resigned the care of the Camp Creek church in Septem-

ELDER J. B. REAVES.
(Photo by Sanders, Waco, Texas.)

ber, 1888, to take the mission work of the Pecan Valley Association. After serving that Association fifteen months he resigned the work to enter school. Resided a short time at Santa Anna, and then with his family removed to Waco, September 25, 1890, and immediately entered Baylor University, where he remained in school for four years. He was called to the care of the Durango church in the spring of 1891, and in the fall of the same year to the care of the Pleasant Grove and Center churches. In 1892 he was called by the White Hall church, which he has served continuously since. Resigned the Durango church in 1893, and in 1894 he resigned Pleasant Grove and Center to take the work at Bosqueville and Flat Rock. The same year the Hewitt church was organized and called him as her pastor. The church buildings at Center and Hewitt were both built while he was pastor of those churches. During his ministry he has baptized 242. He is an earnest preacher and an acceptable pastor. May the Lord spare him many years.

ELDER REID RECTOR,

the pastor of Little Deer Creek church, was born in Caldwell county, N. C., June 28, 1851. He was raised in Burke county, and received good foundation training in common schools. He attended Rutherford College two years. While a youth he read many books, especially philosophical works. Came with his parents to Washington county, Texas, in November, 1871. Becoming associated with Spiritualists, he was led measurably to adopt their views. He then began to question the authenticity of the scriptures, for, clearly, "Spiritualism" is in conflict with the Bible. Soon "Spiritualism" and the Bible were both given up, and he gloried in the thought that he had risen above the ignorance and superstition of all religious creeds. In 1876 he began the study of law, continuing two years, but he never practiced. In 1878 he was married to Miss Lizzie T. Malone. She was born in Brenham and raised in Houston. Her parents were from Ireland. She was raised up in the Catholic faith; was educated in the convent at Houston; was a devoted Catholic. In 1880 he moved to Bell county and settled near Oenaville. Here the young wife read her Catholic prayer book and catechism, and the husband the poisonous trash of Infidelity. The Bible was in the library, kept as a curiosity. At this time Elder John H. Rowland, of blessed memory, became pastor of the Baptist church at Oenaville. During a protracted meeting his burning words led Mrs. Rector to abandon her Catholic faith, and she found peace in Christ. Soon thereafter Major W. E. Penn held a meeting at Willow Springs, near Heidenheimer. Mrs. Rector joined the church and was baptized by M. V. Smith. Reid Rector was in despair. At last the great truth broke in on his soul, "Jesus is the Savior of sinners." He, too, was baptized, and they became members of Oenaville church. He felt that preach he must. He preached at Oenaville and the surrounding country, assisting in revival meetings. November 13, 1887, he was ordained by Oenaville Baptist church. The presbytery consisted of G. W. Green, J. W. Cunningham and A. Clark. In November, 1890, moved near Lott, in Falls county, and joined the Lott church. In September, 1891, he was called to the care of Little Deer Creek church, where he continues till this day. When he began they were a feeble flock, with only 22 members, worshiping in a school house. Since then the membership has more than quadrupled, and they have built a good house. His church went into Falls County Association in 1893. In 1884 he was elected moderator of that Association, and in 1885 his church gave him a unanimous call for an indefinite period of time.

ELDER J. J. RIDDLE

was born in Alabama in 1821. Died at his home in Bosqueville, McLennan county, Texas, January 1, 1881. He came to Waco in 1852. He was converted at Mt. Antioch church, in Limestone county, Texas, in 1857, and was by that church ordained pastor. He preached for Mt. Antioch church nine years. He was again called to that church in 1879. His first and last sermons were preached at Mt. Antioch. He preached for several churches in the Waco Association, and conducted many precious revival meetings. He was pastor of Rock Creek, Mt. Antioch and Marlin at the time of his death, and was moderator of the Waco Association. A memorial page containing touching resolutions of the Association relative to Bro. Riddle's death is found in the minutes of 1881. There it is stated that he always with tears argued the cause of Christ, prayed for its success and labored earnestly in our missionary cause. His heart lived with his flock. If one was in distress, Bro. Riddle was never comfortable till that member was relieved. Even in his dying hour he remembered a sister of Rock Creek church who very much dreaded the hour of her departure. The thought of death haunted her. He had talked with her and tried to comfort her. While he was dying he said: "Tell Sister G— that what I told her about dying grace is true. I told her that while it's God's will for us to live, he gives us grace to live by; but when it is his will for us to die, he will give grace to sustain us in that dark hour. I am dying

ELDER J. J. RIDDLE.

now, and have the precious grace which makes it well." This message was a comfort to Sister G. as long as she lived. Dr. B. H. Carroll, who visited him in his last hours, wrote: "The shadows of death never dimmed his eye nor eclipsed his faith. Even as he entered the cold river that divides the two worlds, he calmly gave his last message of love to relatives and friends, and bore lucid and joyful witness to the comforting power of Divine love." The ship was towed into the last port a dismantled wreck, but with every mast standing and every sail flowing. The last letter he ever penned was written to the Baptist church at Marlin. The following extract from that letter will illustrate his character and fidelity to his people: "I have endeavored to urge upon you every Christian duty, teaching you to observe all things commanded by the Savior. And realizing the goodness and justice of God's holy law and the dreadful doom of the impenitent, I have most earnestly besought them to turn to Christ to live. If to-day I were entering instead of retiring from my ministry among you * * I know of nothing material that I could do otherwise than has been done. And now, dear brethren, I feel that my earthly work is ended. By the grace of God I feel fully prepared for the momentous change, and have no fears for the great eternal future; but look fondly forward to the fast aproaching time when I shall hear the summons to quit this land of sin and pain and enter upon an existence of joy and peace in the presence and society of my precious Redeemer. Not for my good works. No, no! It is a sinner saved by grace. I love the song and would have it sung when I am buried:

"Nothing in my hand I bring,
Simply to thy cross I cling."

"How precious! Oh, how precious, to know that Jesus is my Savior and my all powerful friend."

Elder Riddle was a most excellent physician, and practiced his profession in connection with his ministerial labors. Sister Riddle and two children survive him. His memory will be precious in the Waco Association till time shall be no more.

RIESEL CHURCH.

The Baptist church at Riesel was organized on Sunday, September 15, 1894, in the school house, in the town of Riesel, by Elders J. F. McLeod, C. D. Whitman and Deacon J. A. Akin. The following brethren and sisters went into the organization: B. F. Toler and wife, A. G. Toler, Moses King and wife, M. A. King,

Bro. F. S. Watson and Sisters Lucinda Willingham, Margaret Owens, Annie Owens, Mamie Hunter and M. J. Dew. The Articles of Faith and Church Covenant, found in Pendleton's Manuel, were adopted. During the afternoon Alice Owens was baptized into the fellowship of the church by Elder J. F. McLeod. C. D. Whitman was the first pastor. Elder Whitman was succeeded in the pastorate by B. F. Tatum, the present pastor. Riesel church united with the Association in September, 1894, with 15 members. The church now numbers 35. The town of Riesel, is on the Waco branch of the Houston and Texas Central railroad. It is less than five years old; has about 600 inhabitants and is growing rapidly. It is 15 miles from Waco, in McLennan county; has the rich valley of the Brazos on the east and the great prairie of fertile black land on the west. The deacons of Riesel church are B. F. Toler and James George.

ROBINSON CHURCH.

The first settler in the neighborhood was John Robinson, a Presbyterian. The first Baptist settler was the venerable L. M. Strickland. The first Baptist preaching in the neighborhood was by that noble foundation-builder, Solomon G. O'Bryan. The Bethel Baptist church (now Robinson) was organized September 11, 1866, by the beloved S. G. O'Bryan. The following went into the organization: L. M. Strickland, J. S. Hicks, Martha Hicks, John G. Sanderson, Martha Sanderson, Elder N. W. Crain, Elizabeth Crain, J. Crain, W. J. Evans, Sarah Evans. Bro. N. W. Crain acted as clerk. The first pastor, N. W. Crain, served only a few months, then went to Mexico, leaving the church without a pastor for more than a year. The brethren, however, met regularly. At length a little purse of $5 was made up and sent to Elder R. C. Burleson, at Waco, with request that he come and preach $5 worth. Dr. Burleson said: "They are dead; I will go and give them a decent burial." He went, held a glorious meeting, and was called to the care of the church. He served two years without stated salary, and left the church numbering about 70 members. Elder R. B. Burleson was the next pastor. He was succeeded by the beloved J. J. Riddle, M. D. On September 9, 1876, Elder J. B. Parrack was chosen and served one year. . He was followed September 3, 1877, by Elder John S. Allen, who continued 3 years, after which the church was again without a pastor for about a year. Bro. J. S. Allen sent Bro. C. P. Lumpkin to Robinson, and Bro. R. C. Burleson warned him that the "Robinson brethren would not drink slop." Bro. Lumpkin was called January, 1882. After three years he was succeeded by Elder T. E. Muse. Elder S. B. McJunkin followed in March, 1887. After him was Kit Williams, then Elder John Bateman. Next in order were Brethren C. P. Lumpkin, W. W. Findley and M. L. Davis. J. L. Walker followed Bro. Davis, serving from January, 1894, to September, 1895. The present pastor is Elder H. R. Best. The greatest revivals were during the pastorates of R. C. Burleson and John S. Allen. While Bro. Allen was pastor, the late W. E. Penn held one of his great meetings with the church. While Bro. Burleson was pastor, the sainted W. W. Harris ("Spurgeon" Harris) held a grand revival. The church also enjoyed one of her best meetings while Bro. Lumpkin was pastor. This church from the beginning of her existence has been connected with the Waco Association. The Association met with Robinson church in 1883. The name was changed from Bethel to Robinson in 1877. The first house of worship was of cottonwood boards. The second, a good building, was blown down in a storm. The present house is worth about $700. The deacons have been W. J. Evans, Jno. G. Sanderson, J. S. Hicks, John Majors, Cortes Stubblefield, L. M. Strickland and A. Webb. Elder M. L. Davis was ordained by this church. The Sunday school was organized in 1867 and has never had a vacation. Prior to the organization of the Sunday school, Bro. Strickland kept up a Bible class one year. The first superintendent of the Sunday school was N. W. Crain. Robinson is six miles from Waco.

ROCK CREEK CHURCH

was organized in 1872. Frank Morgan, B. F. Garrett, Smith Bird, T. B. Sparks, Mrs. N. L. Garrett, Sarah Garrett, J. L. Long, J. C. McAdden, Mrs. E. McAdden and J. H. Gilliam were among the original members. V. G. Cunningham was the first pastor, and T. B. Sparks the first clerk. When the church united with the Association in August, 1872, the membership aggregated 34. The pastors have been V. G. Cunningham, three years; J. J. Riddle, nine years; B. F. Tatum, two years; J. L. Walker, six years; T. E. Muse, two years; Joseph Gronde, two years; V. G. Cunningham, one year. The present incumbent, B. F. Tatum. The church numbers about 125 members. Their place of meeting is in the town of Patrick, 12 miles north of Waco, on the west side of the Brazos river. The village was formerly called "Garrett's Mills." The church has a comfortable house of worship in the heart of the village. Hon. Albert Bird, member of the Texas legislature, holds membership in this church. She counts among her members some noble, consecrated brethren, as J. E. Robertson, G. L. Robertson, R. B. Thomas, N. Shaw, etc. They are a dear people, devoted to all the work of the Master.

ROBERT ROGERS

was born in 1799, in Middle Tennessee; moved to Alabama, and there professed religion, joined the Baptist church. Soon afterward he emigrated to the state of Missouri; in 1832 came to Texas, stopping two or three years in San Augustine county; firally came to Rogers Prairie, Leon county, where he located a league of land in the fall of 1835. He was the first white settler in the territory now comprising Leon county. Elder Z. N. Morrell in his travels often made his house his home, and preached to the family and a neighbor or two that lived near. It was at the house of Robert Rogers where Z. N. Morrell and his five companions stopped December, 1835, on their first trip to Texas, when they were reminded by a lad that they were green from the states. He and his family were among those who fled before the invading Mexican army of Santa Anna, in what was known as the "Texas run-away scrape." When the self-styled "Napoleon of the West" was utterly routed and vanquished by the "heroes of San Jacinto" he returned to his home. He was in the organization of the Leona Baptist church in the year 1846, and the organization of the Trinity River Association in 1848. His charity throughout life was only bounded by his ability. Living immediately on the then main thoroughfare through Texas, "the old San Antonio road," many way-worn travelers found a resting place beneath his hospitable roof. He was familiarly known far and wide as "Uncle Bob Rogers." He was a zealous member of the Masonic fraternity. Bro. Rogers passed peacefully and quietly to his final rest, at the advanced age of 72 years. His funeral sermon was preached by Elder John Clabaugh, at an arbor built for the purpose, to the largest audience that had ever assembled in that community.

ROSEBUD CHURCH.

The town of Rosebud, on the San Antonio and Aransas Pass railroad, is in the southwest part of Falls county. . It is in one of the most fertile sections in the state. Rosebud will one day be a large town. It has now about 1,000 inhabitants, and is growing rapidly. The Rosebud church was organized on March 23, 1890, before the railroad reached the town. The presbytery was composed of Elder A. J. Shelton, missionary, and J. L. Walker, pastor, in Waco Association. Elder Shelton was laboring under appointment of the Waco Associational Board. The following named members went into the organization: J. E. Williams, M. E. Williams, A. R. Furguson, M. M. Furguson, Mattie Kemp, Virginia Gott, Bertia Presley, Fannie Dear and Eliza Ann Taylor. The Articles of Faith and Church Covenant, found in Pendleton's Manual, were adopted. Elder Shelton was chosen missionary pastor and A. R. Furguson clerk. The church was organized in the little school house which stood about one mile east of the depot. The church united with Waco Association, at Lorena, September, 1890. The next year W. B. White was pastor and J. J. Williams, clerk. Rosebud did not represent at the Moody meeting in 1891. In 1892 the Association met at Durango. Elder E. F. Brock was present as messenger from Rosebud. The church had at that time 22 members. W. B. White succeeded A. J. Shelton as pastor, and served two years. During the same period L. F. Rigby served as clerk. During the pastorate of Bro. White the meeting house was built. The mission and Sunday school board of Waco Association adopted Bro. White as her missionary to the Rosebud church at the Chilton board meeting in May, 1891,and agreed to pay him $100. This $100 Bro. White generously donated toward erecting the house of worship. In 1895 the membership numbered 50, C. D. Whitman, pastor, and O. Aycock, clerk. Prior to the time when Bro. Whitman became pastor, Bro. Harvey Carroll, Jr., served the church in that capacity a few months. D. P. Airheart is the present pastor.

SALEM CHURCH,

located at Eutaw, in Limestone county, was a member of the Association ten years, from August, 1867, till August, 1877. The membership in 1867 was 75. C. W. Kinnard was pastor. John R. Wilson, Sam Clark and B. H. Hammond were members at that time. In 1877, when Salem was dismissed from Waco Association, she had 190 members. This is one of the oldest churches in Central Texas; was organized in 1855 by Elder Wm. Clarke. The original members were Wm. Clarke, Eliz. M. Clarke, James Tribble, Eliz. Tribble, John Hodge and Alice Hodge. Before the war the pastors were Wm. Clarke, J. J. Haggard, M. Ross and W. B. Eaves. In those early days the deacons were J. Tribble, Sam Clarke and S. H. Abernathy. The first clerk was John Hodge. During the ten years while Salem was in the Association, the pastors were C. W. Kinnard, J. V. Wright, W. T. Wright, A. W. Middleton and W. C. Manning. J. R. Bryant was clerk during most, if not all, of this period. The Waco Association was held with Salem church in 1870.

JOHN B. SCARBOROUGH, ESQ.,

a prominent lawyer, a useful member of society and an efficient member of Waco First church, is a man of broad mind and large heart, and finds time, amidst the multiplied engagements of an active life, to keep posted on the affairs of his denomination, and to co-operate with his church in all her great work. His father and mother were Irvine and Frances Scarborough, of Jackson parish, La. He was born in that parish April 5, 1847. In 1863 he entered the Confederate army and served till the close of the war. Was twice wounded in the Red River campaign in 1864. He was converted in 1867, and was baptized by his brother, Elder M. Scarborough, into the fellowship of Bethel Baptist church. Except one year at Lebanon University, Louisiana, he was educated in private schools. In 1869 he came to Texas and settled in Smith county. Was married August 11, 1870, to Miss Mary A., second daughter of Z. and Emily T. Ellison. Four children are the result of this union. The first son, Ellison B., died in 1872; the three remaining, M. Douglass, Geo. M. and Emily (Dottie), live with their parents in Waco, Texas. Soon after his marriage, he was made clerk of the Carmel church, Smith county, and

J. B. SCARBOROUGH.
(Photo by Sanders, Waco, Texas.)

served in that capacity till his removal to Sweetwater, Nolan county, 1882, at which time he gave up teaching, his former occupation, for the practice of law. Bro. Scarborough and his wife were two of the six who went into the organization of the Sweetwater church. He was the first clerk of the Sweetwater Association. In 1887 he moved to Waco, Texas, to educate his children and practice his profession, and became a member of

Dr. B. H. Carroll's church. He was made a trustee of Baylor University in 1888, and has served as such ever since, and he has been a member of the State Board of the Baptist General Convention since 1887. He has been active in mission and educational work ever since moving into the Waco Association; has felt it to be his duty to give of his means as the Lord has prospered him, and he has discharged that duty well. Bro. Scarborough and his cultured family are loved and honored by their friends, their church and the denomination.

SEARSVILLE CHURCH

united with the Waco Association at the Bosqueville meeting in October, 1862. The church had been organized but a short time previous to becoming a member of the Association. Among the original members were J. L. Sears, for whom the church was named, F. F. Bloodworth, J. H. Mabry and J. K. Helton. All these brethren were prominent in the Association at an early day. In October, 1862, Searsville had eleven members. The next year B. E. Lucas was pastor and the number was 14. J. L. Sears was the first clerk. The third annual session of the Association was held at Searsville October, 1864. Elder Wm. Manning was a member and pastor. The membership was increased to 25. In 1868 the membership was 24. The next year S. G. O'Bryan was pastor. W. A. Ellege was pastor in 1868. He was succeeded in 1870 by B. T. Stevens. The name of Searsville appears last on our minutes in 1874. B. T. Stevens was still the pastor; membership, 43. Searsville still exists in Meridian Association, J. M. Renfro, pastor. The present membership is about 100. Their place of meeting is five miles north of Valley Mills, in Bosque county, in a locality superlatively fascinating and picturesque.

ELDER A. J. SHELTON

came to Texas from Tennessee. He was born in 1846, and found peace in Christ in 1870. After one year spent in the study of the New Testament, was baptized into Shelton's Grove Baptist church, Tennessee. He preached his first sermon December 26, 1876, when the Lord greatly blessed his effort. On

WACO BAPTIST ASSOCIATION.

April 8, 1887, he was ordained to the office of gospel bishop, and in September, same year, was called to the care of Shelton's Grove church, and served that flock till 1880, when he came to Texas. He located on Capt. C. A. Westbrook's farm, December, 1880. Old Salem church, without a pastor and without a house, gave him a call. He preached for that church in the winter of 1880 and 1881 in his own hired house. In summer the meetings were held under an arbor at the "Old Camp Ground" on Westbrook's farm. At this place he held his first protracted meeting in Texas, which resulted in adding 25 members to the Salem church (now Mastersville). In 1881 Bro. Shelton attended his first meeting of the Waco Association at Groesbeck, in Limestone county, and he has attended the most of her meetings since that time. He became missionary of the Waco Association in 1890, and continued till March 31, 1891. During this period, assisted by Elder R. O. Dewberry, he organized the church at Lott. He also organized the church at Rosebud, assisted by J. L. Walker. He organized old Hope church. All these were in Falls county. In April, 1891, he accepted work under the State Mission Board. His field was the vast territory embracing Hemphill, Lipscomb, Ochiltree, Roberts, Wheeler and Gray counties. On this field he organized three churches, the First Baptist church at Canadian, the First church at Lipscomb, and the First church at Mobeetie, all county sites. This field was one of hard labor, and required a horseback ride of 400 miles each month. Here our brother had a hard fight with heresy and infidelity. This work left him and his family in great financial straits, from which he has never recovered. He lives at Bruceville, Texas, and, with his family, holds membership in Mastersville church. He has served several churches in Waco Association, and is now pastor of Shiloh, in Bell county. He has a cultured family, all girls, and all members of Baptist churches. Sister Shelton is blind, but no more patient and spiritual Christian lives in McLennan county.

SHILOH CHURCH

began to exist as an independent flock of Christ, November 17, 1884. There were eight original members. Elder H. F. Curry was the first pastor, serving the church more than three years. Elder J. M. Wright succeeded him, and continued four years. In 1892 Elder R. E. Smith became pastor, and continues as such till this day. Shiloh church first joined the McGregor Association. In 1890 united with the Waco, with 43 members. The present membership is 80. The whole number baptized by this church from beginning is 80. Shiloh has a good house, worth $800. It stands on the bank of the beautiful clear stream of Hog creek. Near by the church door, in this creek, is a most inviting natural baptistry, with pebbly bottom, and shaded by the overhanging bowers of green trees on the west bank, with clean, rocky bar on the east bank—an ideal spot.

ELDER J. CAREY SMITH,

son of J. E. and Prudence Isabella Smith, was born November 12, 1854, 12 miles north of Wetumka, Ala. In March, 1855, his father settled in Fayette county, Texas. Later the family moved near Flatonia, Texas, where J. C. was brought up. During his boyhood days his opportunities for obtaining an education were limited. He attended Concrete College one year. The beloved J. E. V. Covy was president. He had a thirst for knowledge, and spent much time in reading. When 20 years old, he spent one year on the border of Mexico driving cattle. He was married in 1878. He was converted under the preaching of Elder B. E. Lucas in 1879, and was baptized into the fellowship of Beulah Baptist church, in Lavaca county, by Elder J. J. Sledge. The site of old Beulah is now in a Bohemian pasture. In 1883 moved to Colorado county, remaining six years. He felt deeply impressed with the duty of preaching the gospel, but put it off. At length he selected an out-of-the-way place and preached one year. In 1889 he was licensed to preach. And having been called to the care of Antioch church, in Gonzales county, Moulton church, Elm Grove, north of Moulton, and Liberty, near Antioch, he was ordained to the office of New Testament bishop, August 3, 1890. Elders A. S. Poindexter, Pinkney Harris and J. W. Peebles were the presbytery. In 1891 he resigned those churches and moved with his family to Waco, where he now resides. He entered Baylor University soon after coming to Waco.

He is now a member of Dr. Carroll's Bible class. Since coming to Waco, he has been preaching to surrounding churches in and out of Waco Association, and has baptized 400 persons. Towash, Whitney, Osceola, Prairie Dale and Brandon, in Hill county, Center, in Falls, and Prairie Hill and Antioch, in Limestone, have enjoyed his ministerial labors. Through his instrumentality the first Bohemian convert, a young lady, Miss Mary Vrazzel, was

ELDER J. C. SMITH.
(Photo by Jackson, Waco, Texas.)

kept in Baylor University last year (1895-6). She is now teaching among her own people. He hopes through this girl to reach some of these 50,000 people who are marching to Christless graves here in Texas. By the aid of his father's family he has been enabled to induce eleven of these people to enter Baylor University, five of whom are now (March, 1897), in school.

ELDER R. E. SMITH

was the eighth child of J. T. and Lucinda Smith; was born in Randolph county, Ga., February 21, 1866. He suffered the loss of his mother when not 3 years old. A boy without a mother is among the saddest of the many unexplained things in this sin-stained world. Soon afterward his father failed in business and came to McLennan county, Texas, January, 1876. His father's

Elder R. E. Smith.
(Photo by Jackson, Waco, Texas.)

health gave way, and it fell to the lot of young Robert and a brother two years younger to fight the wolf from the door. They were renting land "on the halves" on "Dave" McFadden's place, near Crawford. By accident, young Robert had his leg broken, which was indeed a sad accident to the whole family. While he was convalescing, he would hobble through the cotton field from morning till night and hoe cotton. He afterward herded sheep at $1 per week. He was converted under the preaching of the late Major W. E. Penn, and by him baptized in the Middle Bosque. He was ordained at Shiloh church, near Crawford, and has been pastor of that church five years. He struggled hard for an education, and has made respectable progress. Bro. Smith is teaching and preaching for the people where he was ordained, and enjoys the confidence and respect of the entire community. He was married to Miss Clara McMahan November 1, 1893. He has recently published a most readable little volume entitled "Some Things Under The Sun." Bro. Smith is an acceptable preacher, a young man of noble qualities of head and heart, and one who is doing much good. He is now pastor of Shiloh, China Springs and Oak Grove churches.

DEACON S. F. SPARKS

was born in Mississippi, in 1818. His father was sheriff of Yazoo county, and afterward represented that county in the legislature. He fought in the war of 1812. His grandfather came from Ireland, fought with the colonists against Great Britain in the revolutionary war, and was killed at the battle of Mimm's Ford, Georgia. The family settled at San Augustine, Texas, in 1834. Young S. F. Sparks left school and went with the Nacogdoches company to the war of the Texas revolution in 1835. He was with Colonel Sherman and fired the second gun in the battle at San Jacinto. Sherman's men had driven Almonte some two hundred yards before General Burleson made the attack on Santa Anna's breastworks. Just before the battle of San Jacinto, when Houston crossed Buffalo Bayou, S. F. Sparks and Howard Bailey, a boy of about the same age, conveyed the baggage of the Texas army across the bayou while the men crossed in the ferry boat. They took rope and bound three logs together, and placed on the "raft" as much baggage as it would carry. A rope was tied to one end. This rope S. F. Sparks took with his teeth, swam and pulled it, while Howard Bailey swam behind and pushed. In this way they swam the bayou 21 times and had the baggage all over by the time the men crossed. An anecdote illustrating the humaneness of Bro. Sparks deserves to be recorded. After Almonte had been driven some 400 yards, the pursuers came to a wide, boggy ditch. Into this ditch a Mexican horse had leaped, and sank in the mire all but his head and saddle. An active man could leap to the saddle and from the saddle to the opposite bank. About 50 Texans crossed on this saddle, among them S. F. Sparks. A woman presented herself and begged for mercy. A Texan attempted to bayonet her, when Sparks knocked the man's bayonet off with his gun. "I will shoot her," he cried, "you cannot knock the bullet off!" Sparks leveled his gun and said: "You kill her and I will kill you!" "Are you in earnest?" asked the Texan. "I am," coolly replied Sparks. About this time Captain Segum came up, and Sparks delivered the woman over to him, with two or three others who had presented themselves, asking for mercy. Before the organization of old Union church, which was probably the first Baptist church in Texas, a Baptist preacher, Elder J. T. Bryant, came to Texas and taught a little school, where old Union church was afterward built. During this time he preached one night at a neighbor's house. He was not through his sermon when Mrs. Sparks, wife of S. F. Sparks, walked up and asked for prayer. Sparks bowed by her side. The preacher said he had preached long enough. Six or eight presented themselves for prayer. This was the beginning of a precious revival. This revival resulted in the baptism of 20 and the organization of Union church. Bro. Sparks was among the number baptized. Bro. Sparks came to McLennan county, in 1854, and settled at Bosqueville. He was appointed by Bosqueville church as her messenger to assist in the organization of the Waco Association, but for some reason failed to attend. He was a delegate at second session in Marlin, in 1861, and usually attended the meetings as long as he remained in the bounds of the Association. He was in the organization of the East Waco church, and was one of her first deacons, May 9, 1867. During the year from September, 1881, to September, 1882, Bro. Sparks canvassed the Waco Association in the interest of the Buckner Orphans' Home. This he did without compensation, besides giving liberally to the Home himself. The result of his labors was $261.50 collected for this institution. Sound in the faith, zealous for the advancement of the Master's cause, and liberal with all his means, Deacon Sparks was a power in the Waco Association for good. He still lives at Rockport, Texas, and is waiting the bidding of the dear Lord to call him from labor to rest.

ELDER T. P. SPEAKMAN

was born in Jefferson county, Ala., October 30, 1852. Professed faith in Christ in May, 1867. Was baptized into the fellowship of old Beach Grove Baptist church, in Morgan county, Ala., by Elder C. B. Wilhite, in the summer of 1868. Came to Texas in September, 1872. Was licensed to preach by Pleasant Hill Baptist church, Travis county, Texas, 1875, J. C. Talley, pastor. He entered Baylor University in September, 1876. In September, 1878, he was ordained by the First Baptist church, Waco. He has served as pastor the following churches: White Rock, Hillside, Geneva, Olive Branch, Caledonia, Lone Oak, Oak Grove, Liberty Grove, Greenwood, West and Snyder, in Scurry county, Texas. Preached as missionary in West Texas, in the counties of Scurry, Fisher, Kent and Mitchell, and as missionary of Lavaca River Association from September, 1895, to July, 1896. He was married to Miss Belle Matlock March 6, 1881, Elder John H. Harrison, of Waco, officiating. Bro. Speakman is a safe gospel preacher and an excellent pastor. He has done a great work already, and we trust the Lord has much work yet for him to accomplish. His present home is at West, Texas. Is now pastor at Chilton, Independence and Lone Oak.

SPEEGLEVILLE CHURCH,

located in a rich, black land country, between the North Bosque river and South Bosque creek, at the little town of Speegleville, nine miles west of Waco, and withal in the midst of a prosperous community. Speegleville church has done and is doing a good work for the Lord. The town and church were named for Bro. I. W. Speegle, one of the first settlers in McLennan county. His good wife, Sister Louannah Speegle, is still living, but is very old and feeble. The church was at first called Pleasant Grove, and was constituted August 13, 1859, by Elders Thos. M. Anderson and W. A. Mason. The original members were Campbell Croce, H. P. Hicks, L. P. Standifer, I. W. Speegle, James Hicks,

Mahala E. Groce, Nancy Jane Groce, Louannah R. Speegle, Margaret Standifer, Martha Hicks, Berrilla McLennan—in all 11. The church was afterwards reorganized under the name of Speegleville. Pleasant Grove first united with the Association in 1864, when there were 22 members. The petitionary letter was borne by J. W. Speegle and A. Coates. Elder R. B. Burleson was the first pastor, and continued seven years. From 1870 till 1883 the church was not represented in the meetings of the Association. In 1883 she joined the Association as a "new church," under the name of Speegleville, with but 16 members. Since that time, the pastors have been J. B. Parrack, J. L. Walker, T. A. Mangum, J. P. Kinchen, W. S. Huff and E. L. Compere, present pastor. The membership is now 107, and the church is prospering more than at any period in the past.

DEACON JOSEPH WARREN SPEIGHT

was born in Green county, N. C., May 31, 1825. He was the son of Hon. Jesse Speight, member of congress from North Carolina, and United States senator from Mississippi. He was educated at Stony Point High School, North Carolina, and later finished his course under Dr. R. C. Burleson. At the early age of 20 he began the practice of law, but afterward gave attention to farming. He moved to Waco in 1853. He was inclined toward the Methodists, but after his conversion "the plain, unmistakable, irresistible force of God's holy truth compelled him to become a Baptist." He was baptized by Eld. S. G. O'Bryan in 1857. He was soon afterward elected deacon and clerk of Waco church. The next year he was elected clerk of Trinity River Association, which position he continued to hold till the organization of the Waco Association. He wrote the constitution of the Waco Association. No finer document of the kind is to be found in Texas or the South. In 1859 he published in the minutes of Trinity River Association sketches of Waco, Bosqueville, Springfield, Salem, Friendship, Marlin, Mount Zion, Trinity, Tehuacana, Union, Leona, Concord (Leon county), Sterling (Robertson county), Clear Creek, Caddo, Bethel, Sand Prairie, Pleasant Grove, Rehoboth and Blue Ridge churches. These sketches give in every instance the names of the original members and the first pastors. Deacon Speight was clerk of the Waco church during most of the time from September, 1857, till February, 1876. He was the first clerk of Waco Association during the first seven years of her existence. He was moderator of the Association in 1876, '77 and '78 and again in 1881. He was at one time moderator of the General Association. He was president of the Board of Trustees of Waco University many

Gen. J. W. Speight.

years, contributing much of his time and means to build up and make it a first-class institution. He was a commanding colonel in the late war in the Confederate army, and was raised to the rank of brigadier general. He was once wounded. His home was in Waco, and the stately buildings of Baylor University now occupy the site of his old home. Speight street, running south of the University, perpetuates his memory. "He passed away in the midst of his family September 26, 1888." He has a number of children and grand children, cultured and refined, who survive him and are honored and beloved members of society, most of whom are members of the First Baptist church, at Waco.

ELDER C. EUGENE STEPHEN

was of English descent. In early life he prepared himself for the practice of law, and for a while followed that profession. While he was yet young, he gave his heart to God, and was all his life time through a pious, devoted disciple of the Lord Jesus. He yielded to his convictions to preach the gospel, and became a preacher of unusual power. Occupied many positions of honor and trust in the denomination. His influence and power were felt and recognized all over Central Texas. His home was for many years at Bremond, Texas, where for a time he served Bremond and surrounding churches with great acceptability. He left two sons, Joe and Jim, who are young ministers of pleasing address and great promise; one of them, Joe, is moderator of Little River Association. Bro. Stevens died very suddenly at Franklin, Robertson county, Texas, after many years spent in earnest and successful service in the Master's cause.

DEACON STRICKLAND.

L. M. Strickland was born in Pike county, Ala., in 1832. Moved to Mississippi in 1834. Parents died when he was 6 years old. He was then bound out; remained in bondage about seven years. At 13 he faced the world alone. In 1847 he accepted Christ and joined the Baptist church in Choctaw county, Miss., aged 15 years. In 1853 he came to Bell county, Texas. There were no Baptists there at that time. In about two years he joined the Nolan's Creek church. He moved from Bell county to Coryell, from Coryell to Waco, where he joined the First Baptist church, and was educated. Went to the war in February, 1862; carried his religion all through the war. His captain testified that "old Strick" was never known during the war to swear, drink or play cards. He kept up a prayer meeting and Sunday school when possible, while engaged in that awful struggle. After the war he came to Robinson. Was in the organization of the Robinson Baptist church, and is now the only living member that was in that organization. He has been a Baptist about 50 years; has been a deacon many years. When the Robinson meeting house was blown down some years ago, Bro. Strickland pulled the old pulpit from the wreck and placed it in the new building, after same was completed. His family has been brought up in this community. One noble young son, Scion, bade adieu March, 1896, to father, mother, young wife and babe (only a few

DEACON L. M. STRICKLAND.

days old), and went home to God. There was a melancholy sweetness connected with Scion's departure that was felt by the entire neighborhood. Bro. Strickland is now nearly blind, but while waiting the Master's call to "come up higher," he is not idle. Robinson has no more earnest and indefatigable worker. Bro. Strictland is of Welsh descent, which may account in part for his great firmness as a Baptist. It is a sad, sweet sight to see this feeble old brother going to and from the houseof God led by his little daughter, Mellie. May the Lord continue to be his shepherd, leading him into green pastures and beside the still waters.

ELDER THOMAS D. SUTTLE.

According to the grace of God, as a wise master builder, Elder Suttle laid a good foundation at an early day. The Mart church stands on that foundation, and as the temple of Christ is still growing. Bro. Suttle is by birth a Mississippian, having first seen the sunlight in that state, July 22, 1840. He was born again in Polk county, Tex., in 1861. Elder D. C. Williamson laid him in the watery grave, from which, arising with the Master, he became a member of Pine Ridge church, in Tryon Association. His schooling, six months at Pine Ridge, prepared the way for the self-made man that he is. He is mighty in the scriptures, where for many years the holy spirit has been his teacher. Shiloh church, Houston county, authorized his ordination, and J. T. Williamson, W. L. Gates and E. Shaw set him apart to the bishop's office in September, 1865. His first pastorate was with old Trinity church. He afterward did good work in Cherokee county. In 1876 came to Mart and organized Mart, Battle, Trading House, Prairie Hill, Antioch and New Zion churches; was pastor of all these and others. After many years of successful work in the Waco Association, he went to Northwest Texas, and from there to Indian Territory, and did much good service in those parts, serving churches and holding revival meetings. In Northwest Texas, in connection with Rev. R. C. Farmer, he secured to the Baptists the Jacksboro College, which had been built by the Presbyterians. The buildings, with ten acres of land, worth $10,000, were turned over to the Baptists, and Bro. Suttle secured for the college $13,000 additional. He is now living near Mart, Tex., loved by everybody.

PROF. JOHN S. TANNER.

Few, very few, of our young men set the mark of their ambition high enough. Prof. Tanner is a living example of what may be accomplished, when energy, labor and perseverance are made to do full service. Prof. John S. Tanner, though not yet 30 years old, is the peer of any scholar in the South, if not in America. He was born in Henderson county, Texas, October 9, 1869. Angelic eyes beheld in this babe the coming scholar of America. His youth was spent on a farm, where he received that training in manual labor and industry that is indispensable' to the highest attainments. While a student of the public school at Comanche, Texas, he gave his heart and life to God, and was buried with Christ in baptism. Soon thereafter, September, 1886, he en-

PROF. JOHN S. TANNER.
(Photo by Jackson, Waco, Texas)

tered Baylor University, and graduated with the class of 1890. His means were limited, but he was enabled to keep continuously in school by doing chores for a resident physician, and although this severely taxed his time, he came out easily the leader of his class. Immediately after graduating, he was elected a member of the faculty of Baylor University, and held that position until he entered the Southern Baptist Theological Seminary, 1892. While a student in the Seminary, he was chosen pastor of the Baptist church at Harrisburg, Ky., and was ordained by the Fourth and Walnut Street church, of which he was a member, and of which Dr. T. T. Eaten was pastor. Prof. Tanner's pastorate at Harrisburg was signally blessed. He developed marvelous powers, both as a pastor and preacher. During his second year in the Seminary, he was chosen by Dr. Broadus as tutor in New Testament Greek. After graduating at the Seminary, he accepted a fellowship in the Chicago University, which he held till elected to his present position—that of professor of New Testament Greek and Hebrew in Baylor University. The college degrees of Prof. Tanner are A. B. and A. M. of Baylor University; Th. M. of the Seminary. He has marked executive ability, and his skill as a teacher is not measured by the lessons of the books. He inspires his pupils to higher usefulness and grander conceptions of life. He is a man of convictions, ranks with the best men of our denomination, and we look forward to the day when he will be the highest authority on Baptist affairs.

ELDER BENJAMIN FRANKLIN TATUM.

This brother comes of a family of Baptist preachers. The Tatums came from England in order to enjoy religious freedom. Elder William Tatum was grandfather of our "Ben," and was a missionary Baptist preacher for half a century. He lived many years in Kentucky and died in Missouri, full of years and honor. For many years previous to his death he had prayed that he might have the full, comforting witness of the Spirit in the hour of departure, and he left testimony that he had such witness. Tatum Chapel, on Clear creek, Green county, Missouri, was named for William Tatum. Elder John H. Tatum, father of Benjamin F., was born in Logan county, Ky., in the year 1810. About 30 years of his life were spent in the ministry. He belonged to the old type missionary Baptist preachers. Those dear old brethren labored on their farms and preached the gospel on Sundays. Their ministerial labors and influence contributed immensely toward moulding the early churches of our country. Elder John H. Tatum died in Grayson county, Texas. His sun set in a clear sky. Benjamin F. Tatum was born in Dade county, Mo., September 20, 1853. When he was 8 years old his father moved to Grayson county, Texas. In November, 1871, he was converted and Baptized by Pastor W. E. Holeman into Dripping Springs church, seven miles east of Sherman.. By this church he was licensed to preach in 1872. He was married to Miss S. S. Martin October 22, 1872. In January, 1875, he was ordained by a presbytery composed of Elders E. W. Holeman, John H. Tatum and —. Hart. In October, 1876, he came to Waco. His first pastorate was at East Waco, where he continued four years, till 1881. At the commencement of this pastorate the church had 60 members; at the close, 88. He also served the church at Concord while he was pastor at East Waco. He became pastor of Caledonia church in 1878, and continued six years. In 1880 he accepted the care of Rock Creek church, continuing two years. In 1887, he was again pastor of Rock Creek one year. In 1890 he accepted a third call from Rock Creek and continued two years. In 1895 he accepted a fourth call and continues till this day. He was pastor of Oak Grove some years while that church was a member of Towash Association. In 1884 Bro. Tatum moved to San Patricio county and remained two years. While in that county he served Nueces, Sharpsburg and Refugio churches. In 1886 he returned to Central Texas, and served several churches, Rock Creek, Oak Grove, Smith's Bend and Dripping Springs. In the fall of 1887 he moved to Limestone county, and became pastor of Cross Roads and Independence churches. In 1889 he moved to Mart, and took charge of Mart, Kirk and Rock Creek. He accepted the care of White Rock and Battle in 1892, continuing at Mart at the same time. In 1894 and till September, 1895, he gave full time to Mart. He is at present (March, 1897), pastor of Battle, Rock Creek, Riesel and Armour. When he became pastor of Mart there were 63 members; when he resigned, the membership numbered 231. Bro. Tatum attended Baylor University from 1887 to 1890, three years. Not a shadow has darkened his moral or doctrinal life. He is a Baptist without a crook or blemish. There is not a sounder Baptist preacher in Texas.

ELDER JOHN R. M. TOUCHSTONE

was born in Drew county, Ark., February 6, 1859. He came,

with his parents, at the close of the war to Texas. In 1872 his father settled in Grayson county. At the early age of 17 he was left without parents, money or education. In November, 1876, he entered the Richland Academy, located at Medlenville, Fannin county, Texas. In October, 1878, he was converted, and in May, 1879, was baptized into the Medlenville Baptist church. He began preaching in August of this year. In June, 1880, he finished his course at the academy. April, 1881, he came to Milam county, and began teaching. In 1882-3 attended the Seminary at Louisville, Ky. In 1884 became pastor of Caddo and Chilton churches, and continued until October, 1886, when he accepted the church at Marlin. He was pastor here seven years, at the close of which he returned to the Seminary and spent the first part of the session of '93-4. In February and March, '94, he collected funds for the Sunday School and Colportage Mission Board of Texas. He was pastor of the Decatur Baptist church in '94. Returning to Falls county he accepted the pastorate at Lott. He was president of the Mission Board from September, 1888, until November, 1889. He was the president of the Mission Board of Falls County Association the first two years, and was elected again October, 1895. He has written a pamphlet entitled, "The Church of Jesus Christ, When and By Whom Set Up," which has been well received, and the second edition has been published. In 1884 he married Miss Anna Daffin, of Falls county. She has been a true helper to him in all his work. Their home has been brightened by four little ones, only one of whom remains. He has been for several years a member of the Sunday School and Colportage Mission Board of the state. He now lives at Caddo, in Milam county, and is the pastor of that church.

TRADING HOUSE CHURCH

was organized on Trading House creek, 12 miles east from Waco, in 1881, by Elder T. D. Suttle. There were 13 members when the church joined the Association, September, 1881. T. D. Suttle was the first and only pastor. Next year the name was changed to "Trading House," and the membership was increased to 39. Soon after this Trading House dissolved.

ELDER GEORGE W. TRUETT,

the beloved pastor of East Waco church, was born May 6, 1867, in Clay county, N. C. He received good rudimentary training in Hayesville Academy, in his native state. He joined himself to Christ and to his church at Hayesville in the fall of 1886. In December of that year he was chosen principal of the Hiawassee high school, in Towns county, Ga. Hiawassee was a new enter-

ELDER GEORGE W. TRUETT.
(Photo by Sanders, Waco, Texas.)

prise, "born of the prayers of God's people." He began teaching in the courthouse with 20 pupils. Very soon three school buildings, with boarding houses and dormitories, were erected. The school increased from 20 to nearly 300 students. All this was accomplished under his administration in less than three years. We quote from an article by Dr. B. H. Carroll in the "Youths' Southland:" "The institution had become a power in the land. Boarding students came from more than twenty counties of the Carolinas and Georgia. They were the children of the mountains, whose ancestors broke the power of Cornwallis by the defeat of Ferguson at the famous battle of King's Mountain. The spirit of Christ pervaded the school and sanctified education to the service of God. The school yet lives, ever growing in power and influence, and is to-day one of the best preparatory institutions in the South, and an abiding monument attesting what young and consecrated Christian manhood can accomplish." Bro. Truett electrified the Georgia Baptist Convention at the Marietta meeting April, 1889, in an impromptu speech of 15 minutes on Christian Education. At the conclusion of this speech, a distinguished brother asked the privilege of paying young Truett's way through college. This generous offer was respectfully declined. In the summer of 1889 Bro. Truett came to Whitewright, Texas, where his parents and brothers had preceded him. In the fall of 1890 entered Grayson College as a student, where he continued till the spring term, 1891. Again we quote Dr. Carroll: "But in February, 1891, on the urgent call of the trustees of Baylor University at Waco, Texas, and, as I believe, on the call of God, he accepted the position of financial secretary of this institution. To the arduous work of this responsible position he devoted himself about two years. All over Texas he has with singular power discussed Christian education. He took the work in a dark hour. How acceptable his labors have been to the Board let the following extract from their annual report of 1891 to the Baptist State Convention of Texas, assembled in Waco, indicate: 'Debt was the stone at the mouth of our sepulcher. Divine Providence called upon us to 'roll away the stone,' that the sleeping Lazarus of education might come forth. The situation was a grave one to say the least of it. It was a time of both hope and fear. * * * It was a time of sacrifice. Somebody must make it. That part of it, for Christ's sake, the trustees and faculty took upon themselves. We proposed to pay all agency expense, if the Lord would direct us to an agent. 'At midnight Paul and Silas prayed.' It was night to us. We prayed. The Father heard. The agent was found.

But we found him hungering to complete his own education. Shall he be robbed of life's seed time? Shall we take his years of youth, and send him on this forlorn hope—himself uncrowned as yet with that collegiate education, which he is to make possible to others? What is a money sacrifice compared to this? He laid his youth on the altar. You know him. You have heard him. You have felt his heart-power, his modesty, his humility, his faith. * * * His work will live forever. In the memory of all who heard him, it will be an evergreen, whose foliage the autumn of time will not discolor nor the winter of death disrobe, * * * In November, 1890, he was ordained to the work of the gospel ministry by the Baptist church at Whitewright, Texas. I may be allowed to close this sketch with a personal tribute. The subject of this sketch has been a member of my household. * * * I have never known a young man of more practical piety, profounder humility, and of more amiable character."

In 1893 Bro. Truett was elected a member of the State Mission Board, and has been re-elected each year since. He accepted the care of the East Waco Baptist church in 1893, and is still the much loved pastor of that flock. The church has grown rapidly in numbers and liberality during his pastorate. This brother will graduate at the Baylor commencement next June. His coming into the Waco Association is a blessing to all the churches. He was recently married to Miss Josephine, the accomplished daughter of Judge W. H. Jenkins, of Waco, Texas. In labors, in earnestness and in heart-power no man in Texas takes higher rank.

UNION CHURCH.

It is probable that Union had been in existence only a short while when it joined the Association at Cow Bayou meeting in 1869. The membership at that time was 17. Elder Z. N. Morrell was pastor. Among the original members were H. Kay, J. J. Garrett, N. B. Story and J. G. George. N. B. Story was bearer of the petitionary letter to Association. The place of meeting was in the southeastern part of Falls county. During the nine years while Union church was connected with the Waco Association, the pastors were Z. N. Morrell, J. V. Wright, J. J.

Davis, S. King, J. L. Lattimore. This church represented last in 1878; the membership was at that time 76. Among others who held membership here may be named J. L. Lattimore, H. Johnson, James Teat, W. A. Bennett, H. B. Coleman, T. J. Hair, D. Barclay, J. D. Womack and J. Turner.

UNION SPRINGS

was one of the nine original churches of the Association. It was a strong church in Richland Association before Waco was organized. It was in the organization of Richland in 1847. H. Vaughn was pastor during '59 and '60. At the time of the organization of Waco Association, in November, 1860, this church had 44 members. After the organization of Waco Union Springs did not again represent till 1867, when T. J. Sparkman was pastor, and the membership 54. This church was in the northeastern part of McLennan county. Among the early members were C. C. Clabaugh, O. Barrett, J. E. Long, T. D. Savage, R. B. Anderson, George T. Holman, R. K. Williams. After the year 1867, Union Springs never again represented. It has long ago ceased to exist.

FIRST BAPTIST CHURCH OF WACO.

The county of McLennan was created in 1850, and named for Neil McLennan, an old citizen. The first white man to breathe Waco air any length of time was John Brown—"Waco John"—brother of the pioneer trader and Indian fighter, Captain Henry S. Brown. John was sent by his brother Henry to the Clear Fork of the Brazos to trade with the Indians. He bartered merchandise for over 1,000 horses and mules, and a quantity of buffalo robes. On his return he was surprised on the Bosque by Indians, and all his effects taken. His three companions escaped. John secreted himself, and when daylight came was alone. He was a cripple and tried to make his way to the settlements, but was captured by the Waco Indians, and was kept by them at their Waco village for about 15 months. He was captured in the summer of 1825. Capt. Henry S. Brown, on an expedition in search of his brother, attacked the Waco Indians, drove them into and across the Brazos, killing quite a number. His brother at that time was at another village only two miles above on the opposite bank. He afterwards made his escape from a pillaging party on Cummins creek, in Fayette county. In 1830 the Waco village was taken and burnt by Texans under Abner Kuykendall. About 1845 Messrs. Tory established a trading house at

WACO FIRST BAPTIST CHURCH.
(Photo by Sanders, Waco, Texas.)

Waco, and four years later, in 1849, the town was laid out by Capt. George B. Erath. Lots sold for $5 each; next year for $10. Captain Erath was born in Vienna, Austria, and educated in that city. He went to Germany, then to Paris, and finally in 1831, to New Orleans. He soon afterward came to Texas, settled in

Robertson county; was in the battle of San Jacinto; was in various expeditions against the Indians; served in the Confederate army, and died a few years ago in Waco, honored and beloved. Two years after the city of Waco was laid out, that is on May 31, 1851, the Waco First Baptist church was organized by Eld. N. T. Byars. The original members were Jas. C. Johnson, Geo. T. Holman, Noah Woods and Matilda Johnson. The first clerk was Noah Woods. He was followed by N. W. Crain, who was himself succeeded in 1857 by J. W. Speight. We quote from the "Manual of the First Baptist Church at Waco: "In the latter part of the year 1850, at a meeting of the old State Convention, with the church at Huntsville, Texas, an application was made for a small appropriation ($75 per annum) to sustain a missionary for a part of his time at Waco, then a little frontier village, almost entirely unknown to the outside world. It was natural that an objection should be raised on an appropriation of so much money for such an unpromising field, and as Waco had not been honored with a place in the current geographies it was not strange that some of the members, with just a touch of irony, inquired where Waco might be found. But there were those present who looked beyond that day. They saw the white wings of civilization spreading to the far west. They saw Waco the center of a great, thriving, wealthy section, covered with vast fields of golden grain and waving corn, and tickled by the plowshare of the husbandman, laughing rich harvests of cotton; and as they painted this picture and appealed to the Board to set up the banner of the cross now, and take hold of the Waco country for Jesus, all opposition was withdrawn, the appropriation was voted, and Elder N. T. Byars, the veteran soldier patriot and missionary, was appointed to this field." The sobriquet, "soldier patriot," finds justification and illustration in a little poem written by N. T. Byars in 1835, which begins thus:

"Boys, rub your steels and pick your flints,
Methinks I hear some friendly hints
That we from Texas shall be driven—
Our lands to Spanish soldiers given.
  To arms, to arms, to arms!"

It is said that Judge R. E. B. Baylor preached the first sermon in Waco. Elder N. T. Byars was the first pastor of Waco church. Since him, the pastors have been S. G. O'Bryan, W. H. Bayliss, R. C. Burleson, W. H. Anderson, M. B. Hardin and B. H. Carroll. Dr. Carroll has been pastor 26 years. Before the war there were only two pastors, N. T. Byars and S. G. O'Bryan. The deacons before the war were J. C. Johnson, D. B. Arnold, Edward Kellum, J. C. King, W. R. Kellum, W. Jackson, W. A. Dunklin and Abram (colored). To the above names, these added complete the list: Jas. H. Harrison, E. H. Hardin, M. D. Herring, J. W. Speight, S. B. Humphreys, J. H. Bagby, Richard Harrison, O. L. Battle, J. C. McCrary, E. F. Reese, Andrew Givens, A. G. Prewett, W. H. Long, M. H. Standifer, Jno. T. Battle, M. H. Compere, F. L. Carroll, A. H. Sneed, H. W. Smith, W. N. Griffith, L. Magee, J. C. Lattimore, W. P. Martin, A. Daniel. The church held its meetings in a rude pole and board house till 1857, when the new brick was erected. The first house belonged to the Methodists. "It was by the courtesy of the Methodists that the Baptists were permitted to use it for one Sabbath and Saturday preaching, and afterward for two Sabbaths in the month." The new brick was built while S. G. O'Bryan was pastor. "This building was an excellent one for the times, and continued to be the place of worship until it was consumed by fire, February 22, 1877. What tender memories clustered around that pile of ashes. Thence we had buried our dead. There many of us first heard the preached word. There a majority of the members had given their hearts to God, and their mothers and fathers, sons and daughters had grown in grace and spiritual strength under a faithful ministry of the gospel of Christ. It was a time for memory and for tears. But no time was lost in repairing. On February 25, just three days after the fire, the church met in conference, and under a stirring appeal from our pastor, Rev. B. H. Carroll, resolved at once to set about the work of rebuilding. Never did the zeal, piety and the faith of the church shine forth as brightly as during this period. Without a rich member in the church, and with very few that were not dependent on their own exertions, they adopted plans for a forty thousand dollar house, and determined to build it without incurring a debt. The members followed their resolutions with acts, and as they gave the work progressed. Occasionally a halt was called, and then after a brief period the work would begin with renewed energy. It is a coincidence worthy of mention that during this trying period, when every energy of the membership

TABERNACLE OF FIRST BAPTIST CHURCH OF WACO—INSIDE VIEW.
(Photo by Sanders, Waco, Texas.)

was taxed to the utmost to accomplish the work in hand, yet the pastor's salary was increased, the church more than doubled its contributions to home and foreign missions, remembered the poor, and gave liberally to the building of other church houses. Was it a coincidence? It was rather a fulfillment of the scripture: 'There is that scattereth and yet increaseth, and there is that withholdeth more than is meet, but it tendeth to poverty.' The house was completed in 1883." Services were held in the basement as early as 1880. In 1874 a proposition came to the Waco Association from the Waco church that the church would employ Elder V. G. Cunningham as missionary in the city of Waco on condition that the Association would employ and pay another missionary to labor on the field outside of Waco. The proposition was accepted and the plans carried into effect, Elder J. B. Parrack being employed on the field. Elder Cunningham labored as city missionary, paid by the Waco church, for two years; and he was again employed in 1886, serving till 1890, when he resigned to accept the care of the Second Waco church. The Second church was the outgrowth of Missionary Cunningham's labors. In 1890 Elder J. G. Kendall of Guthrie, Ky., was chosen by the church to succeed Bro. Cunningham, and is the present city missionary at a salary of $1,200, which is paid by the First church. The greatest revival in the history of the church was in the early fall of 1893, when Pastor Carroll did all the preaching. This meeting resulted in more than 100 additions by baptism, and in more than 150 by letter. The First church is far in the lead of every church in the state in benevolence. The stately buildings of Baylor University would have been *in perpetuum non* had it not been for the liberality of the Waco brethren. The tabernacle erected recently by this church points to a revolution in meeting house architecture, a consummation much to be desired. The pastor's salary is $2,500 per annum. The Waco Association was organized at Waco November 10, 1860, in the old brick meeting house. Waco church had at that time 181 members. Ten years after that the membership aggregated 201; in 1880, 398; in 1890, 524; in September, 1896, 972. Her present membership is in round numbers, 1,000. The town of Waco has had a steady growth since the day it was laid out in 1849. It is to-day the great commercial emporium of the famous black land belt of Central Texas. With her twenty-two hot overflowing artesian wells, with her four railroads and more to follow, with her healthful and central location, with her magnificent schools and universities, and with her enterprising citizens, no prophet is needed to foretell the future of the Central City.

SECOND BAPTIST CHURCH.

The Waco Second church was organized in 1888 by Elder V. G. Cunningham, who was laboring as city missionary employed by the First church. A mission was established by the First church in that part of the city where the Second church now meets. The Second church is the result of that mission. When the church united with the Association in 1888 the membership aggregated 83. The present number is 195. The Second church was assisted by the Association during the period from September, 1891, to September, 1893. The pastors have been V. G. Cunningham, S. B. McJunkin, John Bateman and J. H. Roberts. This church counts among her members many spiritual and consecrated brethren and sisters. They deserve the prayers and sympathy of every true lover of the cause of Christ. We hope to see the day when this flock will grow to be among the strongest in the city.

WACO GERMAN CHURCH.

On March 4, 1890, the First German Baptist church of Waco was organized by Elder Joseph Gronde, assisted by Elders R. C. Burleson and F. J. Gleiss. Eleven went into the organization. Bro. Joseph Gronde had been appointed by the Waco Association to labor as missionary to the Germans within our bounds in October, 1889. His labors prepared the way. When the church was formed, there were in Waco about 2,000 Germans. Bro. Gronde was the first pastor, and continued till December, 1891. During this time a beautiful site was purchased, and a neat house built, all worth about $2,000. Elder F. J. Gleiss was the next pastor, and continued six months. Elder H. C. Gleiss, son of the above, supplied the church during the summer of 1892. Then occurred a vacancy of about nine months. The little flock continued to meet, and kept alive both their Sunday school and prayer meeting. Elder F. A. Petereit was the next pastor, and continued 16 months, when he accepted the position of general missionary among the Germans. Bro. F. J. Gleiss is the present pastor. The church is prospering and numbers about 35. They have a promising Sunday school, a woman's missionary society and a wide-awake young people's society. The Waco German church has ceased to co-operate with the Waco Association, and is now connected with the German conference.

ELDER BENJAMIN WALKER

was born November 5, 1819, in East Tennessee. In his boyhood days the family moved to Middle Tennessee, and settled four miles from the mouth of Cypress creek. Here he grew up, received a

ELDER BENJAMIN WALKER.

fair education, united with the neighborhood Baptist church, and was licensed to preach. His father and mother, David and Margaret Pendleton Walker, were Baptists and were with the missionaries when the split came. In 1843 the family moved to Southwest Missouri, and settled in Green (now Christian county). "Walker's Branch," a small, beautiful stream, that empties into Findley river, three miles above the town of Ozark, perpetuates the family name. After moving to Missouri Benjamin Walker was ordained to the office of Elder by Salem Baptist church, on the second Saturday in November, 1843. In his early life he held many protracted meetings, and baptized large numbers. He was married December 13, 1849, to Miss Rachel Lucinda Marley. The Marley family came from North Carolina, and settled three miles west of Ozark. After his marriage, he spent the most of his time for ten years in preaching to four churches, but every year helped in revival meetings. In 1859 he was appointed by the Bethel Association, Southwest Missouri, to ride as missionary. He served the Association as missionary from October, 1859, to June, 1861. We quote from his report to Bethel Association, October, 1860: "Days devoted, 70; sermons delivered, 57; witnessed 100 professions; baptized 49; organized 3 churches; received $7.75." As Elder B. Walker sympathized with the South, he was not allowed to preach in Missouri during the civil war. After being shot at five times, wounded once, and robbed of all his property by marauding bands, he moved with his family north 150 miles to Chariton county. In Chariton he preached one year, but could not preach any longer without taking an oath that he had never aided the Southern Confederacy by action or otherwise. He had never been in the service but could not and did not take the oath. Remained in Chariton two more years with his soul on fire to preach the gospel, but his mouth closed. As soon as peace was made and he could get ready, he came to Texas, arriving in Waco November, 1866. He soon became pastor of Concord church. He held a revival meeting in East Waco in October, 1867, which resulted in many conversions. He was instrumental in bringing about the organization of the East Waco church, May 9, 1868; was in the organization and was the first pastor of that church. He died April 2, 1870, pastor of East Waco, of Concord and Cow Bayou churches. He was taken sick while preaching his last sermon at Concord. He knew his time had come. Was perfectly resigned and perfectly happy. On the day of his death he sang a part of each of three hymns, "Amazing Grace," "Oh, When Shall I See Jesus," (changed to "Oh, Now Shall I See Jesus,") and "Farewell, Vain World, I'm Going

Home." He called his family to his bedside, kissed them goodbye, gave them good advice, then said: "Shave me clean, dress me just as if I were going to preach, and bury me beside my little daughter." He sleeps at Waco, in the old First Street cemetery. There was never a shadow on his life.

ELDER JAMES LAFAYETTE WALKER,

son of Elder Benjamin Walker, was born in Green county, Mo., March 15, 1851. Was converted in October, 1867, and was baptized by his father in the Brazos river, just above the place spanned by the suspension bridge. His membership was first at Concord church, but in May, 1868, he was in the organization of the East Waco church. He was educated partly in private schools, and later in Waco University. He was ordained by Caledonia Baptist church on second Lord's day, in December, 1880, the following brethren acting as presbytery: Elders B. H. Carroll, Thos. Hooker, B. F. Tatum, T. P. Speakman and J. C. Combes. He has given almost his entire time to churches in the bounds of Waco Association. He served four years as clerk of Towash Association, and four years as clerk of Waco Association. He has been pastor of Rock Creek, Bosqueville, White Hall, Lorena, Mastersville, Robinson, Chilton, Speegleville, Lott, Caddo and Oak Grove churches. Is now pastor of Mart. He organized China Springs church. He is now president of the Mission Board of the Waco Association. In 1893, under the administration of Bro. Walker as president, the Association made the largest contributions in its history. In 1887 begining October 1, he served eleven months as missionary of the Association. Was first married January 13, 1876, to Miss P. Evie Neal, whose father died in the Confederate service, and whose mother afterward married Deacon W. F. Umberson, of Caledonia church. Three children made happy Bro. Walker's first marriage, a son and two daughters. In March, 1887, the dark angel of death came to our brother's happy home and bore away the Christian mother of his children. April 15, 1890, he was married a second time to Miss Leila A. Clark, daughter of Elder Anderson Clark, of Bell county, Texas. One child has blessed this union. Bro. Walker is one of the humblest and most self-sacrificing, and consecrated men in our Baptist ministry. He is the author of a number of published articles of merit. For years he has been gathering materials for the "History of Waco Baptist Association," for which work he is eminently qualified, and of which he is principally the author, myself being only recently associated with him in the work. He is regarded by many who know him well as one of our best posted men in Baptist history. He originated the "Baptist Historical Movement," set on foot at Houston, October, 1896. We have often felt that his real worth as a gospel preacher has never been realized. He is modest and retiring, and ever loyal to all our organized work. Doctrinally and morally his life is worthy of imitation.

C. P. LUMPKIN.

ELDER T. P. WALKER.

This brother is the child of Elder Benjamin Walker. Brother "Tommie" was only 3 years old when his father died. He was reared without a father's counsels. But a faithful Christian mother's hand guided the young feet. He was born at East Waco, October 16, 1867. At the age of 14 he professed faith in Christ and was baptized into the fellowship of Caledonia church by Elder B. F. Tatum. He had the best advantages afforded by the country schools, and had also the help of Sabbath school and church services. After a long and stubborn resistance he yielded to the impression to preach. His first sermon was delivered in January, 1889. Soon four regular appointments were made. In the autumn of 1889 he entered Baylor University. In 1890-1 he taught a school in Falls county eight months. Was ordained to the full work of the gospel ministry March 10, 1891, at Deer Creek church, Falls county. The presbytery consisted of Elders J. L. Walker, A. J. Shelton and G. G. Gibson After ordination he immediately became pastor of three churches. In September, 1891, he again entered Baylor University, and continued two years. On January 29, 1893, he was elected Sunday school missionary and colporter of Waco Association, but resigned when the Association met at Geneva, 1893, to enter the Southern Baptist

Theological Seminary, Louisville, Ky. He remained in the Seminary eight months, returned, and was again employed as Sunday school missionary and colporter. During two years Bro. Walker organized more than 40 Sunday schools. Since he entered the service of the Association he has driven 6,000 miles in buggy, made 1,000 visits, given away 300 Bibles and Testaments, distributed 10,000 pages of tracts, delivered several hundred ser-

Elder T. P. Walker.
(Photo by Jackson, Waco, Texas.)

mons and Sunday school talks. His work has been mostly among the neglected, in creek and river bottoms, and in isolated communities. God is still blessing his labors as missionary of Waco Association.

HOMER WELLS

was born in Louisville, Ky., April 9, 1854. United with the Baptist church at Madisonville, Ky., under the ministerial labors of Dr. J. H. Spencer. He became a citizen of Waco, Texas, and member of the First church in 1893. He has been a member of the State Mission Board since 1889. On December 10, 1885, he was married to Miss Ruby Magee, daughter of Deacon Leonard Magee. Bro. Wells' home is on Speight street, in Waco. He is an active business man, but fully alive to the interests of his church and denomination.

HOMER WELLS.
(Photo by Jackson, Waco, Texas.)

DEACON ALFRED WEBB.

In the early years of the nineteenth century Western Georgia was a wild frontier. It was in this wild country that the subject of this sketch first saw the light in Coweta county, January 4, 1829. The place of his birth was in the sombre forest, six miles west of Newnan. Except three years spent in Lumpkin county, Bro. Webb grew up in the old neighborhood near Newnan. In those days it was rare that a boy ever got beyond the "old blue-back spelling book"—Webster's Elementary. Whatever else was studied the old "blue-back" was kept up. Alfred Webb never progressed beyond it. On the third Sunday in October, 1846, he was baptized into the fellowship of Providence church, Caweta county, by Pastor Elder R. E. Flemming. He was married to Miss Mary E. Moore January 21, 1847. The spiritual life of Bro. Webb in Georgia during the next four years, till he left for Texas, was one of joyful sunshine, darkened by no single cloud. He came to Jefferson, Texas, in 1851, and remained till 1868. These were years of darkness and affliction. Sister W. became an invalid. Deprived of church privileges, our brother did not have the spiritual peace that he had formerly experienced and has since enjoyed. He spent three years and two months in the Confederate service in the trans-Mississippi department, with Colonel Ochiltree Walker's division, mostly under General Dick Taylor. He went through the war without being touched by a bullet. In 1868 came to McLennan county. It was a blessed move. His life in McLennan has been one of prosperity, both religiously and financially. Bro. and Sister Webb lived happily in Robinson church for many years. Here was good society. Their children have all given themselves to the Savior. Bro. Webb was ordained to the office of deacon in 1890, and is trying to "use the office well." Sister Webb passed to her heavenly home December 27, 1893. Perfectly resigned, full of faith and love, she went to sleep in Jesus. One of the last acts of her life was to contribute to the Lord's cause. Deacon Webb lingers, waiting the call of the Master.

WEST CHURCH.

The first Baptist to settle in the Bold Springs neighborhood was Elder A. Vaughn. The country was then blushing with virgin beauty and glory. Grass was waving in the sunlight, and cattle were roaming everywhere with happy freedom. Few spots in Texas were more inviting to the settler. Land that could not now be bought for $50 per acre was then offered for $1. Settlers came, and in 1858 there were enough Baptists to constitute a church. It was constituted at Bold Springs, 20 miles north of Waco. There were at that time only four other churches in Mc-

Lennan county, Waco, Bosque, White Rock (No. 1), and Union Springs. Bold Springs united with Richland Association at the first session of that body, 1858. At the second session of the Association Bold Springs reported 32 members. The third session of Richland was held with the Bold Springs church. Before the Waco Association was organized A. Vaughn, Thos. Horsley, B. F. White and D. C. McCauley, ordained ministers, held membership in Bold Springs church. It is probable that these brethren supplied the pulpit in 1858-9. In 1860 J. J. Riddle was pastor. The years of 1859 and '60 were among the hottest and dryest ever known in Texas, yet Bold Springs continued to grow, and numbered 42 in October, 1860. Bold Springs was one of the nine original churches of Waco Association. N. W. Crain was pastor in 1861, and E. J. Billings in 1864-5. At the session of Waco Association in 1866 the church was without a pastor, had 35 members. In 1867 she enjoyed a glorious revival, under the pastoral care of Elder T. J. Sparkman, adding 21 by baptism and swelling the membership to 57. T. F. Lockett succeeded Bro. Sparkman, and continued one year. It was during his pastorate that Waco Association met with Bold Springs church, heard the grand introductory sermon by W. C. Buck, and then adjourned to Waco. In 1870 Thos. Hooker was pastor; membership 54. In 1875 went into the Towash Association, V. G. Cunningham, pastor. In 1879 J. S. Holmes was pastor; membership, 60. Bro. Holmes was followed by T. P. Speakman. The church now enjoyed great prosperity, receiving large numbers by baptism and letter. The Towash Association met with this church in 1880. Bro. Speakman continued pastor till 1887. The church came back into the Waco Association in 1884 with 195 members. At the close of Bro. Speakman's pastorate the number was 174. S. B. McJunkin succeeded to the pastorate, and continued one year, when Bro. Speakman accepted the church; remained two years, and was followed by E. A. Puthuff, who served one year, till 1891. V. G. Cunningham became pastor in 1891, and continued two years. The next year (1893) I. Z. Kimbrough became pastor. He was succeeded in 1895 by J. H. Milburn, who continued only a few months, and was followed by I. P. Langley, who resigned in the autumn of 1896. Bro. Langley left the church in fine condition, with 292 members. In 1896 the name was changed to West. In 1889 the Waco Association met with the Bold Springs church. This church meets in the beautiful little city of West, on the M., K. & T. railroad. The church has contributed to missions, aged ministers and Orphans' Home in all about $2,000. She has church building and lot worth $1,500, and pastor's home, worth $800. The present pastor is W. H. Parks; membership about 275.

JUDGE JOHN C. WEST

was born in Camden, S. C., April 12, 1834. Graduated from South Carolina College, December, 1854. Came to Texas in December, 1855, and taught school and studied law in 1856. Returned to South Carolina and was married to Miss Mary E. Stark, April 14, 1858. Came to Waco from Austin, Texas, December, 1859, to teach as principal in Trinity River Classical High School, and in the spring of 1860 joined the Baptist church, at Waco. He entered as a private in the first company raised in McLennan county for Confederate service, under Captain Ryan, but was persuaded to withdraw as he was the only married man in the company. This company left Waco in 1861 and became Company E, Fourth Texas Regiment, Hood's Brigade, Army of North Virginia. He then joined Speight's Regiment and was at Virginia Point, near Galveston, when his company was transferred to Cook's heavy artillery, and placed on Galveston island. While serving as a private in Cook's Regiment, at Galveston, in the summer of 1862, he was appointed by Hon. Jefferson Davis, president of the Southern Confederacy, to the office of district attorney of the Western District of Texas. This position he filled till April, 1863, when he left the office in charge of Hon. N. O. Green of San Antonio, who was a consumptive. Mr. West then reentered Company E, Fourth Texas Regiment, and went to the command camped on the Rapidan, in Virginia. He was slightly wounded in the great battle of Gettysburg and was severely wounded September 20, 1863, at Chickamauga, but remained with his regiment through the campaign of Longstreet, in East Tennessee, in the winter of 1863-4. When at Bull's Gap, in East Tennessee, in April, 1864, he was ordered by Secretary of War of the Confederate States to return to Texas and take charge of his office of district attorney for the Western District of Texas, extending from the Colorado to the Rio Grande. He never applied for the office of district attorney, nor did he ask or expect any discharge from the army in 1864. Both the appointment and discharge were made without his knowledge. He returned to the

JUDGE JOHN C. WEST.
(Photo by Deane, Waco, Texas.)

practice of law in Waco, January 1, 1866. In 1867 he was justice of the peace and notary public, from both of which offices he was moved by military order during reconstruction period. In 1875 he was mayor of Waco. Has been serveral times elected by the Waco bar as special district judge to try important cases, and has been commissioned as both district judge and county judge by Governors Ireland and Culberson. Judge West lives in Waco on the homestead originally settled by him in August, 1860. No man in Waco has been more punctual to attend the services of his church. For 35 years he has never missed a service if in Waco and able to attend. And he has a statement signed by Thos. J. Selman, Captain Company E, Fourth Texas, that he never missed a roll call, a fight or a skirmish while with the Fourth Texas Regiment. His reputation for honor, honesty and integrity has never been stained. He is posted in Baptist affairs, and has always taken keen interest in all the work of his church.

WHITE HALL CHURCH.

White Hall missionary Baptist church was organized November, 1871, by Elders R. B. Burleson and W. A. Ellege. Elder R. B. Burleson preached the sermon. After which the enrollment of names was called for and the following came forward and enrolled their names, to-wit: A. W. Ellege, B. J. Kendrick, I. H. Earle, M. D. Kendrick, Mary Ellege, Mordie Cobb, J. H. Poague and Lizzie Standifer. The Philadelphia Articles of Faith, as found in the Religious Encyclopedia, were unanimously adopted as the Articles of Faith of this church, after which Bro. Ellege lead in prayer, a song was sung and Rev. R. B. Burleson pronounced the benediction. During the year 1872 Rev. R. B. Burleson filled the pulpit one Sabbath in each month. Also Rev. V. G. Cunningham, in the latter part of the same year, and part of the year 1873, and was the first pastor. In the summer of 1873 Elder John S. Allen held a meeting of great interest, during which there was quite an ingathering. The little church then began to feel like they could keep house for the Lord, and at once procured the services of Rev. John S. Allen as pastor, beginning January, 1874. That was a glorious year of outpouring of the holy spirit. It was in this year that our pastor called to his assistance our dearly beloved and late lamented brother, W. E. Penn. The meeting held by Bro. Penn was one of great power; many joined by baptism, and the whole community was moved by the power of the holy spirit, as it had never before been moved. There were baptized in the Bosque creek at one time 43 converts. That year our letter to the Waco Association showed our membership to be nearly 100. Following are the names of pastors who have served this church since its organization, and the length of time each one served as such: Rev. John S. Allen began his pastorate January, 1874, and continued eight years, with the exception of about one and one-half years, when his place was supplied by Elder S. I. Caldwell. During this term of years White Hall church was greatly blessed, and increased largely in membership; the increase being so great that the old house was found to be too small to contain the congregation, and steps were taken to erect a more commodious house of worship. A building committee composed of the following named brethren was appointed—M. H. Standifer, Winsted Boynton, W. J. Ingram, J. M. Kendrick and B. J. Kendrick. At the June meeting, 1879, the committee made their report, showing that they had erected the house as instructed at a cost of $1,350, and that the full amount had been paid. Dr. R. C. Burleson preached the dedicatory sermon at the July meeting, with his usual power, to a very large and appreciative audience. Having a large and commodious house of worship, the church invited Waco Association to meet with her at her regular meeting, August, 1880, which invitation was accepted. A. J. Shelton served the church as pastor for the year 1883. In 1884 A. A. Hensler was pastor. S. B. McJunkin served as pastor in 1885 and 1886, during which time the church increased in numbers, and was otherwise blessed. Bro. McJunkin preached his farewell sermon to a large and sad congregation, December, 1886. Beginning January, 1887, J. T. Stanton served as pastor five months. J. L. Walker was pastor from July, 1887, to December, 1890. "Bro. Walker endeared himself to the church and community, and we parted with him with much regret."—B. J. Kendrick. Elder J. T Gillespie accepted the church December, 1890, and served until September, 1892. In October, 1892, J. B. Reaves accepted a call of the church, and has served most acceptably ever since. The brethren are now proud to own him as their dearly beloved pastor. The church ordained the following deacons: Bro. M. H. Standifer, February 15, 1874; Bros. W. D. Ish and A. F. Herring, September 17, 1876; Bro. W. P. Crow and D. Moncrief, December 21, 1884. The present deacons of the church are B. J. Kendrick and D. McDaniel. There have been received into the membership of White Hall church since its organization 393 members. During all these years the loss by death has been 14. Present membership, 133. Three churches have been organized out of the membership of White Hall church, to-wit: Middle Bosque, Harris Creek and Hewitt. The Sunday school was organized in August, 1871, and has been a continuous school ever since. Bro. L. A. Trice is the present superintendent. Regular attendance about 32.

ELDER C. D. WHITMAN

was born in Burnsville, Ala., March 23, 1855. He lost his mother when 2 years old, and when 17 lost his father. Was born of the Spirit at the age of 13 years; was baptized by Elder Wm. Green, and received into the Baptist church, at Winchester, Tenn. While attending the high school at Mulberry, Tenn., was licensed to preach when 18 years old. In the fall of 1874 entered Bethel College, at Russellville, Ky., Dr. Leslie, president. He was ordained at New Market, Ala.; presbytery, W. J. Couch, Geo. W. Carmichael and J. J. McCandless. His first pastorate was in Missouri, with a country church called Antioch. Soon also he was called to another church, 20 miles distant. He taught school while serving these two churches. During this time he built up a good school from almost nothing. The school grew till four teachers were necessary. Built up a good church from three members to a membership of 50, owning a good house. He baptized a large number in Missouri. He was missionary of Webster Association two years. Failing health made it necessary to resign his work in that state. Came to Texas in 1885. Spent six months in the Seminary at Louisville in 1888-9. In 1893 accepted the Sunday School and Colportage work of Waco Association, and for nearly a year rendered acceptable service. During this period he preached 87 sermons and sold many hundreds of books. During 1894-5 he preached to four churches in the Waco Association, Riesel, Pleasant Grove, Caledonia and Rosebud. He is now teaching in the neighborhood of Caddo church. He is a good preacher, modest, consecrated, spiritual.

WHITE ROCK CHURCH NO. 1

was in existence in 1858, and was in the organization of Richland Association that year. Among the early members before the war were M. R. Carroll, E. H. Harrington, J. Y. Riddle, M. A. Bates, W. R. Bird and W. B. Park. In 1858 the membership was 31; in 1859, 21. N. W. Crain was pastor in 1859-60. White Rock was in the organization of Waco Association in 1860. Her messengers on that occasion were M. A. Bates, W. R. Bird and J. Y. Riddle; membership, 19. The next year this church united with Bold Springs.

WHITE ROCK NO. 2.

This church was constituted June 26, 1870, with the following members: W. S. Alphin, M. A. Bates, Amanda Bates, M. R. Carroll, Nancy Carroll, William Hardin, E. H. Young, Mary Gross, Josephine Gross and Sarah C. Alphin. White Rock joined Waco Association at the East Waco session, August, 1871. At that time Elder Thos. Hooker was pastor; clerk, M. R. Carroll. The pastors have been Thos. Hooker, J. J. Riddle, J. J. Sledge, J. H. Harrison, T. P. Speakman, H. R. Puryear, T. E. Muse, J. T. Stanton, Holmes Nichols, B. F. Tatum. In 1870 organized with 10 members; in 1880 the number was 95; in 1890, 100; in 1896, 65. The present membership (March, 1897), is about 70. The church formerly worshiped near the White Rock Cemetery. At present their place of meeting is one mile west of the old site. The church has a good house of worship, and counts among her membership many good, spiritual brethren and sisters. E. R. Edwards is the present clerk. W. H. Edwards is the superintendent of a nice little Sunday school of 30 pupils.

ELDER J. M. WRIGHT

was born in Illinois, May 5, 1831. When he was one year old, the family moved to Tennessee. He came to Texas in 1854, and soon afterward was married to Miss Lucy Basco. Was baptized into Mt. Antioch church by Dr. J. J. Riddle in July, 1858, and in 1867 was ordained to the office of elder by that church, Elders H. R. Puryear and B. E. Lucas, presbytery. In 1862 he entered the Confederate service in Company B, Bass' Regiment. Was captured July 17, 1863, at Elm Creek, and taken to Johnson's Island, where he was a prisoner 21 months. He practiced his religion in camp as well as at home. He was a sound Baptist and was ever ready to defend the cause he loved. He was a zealous Mason, and at his death was a royal and select master in the Mystic Tie. He went to his reward on June 9, 1896. During the last six years of his life he had been a great sufferer. His last sermon was preached at Shiloh church (R. E. Smith, pastor), on the subject: "Is My Name Written There?" He called his wife and children to his bedside in the parting hour, and gave them a father's dying blessing and in prayer, commending them, one by one, to the God in whom he trusted. A wife and eight children, with many friends, mourn his loss. At his own request his funeral services were conducted at the Baptist meeting house in Crawford, by his pastor, J. M. B. Gresham, and by T. C. Sammons and R. R. Raymon, Presbyterian and Methodist ministers. He was an earnest preacher and a man of deep piety. He served many churches, and in 1871-2 was missionary of Leon River Association.

"PASSING THE BARS."

(A STORY OF AN EARLY TEXAS COURTSHIP WHICH HAPPENED WITHIN THE BOUNDS OF WACO ASSOCIATION.)

The balmy spring breeze was fanning the early flowers and wafting their perfume through the spacious Burnet mansion. One by one the stars peeped forth. Beautiful Maggie Burnet was gliding here and there, adding a touch of her fairy fingers everywhere. The house was brilliantly lighted, and Maggie was impatiently waiting the arrival of the guests. It was to be only a "tea party," but every heart leaped with delight when the dainty card came saying:

"Won't you come to my tea party?"
"1865."

Hark! the sound of merry voices, and Maggie knew that the guests were near. One by one, in her own charming manner, she welcomed them to her lovely home. The parlors and hall seemed almost like a garden of blooming flowers, so profusely were the sweet scented blossoms scattered about.

Among the guests was a handsome young man from Louisiana, who had lost an arm in the war. His every movement was graceful, and his flashing, dark eyes sparkled with merriment. "Surely," thought the girls, "he is the handsomest of them all; what a sad pity he lost his arm."

He was the escort of Miss Emma Adams. After tea was served, the guests were gathered in the parlor, all seemingly as happy as could be, save the handsome young man from Louisiana. A shade of anxiety seemed hovering about him. All the guests were chatting as merrily as could be. Presently the young man drew his chair close to Miss Adams and fixed his eyes on her lovely face, and looked at her as if he would fix her every feature on his heart. After a few moments of close scrutiny Miss Adams said, with a merry laugh, "Mr. R—, why so pensive? You look as if all your friends had forsaken you, and only a few moments ago you seemed to be the merriest one of all the company."

Mr. R. slowly withdrew his eyes from her face, and with a long-drawn sigh, he commenced in a low tone:

"Miss Emma, I contemplate going on a long voyage in the near future, a journey which will either bring me success or despair."

To this Miss Adams gravely replied: "Indeed! May I ask what distant land you will visit? One would think from the shadow which seems hovering over you, that you might be contemplating a visit to the land of cannibals and wild beasts; if this be so, I pray you take every precaution against such foes."

"It is only the land of matrimony, Miss Emma!" he replied, "and I am fearful of a wreck. Just a little way out on the sea I see a small bar—I am afraid of that bar, and it is with a trembling heart that I make the venture, but it is not so formidable as the large one which I see further out, large rocks and threatening reefs surround it—but it stands in the way, and must be gotten over."

Miss Adams readily understood his meaning, and knew that the small bar was her own consent and that the large one further out was the consent of her parents, but she could not understand why he was so fearful. She mischievously said:

"Well, Mr. R., I'm very much afraid you will either be wrecked or drowned." Notwithstanding all of his fears, he hardly expected so severe an answer from Miss Adams, and he withdrew his chair a little way from her and the conversation ended. Mr. R. looked as if he had already been wrecked, but Miss Adams was as gay as ever.

"Take care, Miss Emma," said a young man coming up to where she sat, "what have you been saying to friend R., that he looks so dejected? I can half guess what is the matter—but never mind, don't be unjust, though."

The evening passed quietly away, and the guests began leaving for home. Soon all were gone except Mr. R. and Miss Adams. Miss Adams went from the parlor, leaving Mr. R. alone. Reaching the hall and meeting Maggie, she said: "What do you suppose is the matter with Mr. R.? I never saw a man look so forsaken in my life."

"Come, now, my pretty innocent," Maggie replied, "you know better than any one else the cause of his drooping spirits. Who can wonder at his sadness when you gave him the answer that you did just now—I've half a mind to quarrel with you for treating him so rudely."

"Really, Maggie, do you suppose that is the cause? I can quickly dispel the gloom if that is all, and I can't let you quarrel with me, so I will proceed immediately to correct the wrong I have done." And with a musical laugh she tripped back to the parlor door and called out in her softest, sweetest tone:

"Mr. R., please don't look so forsaken; if what I said just now has caused a wound, I sincerely repent of it, for I assure you it was not so intended. As to the small bar, it has already disappeared, and I see your tiny boat far beyond the large bar; no rocks or dangerous reefs are now in the way to threaten your destruction, and I see the boat gliding smoothly on."

Mr. R. looked at the beautiful girl a moment, and when he was sure she was in earnest he immediately arose and the "tell-tale" light in his dark eyes showed plainly that the wound was healed, and both hearts were happy and light. He little dreamed that Maggie knew his secret until she called out after them as they were leaving:

"*Un bon voyage,*" and may you pass the 'bars' in safety." The small bar was already past; and soon the large bar disappeared, and ere long the glad wedding bells pealed forth, and the two happy, happy hearts were made one, and the boat glided smoothly on.

One of the many bridal presents received, was more highly prized by the happy pair than any other. It was a simple silver tray, and engraved on it was a tiny boat and beneath it was written:

"The bars, small and great, are safely past, and the boat glides onward."

EVA LUMPKIN.

No. 926, Speight street, Waco, Texas.